A. A. Gill was born in Edinburgh. He is the author of *A. A. Gill is Away*, *The Angry Island*, *Previous Convictions*, *Table Talk*, *Paper View*, *A. A. Gill is Further Away*, *The Golden Door*, *Lines in the Sand* and the highly acclaimed memoir *Pour Me*.

He was the TV and restaurant critic and regular features writer for *The Sunday Times*, columnist for *Esquire*, and contributor to *Australian Gourmet Traveller*. He died in 2016.

THE BEST OF
A. A. GILL

A. A. GILL

WEIDENFELD & NICOLSON

A W&N Paperback

First published in Great Britain in 2017
This paperback first published in 2018
by Weidenfeld & Nicolson
an imprint of Orion Books

3 5 7 9 10 8 6 4 2

A CIP catalogue record for this book
is available from the British Library.

ISBN 978 1 4746 0775 9

Typeset at The Spartan Press Ltd,
Lymington, Hants

Printed and bound by CPI Group (UK) Ltd,
Croydon, CRO 4YY

Weidenfeld & Nicolson

The Orion Publishing Group Ltd
Carmelite House
50 Victoria Embankment
London
EC4Y ODZ

An Hachette UK Company

www.orionbooks.co.uk
www.weidenfeldandnicolson.co.uk

Contents

Drapa of the Sea Fences, The Saga of the Greenlanders

I ask you, unblemished monks' tester, to be the ward of my travels.
May the Lord of the peaks' pane shade my path with
his hawk's perch.

Editor's Note

It was always over breakfast. 8.45 am, the Wolseley. Adrian in his natural habitat, looking the part in a natty tweed, or a bow tie, or a beautifully cut suit lined with something outrageous. There would be three of us: Adrian, me, and Alan Samson, his publisher. Adrian would spring up, grinning, to say hello, and then he was off – news, films, books, TV, plays, politics, history, poetry, gossip, our families, his latest adventures, the countries he'd been to, the people he'd met... He had a reporter's interest in everything. There aren't really words (though he would have found some) to describe how he could conjure an anecdote, or back up a theory with a historical allusion, or deploy a wildly obscure piece of film trivia, or just render you helpless, crying with laughter. There was no conversation like an Adrian conversation: it brought things to life. It made you feel brighter, smarter, more amusing. It certainly never felt like work.

I edited Adrian's books for ten years – six books in all. I was first brought in for *Table Talk*, a collection of his restaurant columns, because he thought it wouldn't be interesting for the readers or fair to the restaurants simply to reproduce old reviews. But as anyone who bought *The Sunday Times* and turned straight to his page knew, the long introductions before he got to the actual restaurant were often the best bits. Could we make a book out of those? So we did. The first time we met I had already sent him some rather tentatively edited samples of his old articles, restaurant names elided and topical references left out. I was nervous he might be precious about this. Actually, I was nervous full stop. But he was charming and hilarious and kind from the first handshake: the only subject that didn't seem to come up was the book itself. Eventually, I asked if he was happy with the sample material. Oh yes, he said, absolutely. It's fine. Thank

you very much. But you're being too respectful. You need to be much
more brutal: cut away!

Of course I didn't have to. Who would want to be brutal with
Adrian's writing? But he said this as a gift, I think: so I wouldn't be
frightened of crossing over some invisible line. And after that, it was
simply fun. The problem was choice – about fifteen years' worth of
articles, nearly all of them gold. But we crammed in as much as we
could: sometimes we spliced two pieces on similar subjects together,
or dug out the 'fragments' – the small shards of criticism that were
the zingers at the heart of a piece; the bits you read out over the
breakfast table. The collections of his long-form journalism were even
easier: we would talk about the structure of the book and which
articles might make the cut, and I would start putting it together to
see how it read. Once he'd read the draft I would sit down with him
to iron out queries. He would read the relevant bit through – slowly,
because of his dyslexia – and suddenly hoot with laughter at some
joke. 'That's rather good, isn't it?', or sometimes 'I think I missed the
mark on that one.' Though he rarely had.

There were also two new original books. *The Golden Door* was
a series of love letters to America. *Pour Me* was the extraordinary
book he once used to say he would never write, until one morn-
ing he suddenly announced that now was the time. 'My Drink and
Drugs Memoir', he called it, writing the title on a coaster in lieu
of a proposal, a mosaic of his life and the last year of his drinking.
For these books, he would spend a breakfast talking to us about
what he was thinking of writing for the next chapter – weaving a
web of stories and themes and associations. And then, a week or a
month later, it would arrive in my inbox. All that bright tapestry of
words distilled and dictated down the phone to his copytaker, perfect,
almost nothing to do but marvel and watch for typos.

His final collection, *Lines in the Sand*, started as unalloyed pleasure.
It was to be a collection of the last seven years or so of feature articles,
but he was particularly keen that it should emphasise a theme that
had become more and more important to him – the refugee crisis.
The writing he produced on this subject lingers, full of moments
that snag the memory – the fey boy on the harbour in Kos, starting

his great trek across Europe; the moment when the weight of the women's stories in the Congo becomes almost too much to bear; the heartbreaking final image of the Lampedusa article.

Early in the summer of 2016, I took the final manuscript down to him as usual, dotted with coloured tags for my queries, and when we were finished we agreed to send the book off to production and said we'd all see each other for breakfast soon. It never happened. We spoke a couple of times over the summer, and then in the autumn he rang to say he was ill. And the illness moved too fast. When he died, that book was just at the final proof stage, and so at the last minute what had begun with such pleasure ended in terrible sadness as we included two more pieces – the restaurant column in which he announced his illness, and the extraordinary last article, which appeared in *The Sunday Times* the day after his death. Only Adrian would make his farewell piece a clear-eyed investigation into the NHS. Always reporting, right from the brink. *Lines in the Sand* was published after his death, and it's a terrific book: a testament to the last years of his writing. But it could not be the final word.

Which brings us to now, and *The Best of A. A. Gill*: an attempt to bring together all the various shades of his writing over the years – funny and excoriating and thoughtful and outrageous. The difficulty, again, has been choice. But how much harder now, with no Adrian to direct proceedings. Reading back through all the articles his laughter has sometimes seemed to echo – 'That's rather good, isn't it?', or, more rarely, 'I wouldn't bother with that one.' The problem is, it's all rather good. Some pieces *had* to be included: the description of his dyslexia, the account of his father's Alzheimer's, the famine piece he wrote in the Sudan in the days when he was thought of as just a restaurant critic, some of the fatherhood pieces that give a glimpse of how his family lay at the heart of things for him, a few of the refugee stories. I once heard someone ask him which article he was most proud of: the answer was the piece about Ugandan sleeping sickness, because it inspired a CNN campaign by Christiane Amanpour that helped change a drug company's policy. But equally typical of Adrian is the account of him driving tanks through Baghdad with Jeremy Clarkson. His final article, of course, is in here, but also a travel article about the last family holiday just before he became ill, an idyll before the shadow fell.

We've started with food, because that is more or less where he started. His knowledge of food – its history, context, meaning – sings out from the thousands of reviews and articles he wrote on the subject. We have included pieces that show his blade whetted to its sharpest, but also the pieces that celebrate what he loved. It has similarly only been possible to include a tiny fraction of his TV criticism; enough to show what made him the scourge of the Tristrams and a must-read for the audience. And enough to show how much he cared about it: he was always enthralled by how much you could see through the box in the corner. Mostly we have avoided his topical, news-driven pieces, but we had to include his astonishing Europe article, written on the eve of the referendum: Adrian at full throttle, coruscating and fervent in equal measure. And no 'Best of A. A. Gill' could be complete without the account of how he once made a porn movie.

Adrian is gone, and we are all the poorer for it: we need that fearless, dazzling, opinionated, provoking and hilarious voice more than ever. But it lives on in the writing he left behind, of which this book is just the tip of the iceberg. I hope it makes you laugh, I hope it makes you gasp, and I hope it makes you miss him.

Celia Hayley
August 2017

FOOD

There was the ever-present steroidal croissant, **the tarts that defy eating**. There were African infant-school blackboards advertising things that might be lunch. There were light classics on the Roberts repro radio, and a girl with pearl earrings behind the till. She smiled, **with just a hint of despair**, as if perhaps there was, under the counter, **a drug-crazed midget** pointing the open Tabasco jar up her frock.

My red miso soup tasted strongly of red miso. If I never ate it again, I wouldn't miss it. If I never had to eat tofu again, I'd be jolly pleased.

Then there was **20-year Gu-yue-long-shan drunken chicken**, which possibly died of cirrhosis and left its body to gastronomic research. In death it amounted to little more than it had in life.

*Service was from the J.R.R Tolkien school of butlering: **everything was an interminable journey and a saga.***

For pudding, a baked alaska for four came to the table with a servile fanfare. **It was doused in spirits and immolated.** After a single taste, the company screamed as one. Bring more alcohol and finish the hellish thing off!

The problem, and I freely admit that this is my problem, is that I don't understand the menu. Since I'm not a gay old Peruvian hand, the ingredients remain opaquely mysterious. I ask you, what are **chia seed? Ghoa cress? Tiger's milk? Algarrobo tree syrup, botija olive, tree tomatoes, sacha inchi oil, yellow ajosecu? Plaintain majado? White kiwicha? Amazonian cashew, muna mint, pisco mosto verde? Huacatay herb? Yellow aji? Crazy pea?** The Blonde enquired what the 'Amazonian fish' was. 'It is,' he said with authority, 'a fish from the Amazon,' confidently adding, 'a big river'.

The temperatures were all wrong, mostly on the chilly side of friendly. **The Blonde's cod was actually hostile.**

. . . the fishiness was strident and discordant, and it gave the dish the unmistakable flavour of cat food. Upmarket cat food, the sort of gourmet pussy din-dins that's supposed to make moggies love you. Still, not really what you want for lunch.

This must be the most depressing restaurant in London, **the echoes of the tinkle and croon of the mournful pianist made it sound even more evocatively suicidal,** like eating in an underpass at the end of the world.

My Colchesters were as broad as hippos' kneecaps, and as **fat and firm and silky as a mermaid's breast implant**. Rock oysters, the long, paisley-shaped ones, taste stringent and invigorating and salty, but natives have layers of taste, fathoms of flavours. They can be quite sweet and medicinally iodine, **and taste of ozone and childish shores**. Each one is a sea shanty.

*...yet another barbecue restaurant. If you live in London and get out a bit, you'll have noticed that fire and smoke are the two on-trend ingredients. **Everybody with a beard and a topknot and a suicide playlist on their phone** is smoking stuff. Smoke is the new balsamic vinegar; it's Soho truffle.*

I started with a duck risotto, a mountain of sloppy rice, full of fatty, meaty bits, as if Jemima Puddle-Duck had flown through a wind farm.

Then there was the beef, the special for two, taken from an aged Spanish cow. It was utterly delicious, **tasting like a repressed memory of the way food ought to be in fairy tales, a taste that is morbid and musty**, the flavour of an oboe played in a hay barn.

This was an object lesson in horrible barbecuing. The wings were like the contorted bodies of strange, bald, blind rodents that have drowned in the vat of the same tinny metallic sticky sauce made from wine gums and boiled batteries. **The coleslaw was vegetables shredded like old prison love letters, but not that interesting**. Puddings were the stuff of every tourist café of every shopping centre in the Western world.

Main courses would have got a Third World Airline grounded. **My lamb would have been of gastronomic interest to a man who had never eaten a sheep before.** The mushrooms wouldn't have tasted wild if you'd soaked them in Ecstasy and given them guns.

*A lobster bisque ought to be the crowning glory of the potager. And this one was excellent. **Silky as a gigolo's compliment and fishy as a chancellor's promise.***

Dinner Parties

(1)

Your shirt is clean, your anecdotes polished, and you've had three glasses of Australian chardonnay and twenty-five Twiglets. On cue, the kitchen door flies open and in a cloud of steam your hostess and your dinner enter like Babette presenting her Feast. Only it's not a feast, it's a small square of supermarket pre-prepared 'fisherman's bake' and four grey mange-touts on a stone-cold plate. It sits there like an unwanted skin graft.

You remember that at home your babysitter is being paid £4 an hour to enjoy a splendid cassoulet. Do you smile cravenly at your hostess and pour compliments on her lazy, undeserving head? No, do what you want to do, what you should do – send it back. Courteously, but firmly, ask for something else, something appetising, something sustaining, something edible, for crying out loud.

Most of us, I know, would rather be caught in flagrante with a farm animal by Jeremy Beadle than murmur even the merest syllable of complaint at a dinner party, but sending your dinner back like a contrary Oliver Twist is not impossible.

I know, I've done it.

We are the only animals in God's creation who share our food with members of our own species to whom we are not related. We are also the only creatures who consider that mozzarella salad (made with the wrong sort of mozzarella), followed swiftly by a fibrous fig, constitutes a dinner party. And it's got to stop. We've got to get militant. We've got to start complaining about being called out after dark on false pretences. Let's get this straight: who's doing who a favour?

The received wisdom is that being a guest is a treat, a pleasure, even an honour. But just think about it: there are eight of us who have taken an hour to get ready and taxi across town in clean shirts with bottles of wine in order to be amusing and entertaining in someone else's dining room. I reckon that when everything's taken into consideration we've spent about £40 each for the pleasure of tucking into the lentil bake and Play-Doh brie. That's £320. And what did the hosts spend? Forty-five minutes and a fiver a head.

There is a kitchen adage that says: 'If the food is the star of your dinner party then you're inviting the wrong people.' Let's face it: dinner parties are social events and the company is the main thing. We've all been to parties where the epigrams sparkled like spumante, where the gossip was riveting and our flirtatious neighbours hung on our every word. We could have been eating carpet tiles for all it mattered. But that's no excuse for serving food that would make the shadow cabinet seem interesting by comparison. It is no excuse for a host to be too busy to shop wisely and cook well. If you're too damn successful to look after your friends, then don't give dinner parties. Take them to restaurants or hire a chef.

The first time I sent my dinner back at a private party, it was a filthy lentil stew. It had been made from the wrong, mushy sort of lentils, with a tin of tomatoes tipped in along with near-raw onion chunks. Accompanying it was one iceberg lettuce dressed with vinegar. The succeeding course, a plate of dead apples and a piece of spongy brie, was already on the table. I said that I didn't think that I could eat the stew. There was a silence you could have spread on toast. The women to the right and left of me edged away and the port merchant on the other side of the table choked on his Bulgarian retsina.

Then the hostess said: 'It is a bit disgusting, isn't it? I've got some eggs . . . ?'

There was a great sigh of relief from the ensemble and we all trooped into the kitchen and cooked each other omelettes. It was a huge success. I was a friend, and if a friend can't tell you that your food is a bilious slop which would be deemed an unnatural punishment in a Turkish jail, who can?

June 1993

(2)

Ten years ago, I wrote a piece about sending back food at dinner
parties. If it isn't any good, I said, ask your hostess to take it away
and bring something else. Perfectly reasonable. The article had the
desired effect – I haven't been invited to a dinner party since.

We should all know that the great Lucifer will tempt and tease
us, not with outright, wanton wickedness, but with a cunning simu-
lacrum of righteousness. And dinner parties are the work of the devil,
the dark side of honest supper, twisting the feeding of family and
friends to malevolence by snobbery, etiquette, envy and pomp.

The dinner party was the dandruff on the shoulder pads of the
evil decade, the 1980s – that explosion of big tits, big hair, big heels
and big heads. People threw their elderly relatives into the snow
and granny flats became dining rooms, while they tied up miniature
vegetables and sprayed raspberry vinegar like tomcats on the pull.

Perhaps at this point we should nail down what a dinner party is.
It's a dinner party when you get dressed up to eat in your own home,
and when you lay the table with things you would never use if it
were just the two of you: specialist exoskeleton removal implements,
butter knives, more glasses than you have hands, napkin rings, silver
pheasants, stags or goat-legged blokes humping fat Greek birds. It's
a dinner party if you write the names of people you know perfectly
well on little Alzheimer's cards and stick them into slots in gilt farm
animals or scallop shells. It's a dinner party if you're cooking some-
thing for the first time and if you're doing it in high heels. And it's
a dinner party if you arrange the food on the plates before serving.

It's not a dinner party if it's a couple of mates joining you for
supper, if the kids are there, if you can pour the wine without uttering
an adjective, and if the first thing you put on the table is brown sauce,
a television remote control, the evening paper or a takeaway box.

In the 1990s, the dinner party seemed to die out, knocked on its
silly hard head by tiredness, diets and a jolt of good taste. But I can
smell the burning polenta in the wind. Dinner parties didn't die –
they just slipped out for a smoke. And they're making a comeback.

The e-mails have started to arrive: would I like to come over for something to eat? And then the telltale date – a month and a half away. That's not spontaneous supper, that's gastronomic flashing, social quail-torturing. It's the thin end of the truffled brie. Duran Duran are back, Band Aid is back, legwarmers and cowboy boots are back. The hell of retro dinner parties can't be far behind.

Those of you who grew up in the 1990s, eating with your fingers, might think, 'Where's the harm? I could handle it.' But before you can say 'kumquat *brûlée*', you've cancelled the new car and taken the kids out of school, just so you can build a conservatory dining room and install an oven with an integrated teriyaki grill and ambidextrous rotisserie function. Remember: it's just an innocent canapé today, but it's the misery of beef Wellington tomorrow. The real sin of dinner parties is that they usurp the most basic human goodness of hospitality and succour and turn it into a homunculus of social climbing. But they also confuse two distinct occupations: cooks and chefs. Cooks do it at home for love. Chefs do it in public for money. Dinner parties are karaoke cheffery.

There are proper places for social gatherings over dinner, for offering hospitality. They're specifically designed to fill all your dinner-party needs and treat your 'mine host' fantasies. These places are called restaurants. A restaurant does everything you want from a dinner party, but better and cheaper. Yes, cheaper – if you factor in your time at the rate you're paid at work, or even at the pittance you pay your daily.

So, where to go? Somewhere local, somewhere they know you by name, that serves food that feeds conversation and doesn't overwhelm it. I'm loath to recommend a dining room to you. If you're old enough to be allowed out at night, you're old enough to find one that suits your tongue, pocket and aspirations.

So that's the recipe for a perfect dinner party: eat in – out.

November 2004

Cabbage

The entry for cabbage in the *Larousse Gastronomique* starts with the heavenly sentence: 'The cabbage seems to have been unknown to the Hebrews. It is not mentioned in the Bible.' I love that – so French. Just the slightest note of disappointment with God; just the merest raised eyebrow and pursued Gallic lip. You can imagine a French chef in confession: 'Bless me Father, for I have sinned – but I'm not the only one: God left cabbages out of the Bible.'

I can still remember my first cabbage, or rather, my first welcome cabbage; my first cabbage that didn't taste like silage boiled in iodine. Pull up a stool and I'll tell you about it.

There are important meals in everyone's life: dinners that are turning points, lunches after which you are a changed man. I can remember every meal that I've ever been dumped over. You sit down full of love, lust and appetite and just after the waiter clears away the starter the object of your desire reaches across and holds your hand in an anodyne sort of way and says 'A.A., I've got something I need to tell you. I love you like a friend . . . I need more space . . . I'm seeing your B.F. . . . .' and then, with the immaculate timing that you only get in the best establishments, the waiter returns with a huge plate of cassoulet, chips and a mixed salad. Your stomach turns to curdled milk and the food looks like someone has been sick on your plate; what's more, you don't know whether to brain the bitch with the bottle of claret or to beg and whimper. And then you remember you're picking up the bill as well.

Bad things always happen over dinner and good things always arrive at breakfast, but the most memorable, most precarious meals are always lunch. When I'm under the number 9 bus and my life flashes before me, the highlights will be a selection of lunches, such as the one where I had my first proper cabbage.

It was in Paris. I must have been eighteen and I was there with my father and brother; I can't remember another time when it was just the three of us together. Nick was sixteen and training to be a chef on the Left Bank, and my father and I had gone across to see how he was settling in. I had been to Paris before, but this time it felt new and original; it was early summer and sunny and we were all pleased to be in each other's company.

Although Paris is a city that my father knew well (he helped liberate it), it was now occupied by the next generation and belonged to Nick. He took us around like Christopher Wren showing off St Paul's. It was a charming reversal of roles. My father had always dragged us around cities refusing to use a map and pointing out baroque whatnots with tears in his eyes while my brother huffed along behind complaining about his feet and wanting Fanta.

This time Nick strutted off, diving into bars and cafés where the patron would shake us by the hand and give us tiny, sweet kirs on the house. Chefs, even very gauche sixteen-year-old commis, are respected in Paris. Daddy had a list of restaurants he had personally liberated in 1944 and which he had been personally liberating two or three times a year ever since. He suggested a few, but Nick said we should eat Alsatian food instead – food from Alsace-Lorraine, the department on the border with Germany that has changed hands once a generation for the last five hundred years.

The restaurant was called the Cochon Noir, the black pig, and I think it was near the Bastille. It might have been next to the Opera; anyway, it was cool and beautiful. We could have gone anywhere, but this was just right. In the entrance hall was a black piglet wearing a pink ribbon (so French, to let tomorrow's lunch smell its mummy cooking). We sat at a corner table and laughed and teased each other and Nick said he would choose, because he wanted to show off, and after a while a huge silver dish was borne unsteadily across the room by a bandy-legged waiter. On it was cabbage, the most divine aromatic mountain of sun-bleached, straw-coloured choucroute. And before you turn up your dainty noses and say 'Ugh, sauerkraut,' let me tell you that this dish had about as much in common with the grey sludge you get in bottles as Juliette Binoche has with Barbara Windsor. On its foothills were base camps of sausages, three or four kinds, and further up were precariously lodged veal chops, anaemic and milky. Closer to the summit were languid, voluptuous strips of fat pork. Ah, but the very best was at the apex: stuck in the top of the Eiger that was lunch was a split of champagne. The sweating waiter gratefully slid the edifice onto the damask and, taking a deep breath, tapped the neck of the bottle with a knife. The champagne erupted, frothing and sparkling all over the mountain. Such a surprise, such a joy, so right for the mood of the day.

That was a life-changing lunch. I never looked at cabbage in the same way after that. It was a bit like the bit in *Now, Voyager* when Bette Davis steps off the boat transformed from a dowdy frump into the most heavenly woman you have ever seen. That's what cabbage had been before: a frumpy vegetable and boring waste of plate space, with a smell that generations of Englishmen associate with floggings, polish, Latin and buggery.

Cabbage is now an almost universal vegetable. From Reykjavik to Canton, you can walk into the kitchen with a cabbage and the chef will smile. The *Brassica* genus (for that is whence the cabbage comes) has spawned a huge number of exotic cousins: cauliflowers, Brussels sprouts, kohlrabis. The cabbage itself comes in hundreds of shapes and sizes and the ones you are most likely to come across in Europe are the straight-leaved green cabbage (school cabbage), the curly savoy, the hard red (best cooked with vinegar and jam) and the white (for sauerkraut).

Cook cabbage gently in a little water, wine, stock or goose fat. It has tons of vitamins, but most of these are lost in the cooking; not that I care. I'm told it's good for the bowels, but since I'm not particularly interested in mine, I wouldn't know. The hard red and the white need to be cooked for longer than the other varieties. The best way to deal with cabbage is to eat it with butter and fresh black pepper; no, the best way is to poach it in wine and water with a piece of salt pork; then again, perhaps the best way is to cook it slowly with potatoes and sausages while you're out at the pub.

Cabbage, they say, is at the centre of the Russian soul. Just as

New York is the Big Apple, Moscow is now the Big Cabbage. A businessman I once met told me it was called that because it has many layers, a hard heart and is full of wind.

October 1994

Morning at the Ivy

6.45 A.M. THE IVY. The day begins. The head plongeur – the chief washer, wiper, mopper, shifter, lifter, stacker, peeler, plucker and muttering-swearer – unlocks the heavy green double doors of the tradesmen's entrance and goes down the stairs, two at a time, past the service bar, the wine cellar, the condiments cupboard, the chef's glass-walled office, to the kitchen.

Outside it's chilly, down here it's warm. The conserved heat of thousands of dinners. A successful kitchen never knows what it is to be cold. Neon flickers and chunters over the room. Everything rests at attention. This kitchen looks like the engine room of a beached battleship, all iron and steel pipes and ducts, thick and corrugated, worn rough and smooth by use. It is a room that shrugs off the word 'design', like oil on a hot pan. It defies order or elegance. The equipment squats like sideboard sumos, nutted and bolted, defending their small territories.

A commercial kitchen is as different from a domestic one as a tiger is from a tabby. There are none of the small rustic niceties of a family home and hearth here. This is not a warm welcome by the stove, no smiley magnets on the fridge, no children's daubs pinned to the wall, hanging herbs, aesthetic vases of wooden spoons. There is not a single chair – no time for one. This is a war room, a factory that manufactures hand-made food with dozens of moving parts, dozens of temperatures, textures, liquid, solid, ice, fire, propelled with pinpoint accuracy and machine-gun rapidity, plate after plate, the same and unique.

The plongeur doesn't look at the kitchen. He could trace every shin-barking stanchion, every apron-snagging tap in his sleep. He gets his brushes, buckets, cloths and sticky acid to attack the canopy. Every morning starts with the canopy. The long steel chimney that stretches over the central island of the ovens, the hot heart of the kitchen. The canopy is a bugger. It sucks the fumes, smoke and hot oaths of service in one continuous day-long intake of breath and spews, exhales, up, up, up and out, into the exhausted sky, to mix with all those other heavenly burnt offerings of London at the trough. The canopy is a bugger. Oil, fat, dripping, lard, ghee, stick and congeal in its creases and seams. The steam-borne smells of root and muscle, allium and brassica, saffron, thyme, turmeric, allspice, nutmeg and cinnamon, caramelised sugar, brandy and sour vinegar, duck thighs and salmon scales curl and emulsify into gobbets that dribble into nubbed stalactites on its galvanised yawn. In other restaurants they try to forget about the canopy, pretend it's not there. Ignore its acquisitive intake of breath, leave it to someone else. Once a week, once a month, whenever the Health Inspector cometh. The Ivy is not other restaurants. At the Ivy they do the bugger every damn day.

A commis-chef arrives, thin and pale as bacon rind, eyes rheumy with untouched sleep. Slope-shuffling feet, he goes to the hob, turns a key, strikes a match. The first hissing blue flame. A commis isn't quite the lowest being in the brigade of chefs: there are apprentices below him, but he is non-commissioned, expendable fodder. Commis is the beginning of the long climb to your own kitchen, your own glass office, but it's a long way away this morning. He bangs down a pan. In every kitchen in the world this is the first thing ever cooked: water. The start of everything, the universal necessity. You can get by without anything but water. Water for coffee. Big tin of instant. Instant, peel away the memories of warm sheets. Instant, wash-the-gritty-eyes caffeine. All the staff here drink from half-pint mugs. The customers have cups and saucers, but this isn't sipping and chatting coffee: this is medicine, this is drugs.

The commis swigs, then collects a heavy sticky blue dustbin on dodgy wheels, a mobile charnel house, full of claggy bones. Big, saw-ended, clubbable veal bones, baked brown and congealed. He puts a pot, big enough to boil a small missionary, onto the wide burner and chucks in skeleton segments two-handed. This cauldron, and another like it, will simmer and bubble all day, washing the knuckles and marrow of flavour, until the bones are bleached dry.

This stock is the fuel of traditional kitchens, the basic sticky, meaty, chameleon goodness, that is the base for soups, sauces and glazes. The Ivy makes and uses up to fifty litres a day. Another swig of medicine. Trays of stacked fresh bones go into the slow oven to be browned off for tomorrow.

The kitchen begins to fill. The morning sous-chef arrives – he is in charge until lunch – and starts going through papers in the crammed glass office. Upstairs, beyond the swing doors that mark the uneasy boundary between the white uniform and the black, the restaurant is still dark and quiet. The tables and chairs are stacked in the middle of the room, silhouetted against the faint grey dawn that pokes through the criss-crossed mullioned windows. An empty restaurant is never a lonely place. The bubble and clatter of service seem to be just a sub-audible echo away. The room hums with the spirit of dinner.

At the far end, through the bar and the doors into the lobby where the hat-check sits, there is a blue window with a moon on it. A street light shines and casts a romantic, dream-like, cerulean glow over the entrance. It is appropriate. The Ivy is a romantic place.

The Ivy is a unique restaurant. In a city bowed down with restaurants, these fretted, scarred, screwed and glued plywood upended tables and chairs are the most sought after in Britain. More people yearn for a round plywood first-night table than a Georgian pedestal table with acanthus carving. In the trade the Ivy has a professional reputation that is envied beyond avarice and mimicked thanks. This is the pre-eminent club of the British theatre, drama's green room. It is also claimed for television, film, publishing, advertising and journalism. This is the room where people who are professionally good in rooms come to be good at what they are good at. The Ivy is a modern, living Poets' Corner. At every lunch or dinner, anyone who reads a Sunday paper will recognise at least a dozen relaxed, smooth-toothed, autocue-animated faces, and the ones you don't recognise are likely to be the movers and shakers, the fixers and dealers of the culture.

Other restaurants may drop a handful of starry names of who eats with them. At the Ivy it would be easier to list the ones who don't. Noël Coward doesn't eat here, Laurence Olivier, Margot Fonteyn,

Marlene Dietrich and Dame Nellie Melba don't eat here, but they did. For most of this century everybody who is anybody has dined at the Ivy.

8.00 A.M. The first delivery of the day arrives. Lay's Fruit and Veg. It's a family business of three cheeky-chappie Chelsea supporters, Cockney enough to warm the cockles of Dick Van Dyke's speech coach's heart. They have been doing 'The Garden' for three generations. Bags of potatoes, boxes of squash, carrots, onions, beans. The sous-chef regards an early parsnip dubiously, Cos lettuce for the Caesar Salad and crates of 'queer gear'. Air-freighted berries, perky ingénue salad leaves dumped in a rush by the larder for the kitchen apprentice to sort.

Breakfast. Bacon sandwiches for the kitchen; sliced white, chin-dribbling, eaten standing.

The first Black Suit arrives. A front-of-house manager, he hurries through the dining room turning on lights. Careful, elegant light, emotive rise-and-fall illumination, not the buzzing flat white-out of the kitchen. Coffee. He fills the machine with the Ivy's special Arabica blend, the water giggles and hisses in through the filter. Customers' coffee, front-of-house coffee.

Downstairs, the kitchen has moved up a gear. The commis who makes the stock is on sauces today. He stands hunched over his little station, surrounded by pots: curry sauce, dark truffle, meat reductions. He chops handfuls of parsley, tarragon and chervil, pours oil into a hot pan, fries off shallots, shovels tomato concassé.

The kitchen may look haphazard and disorganised, but it is formed, cluttered by experience and repetition – not just of eighty years here, but of two hundred years of collective restaurant experience. This is a traditional kitchen, arranged in the old way of stations. Spreading out from sauces are fish, hot and cold starters and hors d'oeuvres, vegetables and larder, pastry and puddings. Every position has a commis going about their small bit of defensible space. You don't ever have to pretend to look busy in a kitchen: from the minute you walk through the doors you just are.

Over by the hellish deep-fat fryer, a big chef takes a small onion bhajee, fries it and presses it, fries it again and takes it to the sous-chef to taste.

'Not enough salt.'

He gives it to me to taste. 'Not enough salt.'

'Better put some more salt in it then.'

There is little chat. Curt hellos, a bit of 'What did you do last night?', 'You didn't, did you?', 'The same,' and some work, 'Have you got a spatula?' There is none of that arch French hand-shaking that takes the first half-hour of every day in Paris. The atmosphere is relaxed because there isn't time to be formal. Escoffier or Carême could walk into this kitchen and feel at home. Outside, the world would be confusion to them, but the kitchen is the last workplace, apart from a museum and the law, to resist rationalisation and ergonomics and employ friendly psychology. A kitchen remains unreconstructed because it works, and because chefs like it this way.

It's a masculine place, incorrect, unfair, hierarchical. A hard-knock, sharp-edges, fat-and-fire place. That's not to say that women don't fit in here, or are not respected, it's just that kitchens don't say please and thank you for a reason. You have to want to work in them very much indeed to get on here. This is not a place to have doubts, want a view, miss fresh air, be squeamish or become a vegan. Kitchens are tough because nobody can fail alone in them: everybody works together or they all fail together. It's not too many cooks that spoil the broth, it's one – the one who forgets the salt.

November 1997

Pomegranate

I have a very strong memory of the first time I ate pomegranates. It was my second year at boarding school, and I was twelve. It was the same year I went to my first dance and bought my first pop record (*Sgt Pepper's Lonely Hearts Club Band*), read *From Russia with Love* and had my first kiss from a girl who closed her eyes and smelt of Johnson's Baby Shampoo and warm winceyette. She played the 'Moonlight Sonata' on the black Bösendorfer in the chilly music room, then leant across and kissed me. I caught a faint opalescent glimmer of her breasts down the front of her nightie. I think she imagined that you should kiss someone after playing Beethoven, and I just happened to be there. I can't hear that piece now without missing the feeling of lips on mine during the silence at the end. Unfortunately, I wasn't there for Rachmaninov.

The day after that kiss was Saturday, and I took my half-crown to the local town as usual, but instead of squandering it on fish' n' chips or a Wimpy, I bought a pomegranate. I really don't know why, as I didn't know what they were. I was at a vegetarian boarding school, so gastronomy was a long way down the list of important things. I do remember being starving at the time, but then a pomegranate isn't what you go for when you're hungry. I'd like to think it was a sympathetic memory of the glimpsed bosom, but perhaps it was because I was unhappy. Homesickness is the worst thing in the world when you're twelve.

The pomegranate was as alien to dormitories – and bells, farting boys, wet socks and the flat, dun-coloured, damp East Anglia that I was stuck in – as it was possible to get. A beautiful russet and rose ball, a comfortable weight in the palm of the hand, it seemed to promise exotic sunshine, distant dusty mountains and warm earth. I took it back to my room and cut it open with my going-to-school penknife, to discover I'd bought a treasure box of beautifully packed precious beads, more delicate and mysterious than anything the ghastly dining room had to offer. I had no idea how you ate a pomegranate, and eventually decided to use a straightened safety pin, spiking each perfect seed and rolling it around my tongue as though it were a sweet-tart tear. It whiled away a miserable afternoon. Every Saturday during the autumn term, I'd buy a pomegranate and eat it, a seed at a time, huddled on the school playing fields watching the house XI kick their opponents' shins.

The flavour of pomegranate is ineffably sad. It's the taste of mourning, of grief mixed with happy memory. I couldn't have picked a better metaphor for how I felt about being away from home, about the girl who kissed me, about my life and body changing from boy to young man. I'd like to say that I understood all this, that I realised that the fruit was a symbolic catharsis, an allegory, but I didn't. I did, however, learn that nice things given when you're unhappy can make you sadder, and that the flavour of sweetness counterpoints bitter-salt sourness.

The pomegranate was a symbol of life long before I got hold of one at school. Persephone, Demeter's beautiful daughter, was kidnapped by Pluto and forced to be his bride in the dark Underworld. She mourned for the green, living world above, and was told that she could return to her mother, so long as she hadn't eaten anything in Hades. But she had eaten six pomegranate seeds. So for six months of the year, Persephone had to remain with Pluto in Hades as a Queen of the Dead, while the earth mourned, and for the remaining six months she returned to her mother and the world bloomed. She also fell in love with Adonis, but that's another story.

The pomegranate grows wild in Asia Minor, and was cultivated by the ancient Egyptians and Greeks about 3,000 years ago. But I'm not sure how they ate it; as far as we know the Greeks didn't eat fruit with meat – it was kept for symposia where wine was drunk. Considering pomegranates have been around for such a long time, recipes for them are few and far between. I've just been leafing through my cookery books and the Greek and Middle Eastern ones often leave them out altogether. Perhaps they've always just been a symbol of sex.

If you want to cook with pomegranates, you need to remove the seeds with a small spoon and avoid the sour-tasting intricate membrane. If you want the juice, simply press the seeds through a sieve. I can hardly ever eat them: they make me sad. Still, the best way to do so is one seed at a time, when the fields are bare and bleak and you think spring will never come. Taste the subtle, ancient flavour and remember Persephone, ruling over the dead as she counted the days before she could return to the sunlight and the green shoots appeared again.

February 1998

Vegetarians

Don't you just hate pandas? Whenever I find myself with a surfeit mouthful of unfocused loathing, I remember pandas and it slips down nicely.

For a start, it's their faces, that childish clown's make-up. And then there's the ingratitude. Panda should be a synonym for rudeness. After everything that has been done for them – the money, the diplomatic initiatives, the four-star reception centres – all we have asked in return is that they mate. Hardly onerous work. And will they? Will they heck. They just sit there turning their backs on us, begging, stuffing their mouths, occasionally relaxing on a car tyre. A tyre, may I remind you, that has been paid for by you and me. How many decent English families can afford to have a recreational tyre? Exactly. Pandas are just taking advantage.

This country has an unparalleled record in offering a home to persecuted pandas. We've been welcoming them since before *Blue Peter*. And, heavens, nobody's suggesting that pandas with a real cause – pregnant pandas – should be refused entry. But in all the years, how many babies have they given in return for our soft-touch liberal largesse? None. Zilch. Zero. I think I speak for all decent, right-minded people when I say enough is enough. No more pandas.

It's not just their ingratitude – they're not like us. Barely human. Barely bear. If my daughter ever fell for those big black eyes and came home with a panda, I'd... I'd... well, I wouldn't be responsible for my sulk. I'd sulk until my nose dropped off. I'd read the newspaper and hum the Dambusters meaningfully. If they've got problems at home, well I'm sorry. We've got problems of our own. The truth is, pandas are just sexual tourists. They've brought it on themselves.

You may be wondering what all this has got to do with a restaurant column. Well, let me tell you the shocking truth: the real reason we hate pandas. They're vegetarians. Oh, you knew that already? Ah, but what you don't know is that they've chosen to be vegetarians. Pandas are unique in the non-human mammalian world: they're animals with carnivores' metabolisms, digestive systems and teeth who have, through caprice, self-advertisement and subverted anger at their parents, become vegetarian. Their brinking extinction is nothing to do with predators, human encroachment, ozone, motor cars or online banking. It's because they won't eat their bloody dinners. 'Oh no, just a few bamboo shoots for me, mum. I'm a vegetarian.'

Well, they're going. Oblivion is staring them in the bowel. Let the panda be a grim warning to all those little girls who think they'll be more interesting if they give up meat. It will only end in black-eyed tears. Nobody will want to sleep with you, you'll never have babies, and you'll spend all day playing back-axles with a Pirelli.

Vegetarian cooking is, it need hardly be repeated, unremittingly vile. It's omelette without the Prince, Rachmaninov's Third without a piano, *Casablanca* without Bogart; it's a kiss without tongue, Christmas without presents – an endless faux-flirtatious cook-tease. One of the little professional tricks of food criticism is to look at a dish and ask: 'Are these ingredients presented in a way that does them the most justice? Is this the best these things can achieve?' With vegetarian food, the answer is always no. It could have been left raw, or it could have been a bridesmaid to some big-hearted, taut-bummed hot corpse. There is always something missing. Begins with M, ends with T.

'Ah . . .' I can hear the frail, ululating voice of a wan and flaccid woman, lying exhausted on a sticky chaise longue. 'You just haven't had good vegetarian food. You should try my mixed-pulse cheesy bake.' Oh, yes I have. I was a vegetarian for a decade. A neat turn-around this. Most children become vegetarians because they hate their parents. My parents sent me to a vegetarian boarding school because they loved me. There is no variation of vegetable muck brought steaming to the table with the exhortation, 'Tuck in, you'll really adore this,' that I haven't tried. And none of it is remotely as good as the stuff I was designed to consume.

The rules of reviewing vegetarian places are not the same as for real restaurants. For a start, vegetarians are people who don't eat things. This is important. Vegetarians ask waiters if they have anything without meat, they don't ask if there is anything with vegetables. Vegetarian restaurants are judged by what they don't cook. The less they cook the better. A vegetarian waiter could come to your table and say: 'Hi! Let me tell you what's off the menu today. We don't have lamb, pork, beef; we have no chicken or fish.' Vegetarians are people who get pleasure from not eating things, and one must keep all this to the fore when breaking bread with them.

Christmas is a bad time to eat lunch in a city. Restaurants are solid with office parties wearing paper hats and shrieking. The Blonde and I decided to try a vegetarian restaurant because we knew a) that we'd be able to get a table and b) that it would be mercilessly free from conspicuous fun and gratuitous enjoyment.

The first thing you notice is the smell: the round, mushy, slightly acidic odour of sanctimonious worthiness. We queued with a tray at the long counter and surveyed the groaning repast set out to tempt us. Vegetarians aren't big on presentation; everything looks as if they've got a bulimic hippo as a food taster. The thing a diligent critic must have, to be fair to vegetarian lunch, is a gnawing hunger. Peckish won't do: you've got to be famished to pass this on to trusting peristalsis.

To start, we were offered tomato and butter bean chowder (let the abuse of the word 'chowder' go) or butter bean soup. Now vegetarians endlessly boast about the endless variety of their cuisine to us carnivores. Veggy cookbooks always promise a thousand and one recipes, a million things to do with a peeler. It's all nonsense. There are just two vegetarian dishes: mucky stodge and stodgy muck. Here, in a pre-eminent vegetarian restaurant, was the proof: a choice of butter bean soup or butter bean soup with tomato.

'Oh, I think I'll have the, er, um, decisions decisions, oh, what the hell, make it the butter bean.'

The Blonde had added tomato. They were both ghastly, tepid, thick, mono tastes, puréed pulse without a heatbeat. What followed was without doubt one of the worst meals I have eaten. The money I have most resented spending. It was all made without apparent love or care or talent. Again, it convinced me that the only ingredients vegetarians care about are the ones they won't use.

My Moroccan potato casserole was a textbook dish. You might like to make it at home to insult the neighbours. Here, as far as I could work out, is how it was done. First boil some lumps of potato in water that other vegetables have been boiled in. When they've absorbed their own weight in liquid, stew them with turmeric (a yellow food colouring for people who can't afford saffron), add some raisins and a sprinkling of chilli, leave to sit for an hour, serve from a great height with panache.

The restaurant itself was a clever functional imitation of a Methodist destitutes' drop-in centre. Every surface I touched was sticky; the cutlery, tables, trays and chairs clung to us like lonely drunks. We sat miserably for the ten minutes it took to taste and discard the food. The bus boy removed our piled plates without a murmur; we obviously weren't the first or he didn't care. Valiantly trying to digest, we glumly watched the queue pass along the counter that says yes to life. I noticed that vegetarians are all marked by their extremities. They have double helpings of freeform set-aside hair, which they arrange in exuberant abstract patterns, and their shoes are cunningly cobbled so that, if need be, an extra pair of feet may be inserted. They also all sniff fruitily. Nobody smiled.

I have a theory as to why vegetarians never smile. Go and smile at yourself in the mirror, now count along your teeth. Two from the middle are a pair that are sharper and pointier than the rest; they are your canine or dog teeth, God's proof that you were born to eat meat. Vegetarians don't smile because their mouths give away their true natures, and are a constant reproach and reminder of their unnatural proclivities. So pity the poor vegetarian, and give one a great big grin this Yuletide.

April 2000, December 2005

Stow-on-the-Wold

Through the miracle of printing, let me whisk you to a gentle fold in the Cotswolds and the soft, lyrically ageless, honey-coloured hell that is Stow-on-the-Wold. Just say it: Stow-on-the-Wold. It's like having a mouthful of the butteriest, sugariest, sucky-glutinous fudge. Stow-on-the-Wold on a Sunday fair takes your breath away, makes you want to hug yourself, wear a cravat, sell your bijou flat in Fulham and move right here, right now. And then set yourself on fire in the market square as a beacon for those who might be foolish enough to follow. Of all the terrible knick-knacky, home-made, detestable places I've seen in this country, Stow takes the biscuit. It will sell you the biscuit first, made from an ancient Gloucestershire granny recipe using only organic pixie nuts.

Where to start? Ah, let's start over there in the organic-food shop with fancy craft den attached. The crafty-wafty shoppy-woppy sells pottery table fountains in runny, pastel iced-cookie colours. I know, I know. How have you ever lived without one? They're £100 each, and together they tinkle like a hymn to incontinence. But the sheer, naked, full-on, peeing nastiness of them isn't the thing that sends you reeling, it's the notices telling you what not to do. Fourteen of them (I counted). Smoking, of course. Eating. Drinking. Babies. Touching. Breaking. Spitting. Loitering. But my favourite is: 'Only serious enquiries, thank you.' Or maybe it was 'sincere'. That boggled beyond Gordian unboggling. How could anyone conceivably be either serious or sincere about portable, moist, plug-in pottery ornaments?

I was brought here by Jeremy Clarkson. It's his neck of the woods – and it needs to be wrung. He not only chose but paid to live hereabouts. They all know him. 'Hello Jeremy,' they say (even the ones with Alzheimer's). 'You're Jeremy Clarkson, aren't you?' Sitting in the only place you're allowed to drink coffee and smoke simultaneously (hotel garden, residents only, unless you're local hero Clarkson), I pointed out that nothing, but nothing, could make this place worse. It had an unbeatable royal flush of horror. And then the Morris men started.

We escaped to a pub in a nearby village.

Country pubs are buried deep in the collective cerebellum, right at the back in the oldest, black-beamed, rustic bit of our brains. We have a country-pub node that feeds sentimental, Edwardian, Wind-in-the-Willows, cloth-cap-and-tankard, ready-rubbed-shag twaddle into our heads to the sound of Percy Grainger. It's impossible to have been born and bred in this country and be dispassionate about pubs. You know they're foul, but you'd die in a ditch to save them. Even New Labour is trying to pass a bill to stop them renaming the Turk's Head the Slug and Stripper.

Sunday lunch in a country pub is one of those things Englishmen with unspeakable tropical diseases in distant jungles hallucinate about just before they die. And this is the pub they dream of. It's perfect in every particular. Hunting prints. Cross-eyed stuffed Reynards on the yellow-stone walls. Inglenooks a gogo. And things growing all over it. There's a garden with barrows planted with flowers. Everything is so exactly right that it's quite obviously a base for invading Martians.

And the lunch was a perfect pub lunch, just the way you imagine it when you've got a temperature. Roast beef that tastes like it has been cut off the bottom of the Morris men's pantomime horse, Yorkshire pudding like dry rot, kedgeree that's hunt-the-fish and the colour of Chinese cowardice, sticky-toffee pudding, and beers that sound like characters from P.G. Wodehouse. 'Ah, Hook Norton, glad you could make it. Do you know Beamish and Tolly Cobbold? Marston is in the gents.' It all cost nothing, or next to a metropolitan nothing.

We happily watched the weekend locals self-consciously talking greenfly in their stiff Country Casuals cords and Viyella shirts, everyone trying as hard as possible to be a character from a 1950s Shell poster, as if the whole thing were being recorded for posterity; as if they were the ghosts of posterity, and 'contemporary' meant chaps you did National Service with and a joke that happened to art. You see, that's why I could never live in the country. I wouldn't have the stamina to keep up the continual collective pretence, the delusion, that all this was normal.

July 2000

Starbucks

Have you ever been to a Starbucks? (God, I'm beginning to sound like those judges who say: 'Pray, what is a Rolling Stone? And could you enlighten the court on the exact nature of a T-shirt?') Of course you've been to a Starbucks. Starbucks is your second living room. The question I should have asked is: why?

I'm not a habitué of these West Coast coffee shops. Not for any snobbish reason – just because I like coffee. An American café sounds like the punchline to one of those jokes in which the Germans end up the lovers, the Italians the soldiers, the French the marriage counsellors and the Greeks the cooks, architects or hairdressers – in fact, anything at all. I can't think of a single thing I'd trust a Greek to do professionally, except make Turkish coffee. (That should get the postman's hernia pulsating.) Asking Americans to make coffee is like asking them to draw a map of the world.

'OK, so this is your house, that's Disneyland, and what's this squiggle over here? Right, that's everywhere else.' American coffee is only coffee because they say it is. It's actually a pale, scalding infusion of junior-school jam-jar brush water. Americans who drink one a week imagine they're in the grip of a vicious caffeine frenzy that prohibits them from signing legal documents, operating heavy machinery and adopting children, but, oddly, helps if they want to plea-bargain a murder – or bomb developing countries. It's not a drink for grown-ups.

Anyway, I did go to a Starbucks recently. And I'm still reeling. I can't remember the last time I was served something as foul as its version of a cappuccino. I say 'version', but that's a bit like saying Dot Cotton's a version of Audrey Hepburn.

To begin with, it took longer to make than a soufflé. I was the only customer, and asked the girl for a cappuccino. There followed an interrogation that would have impressed an SS Scientologist. What size did I want? Did I need anything in it? Was I hungry? By the time she'd finished, I felt like sobbing: 'You've found Tom, and Dick's under the stove in D Hut, but I'll never give away Harry – he's got Dickie Attenborough up him.'

Suspiciously, she passed the order, written in Serbian, to another girl standing all of three inches away, who, in turn, slowly morphed into Marie Curie and did something very dangerous and complicated behind a counter, with a lot of sighing and brow-furrowing.

An hour and a half later, I was presented with a mug. A mug. One of those American mugs where the lip is so thick, you have to be an American or able to disengage your jaw like a python to fit it in your mouth. It contained a semi-permeable white mousse – the sort of stuff they use to drown teenagers in Ibiza, or pump into cavity walls. I dumped in two spoonfuls of sugar. It rejected them. Having beaten the malevolent epidermis with the collection of plastic and wooden things provided, I managed to make it sink. Then, using both hands, I took a sip. Then a gulp. Then chewed.

I had the momentary sense of drowning in snowman's poo, then, after a long moment, a tepid sludge rose from the deep. This was reminiscent of gravy browning and three-year-old Easter eggs.

How can anyone sell this stuff? How can anyone buy this twice? And this was only a small one – a baby. The adult version must be like sucking the outlet of a nuclear power station.

I slumped into a seat. There was a pamphlet about fair trade, and how Starbucks paid some Nicaraguan Sancho a reasonable amount for his coffee so that he now had a mule to go with his thirteen children, leaky roof and fifteen coffee bushes. It made not screwing the little no-hope wetback into penury sound like the most astonishing act of charitable benevolence. And they just had to print a pamphlet about it, so we all know the sort of selfless, munificent, group-hug people we're dealing with.

I've just looked up the origin of cappuccino. I always imagined it was nineteenth-century Italian. Actually, it appears first in 1683, just after the relief of Vienna from the Ottomans. The retreating Turks left behind sacks of coffee, and an enterprising double agent, Franz

Georg Kolschitzky, opened the first European coffee shop (disputed with Caffè Florian, in Venice). It was not a success until he added milk, honey and cinnamon. The cappuccino was born. He needed something to go with it, so he got his neighbour, the baker Peter Wendler, to turn his excellent butter buns into Turkish symbols. Ta-ra! The croissant.

All that history, all Sancho's effort, and it ends up as Starbucks. Oh, the pity and the shame. The name, by the way, comes from Capuchin monks, who had white habits. Interestingly, they also donated their name to a monkey, simply by adding a syllable.

February 2003

Concert

Took my boy Ali to see Eminem. 'Are you sure?' cautioned other parents. 'It's pretty unpleasant. Urban nihilism. Drugs. Violence. It could get very ugly.' Yes, I'm aware of all that – but I think he's old enough to make up his own mind about Milton Keynes. Anyway, I'll be there to remind him to just say 'No ... tting Hill Gate'. Eminem, by contrast, is a poppety socks.

Now I'm about to do one of those things that annoyed the loons and grandpa vest off me when I was a lad. I'm going to patronise young people's culture. I once had an old in-law who would smile with a manic serenity and say: 'You know, I'm not shocked. You think you're all so clever and on your face.' But it's gay-porn Nazis, I'd say, doing it with cripples in the middle of a christening. 'No, no, I saw far worse than that during the blackout.'

Anyway, Ali and I stood in the bowl of Milton Keynes, shouting 'Fug chew, muddyfugger!' as instructed. It was a bonding moment. I know other fathers take their sons to chalk streams and tie small bits of handmade bellybutton fluff to hooks, but, for my boy and me, the father-son thing is woven by singing 'Two trailer-park girls go round the outside.' I love the pantomime audience-participation stuff. Instead of shouting 'Behind you!' and 'Oh, no, he didn't!' we go 'Yo! Fugger pig!' But what I like best about Eminem – and I'm not sure a lot of the audience quite understood this – is that he is, in fact, the second coming of Gilbert and Sullivan.

Now, I can hear you snorting all over the Home Counties. But bear with me – I'm not coming over all Tom 'Contrary' Paulin just to get a rise. Eminem sings patter songs: they could be from *The Pirates of Penzance* or, indeed, *Ruddigore*. The Lord High Executioner's little list is plainly proto-rap. Eminem just adds a modern touch of Grand Guignol (a theatrical form that has been sadly and shamefully ignored

of late) and auto-testicle clutching, which I've always thought there
was far too little of in *The Mikado*.

'What has this to do with food?' I hear you say. Or, more likely,
'Yo! Muddyfugger, wheredy fugdy food, bitch?' Well, I was planning
on doing an archly amusing little review of the luncheon bazaar that
circles the bowl of Milton Keynes. (By the way, I'm sure I'm not the
first to point this out, but was it the civil servants' famed sense of
humour that named this place after the two Englishmen who would
have loathed it the most?) But they're not paying me enough to put
this stuff in my mouth ahead of a four-hour traffic jam. And, anyway,
it's the one cuisine that you all know intimately: the caravans of
burgers and sausages, pizza and lardy ice cream, and a stand with a
sign that was as unequivocal as it was untrue: 'Chinese Food'. Given
the enormous changes in gastronomy and our growing sophistication
about food, it's amazing that the catering at large, popular events
remains doggedly doggy. It's essentially the same as it was when I first
came across it in the 1960s, and probably longer ago than that. It's
the nastiest food in Europe. That smell of onions sweated in fat and
water, then seared on a greasy hotplate, is the abiding scent of the
English en masse. I'm sure that's what the Crusades smelt like – all
the way from Tilbury to Acre.

In Milton Keynes there were 64,000 people, all of whom can now
find their way round menus in half a dozen languages and three or
four continents, who have watched a thousand hours of cookery on
television, who use a wine list, who travel abroad. But this event cater-
ing is still all people think they deserve when out having communal
fun. The problem with it is that it's still very white food. Indeed, the
audience for Eminem was extraordinarily white. I saw only half a
dozen black men, and most of them were on stage. This just added
to the *Mikado* nature of the event. It's fusion pop culture: the way
Fred Astaire fused with black dancing and Elvis fused with the blues.
Fusion is never a 50:50 deal. As heat passes from the hotter to the
cooler, so popular culture passes from the black to the white, from
the gay to the straight, from the street to the square, from angry to
amused. It's social thermodynamics.

I was just trying to remember what it was my dad took me to

see when I was ten. It was *Coppelia*, with Robert Helpmann, who resembled Eminem in not a single atom. As I recall, it's the story of a dirty old man who falls in love with a mechanical underage sex doll. And you really imagine that's more suitable than Eminem singing about cleaning out his closet?

July 2003

Pubs

I've spent more time in pubs than in any other public building. More than in restaurants or cinemas, theatres or magistrates' courts, libraries, museums or churches. More than in all of them put together. That's an amazing testimony to the power of the pub – and a savage indictment of my social sophistication.

My abiding memory of pubs is not the Hogarthian jostle, the elbow-nudge and spittle-spray or the claggy dampness that implies every surface is the sickly skin of some giant comatose creature. It isn't the bellowed bollocks, the charmless flirting or the desperate, choking camaraderie with geezers whose surnames I never knew, but whose girlfriends I'd shagged.

No, my abiding memory of pubs is the wide open emptiness, the motes drifting in the cue of sunlight above the pool table, the luke-bile gag of the first rinsing mouthful of beer and the fingered and folded *Daily Mail*s, passed from bacon-smoked hand to redundant hand. ''Ere, you went to boarding school. What's the capital of Nigeria? Five letters. First letter K... Bugger. That means wanker's wrong.'

Some – actually, lots of – people have asked me why I spent so much time in pubs.

The answer is that I was a drunk, and that's where drunks go. But that's only half an answer. One of the few perks of being a full-time professional drunk is that you can do it almost anywhere – benches, emergency stairs in multi-storey car parks, other people's spare rooms. And yet I would assiduously get up every morning and go to a pub, the way my grandfather went to the bank. I was never late and I never took a day off sick. I'd sit and wait till they rang bells and threw me out.

It's the waiting I remember most vividly, waiting for something to happen. The pub was a metaphysical airport lounge and, standing at the bar, I was like those drivers with a passenger's name scribbled on cardboard. I stood there for years with this invisible sign that just said: 'Anyone. Anywhere.' At the core of the Wagnerian despair of your committed drunk, there is a Micawberish glimmer that something will turn up.

It's a long time since I've been to a pub with intent. Like all folk who make, or are forced to make, life-fracturing decisions – the defrocked priest, the refrocked transsexual, the refugee, the divorcee – I'm ambivalent about the rooms I've left behind. Going into a pub is like revisiting the scene of a crime, being both victim and perpetrator. One of the things I hated at the time was any confusion of the pubbiness of pubs; the trendy pretence that the pub might be a family recreation lounge, a French-ish boules park, a part-time disco, a Cuban cocktail bar or, worse – much worse – a restaurant.

Food and pubs go together like frogs and lawnmowers, vampires and tanning salons, mittens and Braille. Pubs don't do food; they offer internal mops and vomit decoration. The idea that the gastropub is the answer to a lack of reasonably priced decent public food in suburban Britain, and the declining fortunes of public houses, is a Tony-ish mule of an idea.

Pub kitchens are invariably tiny and ill equipped to produce much more than a toasted sandwich. The dreams and desires of drinkers and eaters aren't complementary. A drinker needs room to get clumsy, flick fag ends and do Sean Connery impressions, which tends to get in the way of the organic English spotted loin in mustard and balsamic jus. And what about fighting? You can't have a fight in a gastropub. It would be all Hooray Billy Bunter bun-chucking.

We've had a decade of pub restaurants, and they're virtually all horribly splod and tish. But still they come, little upstairs rooms with a couple of tables, a snug made into a kitchen, barmen doubling as waiters. So it was with less than vaunting enthusiasm that I shuffled down to Lambeth to try the latest one. I couldn't even get the Blonde to come. She said she'd see me for real dinner later.

I walked in and discovered it was a pub: a very pubby pub, pubbled with after-work drinkers. The restaurant bit was in an adjoining room. At 6.30 pm, it was packed – and I was amazed. The waitress found me a spot on a table with two couples. The kitchen was a cage the size of a Monopoly board, with a pair of cooks running around like the top hat and the iron. The menu was to the point and very good – modern, non-dainty-Rhodes English. It had that distinctive, meaty smell of Fergus Henderson. I think maybe both the hat and the iron trained with him at St John.

I started with a dish that made the whole room go quiet.

The lights went down and a single spot illuminated the bowl in front of me. In the distance, there was a choir singing the Angelus, and I knew, the way you just know, that I was going to love this dish with all my heart for the rest of my life – or its life, whichever was longer. It was a heart-clutchingly thick potato soup, and nestling in it was a slab, a plinth, an altar of pressed foie gras, gently melting. It was properly brilliant. Every descriptive illustration I can think of to make it live for you is so intimately sensual that we can't print it on a Sunday. It was rough'n'toff.

February 2004

Turtle

'This must be the worst thing you've ever put in your mouth,' said a travelling companion as the waiter presented us with the turtle. We were in the middle of a paddy field outside Hanoi, in a restaurant that was no more than an agricultural, corrugated iron barn on a concrete floor with that ubiquitous light of Asia, neon. It specialised in what my Vietnamese guide euphemistically called 'exotic food'. What he meant was stuff fished out of mud – frogs, rats and this turtle, which is what Americans call a turtle and I call a terrapin.

They come, of course, with their own handy serving suggestion. We chose a live terrapin doing its impression of a dead terrapin in a plastic paddling pool. Why anyone wants to keep these things as a pet is beyond me. Anyway, half an hour later it's back at the table, looking remarkable unfazed. Only the waiter goes *voilà!* and lifts its lid off with all the swagger of the Tour d'Argent. After half an hour of sucking the metatarsals out of gelatinous feet and fiddling about in its incredibly rudimentary digestive system with chopsticks, I realised that turtle on the half-shell is more of an event and an anecdote than a meal.

I also had the hard-boiled fertilised duck egg. This is a 12-day-old Jemima Puddle-Duck abortion and, frankly, though edible, it's not an improvement on the before or the after. We were offered scentweasel, a cat-sized animal wrapped in a straitjacket of bamboo, and whose furious eyes gleamed in the neon. I declined, not because I couldn't have eaten it, but because I probably wouldn't have finished it.

All of these things weren't served for sustenance or pleasure, but as mystical medicines. Medicinal food in the Third World usually promises one of two things: boy babies, or an erection you can open a packing case with. I'm continually astonished at the number of things that are supposed to be aphrodisiacs in the Far East in societies that, leaving aside Western sexual tourism, are generally rather prim and conservative.

We left. The waiter gave me the gall and blood of the terrapin in rice spirit to take away. I gave it to my driver, a man of unsurpassed hideousness. The next day he told me he'd shared it with his 70-year-old father. Together they'd had a night of depraved Dionysian excess, he winked and leered. I strongly suspected he'd got dumpling-faced and did karaoke.

The things people always imagine will be vomit-inducing usually aren't. I've eaten white flying termites, salty ants, scorpions, jewelled beetles, locusts, armadillo in the shell, agouti, warm Masai cattle blood from a gourd rinsed in urine, and giant African frog. All of the insects were delicious. In fact, I'd stop for flying ants or jewel beetles. Armadillo was tough and metallic. The agouti, a large guinea pig, was really delicious, with a thick layer of fat. The frog was filthy, the size of a green meat pie, with devil eyes. I carried it in my pocket for a day. It made a lunge for my willy; frogs will eat anything. I've never been so pleased to see anything die. It tasted like pond slime and forgotten face-flannel.

A food critic really only needs two things in order to do his job properly: no eating disorders and the gastric morals of a hooker with a mortgage. You gotta eat everything, and mostly more than once. I actively try to keep my prejudices down to a minimum. I got over my round-eye revulsion of durian fruit. It tastes of garlic, wine gums and rotting liver. I quite look forward to it now.

I think in the First World we have the illusion of choice and sophistication, whereas in fact the range of flavours and textures we consume for pleasure is getting smaller and fewer: we're down to dumbly bold and inoffensively bland. So many things have single, polite flavours; we're cutting out the complex and the strange.

In Iceland, they eat what is probably the most difficult thing I have ever had to put in my mouth: year-old buried shark. The flavour of ammonia so strong you can taste it behind your eyeballs. And seal hand-preserved in whey. In Reykjavik these are dishes of identity – they link modern Icelanders with the astonishing hardships of their past. It's edible heritage. They're also ferociously drunk when they sit down to the table.

There is the shock of the new, and then there is the shock of the familiar but hidden. The truth is that when you eat something threatening, disgusting, poisonous abroad, it's sort of straight up in your face. When they offer you dog, they don't call it low-fat, organic, hand-reared, street-smart meat, they call it dog. And you can go and see it out the back. They serve stuff with its teeth in and its fins on. A durian is a durian, and you can tell it's coming three rooms away.

But at home, food arrives by stealth. You never quite know – it's cloaked in euphemism and simile, wrapped in advertising and association. You never can be really sure what this more-ish thing is actually made of. William Burroughs said that the naked lunch is when each of us realised, properly realised, what was actually on the end of our forks. The most shudderingly disgusting thing is food that's pretended to be your close friend, but is really a sordid, child-molesting, gut-rotting sociopath. The naked lunch, the vilest thing you put in your mouth, is when you realise what mechanically recovered meat actually means.

And the worst thing? Well, the worst I ever heard of was a friend who'd spent three months in Pakistan and craved chocolate beyond reasoning. At the airport, she found a stall selling Rolos. With nerveless fingers, she shoved four into her mouth. They were fakes, frauds, copies filled with gutter water. The glissando from expectation to fathomless disgust in that is pretty unbeatable. But my worst? Honestly? It was the hamburger from a caravan at the Eminem concert. Without doubt, by a country mile, the most disgusting thing I've ever put in my mouth.

September 2004

Ramadan

At the heart of all religions, there is food. Actually, that reminds me of something a Quaker woodwork teacher once told me. We were looking at the simple cross in chapel and he said quietly (Quakers say everything quietly, with an Eeyore-ish emphasis): 'You know what's at the heart of Christianity?' The Holy Ghost? Love? Redemption? Grace? 'A mortise and tenon joint.' It was an opaquely Delphic pronouncement that still niggles, like a paper cut in the corner of your mouth.

Anyway, I can't think of a religion that doesn't use food as part of its ritual. For Christians, there is obviously the Host (or mein Host, as it's known in German churches): the bread and wine. But there are also pancakes and Easter eggs, simnel cakes and hot cross buns, thousands of European Catholic sweetmeats and tarts (both risen and fallen), and enough marzipan saints to make you sick. Hindus have lentils and chapatis. Judaism has its bitter herbs and Passover lamb. And in Guatemala, I once saw animist offerings of rum and fags.

I have a theory – no more than a guess – that religion and the preparation of food arrived together and grew, temporally and spiritually, hand in hand. Cooking is a profound transformation. It's only a spiritual hop and skip to burning heretics at the stake. And the food that was probably at the heart of nascent religions was your neighbour's heart, liver and thumb muscle (apparently a particularly moreish delicacy). Men with beards posit that the original reason for Leviticus prohibiting pork was that pig and human are indistinguishable when thoroughly barbecued.

In many religions, there is also the absence or denial of food. Fasting has generally dropped off the Christian calendar. There were once two fast days a week, as well as numerous saints' fast days and

Lent, which, when there was less to eat, was far more rigorous than just giving up drink or chocolate or Indian takeaways.

Medieval monks were canny at getting round the 'fish on Friday' thing. They made conies (rabbits) into honorary fish, because they lived in holes, like puffins. And puffins were obviously fish. Look, if angels can dance on the heads of pins, then puffins can be fish, OK?

The most dramatic religious fast is Ramadan, which sounds like a Bill Haley chorus. I took the kids to Oman, not for Ramadan, exactly, but during Ramadan. It's a tricky time to travel in an observant country. All the restaurants are closed. You can't eat in the street. Tourist hotels have secret locked-and-darkened midday dining rooms. I had to tell the children not to drink in public, while at the same time making sure they drank enough.

I asked my guide, who was fasting, what the point of Ramadan was. I thought it would be the same self-mortification as Christian fasting: to rarefy the ethereal reverie. 'Up to a point,' he replied politely. 'Actually, it's self-restraint. It toughens us up. The Koran says we need to be strong to withstand hardship.' I had forgotten what an earthy and practical religion Islam is. Not drinking from sunrise to sunset when the temperature is in the 40s is properly tough.

We were invited to breakfast with a family of Bedouin. In that rather over-polite, respectful, smiley way that white Westerners have when taking part in other people's rituals, I hissed at the children to behave and only eat with their right hands. 'We know,' they sighed. 'We've done religion and other cultures and bum-wiping.'

The first thing that is eaten is dates. I watched an old man stone his with a magician's sleight of hand. The elegance and delicacy of eating with your hands from a communal plate is beautiful, respectful and amazingly neat, if it's done by neat, respectful and beautiful people. I was left cross-legged in a midden of dripped and spilt food. We drank orange juice and laban, a thin yoghurt. Despite the hunger and thirst, nobody grabbed or rushed or stuffed or chugged or gulped.

It was a thoughtful, timely and surprisingly frugal meal. I envied them the appetite that comes with forbearance and faith. I even considered joining in Ramadan for a weekend, but you can't be a tourist in other people's souls.

We finished with a farinaceous soup that was thick and warm and blandly delicious. 'What is this?' I asked. 'It reminds me of something.' A child was dispatched to the kitchen tent to get the recipe, and came back with a tin of Scott's porridge oats. As the huge and miraculous Arabian night sky rolled out over the cooling desert, not for the first time, I was reminded that we are all connected by more than divides us.

September 2005

Markets

My weakness, my pleasure, is markets. Whenever they say, what would you like to see? The museum, the opera house, the red-light district, the bridge over the river? I always say the market. I want to see where the women buy their vegetables. I want to see the fish, the butchers, the quarter of cobblers and tailors. You can't fake a market. You can't make it what it's not. It is as true a reflection of the people it serves as anything; what they have, don't have, what they make and import, and what their pretensions and weaknesses are.

The Mercato in Addis Ababa, biggest market in Africa: dangerous red-eyed tribesmen, maddened and delusional on khat, unloading bushels of the stuff flown in daily from the ancient cities on the Somali border. The stalls selling coffee and the winding lanes of incense dealers, the gifts of the Magi, smelling of martyrdom and plainsong.

Tsukiji, the Tokyo fish market: miles of frozen tuna, lying like a thousand unexploded bombs steaming in the dawn as the auctioneers paint red characters on them, buyers cutting tiny nuggets of flesh from their tails to knead for water content. The unspeakable nameless denizens of a dozen oceans flapping and squirming in brine, all the height of gustatory sophistication, or speechlessly depressing, depending on where you stand.

The fish market in Zanzibar: a slithery soup of scales and guts and too-few fish, the spindly outrigged dhows having to go further and further into the Indian Ocean to find a catch. And then the fish markets of southern Spain, where everything is kept alive, the skate laid on their backs with their squashed baby faces, dribbling blood from their severed tails, looking like mortifyingly religious parables.

The dawn markets in Saigon: vast and frantic, but beautiful. Thousands of ducks and chickens waiting to be plucked, mountains of flowers. The Grand Bazaar of Istanbul, with its streets of gold-dealers and ziggurats of pastel Turkish delight, the caviar merchants, the bags of nuts and dried fruit. Peshawar's many, many markets: older than civilisation, leatherworkers making bandoliers and sandals with the soles of old Russian tyres, the pomegranate-juice sellers, and the boys trussing and skewering sparrows.

Crawford Market in Bombay, the book market in Calcutta, the bird market in Denpasar, the karaoke market in Tashkent. All markets are vitally and vibrantly different, but they're also fundamentally similar. They work on the universal principles of supply and demand, daily bread, bargains, extravagance and thrift. Markets are the true face of cities and of countries.

But of all the markets in the world, there is one example that stands as a template for markets – the market's market, the perfect market against which all others are measured: the weekly markets of southern France. Most white, Western, middle-aged tourists travel to France in the belief that here they will find the apogee of domestic sophistication and taste. Apart from all the hot and tedious haute couture, the museums, the churches, the ruins and the endless, endless art, which must of course be genuflected to and murmured at reverentially, the true civilised genius of France is not what it has made and done, but what it doesn't do. And not doing anything, with a languid haughtiness, is France's great contribution to the Western canon.

The great places of pilgrimage for masterly inactivity are France's markets. The markets entrance and astonish and comfort the rest of the world because somehow they manage to encompass and impart a way of life that is particularly, peculiarly French. No one outside France has quite managed to codify or explain cogently what this uniquely French existence consists of, so they come up with a French phrase to encompass it all: *je ne sais quoi*.

Je ne sais quoi is France's abiding gift to the world. More *je ne sais quoi* for your euro is to be found in a French market than anywhere else. We wander down the aisles of trestles and stalls aghast at the marvellous repose of produce. There are peaches warm from the tree, ripe and golden. Figs, green and black, bursting with sweet, ancient, darkly lascivious simile. The smell of fresh lemon, the bunches of thyme and lavender and verbena, the selections of oil and olives, pale green and pungent, and the honey, from orange blossom, from heath and orchard, and the beeswax. The charcuterie, the dozens of ancient and dextrous things to do with a dead pig, in all the hues of pink and pale, fatty cream.

The smell of the complements of pimiento and fennel, the strings of sausages, of bones, of pâté and rillettes. And then there's the ducks, with their unctuous, giving, bloated, lustrous livers, poached in sealed jars cuddled around truffles and cognac. And pirouetting chickens, like couture birds smelling of very heaven with delicate legs poised on a spit. The boulanger, with loaves crisp and hard, plaited and rounded, wheat and rye, malted and dusted. Bitter crusts and soft sour centres, the pastries and sweetmeats, the plates and bowls of little titbits in sauce, the oeufs en gelée, the asparagus, the snails with their puffy green butter stuffing, the store selling napery and embroidery, the beautiful rustic starched pride of peasant tables and French rooms. The fussy caps for confitures and cake trays, the chocolatiers with their outré soft-centres, and the cheeses – the land of a thousand cheeses. The market will wind its way around a boules-rabbled square with pollarded planes and uncomfortable ironwork benches, and at its corners will be the most holy of holies in the *je ne sais quoi* market: a café. A café with cream and pink woven chairs and little metal tables and a waiter with a long apron and the look of a man who is beaten by his wife. And here you will meet the rest of your party after two hours of worshipping at the long temple of Frenchness and order your café au lait and perhaps just an Armagnac, if you're having one, and perhaps a tasse of the rough but immensely agreeable local wine – just to smell it is to understand utterly the superiority of terroir over mere talent.

And you can examine the rewards of your forage, the amulets of pilgrimage. Oh, I didn't get much – just this artichoke, because I liked the colour. Oh well, we got this marvellous chèvre. The man said it was made with his grandmother's goats, or perhaps that his grandmother was a goat. And this charming gingham bag for hanging on the back of the kitchen door and keeping old plastic bags in. Not, of course, that we now use plastic bags anymore, on principle. And no, you're right – we don't actually have a kitchen door, either. But still, it seemed so here, so right. I'll give it to the daily; she's from the Philippines. Did anyone get any olives? I tried to get some of that divine-looking pâté, but I think I bought an eggtimer instead.

And here is the truth of French markets: it's almost impossible to actually buy anything in them. If you had to really do your entire weekly shop in one, it would take you a fortnight. So consequently the French don't – they use supermarkets like everyone else. This isn't for buying, it's for worshipping. France isn't really like this at all, it's just an idea of a France just like this. This is where they teach their *je ne sais quoi* before they go to the convenience store, the gym and the office and figure out how to be more like the Germans and the English and the Irish and the Americans. I said that what I liked about markets was that you couldn't fake them, that they're immutably driven by commerce. Except for these ones. They are the exception that proves the rule. The French are not like their markets at all. Their markets are actually like the rest of us, or our ideal selves. Somebody once said that when good Americans die they go to Paris. Well, the rest of us go to a market somewhere in the south of France.

July 2007

Last Suppers

Two double-cheeseburgers, two large servings of French fries, half a gallon of vanilla fudge ripple ice-cream. Or perhaps cheese pizza, cheese omelette, green peppers and onions, white cake with white icing. Now these probably aren't anyone's choice for a last meal, ever – except they were for John Schmitt and David Dawson, two executed American murderers.

Reading through the last-meal requests from death row is one of the most gastronomically and socially depressing things you can do. I really don't recommend it. Rubbish food. Yards of enchiladas. Stacks of well-done steaks. Towers of pizza and buckets and buckets of fried chicken. Swimming pools of ice-cream, root beer, Coca-Cola and fruit juice. Tenements of pies and peach cobblers and vast ranges of chocolate cake.

Very occasionally you come across something out of the ordinary. Farley Matchett asked for four olives and wild-berry flavoured water. Arthur Rutherford had fried catfish and green tomatoes. Unusually for a last meal, he had it twice. The first time he was reprieved. The second time, not.

Philip Workman asked that a vegetarian pizza be delivered to a homeless person. The prison refused. On the day of his execution, Nashville's Rescue Mission received 170 pizza deliveries.

These meals are small windows into the lives that led to their consumption. Almost everything in them, you could get from convenience chains or diners. This is food without grace, without joy, without hospitality.

Johnathan Bryant Moore's life culminated in the self-inflicted dinner of Kraft cheese and macaroni and beef-flavoured Rice-A-Roni. Obviously, junk food doesn't necessarily make a drug-addled premeditated murderer, but it's an inescapable truth that with every last meal ordered at all executions over three years, not one of them was what you'd call home-cooked. At the moment when a man might be expected to reach for comfort and a final taste of hearth and a family kitchen, something that his mother made, they only have franchised convenience food available. Almost all of it can be eaten with their fingers.

Only Sedley Alley, with an infantile pathos, asked for milk and oatmeal cookies. I was interested in this because 'What would your last meal be?' is one of the most common questions asked of food critics and chefs. Keen young home economists are always looking to turn out a celebrity cookbook of last suppers.

If your last supper includes something that isn't fried or you need to eat with a knife and fork and it doesn't come with ketchup or barbecue sauce or chilli, then it's almost certain you won't ever be asked to make the choice for real. Asking for a napkin to go with that would probably be grounds for a retrial. Bad food doesn't lead to bad lives, but rotten lives eat rotten dinners.

I always dodge the last-supper question because I think it's in bad taste. It's one of those things like 'Make up a list of the 10 sexiest women ever'. You have all the anxiety of the choice but none of the pleasure of the execution. You're never going to get a date with Uma Thurman and, in fact, your last meal will probably be an uneaten cold tomato soup.

Much more interesting from a foodie point of view is the question 'Which food would you choose for the rest of your life, if you had to live with one other people's national cuisine?' You can't choose your childhood food or a neighbour's that's too similar to make no odds. So if you're Irish, you can't say Scottish. And you can't just say Italian because everybody just says Italian and there really isn't such a thing as Italian food: you have to specify a region.

I've thought about this a lot. In fact, sitting in airports and traffic jams and editorial pep talks, I think of little else. And I've got it down to four cuisines. Fourth is south-western France – foie gras and cassoulet, all sorts of duck, figs and Roquefort. This is the home of the French anomaly. People here eat more saturated fat than anyone else on earth and have a very low incidence of heart disease. This is the food of old Gascony, of Cyrano de Bergerac: a cuisine for the last leg of life, of post-prandial naps, of meals that soak into each other, of a languid, replete and easy life. I could live with that.

In third place, there is the food of Piedmont, of northern Italy and the Po Valley, where they grow rice, make risottos, collect truffles, cook with butters, lard and the light olive oil of Genoa and have the youngest veal. I'd have to stretch it a bit to Parma, to take in hams, cheese and ice-cream, but that would do me. This is the origin of the Slow Food movement that grew to become the Slow City movement and now has a slow university where presumably they don't care much if you turn up for lectures or not, and you can take your exams over three or four hours or perhaps three or four weeks.

Second is the food of the North-West Frontier, the mountainous tribal lands of northern Pakistan and Afghanistan: the very best lamb curries, biryanis, pilaus, apricots and quail, Peshawari naan, yoghurt and pomegranate juice eaten with gusto and arguments and your fingers on the roofs of mud-brick houses, in a confusion of power lines and washing, the smell of charcoal fires and the call of the muezzin.

And in first place is Vietnam. I love the food in Vietnam. I love it so much I've invented new meals. It is an ideal combination of delicacy and panache. It has enormous variety of flavours and textures without being irredeemably twee. It's refined but it's also assertive. It has tiny little finger food and dog. But what really did it for me was breakfast. When you consider a cuisine for life, you have to start with breakfast. Your home style is the most difficult thing to give up. I defy anyone but a Japanese person to enjoy the breakfast of the rising sun. My sub-continental Afghan breakfast of dhal, curry and chapatti is difficult to swallow. Italians don't do much more. They have a minute syrupy coffee and perhaps a bad bun. But in Vietnam, they have a pho. The divine broth with do-it-yourself additions of coriander, mint and chilli. It's perfect. Actually, if you're going to have a perfect food retirement, it would be Vietnam for breakfast, northern Italy for lunch and then alternately south-west France and the North-West Frontier for dinner.

But if you want to start a real food fight, just ask your next dinner table which of the three great staple carbohydrates they would choose forever, to the exclusion of all others. Wheat, rice or corn, that is the decision that formed empires, made history and grew civilisation. So take your time.

September 2009

Noma

All great cities have their defining object, the thing they put on postcards and stamps, that kids subvert on T-shirts, the image the visitor has to see to prove they've been and done the burgh. And they're always, to a greater or lesser degree, disappointments. Parisians hate the Eiffel Tower, pointing out that the only reason to climb the hideous telephone mast is that it's the only place you can get a view of the city without the Eiffel Tower. The Brandenburg Gate is a dull little arch. The Statue of Liberty is impressive, if a bit bonkers. And it's odd that Gustave Eiffel is responsible for the icons of two pre-eminent cities.

Our own Tower Bridge is impossible to see unless you're on a boat, and Big Ben is a hideously misproportioned novelty clock. But nowhere is the sense of anti-climax quite as intense as the one that overwhelms the visitor to Copenhagen, when they first set eyes on the city's letterhead, the Little Mermaid. The maudlin fish is set off the road, on a bit of rock a few feet from the shore, in a ferry terminal. Behind it, factory chimneys spume and the lazy wind farm tries to blow away the smoke. She was put here to commemorate the city's bestselling son, Hans Christian Andersen, a tortured and bad-tempered git. It is a literary law that all people who write for children are weird malcontents, and while parents may read their stories at bedtime, they wouldn't for a second allow the authors to babysit. Who would leave their child alone with Lewis Carroll, or the Brothers Grimm, or the crazy rural bag lady Beatrix Potter? And don't even go near J.M. Barrie.

The Little Mermaid sits on her rock with annoyingly indistinct features, looking like a half-caste seal. She was surrounded by Chinese tourists, who appeared to have eaten all the Japanese ones, trying to get into the same frame as Homo pescator without falling in.

Andersen, with his pitiless stories of abandonment, greed and death, was Copenhagen's most famous citizen only because they couldn't sell the works of the real greatest Dane. 'Come and visit the home of the father of existentialism, Søren Kierkegaard.' Doesn't have a ring to it, not like the bloke who sang, 'There Once Was an Ugly Duckling'. But Kierkegaard is Denmark's real hero, and far more typically Danish. He was the bloke who pointed out 'the leap of faith', that junction where you have to step off the rational pavement of provable fact into the motorway of belief. He says that to have faith you must also have doubt, that doubt is the natural and inescapable condition of faith. To have belief without doubt is not devout, it's being a credulous cretin. He also had hair like Jedward, which in itself beggars belief.

I glared at the supine sprat-girl and wondered why the sensible Danes hadn't put up a statue to Kierkegaard. Then I realised that this impossible half-human, half-fish was one herself: a perfect metaphor, a symbol for the contradiction he spent his life struggling with. Suddenly she looked nicer, not indistinct but indecisive. Instead of a sentimental garden gnome, she was the realisation of a conflict between empiricism and faith.

I was in Copenhagen for the climate conference. You might have read the piece I wrote. (It doesn't matter; even my mother couldn't be bothered to read it.) I was surprised that not one of the hundreds and hundreds of commentators bothered to have a look at this beautiful city, or the Danes, and the way they run their lives. Because in many ways, they have, for a century and more, been the model for how societies should be, and may be forced to become. They are people with a deep modesty in all things. You can't tell anyone's income or social position by looking at them. Everyone dresses with a utilitarian blandness. There is a conspicuous absence of ostentation, in both appearance and behaviour. They all drive clapped-out cars and ride shabby sit-up-and-beg bikes with impeccable manners. They are discreetly proud that while almost everyone has enough, few have too much. This is the safest city in the world, and the cleanest. Danes are polite, helpful, concerned and innately co-operative. This is a liberal society that legalised pornography and freedom of speech and behaviour, yet personally they are conservative and old-fashioned.

This is a libertarian nation governed by the most right-wing coalition in Europe, that has reached an admirable accommodation between public freedom and private responsibility. And the home of Carlsberg may also have probably the best restaurant in the world.

To get a table at Noma I didn't just have to drop my own name, but fling it with force, repeatedly, at the windows. Finally a table was found, for one, in this low building at the end of a pier, looking out at boats and the beautiful slanting golden light, when there is any. Inside there's an open kitchen and Danish style. Arne Jacobsen, the third greatest Dane, said design should be simplicity and function equalling beauty, adding that not all functional things are necessarily attractive. (Think Tessa Jowell.) The room was full of families, a lot of couples on pre-big-question dates, all candlelit. Danes are besotted with candles. It exuded hygge, which roughly translates as convivial, relaxed cosiness. What we might call tipsy frotting. Because they knew who I was and why I was there, and most of the kitchen seemed to come from England and Ireland (which, of course, were both once Danish), I asked them to forget the menu and bring me what they'd like me to eat.

Now I'm going to rush through this, but I don't want you to miss out on any of it, and it doesn't need a lot of five-quid words. I started with a biscuit with lardo and currants, and then a finger sandwich of rye bread and crispy chicken skin filled with split peas and smoked cheese. A quail's egg, soft boiled and mildly pickled, then warm-smoked, served on hay. A flower pot of earth with seedlings in it that turned out to be turnips and radishes, the most perfect realisation of a turnip, a Baby Jesus turnip. The earth was roasted hazelnuts. Smoked cod's roe and vinegar on toast. A salad of apple, nut and marjoram, with hazelnut milk. A razor clam in a tube of parsley jelly with dill, and the excited juices of mussels. Steak tartare, with sorrel, juniper and tarragon. One perfect langoustine, with sea water and parsley. Fresh cheese with indigo mushrooms, with watercress and sorrel. Spinach and rose hips with lovage. A melange of onions with chickweed and onion bouillon. Salsify and Gothland truffle wrapped in the skin of milk, with rapeseed oil. Turbot with stems of vegetables and cabbages, and spectacular unripened pickled elderberries. Musk ox and horseradish with ramson capers. Carrots and buttermilk and liquorice. A meringue snowman with cloudberries and wild thyme. Øllebrød: a granny porridge of dark rye bread steeped in beer and cooked with sugar, served with frothed milk, skyr (a particularly wonderful Scandinavian yoghurt) and toasted rye kernels.

There are wines with all of this, but I don't drink, so the waiter suggested fruit juice. I was offered glasses of cucumber, apple and pine, carrot, celery, elderflower, and a number of berries of Nordic origin with unpronounceable names. If you have the meagrest ability to transubstantiate words into sensation, you will understand that this is a palate-tattooing dinner. The ingredients were of an irreproachable freshness and quality; every single one gleaned from Scandinavia, all in season, all with a sense of place and a commitment to this frugal-but-generous society that's always lived on the thin edge of the environment. These things were memorable and emotional. Food is always a coming-together of the prosaic and the sublime. It is the combination of a lot of crafts and husbandry, chemistry and physics. What it makes is transformed into an essence that is more than a list and heat. This is where the mermaid gets her chips. Noma is the real and the unreal deal.

December 2009

Hotel

Two of the first reviews I ever did for 'Table Talk', a brace of decades ago, were country house hotels. I was dispatched to a Welsh place where Hugh Grant had stayed and given one of the maids a nickname: Crustyknickers, or Poo Breath, or something. I made the 14-hour journey to Wales, sat in an empty dining room, watched the RAF practise aborting livestock, ate a perfectly mediocre and forgettable lunch, and went home.

The next one was a dingy suburban warren that was the favourite of businessmen and advertising executives wanting a satisfyingly snobby, spenny piss-up. It was Jacobethan, like a Stygian wardrobe. The food was deeply unlovely, the service resentful. At the time I thought there was something weird about these places, these hotels that were their own destinations, that sat impervious to the real world, little stage sets of make-believe. You didn't come here to visit something; it wasn't like going to Venice or New York. They were portals to alternative realities, a place of chintz fascism that was dictated by romantic fiction and the formal etiquette that had intimidated our parents.

You arrived and a passed-over major in assertive tweed would meet you in the hall, and start bellowing. He'd make a fuss about picking up your bag and tell you that both he and Marjorie were immensely pleased you'd come, and that you were to treat the place exactly like your own home, adding that, in fact, it was his home, and there were one or two small rules. 'Drinks in the library at 7.30, dinner eight o'clock sharp. There's an honesty bar: please write clearly. Don't smoke in the Chinese drawing room; we discourage mobile phones and computers; jackets and ties in all the public rooms. I'm sure you don't need to be told, but our transatlantic cousins are woefully informal. Apart from that, try to relax. Please check with Samantha if you need wellingtons, and we'd like you to be out of the house after 10 o'clock so that Padma and the housekeeping team can get on. You have 23 minutes before tea in the conservatory. Earl Grey or builder's? I need to tell Pedro.'

The high point of my journeys among the country house hotels was once being offered a complimentary labrador for my postprandial walk down to the lake.

Well, that was all 20 years ago. It all seemed so desperately last century, these raised-pinkie knocking shops with their insecure fantasy-weekend lives, so absurdly 1990s. I really thought they'd wither and die, along with daily blow-dries and turned-up collars. But last week, I was in the West Country in need of lunch, and I asked the office if they could find somewhere halfway decent. Yes, they said, it's only 100 miles away. Result! Virtually round the corner. I was with Tom Craig, my photographer (David Cameron's got one, too); he suggested some pub he'd once been to in the middle of Salisbury Plain that did a pretty decent sausage. No, I said, let's trust the collective wisdom of *The Sunday Times* restaurant guide and drive hell for Velcro to a hotel, restaurant and spa, set in the scenic rolling suburbs of Jane Austen's favourite city.

It was harder to find than we expected: Tom cursed the satnav for never getting hungry. In fact, we were there: it just didn't look like a country-house hotel. It looked like a provincial dentist's practice, or the headquarters of a small prosthetics firm. We parked the car in the little gravel drive, as far away as possible from the signs saying 'Invalids Only', and 'Deliveries Round the Rear, Drivers Remove Your Cloth Cap'. The sound of gravel underfoot is an intrinsic and vital element in the country-house hotel experience. We stepped into the small and rather poky foyer, or perhaps it was a vestibule, where a plainly annoyed woman appeared and said 'Yes?' in a pre-emptory, accusatory sort of way. Lunch, I smiled. 'What?' she replied, as if I'd offered her a speculative introductory D and C on the carpet. It's amazing how many provincial hoteliers think that *Fawlty Towers* was a training video. 'Have you got a reservation?' Dozens. Quite a lot of them about you. I also have a booking: Major Quim. My editor's little joke. There's a thorough examination of the ledger, as if it were St Peter's appointment diary, hoping against hope to find a discrepancy. 'I'm sorry, we have a Major Kim, but nothing with your spelling. Take it up with your lawyer.'

In fact, she said would we like a drink in the drawing room? I never, ever want a drink in the drawing room. It's like going to the barber's and being asked if you'd like to see their etchings. We sat in the drawing room, which was really a dentist's waiting room, except for the vast number of weird and competitive paintings on the walls. It was a bit like being pasted into a consumptive girl's decoupage screen. The canvases all bellowed empire and service and duty, handwritten notes in lavender ink, bonnets and buttoned gloves, solar topees and proper luggage. Yearning and longing, exclaiming and declaiming, hiding and abiding. Stiff upper lips and stiff lower lips. Sighing and fainting, the sound of distant bells and bad-news telegrams. After 10 minutes, I was ready to go and shoot Archduke Franz Ferdinand myself, just to put an end to it.

We were ushered into a dining room by a waiter who waved his hands like Thomas Hardy trying to herd geese into an abattoir. The room had more huge paintings, and bits of decorative nostalgia. The menu was short and had a reasonable set lunch and an à la carte. But here's the thing: it was all so long ago, so sepia, that I can't remember any of it. Normally I have a pretty engraved memory for food, but whatever this was, it slid past the alimentary recall without leaving an impression. There was some venison, a lobstery crayfish thing with foam, a partridge that had been dismembered and teased. Was the pudding chocolate? Is there honey still for tea? Can't remember. I think it was all quite good.

What I do remember are a lot of waiters, and a marvellous tintinnabulation of exotic accents, all of which are mocked by the old English ambience. They offered selections from the bread basket, little glasses of things that I hadn't ordered and didn't want. They told me where the fish had lived, and that today's special words were 'nestling' and 'drizzled'. And I can see from the bill that, as they put it, the grand total for this pre-memorable experience was £166, including a £9 glass of wine. What amazes me is that anyone is still trying to flog this ridiculously laughable theatre of life, this Princess Di memorial version of an elegant age. It's two hours of your life that are taken over by Gilbert and Sullivan. The place they tried to re-create never existed. It's a Sealed Knot reconstruction that I thought had died. This national culinary embarrassment should have had a Spanish, Italian, Japanese and modern British stake through its miserable jingoistic heart. But apparently not. I suppose that's the truth of nostalgia: whenever you kill it, its teeth just return, more winsome and fey.

December 2010

Paris

When I was an art student in the 1970s, I used to doss in a squat in Victoria.

Going back drunk at night, we'd take a short cut to the station, where a big, beautifully glowing, aquamarine sign promised the 'night train to Paris and Brussels', and sometimes we'd be drunk enough to get on it. The train was slow and had that blissful sense of escape that only the rhythm of a track can impart. Planes and cars are always going someplace; trains leave somewhere with the feeling of putting it all behind you, and the lightness of anticipation.

At Dover, we'd get on the ferry, then the French train would wait for hours before trundling across the First World War battlefields of Amiens and Picardy. We'd arrive at the Station of the North, the light would be wearing grey, the street-sweepers wearing blue, damming and diverting the flush of water that came from the drains. Hungover and tired, we'd slip into the station bar for a *pression*, and then make our way to the Left Bank, where my brother was a chef and had a cold-water walk-up. I'd sleep on his floor and we'd talk about food. I remember going to see the great Bacon exhibition and the newly opened Beaubourg, and I'd eat in cheap bistros. I learnt about food from 9F menus.

The onion soup of Les Halles, the breakfast of market porters, with a shot of marc tipped into it, grated celeriac with Bayonne ham, a plate of pink cutlets, a dish of brown tripe à la mode, a sliver of camembert, a glass bowl of îles flottantes, and the coffee that was stewed with chicory before espresso machines became ubiquitous.

Restaurants were invented by the French, there's no getting around it. They spring from *Liberté, égalité, fraternité*, and although they instantly and typically became a focus of snobbery, of class distinction and exclusion, Paris always had good, cheap public food for the men in blue. It was a cause of French pride that the *clochard* knew as much about his pistou as the banker. Gastronomy was a pleasure and an expertise that came from peasants and reached to presidents, but was shared by all, a right of culture and birth. And the 9F menu meant that, as an art student, I could learn about the greatest and most profound part of our civilisation: what we put on the table. All of the rest is simply the *mise-en-scène* to dinner.

It was never the same here. The top table ate French, or something whose autopsy was written in French. The lower orders ate mince. There was that brief time after rationing when English food patently got better for everyone, and we could all learn how to cook again and eat together again. Food never lost its potential to be made out of snobbery, but it was also aspirational and convivial. The most distressing thing about eating out now is that we're slipping back into an apartheid of 'us and them' plates. London restaurants are so expensive that most Londoners can't afford to eat in them.

This recession has had very little effect at the top of market, but there are precious few concessions for feeding the neighbours, who might like to take part in the culture of eating out. The cheap ingredients aren't made for the young or the minimum-waged, for students or the old, they're made chic and expensive for the rich. And the most unpleasant thing about dining in London today is not the careless, grease-smeared George Grosz faces of the gob-stuffing rich, it's the absence of everyone else.

One of my favourite restaurants in Paris was Chartier. It was ridiculously cheap, but the food perfectly good – you could eat foie gras or grated carrot. The service was perfunctory and the bill was written on the paper tablecloth; it was first come, first seated, and you shared your table with strangers. But it was set in the most beautiful and grand dining room – it was not a restaurant that had fallen from high society, it had been built like this for working people and students. It was eating with Victor Hugo.

Occasionally someone will raise a fist and call for statutory prix fixe menus in London restaurants, but really this misses the point. It's not about ordering it, it's about wanting it. I really wish the grander enterprises wanted to feed their neighbours, or the men who deliver their ingredients, or the families of their waiters, to offer something to the good of all. I also wish I didn't have to sit in quite so many rooms that give me the queasy feeling I spend too much time on the wrong side of the barricade.

Abraham Lincoln, quoting Genesis, asked how could any man wring his daily 'bread from the sweat of other men's faces'. Surely, in hard times, it's even more important to remember we don't start dinner until everyone is seated.

July 2012

Steak

I once dined with the Masai in the Serengeti. Seven thirty for eight, smart safari casual. I tiptoed up to the thorn enclosure, shook hands, smiled, talked about the weather and the flies and the children's beadwork, admired the big lotus-bladed lion spears, and then my host said, 'Shall we go through?' We went into the dining room, which was also the cattle pen, where dinner was standing with a tourniquet around its neck and a lad pulling its tail. A boy took a bow with a blunt arrow and shot a hole in the animal's jugular vein, which spurted a river of blood dexterously into a long, bulbous gourd that had been cleaned for my benefit with cow's urine.

After about half a pint had been tapped, the tourniquet was released, a finger of dung applied to the hole, and the steer was reunited with his mates to complain about the greed and cold hands of cooks. The dinner soup was briskly whisked with a stick to keep it from clotting, the stick was handed to a child in the way your mother gave you the cake-mix spoon, and the gourd was hospitably given to me. It was heavy. The family watched with a host's nervous expectation. Cheers, I said weakly, and lifted it to my mouth. The smell of the disinfected pot reeked rank as I felt the blood move and lurch in the gourd's neck like a slinking dark animal. And then, before I was ready, my mouth was full, cheeks bulging with body-heat gore the texture of custard, silky and vital and forcing open my constricted throat. I swallowed. Great visceral chugs.

Imagine what it tasted like. Just think. Because, actually, you already know. You know what warm blood straight from a bull's heart tastes of – it tastes of steak. Not merely like steak. Not just a little meaty. But of the very finest, perfectly velvety, unctuous steak I'd ever tasted. But it isn't the blood that tastes of steak, it's steak that tastes of blood, and that's all it tastes of. I never eat a sirloin now without thinking, This is good, but not quite as good as the real oozing liquid thing. My Masai dinner was, incidentally, the only steak a vegetarian could ethically eat; no animals were killed. It was organic, and it was wholly sustainable. The Masai's cows owe their long and treasured lives to this occasional painless cupping.

We live in the steak age; marbled fatty buttock is the defining mouthful of our time. Smart cities are being stampeded by herds of restaurants devoted to cows' arses. This is the bovine spring of red meat, and it's not just America or the West. Around the world, communities that a generation ago rarely or never ate steak are now craving and demanding the taste of blood. In 1950 there were an estimated 720 million cows in the world. Today there are nearly 1.5 billion. In America there is one cow for every three people. Think of a third of a cow – that's what's on your plate, and you're not getting up until you've finished it.

Why have we fallen in such greedy love with beef? What does steak say to us and about us? Well, it's manly. If food came with gender appellations, steak would definitely be at the top of the bloke column. Women can eat it, they can appreciate it, but it's like girls chugging pints of beer and then burping. It's a cross-gender impersonation. Steak is a high-value food that doesn't need a chef. You don't want some twiddly-accented, *jus*-dribbling, foam-flicking chef mincing about with your meat. You want a guy in a checked shirt with his sleeves rolled up forking and tonging your T-bone. Steaks even come with their own butch utensils. It's more like engineering or Lego than cooking. It's boy stuff. The porterhouse used to be the dining choice of a gauche out-of-towner, a man who was uncomfortable with chic urban menus and didn't know how to order – 'Oh, I'll just have the steak. Wipe its behind and bring it to the table,' they'd say, just to let the rest of us cheese-eating sophisticates know that they weren't intimidated hicks. Restaurants would keep steak on the menu just for them because they knew there would always be a certain sort of guy who didn't think it was an acceptable date restaurant if he couldn't get a New York strip. Chefs hate steaks because their reputations are left in the hands of their butchers – two cuts off the same muscle can eat quite differently.

But today steak is, if not chic, then at least modern. Steak houses used to be leathery, clubbable lounges with cartoons of dead customers on the walls and faux Victorian paintings of obese cattle, staffed by ancient, permanently enraged waiters with faces as livid as well-hung sirloin and aprons that went from nipple to ankle. Now a steak restaurant is more likely to be James Bond luxurious and internationally expensive, a setting for chiselled-jawed, silver-templed seduction and couples with multiple passports. A place for men – who might fear that their testicles would pack their bags and leave if they caught them talking about *terroir* or heirloom tomatoes – to have a detailed and exhaustively knowledgeable discussion about dry-aging, grass-fed versus corn-fed, and the state of Wagyu-Angus cross-breeding. Steak has become the butch foodie communion, and tellingly not just for flinty-eyed, Armani-suited leaner-than-thou businessmen, but for metrosexuals who wish to beef up their cultural testosterone.

In lean times, when we're keeping a white-knuckle grip on the rungs of the middle-class ladder, steak comes as a small vote of self-confidence. It's an emblem of victory, of survival. A slab of bleeding meat is symbolic of something fundamental, something pre-banking, pre-mortgage, pre-downsizing, prehistoric. It is a metaphor for the most basic achievement: to kill for sustenance, to be strong, to man up. Watch a guy in a suit look at his plate when the waitress brings his steak. He glares at it just for a moment. It's not even conscious, but it's the look of ownership; it's the pride warning, 'Don't touch my meat.' A lot of men do something called mantling – that is to lean over the plate, surround it with their arms just for a second. It's body language that comes from a time before speech. The bit of our brain that deals with taste and appetite is the most ancient in our heads, the bit we share with lizards. Nothing about our menu choices is purely cultural, civilised, or rational. A steak feels, looks, and tastes like winning – a direct connection to our bipedal ancestors. The original reward of victors.

Actually, steak is quite modern and very American. The great boom in beef-eating came during the Civil War as a way to feed large groups of peripatetic men living in tents. Steak became a fad when the first refrigerated train cars pulled out of the Chicago stockyards and headed east. Steak houses appeared and gave fancy names to the slabs of flesh. Before the Second World War ordinary Joes rarely ate steak. It was the occasional meat of millionaires and cartoon characters. Steaks were dreamt of and fought over; they were the muscle of a better tomorrow. Today the prices being charged for prime cuts in prestige dining rooms – where the raw material is paraded to the table like a Premier Cru – can equal a day's pay for the waiter. The expense adds to the special pleasure, the achievement, and is the secret ingredient of the filet mignon.

Around the globe, particularly in the East, in cultures that are more attuned to the semaphore and simile of ingredients, more steaks are being ordered. They are the taste of the free market, the blessing of Western capitalism, a celebration of consumerism and modernity and the arrival of the middle class. Thirty per cent of the world's land surface that isn't frozen is given over to livestock production, and most of that is for grazing cattle. We eat the cows, and the cows eat everything else: horizons of corn, the rain forest, the plains and pampas, and the habitats of other species. They poison the water, and their flatulence contributes to global warming.

Like us, the Masai believe that their cattle make them superior to those who grub in the dirt or eat fish or fowl; the blood makes them special. Steak may be the taste of victory, but that sizzle is also the smell of fear.

May 2013

Burger Pizza

The hamburger owes its rise to Henry Ford and the affordable car, and the roads that had to be built for salesmen, families and the migratory dustbowl poor to motor down, and the gas stations and diners that filled up man and machine. So the hot meat sandwich was the answer to a modern need, pit-stop petrol for humans.

The pizza is rather older, possibly Greek in origin, its etymology unclear, though not its ingredients. It is bread with some flavourings plucked from the surrounding lands – thyme and laurel, goat's cheese, olives. Something like pizza was made by the Romans with focaccia. In the incarnation we know, pizza had to wait for the discovery of America and tomatoes. Italians were the first Europeans to bravely eat the love apple, realising by brutal trial and error that it wasn't a type of deadly nightshade. Pizza is a dish of the poor south, used like yorkshire pudding to pad out hunger so that the more expensive ingredients will go further. It is always simple, cooked in a kiln-hot oven, far hotter than your domestic cooker will ever manage.

Pizza travelled with Italian migrants back to America where it got bigger and fatter and floppier and sloppier and competes with the hamburger. They remain friendly but separate, integrated into the fast finger food but never amalgamated, until the Doctor Moreau, horror-food eugenicists came up with the burger pizza.

What hellish new super-chew orthodoxy, what fundamental-ist mullah of taste decided that the world needed this nightmare pushmi-pullyu, this pit-spawned, misbegotten basilisk, this sticky chimera, this foul, unnatural, Caliban union of dribble-chinned fast food?

You could imagine the mad Pizza Hut scientists in their jackboots and white coats, in their secret lair where nothing grows, cackling with satanic glee as the lightning flashes over their pestilential confection.

Nothing as gastrically heinous as this can be made without first doing a lot of market research. Pizza Hut hasn't got where it is today without pandering to the baser appetites of its customers. I imagine they sent out questionnaires with the deliveries asking: if you could put anything on top of a pizza, what would it be? A) more pineapple; B) a generous scraping of white truffle; C) Viagra; D) quinoa and kale; E) a hamburger; F) half a dozen hamburgers; G) other. In the 'other' suggestion box I suspect most responded with: 'A packet of extra-large Rizlas, mate.'

So on your behalf, because someone has to step up and try it, to bring back the vivid truth, because *The Sunday Times* has a proud tradition of investigative journalism, and because hacks have just had a bit of a bad week, I voluntarily put myself in harm's way so you can know the truth about the burger pizza.

It comes in the night. Actually close to teatime in my case, delivered by scooter, the urban drone of collateral calorific damage. Someone somewhere just puts these things in a box and pushes a button. They never see the destruction, the children with smeared faces, and they make their victims sign for it. So the first thing you notice, even before it's out of the box, is the smell, the overpowering aggressive thuggish smell. From three floors up, the Blonde shouted: 'Christ, what's that smell?' It's organic, but not like food. It smells of farm and rot and armpit. If the Gruffalo farted, this is what Gruffalo fart would smell like.

Open the box and it gets a whole lot worse. There's the added nidor of damp, warm cardboard. What I've been sent is the barbecue steak pizza with mini cheeseburgers and Heinz dipping sauce. I expect UN chemical warfare officers to knock on the door any day. The thing is huge. I had no idea they came this large. How many people is this supposed to feed?

As a piece of Willy Wonka engineering it's quite something. The edges are crimped into divots in which nestle a ball of burger, like the ball bearings put into suicide fast food. They are the size of infant fists, topped with a congealing pustule of splat, of yellow cheese-style gunge. I haven't eaten all day and am quite hungry, but the smell has grabbed my appetite and dragged it into a narrow dark place where it is being beaten unconscious.

The pizza crust isn't actually pizza at all, or indeed crust. It's a coarse, pale cake, and the first and pretty much the last mouthful is a real surprise. No, it's a poleaxeing shock. I can't remember the last time I was so flabbergasted by the difference between plummeting expectations and hideous actuality. It's sweet. Not just sweetish, or sweet and sour. It's tooth-curlingly, diabetically sugary. There is a mild background flavour of tinned tomato and a hint of malt vinegar. There is a texture of something dead and mutilated, possibly dragged from a canal, but without a pathologist and a chemistry set it would be impossible to identify what it once was, or indeed the genus of any of the other things that may or may not be vegetable but could also be whatever it is that clogs shower drains.

The meatball burger is brown. It tastes brown and gritty, something that has passed through many colons with a grimace. It's like chewing old man's corduroy. If for a year you had eaten only Siberian gulag rations it would be merely unpleasant. My children wouldn't touch it. The Blonde wouldn't be in the same room as it. I suggested donating it to the homeless man who sleeps outside the local hospital. With her finest nightingale voice, the Blonde hissed: 'Don't you think he's probably suffered enough? And we can't just put it in the bin. It'll poison the foxes. We'll have to double-bag it, like casual rough sex.'

Given my job, this isn't the worst thing I've put in my mouth, but it is probably the worst thing that was pretending to be food and made you pay. It's not that I'm against binary cross-cultural combinations of ingredients or dishes. When Miss Strawberry Jam threw herself on top of Mr Peanut Butter, it was food porn of the highest order.

The marvellous thing about grub is that it is no respecter of borders or prejudices or manners. There was a UN on the table long before politicians got round to it. But each time you mix and match, you have to ask: is this an improvement that is greater than the sum of its parts? And in this case, the regurgitated answer is a glottal no. And the parts weren't particularly toothsome to begin with. Forget the benign tinkering of GM, this is real Frankenstein food. This is a glimpse into the stinking box that contains the end of civilisation as we know it.

November 2013

Fäviken

The taxi driver has the guardedly stony, pale-eyed face that's familiar from a dozen Scandi detective series. He could be the victim's father, or the killer, perhaps both. His board says he's waiting for 'Mr Gyle'. That'll be me.

I can't pronounce the name of this tiny airport: it's a random, runic collection of vowels. Outside, the snow is fresh and powdery, as if a suspicious god were dusting the country for fingerprints. This is an hour's flight out of Stockholm, halfway up Sweden's sparsely populated spine. It is also the shortest day of the year. We drive for another hour through a bleak landscape where the Garbo moon wants to be alone with the frozen lakes and hissing trees. The windows of stoic farmhouses glow with promising stars and Advent candles. 'You know there's a body in every cellar,' says the Blonde. Amazing how potent cheap fiction can be.

This is Jamtland: once a semi-independent state with its own law, it broke away from the bloody reign of the marvellously monikered Eystein the Evil, and still has its own flag and a reputation for cussed contrarianism.

Finally, we pull off the main road to either a shallow grave or dinner. The snow eddies and whirls like a ghost stream and we drive up to a solid wooden farm that has flaming torches outside and a fir tree draped in Christmas lights, as much a lighthouse as a celebration. Welcome to Fäviken, probably the most gastronomically chic, fashionable and dribblingly mulled-over restaurant in the world, though you'd be forgiven for not knowing that. If you asked a hundred Michelin-starred chefs where they'd most like to eat, most would say here.

Foraging is this season's must-have thing, and Scandinavia is hedgerow Valhalla. Even other Nordic chefs talk of Magnus Nilsson, the cook, with the reverence of a semi-mythical hero, the man who holds the torch. We are shown to our rooms (you have to stay overnight or you die): simple beds, a sauna before dinner and I resist the suggestion of an invigorating naked roll in the snow.

The restaurant is an 18th-century barley barn and is a suitably sparse space: wooden walls hung with drying flowers and herbs, dangling tobacco, ham and smoked trout. There's also a huge 19th-century wolfskin coat. The dining room under the eaves seats 14, 16 at a push. The kitchen brigade is eight, but two are interns. You eat what they're cooking, and before we go to the table there's an array of things to nibble with drinks: flaxseed and vinegar crisps with mussel dip; wild trout's roe in a crust of dried pig's blood; pig's head dipped in sourdough, then deep-fried; pickled gooseberry with pine salt; slices of cured sow; salted herrings aged for three years with sour cream and rusks.

Sitting at the table in the candlelight, we start with huge scallops cooked in their shells with broth over burning juniper. Then a lobster tail, served with a cream made of its own claws and a rosehip and mushroom sauce. Poached turbot with sunflowers, then turbot again in a cup of buttermilk; brussels sprouts with lupins; cockles with beer; barley pancakes filled with onions; fresh potatoes boiled with, and served under, a mound of last year's semi-decomposed autumn leaves; a small egg coated in a skin of ash with a sauce made of dried trout. Then porridge of grains and seeds poured over a lump of salty butter with fermented carrots, and a meat broth filtered through moss.

Pause here. We're not quite halfway through, and while you're reading it out loud for the hilarity of your breakfast table, let me tell you not a single mouthful is awkward or tricky, or involves bushtucker bravery. All of it is warm and hospitable, softly spoken with a great blanket of elegant flavours. The setting, the flickering light, the lowing of the moose outside and the moonlight make it all seem hyperreal, a scene from a fairy tale. The singsong ingredients come as incantations as much as recipes.

The nature of Scandinavian food is a very short summer from which you must glean enough for a very long, immobile winter, so preservation is all. Salting, pickling, drying, packing, smoking, sugaring ingredients: these are the central kitchen skills and, to the palate, every mouthful comes with a taste of hope and a wish, and the memory of dexterous skill.

On to bread made with blood, moose broth, backfat and onion; a rib-eye of 10-year-old milking cow that's been aged for five months with bird cherries (my book says these are only edible by birds); then colostrum with blueberries. Colostrum is the first milk a cow gives to its newborn calf, much fatter and sweeter than ordinary milk. I'd never tasted it: it's heaven, almost as rich and deep as a 10-year-old mother cow's moo. Then curdled woodruff milk and egg yolk preserved in sugar syrup with crumbs from pine-tree bark and meadowsweet ice cream.

The Blonde tells me the wines are marvellous, old and round and mostly French, and because I don't drink I ask for Swedish apple juice but am also given an infusion of birch leaves with red clover and blackcurrant leaves, cold rosehip, and blueberry and lingonberry juice. After dinner, in the drawing room with the fire and the wolf, there's a tray like a witch's toolbox of spells: miniature reindeer pies; raspberry ice wrapped in paper; tar pastilles; sunflower nougat; smoked toffee; pine resin and the *snus*: fermented chewing tobacco stored in a bitter barrel.

Magnus Nilsson is a man who looks the part, a character from a children' s story. He is convivial and modest. He's also exceptional. He cooks intuitively: the kitchen is small and bare of folderols or technology, his storeroom has racks of preserved food and vegetables in jars, gibbets of ham hocks, and coffins of beetroot and turnip. The essence of this food is its rootedness and identity. It is the accumulation of tiny ingredients. He has more than 120 suppliers, not through epicurean vanity but because there is nowhere else to go: no supermarket, no commercial catering supplier. Some may give him only a handful of herbs or find a crop of berries that have little intrinsic value, but which the kitchen must make worth everyone's while.

Fäviken is memorable, a joyfully comforting, questioning saga of a restaurant. The long journey to get here becomes a story, its dishes are illustrations that capture the eternal and metaphysical, tough and touching truth of food that is its culture and history, survival and hospitality, its hope, faith and hardship, its skill and craft and patient inheritance, pleasure, memory and communion. Nilsson has without a drop or dab of pretension put all that on a plate.

In the morning, there is a splendid and excessive breakfast. The taxi driver returns. 'How was the restaurant?' he asks. 'Very good.'

'Ah, yes, they all say it's not bad.' And he cracks a smile that makes him look even more sinister.

January 2014

Scotland

Before I wrote about food, I taught cooking. Not terribly well, but just a bit better than the people who came to learn. The first thing I insisted on was that nobody ever wrote anything down or looked at a book. You cook ingredients, not recipes. For thousands of years, people have learnt to cook by example, memory and taste. Most food was invented, perfected and passed on by illiterate women with one pot over a flame. I was particularly interested in Scottish food, because it's the earliest mouthful I remember.

My first kitchen instruction was how to stir with a spurtle porridge made with water, eaten with salt and butter. So, for a couple of summers I taught up a glen in Ross-shire, beside the River Conon. We cooked ingredients only to be found locally – tatties and soft fruit, deer and grouse from the hills, salmon and trout from the river, crab and mackerel from the coast.

To stay ahead of the students, I'd trudge up the hill in the afternoons and sit in the kitchen of Peggy McKenzie, a retired gamekeeper's wife who was one of the most naturally in-tune, modestly perfect cooks. I'd watch her make food and listen to her talk about the family and the seasons and the events and the hardships and the triumphs that were marked by her labours. She did everything with an ethereal lightness and the elegant dexterity of ancient practice.

She knew all her frugal kitchen equipment by touch and made miraculously simple yet soundly surprising food, from slow-baked jams as clear as precious stones to boiled cakes and slow soups. She taught me how to stuff a sheep's stomach to make mutton black pudding; and black bun and clootie dumpling, braw bree, skirlie, crowdie and oat farls. She wrote nothing and I wrote nothing. All the food was sourced, invented, aged, matured, smoothed and perfected over years and years by hundreds and hundreds of hard, gentle hands and hungry mouths within a day's walk of her bungalow.

I learnt more about cooking and the value and meaning of food and hospitality, sitting at her tin-topped table, than in all of the next 30 years of menus, reading, writing and eating. The great dichotomy of Peggy's kitchen was that what it produced was entirely private, almost secret. There was nothing comparable in public cafés, bars or restaurants. And there still isn't. Scotland remains the worst country in Europe to eat in if you're paying – and one of the finest if you're a guest.

People who have only been tourists here laugh when I mention the heritage of Scots' hospitality. They know only the hot box pies and late-night souse of vinegared fish suppers, the grim tourist interpretations of guidebook food, the dumb blanding of the Scottish board into the polite ethnic experience of haggis-stuffed tomatoes.

I was up in the Highlands a couple of weeks back, banging about in the heather. At the end of a day, I stepped into the kitchen to a smell that reminded me of Peggy – mutton being braised by Fiona, another miraculous Scottish cook. I, like you, had forgotten mutton. With a great marketing and agri con, it was replaced by lamb. If you look at 19th-century cookbooks, you'll see very few recipes for lamb and hundreds for mutton. Wool was what made England its first fortune. Fluffy gold, sold to the weavers of Ghent. Sheep weren't slaughtered till they were four or five years old. The most valued were gelded rams. But today, wool has no value, and farmers want an immediate return on their animals, so the sooner they can slit their throats, the better. And the more they add value to young, tender meat, the better. Except it isn't better. Lamb is a bland, short, monoglot mouthful compared with mutton's eloquent, rich, euphemistic flavour. We've been cheated by agri-expediency to eat an inferior, flannelly, infantilised alternative. In fact, we're led to believe that younger is better for all meat, when the opposite is the truth. Flavour, richness, interest and complexity come with age. Mutton is the true base taste of our national cuisine, and it's gone. But you can still find it – go and order some, cook it slowly, be amazed.

I spent a day in my home city of Edinburgh and had one dinner.

Afterwards, we went to the Ensign Ewart, a tiny, low, ancient pub under the castle, named after a soldier of the Royal North British Dragoons who captured a French eagle at Waterloo. There, I sank a happy can of Irn-Bru, which is everything I love and loathe about a Scottish mouthful.

There was local music being played conversationally around a table, by, I think, Sandy Brechin, a magical accordion player. And it struck me as strange that the accordion can be a brilliant purveyor of emotion and pleasure in the hands of a Scotsman, but an instrument of aural torture when given to a Frenchman – and that exactly the opposite is true with frying pans. Phew.

October 2015

Refugee Camp Café

The first refugee story I covered was a famine in southern Sudan. An editor on the paper (now departed) implored me not to go. Sending a food critic to report on a famine was just bad taste. But who would you trust with bad taste if not a food critic?

In the Calais Jungle a few weeks ago, I was reminded of this by a trio of doers-of-good, who were walking up the muddy main drag when one of them saw me and did a theatrical double take. 'My God, I was just saying A. A. Gill should come here and do a review. And here you are.'

'And here it is,' I said. They were working in the tented theatre, run by a pair of playwriting Joes, called the Good Chance because the refugees say: 'Tonight, there's a good chance I shall get to England.' Of all the things I have told people back home, the stuff about the theatre has caused the most eye-rolling, brow-furrowing, exasperated exhaling. What a monument to bleeding-heart liberal pretension, a theatre in a refugee camp, I was told. Well, yes, but if I ever find myself lost and penniless, I hope it's the liberals with leaky valves and a penchant for quoting Shakespeare that find me, and not the sanguine, pity-tight realists. But I do want them to tell me where they imagine the Plimsoll line of culture runs. When are you too poor, too bereft, too unappreciative to need or deserve art? Is this culture stuff really only the property of those who can pay for it – only ever bourgeois decoration?

The camp also has a touchingly divine Ethiopian Coptic church, built from tarpaulin and bits of lost wood, painted with the clear, strong and bright fresco saints of Africa. There was a boy, pressed tight against a bold St George. I think the church has just been bulldozed. There is a street of small tented cafés, most of them run by Afghans or Pakistanis from the North-West Frontier. There's one called 3 Idiots. A man stood grinning in the door. 'I'm one of the idiots. We're all called Khan.'

Next door, a Peshawari man makes rotis in a small bread oven, taking the tennis-ball-sized white dough, patting it and flipping it onto a cushion and then sticking it to the inside wall of the stove. Some of the best unleavened bread I've ever eaten was in Peshawar, and this was as good as I remember. I bought two for €1. The baker made the long and difficult journey across to Libya, got on a boat over the Mediterranean and ended up in Bari in Italy. I asked where he wanted to get to.

'Oh, I live in Bari,' he said. 'It's lovely there, nice people, wonderful weather, good food.'

'Well, what are you doing in a freezing, wet refugee camp in Calais, then?'

'Well, the only problem with Bari is that there's no work, so I come up here for a couple of weeks at a time to make bread.' He makes about 400 roti a day.

'Where is your oven from?'

'Ah,' he laughs, 'that came from England.'

Next door is a caff without a sign. I ask the owner what it is called. It has no name. Everyone knows it's here. A name would imply permanence. 'My name is Mohammed Ali. But I am not Cassius Clay. Don't be mistaking me for him,' he laughs.

Mohammed is also from Peshawar. Today, for lunch, he is offering red bean curry, reheated fried chicken and a stew of chicken livers. I'm here with Natalie, an absurdly and insouciantly brave doctor from Médecins Sans Frontières; Jon, my photographer; and Bana, an optometrist, translator, Kurd and child of refugees. The room is a tent, with a make-do kitchen in one corner, a couple of gas rings, a banged-together counter, a kettle, some pots and pans. There's a television and a deep bench around the sides where a handful of young men recharge their phones, text and scroll, the unchecked great diaspora of displaced information. The phone is everything for refugees, and anywhere that wants to attract their business must have charging points.

The dishes come hot and generous, with fluffy, nutty white rice.

Bana is a rice stickler – she's particularly appreciative. The red beans are a great, solid, aromatic dose of slow-release carbohydrate, as warm and uncomplicated as a hug. The surprise, the great surprise, is the chicken livers. They are perfect. Soft, with that mysterious, renal flavour that is medicinal and industrial, but also like earth and grass and licked copper. The sauce is pungently hot, but still a negligée, not a shroud, for the meat. This was a properly, cleverly crafted and wholly unexpected dish, made with finesse and an elan that defied the surroundings, but at the same time elevated them. Ali smiled with a rare pride.

'Where do you want to go?' I asked. He shrugged and the smile became sad.

'You know, you know.' As if to say the name out loud would be inauspicious.

A cup of coffee – Nescafé, with a lot of milk and even more sugar. After years of po-faced hipster coffee, the sweet, thick Nescafé comes like a mouthful of remembrance. It is the taste of the south, of the Third, left-behind World. I have sat in the make-do shade on the red earth in so many refugee camps and roadside temporary halts and sipped this bittersweet, mothering coffee. So many slow, hopeful journeys.

So if you find yourself in the Jungle, ask for Mohammed Ali. The blue tent. He gets his bread from the chap from Bari next door. The desperate desire of everyone is that this is a temporary stop. A brief, cold and trying moment. But despite the best intentions, the Jungle is beginning to become a place, with churches and theatres and art and restaurants. It is germinating into that collective home. But then, isn't this how all places once began? With refugees stopping at a river, a beach, a crossroads and saying, we'll just pause here for a bit. Put on the kettle, kill a chicken.

February 2016

AWAY

Sudan

'There is no famine.' Marc Hermant, the lugubrious Belgian head of mission for Médecins Sans Frontières (MSF), South Sudan programme, wipes his tired eyes and repeats himself like a patient schoolteacher explaining basic grammar to a thick nine-year-old. I am sorry, no famine? There must be a famine. 'Not a Famine in Africa' isn't exactly news. I've seen the footage, it looks like a famine to me, Bob Geldof said it was a famine. 'Bob Geldof said that?' Hermant gingerly sips his bright yellow mulligatawny soup. 'No, what we have is a potential famine. If something isn't done now there will be famine next year.' Ah, so it is the foothills of famine? The preview of famine? A promise of famine? 'Yes, now is the hunger gap.'

Don't you just love the hunger gap, such a great phrase? It sounds like an advertising slogan: 'Mind the hunger gap', 'Fill that hunger gap'. One hundred years ago the hunger gap would have been familiar all over the earth. It is that lean time when the store food runs out before the harvest has ripened. In Britain, late spring was the time when it was dangerous to be young or old or alone. In Sudan, they plant with the rains, in normal years about now, and harvest in October. The hunger gap should be a month or so – nature's organic cull of the feeble and the halt and the sick and the unlucky of a species that has no natural predator but itself. This year the hunger gap has come early and the rains haven't come at all – yet. In the lexicon of professional aid, famine is a technical term. It squats darkly over the horizon, collating its misery, biding its time.

We're sitting in the terrace bar of the Norfolk Hotel in Nairobi, 500 miles from the Sudan. It is spitting rain emetically, and has been for a month. El Niño, this year's pan-global excuse for everything, suits the Norfolk, which looks like a down-at-heel Hampshire golf club, suburba-bethan: black beans and steak-and-kidney pudding, faded framed caricatures of long-dead ex-pats with smug grins and neat facial hair. In the lobby the souvenir carry-on of carved giraffes and smiley rhinos graze among the silver boxes of film crews, neatly encapsulating Africa's two great exports: anthropomorphism and bad news. The bellboy hurries back and forth, piling up the delicate technical kit and telescopic legs of investigation and concern. There are a lot of film crews here: the BBC has three; ITN has one, with another on the way. CNN and ABC and a host of others are passing through. Famine always draws a crowd.

Here's how a promise of famine works: people start to die. Charities on the ground blow the whistle, Khartoum wants to show international goodwill, so, despite a civil war, it allows strictly limited food drops. Thirty-six charities and the UN form an umbrella group called Operational Lifeline Sudan and make a deal with the guerrillas, who need to feed their soldiers, and then turn to the world media to provide the advertising. Khartoum says no one is allowed on a charity flight without its visa, which takes months, so forget it. The rebels won't allow anyone into their areas without a pass from them and they won't give it to anyone who has got a stamp from Khartoum, so the film crews have to charter their own aircraft and it is a very expensive operation. Bad news is the province of the rich. Charter prices have gone through the roof: the BBC has leased a Dakota; back home, editors are screaming about vanishing budgets, but like two bluffing poker players, ITN and the BBC won't back down. They need a story and so do the charities. Charities may work as a selfless consciousness of the world at the sharp end, but at the tin-rattling end, they exist in a deeply competitive capitalist market: an appearance by a logo and spokesman on the *News at Ten* means donations. An American religious charity went to an MSF feeding centre and put their T-shirts on the hungry kids to film them – cash in the tin back home. Someone sent a plane-load of anti-hypothermia suits made for Bosnia; ah, well, beggars can't be choosers. Brenda Barton made the front pages and the *Nine O'Clock News* in her logo T-shirt by feeding two malnourished children with her own breasts. It was a great picture. The fact that she had presumably taken up 10 stone of food space on an aid plane to transport a pair of pint-sized breasts to the starving wasn't mentioned. Nor was the horrible symbolism of a fecund European dribbling largesse over black babies, or the sensational tastelessness of flashing gravid teats in front of mothers whose own milk has dried up. 'I didn't do it as a publicity stunt,' she said. Barton is the press officer of the World Food Programme (WFP) and just happened upon a BBC camera crew in the biggest, emptiest country in Africa.

The journalists at the bar consider starting a charity called Lactaid and holding a red nipple day. Over the cold beers they talk about there not being enough 'skellis': skeletal people. ITN coaxed an old woman into a tree to pick leaves. The humour is callous and black but it is forgivable, it is the flak jacket of people who have only their own hard-bitten cynicism to protect their dreams.

The press and charities have a mutually beneficial symbiotic relationship: hacks need the charities to find the eyebite-worthy starving; the charities need the publicity. Apart from the familiar charities there are some very weird organisations out here raising money while the sun shines. They have alarming names like Safe Harbour, A-Cross and Victims of the Martyrs. Because, at least in part, the civil war is religious: Christian and animistic south rejecting the imposition of northern Muslim law. There is an absolute prohibition on Bibles. It is a stipulation for continuing aid, but an air traffic controller at Wilson airport in Nairobi tells me she has seen American religious charities smuggling them in anyway. Now explain to me what sort of missionary zeal fills a plane with books when children are dying for milk?

Others smuggle guns, butter and psalms across the Ugandan border with the connivance of a bunch of bona fide foaming dingbats called the Lord's Resistance Army, who kidnap children, and give them Kalashnikovs and the belief that bullets can't touch them. There are rumours of CIA involvement and of links with the Tutsis. Saddam and Gaddafi have their fingers in this pie. Fifteen years of civil war, dislocation, drought, double-dealing, burnt crops and regular bouts of world amnesia have made South Sudan a rich Petri dish for all the fungus and corruption of every conceivable form of apocalyptic, man-made misery.

Paul, the photographer, and I cadge a lift north with an ITN crew. From the air, northern Kenya could be the Scottish borders. This is *White Mischief* country, Isak Dinesen – I had a farm in Africa, the landscape of lachrymose colonial bathos and excess. But it exhausts the romance and the bedside literature to peter out into rough khaki scrub that stretches like mouldy pebbledash across the horizon. We are flying in a caravan, a squat, slow, single-engined workhorse, with a pilot who has aviator engraved on his shades. It's no comfort to be flown by someone who has to have their job description etched on their spectacles.

Bahr al Ghazal is a state twice the size of France with a population of perhaps less than a million, but no one's counting. This is where the worst of the proto-famine is. Six hours from Nairobi, it is like flying to Washington in a Morris Minor without a toilet. Tim Ewart, the ITN reporter, slowly does the *Telegraph* crossword, then gives up to read Mario Puzo (he's on page 20). Paul and I haven't got passes from the Sudanese People's Liberation Army (SPLA) guerrillas – the office in Nairobi was closed – but we are assured we can get them at the refuelling stop in Lokichokio. It's a formality, no problem. Lokichokio: crazy name, crazy place, a border town dropped in a fold in the hills between nowhere and nothing. The line that separates Kenya from Sudan is purely notional. A year ago this was a collection of huts baking in the wilderness, with a landing strip. Now it is a frontier town, a burgeoning collection of tents and hastily built breeze-block cantonments with bars and swimming pools and rooms with showers. It is a boom town, growing to service five Hercules aircraft, tied to the outside world by a thin, potholed, crumbling, rain-washed, bandit-harassed road that winds 1,000 miles to the coast at Mombasa. Everything – fuel, food, loo paper, Coca-Cola – has to be driven into Loki. This is Charityville.

In the West, we don't get to see the UN at work. We probably think it is a good idea, a bit wasteful, a bit blunt and slow. But we never get to see where all that money and effort actually goes. It goes here, into these ranks of Toyota Land Cruisers and bubbling Tarmac; and guards with walkie-talkies and gangs of black labourers, humping white sacks in the midday sun, and the pilots hanging out with a cold Coke in the Trailfinders bar. And the long lines of dusty tents, each the size of a football pitch, with the letters UN like a 20ft-high expletive painted on the sides. When this much neat charity lands on your doorstep, it changes everything: the economy, the social structure, the landscape. UN, the Ultimate Niño. Looking at Loki, it is impossible not to draw the trite conclusion that Africa has simply swapped colonialism for charity and there is very little difference. Both are buttressed with fine words, both in practice are paternalistic and divisive. It is still the white folk in the shade and the black folk humping the sacks.

There is a problem. A big problem. They won't give us a pass. The SPLA has changed the rules: it says it doesn't have authority, we've got to go back to Nairobi. 'What do you want to do?' Stick here in Charityville, cadge a lift back tomorrow or the next day, then rent a plane sometime next week, or go on? 'You're welcome to wing it,' says Tim Ewart. 'Basically, if we don't go now, there's no story.' Someone says we'll risk it. Startled, I look round, what fool was that? Idiotically, it was me. As the plane takes off Paul says, 'What can they do to us? Send us back?' I spend the next three uncomfortable hours thinking of all the things they can do to us. For some apparently good reason, we have left our passports behind. I am travelling across an international border into a war zone illegally, without a passport or a pass. I am going to a place that is 20 miles from the front line, that was evacuated a month ago because it was attacked by the Popular Defence Force. I don't mention the PDF, aka the Murahaleen, light cavalry mercenaries employed by Khartoum to ride down the single, vulnerable railway track and do a bit of entrepreneurial terrorism on the side. They came at night, killed 200 and rustled cattle. No one has been up here since. What can they do to us? Plenty.

Suddenly I'm moved by an unarguable need to pee. There is nowhere to pee. We brought our own water (five inflated dollars a bottle from the hotel), but the bottles are still full. We land in Ajiep. I am hyperventilating with fear, the doors open and the heat greets us like a long-lost relative. 'There is some bad news, I am afraid. Mawir Myok Lyal from the SSRA is here.' That's bad? 'That's bad.' The SSRA is the political wing of the SPLA, sort of their Sinn Fein. This Lyal is Gerry Adams. That's bad. Tim Ewart says, 'Look, no offence, but I don't know you, I can't risk my story.' 'We don't know you,' says the charity worker. 'We can't risk the team on the ground.' Quite. 'You can hide in the plane,' says the pilot, 'I'll fly you back.' A court martial is better than another six hours in this thing. Sod it, at least I am going to stand in Sudan. Secretary Lyal is sitting at a roughly made table under a shade-tree. He is surrounded by lieutenants in T-shirts and bits of fatigued militaria. One bloke has a baseball cap that advertises *Men in Black*. Lyal is precisely what Central Casting would have ordered for *The Wild Geese:* imposing, cunning, tough. AA Gill, *Sunday Times,* London. There has been a bit of a mix-up, I'm afraid. I shake his hand with a firm confidence and squat at his feet, cod psychology. He opens his mouth to reply, but he hasn't got any front teeth and it rather spoils the effect. Have we got any identification, he lisps. I give him my press card. He examines it, flips it over and reads, 'If found, please hand this card in at the nearest police station.' Pauses for a moment. 'OK, you can stay, I'll fix it.' Manfully, I restrain myself from French-kissing his hand.

We look round for the first time. Nothing prepares you for mass starvation, for the promise of famine. Or rather, everything prepares you for it, years of photographs and terse newsreel, skimmed journalism, accusing posters and award-winning photographs. They all prepare you for it, but none of them protects you from the truth of it. The terrible, terrible, pitiful shock of it. It is not staring at the face of starvation that thuds like a blow to your heart, it is having starvation stare back at you. All our lives, we've examined these people and swallowed the lump, turned the page, been quietly moved, but protected by the one-way mirror of news. We have averted our eyes to the grinning photos of our own plump children framed on the mantel, and felt the shaming relief of the uninvolved. Nothing protects you from the quiet scrutiny of a thousand fly-blown, bloodshot, liver-yellow, starving eyes, and nothing protects you from the smile of welcome. What have the Dinka got to smile about?

Ajiep is where the buck finally stops. Having been passed from hand to mouth around the world it comes to rest in the shade of a thorn tree in this dry, hot earth. Here, finally, is that mythological, nursery tea-time place: 'Remember all the starving people in Africa.' This is what we left on the side of our plates. Here is the end of the longest queue in the world. 'The people less fortunate than yourself.' When the Dinka look round, there is no one behind them. They are refugees in their own land wandering in an arid, featureless plain, waiting for famine to organise its paperwork.

Technically this isn't a famine because the starvation is only patchy. Some of the Dinka, one of the three main tribes of South Sudan, are less malnourished than others, but the hunger gap is working overtime. Ajiep is the worst any of the aid workers have seen. There has been no food here for a month. Lifeline Sudan flies its Hercules in broad circles over the area days before food drops. In this land without electricity or even the last century's communications, it is the semaphored signal for people to start walking. They walk enormous distances in an oppressive heat that makes every foot feel like a yard. Through a bush so bereft of natural features, I am lost within 50 paces; they do it carrying their children and with barely any water. We have to drink eight litres a day to avoid dehydration, but the Dinka carry only little carved cups around their necks and sip occasionally. The hardiness is beyond anything you have ever seen on a sports field or running track. And nothing can protect you from their awful beauty.

You couldn't have chosen a more handsome tribe to starve to death: they are tall and rangy, blue-black with high cheeks and broad foreheads with beautiful chevrons scarred on their brows. They wear elegant earrings and bracelets and simple silver crosses; the men carry orchid-leaf-bladed spears and stripling-thin cattle whips. They wear a mixture of swathed and swagged traditional togas and cast-off Oxfam rags. The young girls seem to like slips and nighties, and the mixture of beads and silver and silk petticoats in faded pastels disconcertingly makes them look like this year's Paris catwalk. Everyone moves with a slow grace. The Dinka are incapable of doing anything without a poised elegance. They arrange their limbs with fluid ease; you are always being drawn to the curve of a neck or the etiolated fingers cupping a child's head. They gather in tableaux, like Renaissance frescoes with occasional splashes of cerulean from the men's jellabas.

ITN go off in search of 'skellis' and tree-climbing grannies, wrapping their poor-taste cynicism around them like a mackintosh against a storm of pity. I walk to the children's feeding centre, a collection of grass huts, where young mothers sit in the sun cradling their infants. The starving children are beyond words. They lie limp and exhausted in the young women's laps, eyes half-closed, limbs like so much kindling. Most are silent, and occasionally tears streak the dusty-sallowed cheeks, attracting the constant flies. Inside the longest hut in the stifling dark a French nurse tersely and efficiently logs the proximity of death. She does a MUAC test (middle upper arm circumference), where a calibrated circle of card is placed around the child's upper arm and slid tight. It is coloured green, yellow, orange and red. The orange section means the child is at risk, the red means the child needs therapeutic feeding. The circle is the size of an expensive cigar. She measures weight for height: children who have fallen to 70% of body weight are given supplementary rations. At 60%, they are kept at the centre and fed milk eight times a day under supervision. There are five-month-old babies who weigh the same as they did at birth. An infant who is 60% of body weight looks virtually dead. The fragile signs of life flicker like a guttering candle. Their skulls and joints are perfectly drawn through their baggy skins. The hair is as parched and sparse as an old man's, slitted eyes glint through well-like sockets. They exist from moment to moment, small bird-like gnarled hands resting on exhausted breasts. 'A Western child wouldn't live two days in this condition,' the nurse says. 'Here, the ones we can feed have a 90% chance of surviving. The transformation over a month is miraculous. They are very resilient, but of course they may have less resistance to illness later.' Measles and diarrhoea are famine's little helpers.

She has seen 815 children under five: 167 are moderately malnourished by African standards, 404 badly and 234 severely. The centre works on a 5% higher threshold than anywhere else on the continent, otherwise they would be overwhelmed. All through the bush the Dinka are walking, moving in straggling lines to converge on an open, treeless plain where the food drop will be distributed. In normal days they are pasturalists who plant single subsistence crops and herd cattle.

Cattle to the Dinka aren't food, they are everything. They're money, property, holidays, shops, golf clubs, arcades, multiplex cinemas, trips to the pub, walks in the park. A wife costs about 40 cows and five bulls. Cattle are life. And now they are eating them, or they are being stolen and shot. If someone took away your home, your income, and set you on the street in your pyjamas, you would still live in a place that was functioning and solid, in a society that doesn't even count hunger as a measure of poverty. Without their cattle, the Dinka have less than nothing. If these young people want to be homeless together, it has to be on tick, on the promise of future calves.

A gaggle of girls walk beside me, straight backs and high breasts. They move with an easy, undulating rhythm. Little plumes of dust are kicked up by their feet. They giggle and whisper to each other, as cool and direct and blushingly unnerving as any group of pretty teenagers. They flirt. Nobody prepares you for flirting in a famine. While there is life, there is still living. One strides close and does a rolling lumpen imitation of my gait, and her friends bridle and shimmy in peals of laughter. With long, strong fingers, she touches her heart and then her lips and gives me a glowing white smile.

On the plain the Dinka line up in a milling band. They stretch across the horizon like a David Lean panning shot. Facing them 200 yards away are the neat files of white sacks containing split peas and maize, each attended by companies of askari. Standing on a pile of food, a fat WFP officer with a plastic water bottle over his shoulder shouts orders and waves a fly whisk: a martinet that is depressingly familiar all over Africa. Small boys, self-important with red rags of office tied to their wrists, dart back and forth, prodding women with cattle sticks. This is the lottery of life, the rough end of charity. Not everyone will be fed. And considering its mortal importance, the choosing is remarkably good-natured. The sacks are broken open and each divided between nine women: they fill their calabashes with pulses and tear up the plastic to make bundles to put on their heads.

Each of these little groups comes from one village – the women are responsible for the food but the head man chooses who will be fed. There is a lot of shouting and gesticulating, and the process is meticulous and desperately slow. But the Dinka have nowhere else to be. They stand in the hot sun and wait: it is not so much stoical or fatalistic as a worn-out realism. Each of the women carries a small brush made from sticks to sweep the spilt grain. They are loaded with 28 days' subsistence and, balanced as finely as tightrope walkers, they slowly move off into the bush, their small, naked children trailing behind. They will return to their villages if they still exist, or find a spot under a tree. An aid worker says, 'I wonder what those women have to do to be chosen and how much of that food goes to the army.' As the interminable business grinds on, I lie in the shadow of a termite hill with a group of men. They smile and nod. I hand out the last of my cigarettes, we sit for ten companionable minutes, watching. The choosing and rejecting, the spilling of seed. There is a light touch on my shoulder, and a man about my age in a shirt that is just dirty ribbons, with bony elbows and ribs like the ruts in a baked road, leans forward and smiles. The taut parchment skin wrinkles over his cheeks, his eyes are the colour of weak tea. He holds out the little gourd that is slung round his neck: would I like a drink? It is a small epiphany of sorts, to be offered hospitality from the very back of the earth's queue. Think of all the starving in Africa. It was as if the Good Samaritan had been offered succour by the man overtaken by thieves, and it was the most gravely humbling gesture. I was glad to be wearing sunglasses. I didn't trust myself to speak, just shook my head and dragged deeply on my cigarette.

Biblical analogies come easily here, the exodus of the Dinka, the flight across the desert, the ancient heroic look of them, a chosen people. Every so often a flash of metal spikes the eye: invariably it is a silver cross. Unbidden, I remember the Sermon on the Mount. I never thought I would actually see it played out quite so literally or with such grace. 'Ye are the salt of the earth.' 'Sufficient unto the day is the evil thereof.'

I was dreading dinner: how do you eat in a promise of famine? Actually, it is not difficult; not to eat would be a silly act of self-mortification. And we are hungry. The relief camp was a collection of little tents set behind a low palisade of thorn bushes; on the other side the starving stood and watched as we shared out the contents of bags: trail mix, repellent muesli bars, apples, chicken legs, packed lunch from the Norfolk Hotel with weirdly surreal lamb sandwiches cut into triangles that Paul said reminded him of childhood. There was a bit of rather good boiled goat. ITN provided a bottle of whisky and told with glee of the American network crew who had set up a grand tent with an awning and a collapsible dining table, napery and candles, and toasted each other with claret while the Dinka stood in a silent circle. It was the French nurse's birthday: she slumped exhausted into a chair and ate a boiled egg. When next you hear someone talk sneeringly about the high moral ground, remember the field workers of MSF, the only charity to have staff actually living in Bahr al Ghazal. These are volunteers who work because MSF pays the lowest subsistence salaries of any international charity, not despite it. Who have to be rotated every two months because no one can bear it for longer but who sometimes have to because they can't be pulled out. Who have to sleep in their shoes with a water bottle because their camp may be overrun. Because if you do find yourself living at the very pinnacle of the high moral ground, there are any number of people who would slit your throat for a moral and a watch.

We turn in. I haven't brought a tent so I lie under a mosquito net. Sleeping out in the African bush under a sickle moon is one of the most awe-inspiring experiences – as long as you have a choice, of course. Men have lain here in the hot wind looking at the stars for as long as there have been men. This is where we come from, this swathe of thin earth, brittle grass and thorn stretching from the Rift Valley to the filigree marshes at the source of the Blue Nile. This is our ancestral home. The sour-sweet smoky body smell of Africa drifts on the breeze. The cooking fires of the Dinka flicker like earthed comets. There is a sound of crickets and a distant drumming and the exhausted wailing of hungry children. And the temazepam-induced snores of an ITN reporter. Just as I was dozing off I turned over and came face to face with a wild beast. I made a noise not unlike a stuck heifer. The bone-questing dog and I were frightened in equal measure. Paul in the fastness of his tent laughed so hard his film rattled.

South Sudan is the line in the sand where Arab and black Africa meet, but it is also the place where the First World, north world, blue-eyed haves meet the Third World, south world, dark-eyed have-nots.

It is the front line, the raw edge of our conscience. I had expected to feel guilty, angry, horrified and depressed, and in varying degrees, I am. But the abiding sense is one of dignity. The dignity of a Dinka standing patiently in the sun and the workers who risk so much to help them. It is not that suffering is dignified, it is that here the fat and panoply of life are stripped away to reveal a fragile but resilient shared humanity. When I got home, I tried to explain to my young daughter where I had been and what I had seen. 'Are they dying?' she asked. Yes. 'Where do they bury them?' Where do we bury them? In Monday's rubbish, in the commercial break, in the turned page and the changed subject in Sunday lunch and under the prune stones on the side of your plate.

In the grey light before dawn I woke and saw a line of women pass silently in single file with calabashes on their heads going to collect water from the muddy hollows of a drying river. They looked like so many ghosts. As the sun rose it caught the shadows of a thousand bare footprints in the dust. A mother was washing her son. He stood in an enamel basin, his arms raised, and gently, with a tin cup and infinite tenderness, she sloughed the dust off him. In the golden light, he glowed and shone like the child in an icon.

May 1998

India

Here is my one traveller's tip for those of you considering going to India: don't tell anyone. Pretend you're spending a fortnight with your decaying mother in Torbay, really. Announcing you're going to India is like saying you've got a bad back: everyone has an address, has a cure. The very mention of India turns half your friends into travel moonies. 'You are going to Dhinki Dhoobre, aren't you?' they say, with barely contained missionary zeal. 'Well, you simply must rearrange everything.' I jest not. I had 20-page faxes of handwritten itineraries, imploring phone calls in the middle of the night, notes from strangers, the itinerant yogis of subcontinental tourism. And they all end with the same damning phrase: 'If you're not going to see the palace at Mollycoddle, then you're not going to see the real India, and you might as well not bother.'

As if all India seen through Western eyes isn't sensationally unreal. I tried to imagine Indians saying to each other, 'Well, of course, if you're not going to Sheffield and the Arndale Centre then you're not going to see the real England.' The rest of your friends, those who aren't born-again sahibs, will say, 'Oh, India, how wonderful, I'd love to go, but I don't think I could face it, the beggars you know, how do you handle the poverty?'

India has an unassailable position at the head of the world's poverty league. It is a perceived truth, an unarguable rubric, that this is the poorest country in the world. In the rich West, the implication is that to confront it, you need to have had a caring gland removed. It will be too much for sensitive, charitable folk, so best not go, best not look. How do you cope with poverty is the most asked question about India – the best answer comes from Mark Tully, the veteran foreign correspondent, who lives in Delhi: 'I don't have to cope with the poverty; the poor have to cope with the poverty.' To which I would add that actually the poverty is what you and I go to see. Poverty is what formed India, made India what it is. If Indira Gandhi's dream of a modern, thrusting, industrial tiger economy had been realised, and it had become a bigger Malaysia or Singapore, you wouldn't be that interested. It's the grinding lot of the vast majority that makes the opulence, the splendour, the architecture, the decoration, and the trappings of the princes and history so awesome. Always in India you're confronted with these juxtapositions of wealth and poverty; power and hopelessness; of sublime beauty and shocking ugliness. Everywhere you look there is binary metaphor, an encyclopedia of contradiction, dichotomy and counterpoint. Indians, all Indians, are the cleanest people in the world; you see them washing in the morning and evening, like obsessive surgeons scrubbing up, and then they work all day in streets that are no more than baked open drains, with rooting pigs and mange-crippled dogs. It's a contradiction, it's India.

Go to Agra – Agra is the one place the born-again sahibs back home will never recommend. 'Oh well, of course, there's the Taj Mahal,' they'll say, 'I suppose you want to see it. It's wonderful, of course (they sigh), but quite spoilt.' Don't believe it. Agra is an industrial military town, noisy and dirty, a real place where soldiers inhabit the old colonial officers' quarters and the town is modern, in the sense that in India even things that were built yesterday have a look of ancient exhaustion. But it is also a place that has more bona fide world heritage sites than anywhere else on the globe: it was the capital of Mughal India. And sitting in the middle of it is the Taj Mahal, Shahjahan's tomb for his beloved wife, but like everything in India, it's not that simple. She was his second wife and she died in childbirth, and then one of her sons killed all his brothers, and locked old Shahjahan up in a castle till he died. From his terrace he got perhaps the best, most heartrending view of his wonderful white tomb. Everyone should see the Taj once. It is an absolute, there are few absolutes in this world, it is absolutely beautiful, absolutely stunning. Set in the corner of a garden laid out in Arab fashion, but – with Victorian confidence and hubris – replanted by the Victorians like an English country garden, the Taj sits against the sky on the middle banks of a river. Its absolute symmetry, the maths of perfection, is almost painful to contemplate. It is the most complete thing ever built by man and nothing can diminish it: not the queues; not the crowds; not the kitsch of endless reproduction and familiarity; not the sneers of Noël Coward or the epicurean India snobs; not the clicking lines of newlyweds waiting to be photographed on Princess Diana's bench. Nothing can touch it and nothing adds to it; not moonlight, or dawn, or dusk, that's just weather and light. If you go to India for just one thing, if you go to just one place abroad in your life, it should be the Taj.

The other place born-again sahibs will never recommend is New Delhi. Nobody does, even if they live there. Like Pretoria, Canberra and Washington, it's a capital without a soul, only a name, because civil servants and embassies were dumped there, but, if for nothing else, Delhi is memorable for the finest example of English architecture. You'll see Lutyens's viceregal palace and its approach from India Gate, a red-stone Arc de Triomphe which beggars the Champs Elysées, or the Mall, or any other street built by swagger and power. A mile away is Chowpatti Street in Old Delhi, where traders from all over India buy and sell wholesale. It's a frantic stasis. The last word in free-market economics and capitalist chaos, it makes Cecil B De Mille look like Ingmar Bergman; to see the impossibility of organising India, coping with India, imposing a logic on India, Chowpatti Street is the answer.

Simla is a hill station – it was the summer residence of the viceroys – and it scampers up the nursery slopes of the Himalayas, surrounded by pine forests and vertiginous views. The town is like a cross between Godalming and Alice Springs, Tudorbethan home counties with corrugated tin roofs. A big billboard welcomes you to India's Switzerland; well, Switzerland should be so lucky. Simla is now where the new Indian middle class comes to relax; we didn't see another white face. Families who've done well out of foreign trade and old-fashioned metal-bashing industry, avaricious for the West. The men don Pringle sweaters and Sta-Prest slacks, but again the contradiction; the women wear *kurta pyjamas* and saris. They make odd couples: the men look like dowdy, Sunday afternoon Milwaukee plumbers and the women splendidly, riotously Asian, and they promenade, as the Englishmen sahibs used to, to Scandal Point, where tough, bigoted, disappointed paragons of empire had collected in covens to pass vicious gossip. The Indians are too polite, they smile and laugh and pass exaggerated compliments.

I came here in search of Kipling's India. It's here that Kipling's father built an amateur theatre, and here, in the splendid Cecil Hotel, that Kipling wrote. It's been lovingly restored to an imperial grandeur and comfort. I found a second-hand bookshop and curio dealer in a dark nook that could have been straight out of *Kim,* but the more you look, the further the stories and the ghosts slip away. Kipling's India, I realised, only ever existed in the slow, damp afternoons of home counties vicarages. To search India for it is as pointless as looking for Graham Greene's France. Kipling, after all, wasn't looking for Kipling's India, but I bear the literary baggage of empire and my family's clubbable mythology of tea-planting and pith helmets. India infected our souls far more than the Raj ever infected theirs. A polite and kindly people, Indians will say what they know you want to hear, that they are terribly grateful for the railways, and the post office, and the civil service – but how often do you think about your post office, or your railways, or your civil service? The Raj hasn't been wiped away on purpose with anger or resentment, it's just sunk beneath the seething surface, beneath the daily grind for dhal and a few rupees. India's poverty absorbs everything and uniquely reinvents it. Reincarnates it and decorates it. The vaunted babus and the civil service that we left behind have become an intricate, impossible filigree of forms, carbon paper, rubber stamps and towers of files. It's as impossible to conceive constructing India's civil service as it is building its temples.

Leaving Bombay airport, I collected nine separate rubber stamps, the last one applied with a grinning shrug to my hotel baggage label because there was nowhere left for it to go.

Walking around the pine-scented streets of Simla, I thought with what quite good manners the Indians had buried our lauded shared two centuries. How little was left – and then, from a parade ground somewhere below, a military band struck up a hymn, the sun was setting, catching the spire of the Surrey church, and the gables of the officers' club, Gurkhas stood on starched guard, 'rock of ages cleft for me' words, and the years rolled back, and I was awash in a remembrance of things past, a reverie for a time and a life that I'd never actually lived, that existed only in print and celluloid, of burra pegs and punka wallahs, sepoys and redans. The ghostly echo of our finest hour – but only I felt it and that's another thing about India: everything you can or want to dream is here, everything anyone tells you is true. It's a place that accepts all visions, all interpretations, all are true, but none is the whole truth, like Hinduism, that most beguiling and infuriating of religions. It's endlessly accommodating but rigidly fatalistic. It starts with a simple trinity and then there are 30 million, or 300 million, or 3,000 million lesser gods; I was told all three figures with absolute authority. India has a civil servant's religion of numbing complexity and awful simplicity; no other country in the world believes this, or could afford it. You can't convert to be a Hindu, you can't join the reincarnation train halfway through its endlessly slow, circular journey. Plenty of Westerners come, though, to pick through its jumble for something off the peg that fits; they do yoga as exercise, which is a bit like walking the stations of the cross as aerobics.

This is not an empirical, rational place. Here a spade is not a spade, it's a two-man spade, it's a two-man tool. One man holds the handle, the other pulls a rope tied to the blade. In 40-degree heat, I watched a pair of men, one with a small chisel, the other with a lump hammer, chip away at a rock the size of the Taj Mahal's dome. They were planning on flattening it. It was a Sisyphean task of epic proportions that defied a normal life expectancy. But they worked with the slow rhythm of men who know that all life is just an illusion, there is only karma, only rhythmic chipping away at this existence in preparation for the next, when perhaps they'll come back as a JCB.

Everybody agrees you must see Rajasthan, although again, born-again sahibs will recommend spectacularly inaccessible places. Travelling on Indian roads has a funfair-like, heart-in-the-mouth excitement. The gaily decorated lorries swerve across the rutted roads and all have the imperative 'horn please' painted on the back. Eight or nine hours on the Asian equivalent of the wall of death, where you know that every other driver has the ethereal air bag of reincarnation for added confidence, is a little more nerve-jangling than most of us want on holiday. Rajasthan is palaces and forts. In a remarkably short space of time they fuse together into a rummage of blinding opulence. You don't lose the ability to be awed, just the ability to rise to the awesomeness. I'm sorry, my jaw has dropped as far as it will go and my eyes have reached the ends of their stalks. The guides' mantra of impossible facts come round for the second, third, fourth time: 'all from a single piece of marble, all laid by hand, all real gold, real silver, the biggest, longest, highest, most expensive'. It rolls over you like the blindingly reflected light, and the cumulative effect is of slowly being drowned in decadence. But there is none of the bated, reverential, national trussed-up preciousness of English country houses. One place stood out for its contrapuntal oddness. A man in a hotel said we should see the largest gun on wheels in the world. Now, you know, I'd thought I'd give it a miss. The biggest gun on wheels in the world is not what I'd come to India for, but, somehow, we found ourselves there in front of it, a vast, ornate sewerage pipe on bossed wheels with a soldier asleep in its shadow. As uninspiring and unmemorable as anything you care to forget. But it was set in a place called Jagger Fort, a dilapidated 17th-century barracks on the crest of a mountain, home to nesting pigeons, green parrots and langur monkeys. Scattered in its ruined, crumbling courtyards were mouldering Victorian barouches and state sedans, a fading theatre, an overgrown garden, a wall of curling, bleached photographs from durbars and forgotten polo games, all dozing in the heat. From the battlements you could see across Jaipur and out over the dun-coloured desert, kites and eagles hanging in the thermals and wild figs and banyans slowly, slowly pulling apart the teetering walls. It was a moment heavy with reverie.

The first time I came to India, 25 years ago, the rule was eat first. Public food was either poisonous or disgusting, often both. The biggest change in India is that you can eat Indian. The food in hotels is universally adequate, often good and frequently exceptional. Food on the street, though it looks enticing and smells better, is still just too risky to consider, not because the cooks are dirty, but because the vegetables by necessity are grown in human manure. Our soft

Western guts are just too vulnerable. Gastric liquidity is the second most commonly asked question about India, and indeed you should only travel with people who you feel comfortable talking stools to. Personally I will happily indulge in toilet talk for six or seven hours at a stretch. Indian food tends to be gassy – slow-cooked vegetables and pulses – so you see lines of Dutch tourists who at every step sound like an RAF motorbike display. They wear expressions of pained concentration: farting in India is playing Raj roulette with the linen. I came away with the rarest of all tropical afflictions: constipation.

I finally found my Kipling connection in Bombay. I adore Bombay, a cross between New York and Gomorrah, the most exciting and walkable city in the world. I love the Mutton Street junk market and the red-light district with its filthy streets and brightly saried eunuchs and the chaos of Victoria station and the dhobi ghats, the biggest launderette in the world. The monsoon still lingered and in the afternoon there was a downpour. I'd been taken to see the house Kipling was born in, now an art school. Outside, in the teeming gutter, a small, naked child crouched and washed itself, its black hair cut roughly to the shoulder, the little body wriggled like an eel, and I was transported back to my grandmother's house with its Benares brass, worn leopard skins and Turkey rugs and my favourite bedtime story with its wonderful pen-and-ink drawings: this little child just was Mowgli, the little frog, fishing in the Wainganga river, with taxis and scooters rushing past.

One last word on the poverty. There are more beggars in Soho than there are in Bombay. They're not as good at it, they don't have as much reason, but there are more. And you will be bothered by more peripatetic salesmen in Morocco or Naples than in India. And if you're really worried by poverty here, then allow yourself to be ripped off. Don't argue with taxi drivers or curio sellers – you don't start from an even bargaining position. The most cynically embarrassing thing to hear from born-again memsahibs is that the poverty is terrible but 'do you like my shawl? I managed to beat him to half the price'. India is a poor place but only in economic terms. On any other scale you care to think of, it's rich beyond the dreams of avarice. Any fool country can have democracy and freedom of speech and a rudimentary social security system when they've got the cash, but to achieve these things when you don't is humbling. India is that most miraculous of all modern states, a secular, democratic theocracy. And if we measure wealth in terms of any of the things that really matter – family, spirituality, manners, inquisitiveness, inventiveness, dexterity, culture, history and food – then India would be hosting the next G7 conference and sending charity workers to California. Of all the places you'll never get to because of squeamishness, trepidation, laziness and a dodgy bowel, India is by far and away your greatest loss.

In the frantic scurry and crush of Bombay's railway, where there is a fatality every day, a man bumped into me. I mention this because it's rare. Indians are dexterous in crowds. As our shoulders jarred, he touched his heart with his fingers. It's a silent apology and a prayer. There is a spark of God in all of us. He was saying sorry to his bit of the deity for bumping into mine. We may have given them the iron of the railways, but they filled it with 3,000 million gods.

January 1999

The Aral Sea

The man behind the desk has a bandaged ear. Perhaps a previous guest let him keep the rest of his head as a tip. He holds my passport and press accreditation as if they are fortune cookies containing death threats. He licks his fingers, then his lips, then the ballpoint and begins very slowly copying out the letters and numbers in triplicate on three ancient, moth-winged ledgers. He has no idea what he is writing, it's all English to him, awkward for his Cyrillic-conditioned fingers.

Finally, he writes US$40 on a scrap of paper and rubs his thumb and forefinger together. Forty dollars. That's more than a month's wages for a middle-class man here – if they had anything as outré and modern as a middle class. He hands me a receipt on a square of brown lavatory paper, which is useful because it's the only lavatory paper in the place. This is only a hotel because they charge you $40 to stay. There's no furniture and no soap. The water comes in a prostated, rusty dribble. The bath has been used to interrogate sheep. The towel is a bar mat. There's a blanket, a chipped tin teapot and a carpet that looks like tar applied with a comb. All night, lost herdsmen bang on my door and stare as if they've seen the ghost of tsars past. Welcome to Nukus, rhymes with mucus, twinned with nowhere. Nukus, no mates.

Nukus is the capital of Kara-Kalpakstan. Don't pretend you've heard of it, a semi-autonomous republic in the far west of Uzbekistan. One of the 'stans', shires of the former Soviet Union. A vast area of vast land. Desert, mountain, broken promises and wrecked grand plans once known collectively as Turkistan or where-the-hell's-that-stan. Now cut into five post-meltdown new countries – Tajikistan, Turkmenistan, Kyrgyzstan, Kazakhstan and Uzbekistan – which stretch from the Caspian Sea in the west over Iran, Afghanistan,

Pakistan and the Tien Shan mountains of China to Mongolia. This was the Russians' back yard, not open to the public – a place to dump rubbish, people, embarrassments and five-year plans. Up there somewhere in the desert is Star City and the space programme. Also the glowing half-life of above-ground nuclear test sites and their collateral seeping, cancerous waste. But right here is the big one – the stans' main claim to an entry in the *Guinness Book of Records*. The Kara-Kalpaks can boast the Biggest Ecological Disaster in the World, Ever. Nothing else, no smoking rainforest, no solitary carnivore, no home-county ring road, comes close to the majesty of this disaster. Not just the biggest, but the fastest. Organised and executed with the precipitate callousness, greed and sheer eye-bulging stupidity that only hands-on communism can muster. They've managed to drain the Aral Sea, the fourth biggest inland lump of water on the globe, and they've done it in 20 years. The southern Aral was created and maintained by the Oxus river (now known as the Amu Darya), which rises in the frozen attic of the Pamir mountains and meanders across grassland in search of a coast, finally giving up and creating its own terminus. The Oxus is/was one of the great rivers – the ancient Persians thought it the greatest. Along its banks the towns of the silk route flourished. The orchards and spice gardens, the mulberry trees and roses of Samarkand and Bukhara and Khiva.

Cotton has always been grown here, mixed with silk into a bright material that made Bukhara famous. Then in 1861, across the Pacific, something apparently utterly unconnected with central Asia caused the flutter of chiffon that grew into a wind that became a dust storm that changed everything: the American Civil War. Russia was one of the few supporters of the South (we were another). Russia bought its cotton from the South – to make up the deficit they increased production in the stans. When the communists took over, they decided to bury capitalism in a generation, and turned the whole of this vast area into a mono-crop culture of the stuff. In 1932, they started the Fergana valley canal, one of the huge, murderous, wasteful engineering achievements of Stalinism. It was only the beginning. Soon the apparently inexhaustible Oxus was gashed and slashed with thousands of miles of arbitrary irrigation, canals and dams, hydroelectric plants and repetitive ditches. They did the unthinkable, the unimaginable: they bled the river dry. Now it does not even reach the Aral Sea.

Oh, but that's not the half of it. Cotton is one of the thirstiest crops, and all mono-crops are prone to disease and infestation. Cotton naturally is particularly weedy. The haemorrhaging river leached salt that should have gone to the sea into the earth. The water came on and off the field up to 15 times in its course and sucked more salt to the surface, salinating the water table. Now a crystal layer sits on the exhausted earth and the tea tastes like a practical joke (oddly, it improves the coffee). Here, the drinking water is three or four times more saline than is considered healthy or palatable. To salt the land is a biblical horror, the final murderous curse of a place. Kara-Kalpakstan has become the largest cruet set in the world. Ah, but we are not finished: terrified managers facing falling yields sprayed tonnes of phosphates, nitrogen and, worst, DDT indiscriminately over the fields, and it's still all here, blowing in the wind.

Step out onto the wide, grim, grey streets of Nukus, and in one slow pan you can see all you will ever need to know about communism. It is not so much that this place of hateful, cheap Soviet architecture fills the soul with gloom: it's that it sucks everything remotely beautiful or sensitive from the soul, leaving a vacuum of low-grade depression and the tinnitus of despair. Seventy years of communism, all that hardship, terror, death. All that effort and hope and promises, the forced migrations, the cruelty, exhaustion, misery and rationing, the starvation and privation, the mechanical, imperative certainty of it all, ended up with this baking, grim bleakness.

A few bronchitic, gaseous Ladas career along its broadly potted and rotted roads, every one a taxi. An old woman squats beside an upturned box, selling individual cigarettes, sunflower seeds and sluggish, dusty cola. She is the summit of independent Uzbek private enterprise. A man in a traditional skullcap pulls a reluctant goat on a rope. The goats bleats piteously – it knows this is not a good day. Soviet-style posters of happy storm troopers and peasant girls fondling potent sheaves fade and curl in the hot wind. Bits of folk-painted hardboard clap against iron and cement like early drafts for BA tail fins. This is a bad place, a sick place. The damage to the land is as nothing compared with the damage to these people.

Here is a brief and incomplete list of what the Kara-Kalpaks can expect in return for their cheap cotton and blasted land: bronchial asthma, allergic rhinitis, infantile cerebral palsy, chronic lung disease, kidney disease, endocrine disease, urogenital disease, diseases of the nervous system, all of them way, way beyond what would be considered acceptable in a normal, moderately developed world, and chronic anaemia. Even before they're born, Kara-Kalpaks are cursed by their habitat: 97% of pregnant women are anaemic, 30% of births may have defects, 1 in 10 babies may already be dead. These figures, as with all statistics in this piece, are educated, conservative guesses by outside agencies. The Uzbeks don't make a habit of washing their salty linen in public or letting their citizens know what's sitting at the end of their bed. But there are special wards just for birth defects here that no outsider has ever seen, the consequence of DDT and salt and malnutrition – thin bread and tea is the daily diet of most Kara-Kalpaks. What makes all this more ironic is that these exhausted women were the original Amazons, the warrior caste Alexander supposedly would not fight. If a child makes it past birth and the 30% infant mortality rate, then it had better pack its experiences and fun tight, because life expectancy is probably only 38 choked, grim years.

The microscope I'm looking through is a gift from Médecins Sans Frontières (MSF). Through the mist of blue, stained lung gunk on the slide swims a bright red spot. That's it. Yes, that's definitely it. The red spot that marks your card for life: tuberculosis. TB is the number one top-of-the-pops killer in Kara-Kalpakstan. New cases in Nukus come in at a hacking 167.9 per 100,000 of the population (50 is considered an epidemic elsewhere). The microscope is the only piece of equipment in Nukus's TB hospital that couldn't have been made by a carpenter or farrier. This rambling institution, like the hotel, is only a hospital because someone says it is. There is no equipment, nothing that plugs in, just iron beds and broken tables and Cyrillic posters warning against Aids, which hasn't got here yet. The distempered walls flake and sag.

There's an overwhelming smell of sick, hot sewage. A truck pumps out the open latrines. Most patients sit outside in the baking dust, catching what passes for fresh air. The hot wind gusts with thick, poisonous lungs. The stoic sick hawk and spit. Spitting is a national sport. When I suggested, all things considered, they might be asked to stop, I'm told it's delicate, it's a cultural thing. Yeah, and Genghis Khan thought kicking people to death in sacks was a cultural thing. TB is very, very infectious. We walk around wearing paper Donald Duck masks.

As ever, the children's ward is the most depressing: little girls wheezing on beds, watching the motes dance in the sun; the hospital cannot even feed them properly – a little yogurt if they are lucky; mothers in bright headscarves hover in corners, desperately grateful for even this, not wanting to draw attention or make a fuss; infants as young as nine months are brought in with TB. In children, it's likely not just to be pulmonary: it affects the other organs, the bone, the spine, as meningitis.

A small lad tags along with us, pretty, pallid, central Asian features with a mop of black hair. Whenever I look round, he's there, sneaking with a tyke's smile and a slight squint. His name sounds like Gary. Gary's bright as a button, except he's not: he's got TB and the complications of pleurisy, and he's brain-damaged; and he's an orphan; he's seven.

Today, by chance, is my son's seventh birthday. Thousands of miles from here, his healthy lungs are blowing out candles. I should be there but I'm not; I'm here with Gary, who puts his face close to mine and laughs – the first laugh I've heard in days, a tinkling, rippling noise, an echo from another place. I smile back but realise he can't see it, because I'm wearing this antiseptic muzzle to protect me from his breath.

Being dealt TB, pleurisy, brain damage and a family of one in Nukus is about as low a hand as God can offer a seven-year-old. We walk on through the wards, the little hand fits into mine and breaks my heart. TB is not an illness like cancer or malaria or cholera. It's not the result of bad luck or bad drains or genes or insects. It's a consequence, an indicator of something else, something we've got loads of – money. More exactly, the absence of it. TB hitches a ride on the back of extreme poverty. Only the poor and malnourished, the weak, are susceptible. It's as if they read the instructions on the box the West comes in wrong, and went and got inconspicuous consumption. That it should have returned so violently and comprehensively in what was, until a decade ago, part of a superpower, is a symbol of how precipitous the collapse in central Asia has been.

MSF is treating TB with some success, and for every patient, of course, that's a miracle. But in the general walk of life in Uzbekistan, it means little or nothing. MSF is here because someone should be here to show that someone out there noticed and cared. They can't tell how many of their failures have the terrifying new variant of drug-resistant TB. Oh, it's out there. Prisons have about 40% TB, one in five of those drug-resistant. The only laboratories that could do the tests are in the West. Incidentally, my local Chelsea & Westminster Hospital had a rare case last year: an immigrant who was kept in locked isolation. He escaped, and the health officer ordered a police search. Here it could be anyone: the waiter, the man who spits at your feet, the policeman who leans in the window to check your papers. The treatment for drug-resistant TB costs £8,000, has side effects of kidney failure and blindness, lasts five months and then it's only 50-50, a toss-up.

Don't stop reading yet. The best bit is still to come. We haven't got to Muynak yet, the destination of this piece, the real reason I came here. Someone said to me in passing, apropos of nothing, over lunch in the Ivy: 'Hey, why don't you go to the worst place in the world?' The worst place in the world has an emphatic ring to it.

We leave Nukus in an ancient Volga. The driver loves it. A fine car. A good car. It's a deathtrap heap: the safety belt is attached to the chassis with gaffer tape. On the outskirts of town, a bridge crosses the Oxus. The river is a brown, turgid worm as broad as a peaty salmon-spawn stream. 'There are the old banks where it used to run,' points the driver. Where? I look and can't see. And then, pulling back for focus, the width and depths of the once-upon-a-time river are revealed in the distance. It was huge, wider than the Nile – a dozen motorways across. Awesome, appalling. The road traces the crippled stream north, through the horizon-shoving flatness of semi-desert and large, vacant fields with a frosting of salt. We pass plunky, unstable three-wheeled tractors, sand-matted camels, men in traditional long coats and boots with galoshes riding dusty, ballet-toed donkeys, and patient families with small, plastic bundles waiting for lifts. Every tree in Uzbekistan is painted white. It's the literalism of communism. Someone once wrote an after-lunch memo, and the next day they started painting all the trees. We stop in a village to visit the hospital. The doctor in his white coat, boiled thin and translucent, and the tall chef's hat that medical folk wear here, stands in the dust. A cleaning woman is tearing a strip off him; the patients stare at him. For a moment, he looks at the ants and silently turns back to his barren, distempered office. His one medical assistant has just got TB. He hasn't been paid his pittance of a salary for seven months. The health ministry has fined his under-resourced hospital for not disposing of its rubbish properly. He hasn't got an incinerator, a tin can belches greasy sputum smoke. He drinks. All day, every day, hopelessly.

When the Soviet Union finally collapsed with exhaustion and horror, the stans were the only constituent part that didn't want independence. They actually asked to stay – better the devil... Russia had to push them out like reluctant teenagers, so they waited till they had half a dozen Aeroflot planes on their provincial runways and declared independence and a national airline. Nothing else changed much – it just got smaller and meaner. Uzbekistan is still a one-party command economy. It recently came top of a business magazine's list of the world's most corrupt countries (when that was reprinted in the local press, Uzbekistan's name had miraculously vanished, that's how corrupt it is). Every cotton harvest, schools, universities and offices are emptied into the fields. Everyone must pick and sleep in freezing barns, beg food and drink salty ditchwater. It gets harder: every year the fields are scoured for every wisp of cotton. Yet the people don't yearn for democracy. Democracy is an indecipherable foreign language. Since before the birth of Christ, this swathe of earth has suffered under waves of light-cavalry dictators: Macedonians, Persians, Arabs, Scythians, Mongols, Russians. A word was invented for them: horde.

This place is antidemocracy, the opposite of democracy. What people yearn for is a new, better, stronger megalomaniac. There are rumblings of infectious, fundamental Islam coming from out of the desert, and the government is keen to associate itself with the personality cult of Tamerlane, or Timur, as they call him, erecting hideous, *über*-realist statues, gaining strength by retrospective association. Timur was Uzbekistan's home-grown 10th-century monster, creator and desecrator of the biggest land-base empire ever seen. A man who made Stalin look Swiss.

Muynak quivers out of the dust. It looks like solidifying dust, shimmering in the heat haze. It's a seaside town, a spa town, a summer holiday place with a promenade that's also a fishing port with a flotilla of big trawlers and cargo barges in a harbour. There's a huge fish cannery that's won international awards. You can tell instinctively it's a seaside town. It has that sense, that rather tatty, low-rise feeling; light and air, bracing.

We walk up a dune to the edge of a beach and look out to sea. It's desert, as far as the eye can stretch – flat, scrub desert with shells. Muynak is now 100 kilometres from the water. It's as if you stood on Brighton pier and the sea started at Paris – truly unbelievable, shocking. In the distance, dust storms twist, a family walks across the sea bed, the father's angry: 'Wolves,' he shouts. Wolves took his cow in the night. His son carries its head in a congealing sack. Sea wolves, sea cow. Muynak is a town in shock. It feels the sea like an amputated limb. Still aches for it. Men sit and look out at the waves of sand and hear the surf. The Aral Sea, with its thick deposits of salt and chemicals, is now the biggest single collection of dust in the world. It's the equivalent of a friable, airborne, choking Holland. Every year, suffocating toxic clouds blow into town. Man-killer dust. And I forgot to mention, out there, just over the curl of the earth, is an island that, in the way of this country's negative absolutes, has the biggest chemical weapons plant in the world, that contains the largest dump of anthrax on the planet – abandoned, waiting for the wind.

Of all the ills that have been dumped on Kara-Kalpakstan, it seems invidious, unnecessary, to mention unhappiness, but Muynak feels grief-stricken to the point of madness. The people move with a slow, pointless lethargy. All around, there are signs of psychotic, repetitive

comfort: men sit rocking like caged bears, women with short reed
brooms sweep their doorsteps maniacally for hours. I watch a man
wash an ancient green van from sunrise to sunset, the corrosive dust
falling as fast as he can wipe. Early one morning, I notice an old chap
sitting on a bench staring at the absent coast, legs crossed, arms folded
in his lap. At dusk, he's still there, hasn't moved a muscle.

The town itself is worn out, all its constituent parts loose and
sagging; hinges rasp, the edges of things are darkly rounded with
abrasion. It's coming to the end, the factories and canneries slowly
sink into the grit. The darkly empty fish fridges are slumped saunas
in the heat. Steel hawsers and bits of black metal grow out of the
rising earth like hardy plants or drowning hands. Even imagining
the effort that once invigorated them is exhausting. Stunted cattle
plod the street, cudding dust and mud, so scrawny that at first I
wondered why they were all calves. Large, hard-boned dogs crack
their skulls on the smoky rubbish wasteland on the edge of town,
hanks of gory sheepskin lie in the turgid filth and multi-species dung.
Only the children run and shriek and throw stones and wrestle like
children everywhere, making balls out of rags. The three, parallel
Tarmac streets are their playground. The road is covered in chalk
drawings: hopscotch and football pitches, pictograms of dolls and
soldiers, houses, cars and ships. Ships they'll never sail in. It's a long,
black wish-list letter to Father Christmas, the one dictator who never
visited these parts.

They're still here, the ships – huge ships, blackened and callused.
They lie askew in their dry beds, at anchor for ever, their plates
wrenched off to make defensive stockades for houses. Their ribs are
like the bones of extinct animals; brave and boastful names peel off
their hulls. I lie in the dunes and listen to them, the wind plays
them like a sad band: hatches boom, metal keens for the lost sea. A
hawk hunts the sparse grass where seagulls should call, runty cattle
move silently in line astern. You can still hear it, the echo of the surf
hissing on the hot shore. It is the strangest, most maudlin place I've
ever been. There's something particularly awful about dead ships. All
other discarded man-engineered metal is eyesore rubbish, but not
ships. They retain a sense of what they were: a majesty, a memory of

the lightness under their keels. Of all the things sailors dread, carry superstitious talismans against, weather and wave, snapped hawser and hidden shoal, none, even in his wildest dreams, imagined that the sea would leave him, would get up and steal away.

This town thought many things, worried and dreaded plenty, but it could not conceive that it would one day be abandoned to dust. Up on a dune overlooking the mirage of water is the Russian sailors' graveyard. The crosses made out of welded iron pipe have, in the Orthodox way, three crossbars. Unkempt and crooked, they look like the spars of tall ships ferrying the dead. All the Russians that could go have gone now, leaving the Kara-Kalpaks. But the old Russian harbour master is still here, living in a dark hovel of memories and smells with his babushka wife, a painting of Stalin and a map of remembrance with fathom markings that are thin air. He has his uniform and grows garrulous about the good days when there were 40,000 people here. Holiday-makers, work and play. 'It took a day, a whole day, to sail across the Aral. We knew it was shrinking; we built canals out to it; we chased after the sea.' And then, one day in 1986, all the fishing boats went out, cast their nets in a circle, and when they pulled them in, there was nothing. 'We knew it was the end.'

A story like this, a story of such unremitting misery, ought to end with a candle of hope. There should be something to be done. Well, I'm sorry, there isn't. Plenty of better men with clipboards and white Land Cruisers have been here to put it back together again, but they've retreated, dumbfounded and defeated. The World Bank has just spent $40m on a feasibility study and come up with a big idea. The big idea is a wetland bird reserve. Thanks, that would do nicely. You can't cry over spilt water: it just adds more salt. The sea will never come back to Muynak. The river will never repair its banks to meet it. The people of Muynak have nothing to do and nowhere to go; surrounded by thousands of miles of dust, without money or health or expectations, they'll just wait to die. The children will stop drawing in the street, grow up and give up, and the town will give up with them.

I said at the beginning that it was an ecological disaster, but that's not right. That puts it at a remove, makes the Oxus and the Aral Sea a piece of cowboy exterior design, a cock-up with fish and minerals. It's not that. It's a human disaster of titanic proportions. This hard earth of ours doesn't care if it's a sea or a desert, a river or a dune. It has no game plan, no aesthetic. Eagles will replace the gulls, and there are plenty of salt-loving succulents that see this as a golden opportunity. Rivers and seas come and go, there's just no space for people here. For them, for us.

In the hospital a young lad sits on the edge of his bed. He is frightened, his eyes are like saucers. His breath is as quick and shallow as a trapped bird's. He's right to be frightened. He's very, very sick. His bones incubate a mortal malevolence. His mother has pinned a little cloth triangle to his shirt. I ask what it is. 'A protection against the evil eye, for good luck.' It holds salt – cotton and salt. Boy, was she ever misinformed.

July 2000

Uganda

Nowhere wakes up with a greater sense of optimism than Africa. Good morning, Africa is one miraculous experience. The sun arrives bright and smiley as a kid's magician, there's none of the somnambulant slow-fade greyness of the north. A fresh gold light slants through the palms and acacias. The air is clear, the dust gauze and thermal shimmy are still a few hours away, the country glows with a new-minted radiance.

The early-morning sounds of Africa: kung-fu cockerels straining to out-crow each other, frantic weaver birds in the thorn tree like an immigrant tenement, mnemonic doves, bleating, hungry goats, chuckling children being bathed in tin buckets, men coughing and spitting into shards of mirror to shave outside daub-and-thatch huts, radios searching the static for distant news and Mali pop songs. Gaggling women at the wheezing water pump filling the first of interminable four-gallon plastic cans, and the smell, that most evocative essence of this bright continent: hardwood smoke, hard-work sweat, animal fat and the yawning breath of the hard red earth. Nowhere starts each day with more hope than Africa. Or needs to.

Uganda, the garden of Africa, is a shock of greenery. Compared with its neighbours across Lake Victoria, Kenya and Tanzania and Sudan in the north, it's a revelation of fecundity. Everything grows. Lean too long on a walking stick and it sprouts. Travelling north, you cross a faintly familiar patchwork of fields, a rare sub-Saharan glimpse of promised bounty. Up in the corner, where the country marches with Congo and Sudan, the cash crop is tobacco. Strip farmers' plots are mixed with maize, cassava, potatoes, bananas and leafy green vegetables that only have indigenous, sonorous names. In the margins of fields are tethered shiny, fat goats; chickens and ducks peck at the earth.

Every family steading of low, thatched huts has its own broad, shady mango tree. The fruit is small, sun-coloured, dizzyingly sweet. On its smiling face, Uganda is the African dream, a self-sufficient mixed agrarian economy, but it's only skin-deep. In its short independence, it has also been cursed with a brace of top-of-the-range monsters. Even by Africa's unimpeachably high standards, Milton Obote and Idi Amin stand in a class of their own. But progress is all relative, and after years of terror, pillage, civil war, invasion and the nightmarish buffet of bones there is now a sense of stability, a fragile hope for peace.

I'm in Omugo, a one-street town. There's a hospital, a collection of half-finished, half-started grass-roof barracks that is the town's biggest building and the biggest employer. As well as being a vegetative Eden, Uganda is also a medical theme park that can send the pulse racing and the temperature soaring. The hot, damp climate incubates some really world-class illnesses. There are, of course, the old rollercoaster favourites – malaria, TB, river blindness, and a comprehensive selection of parasites – and there's something for the kiddies: measles and diarrhoea to keep infant mortality rates right up there, and poliomyelitis, the experience that stays with you for life. But what really draw the enthusiastic pathology tourist to this corner of the continent are the specialist haemopathic diseases: Ebola and Marburg disease, the Ferrari and Lamborghini of sickness. You go from feeling fine to repulsive death within days, something that in the rest of the big-girl's-blouse world only toxins can do. An outbreak of Marburg will bring private jets from medical centres in the United States to Africa, then executive helicopters up into the bush, carrying men in all-in-one, head-to-toe anti-contamination suits breathing bottled American oxygen. Hell, it's not just don't drink the water, it's don't breathe the goddam African air.

Fearlessly they'll go right up to the no-hope, infectious poor bastards whose internal organs have turned to sludge and who are bleeding from every orifice, crying blood, and who, as a finale, will ooze claret through their pores. The First World billion-dollar experts delicately swab for souvenirs, seal them in nitrogen-cool attaché cases, and then get back on the whirlybird and go home to Atlanta or

Boston in time for breakfast and some really thrilling, reputation-making research. They're thoughtful eco-disaster tourists, so they leave nothing behind except a rubber-gloved wave. Not even an Elastoplast.

And there's the big one, the crowd-puller, the disease that made Uganda famous, an immoral dictator that beggars the puny efforts of Amin: Big Slim.

Aids. Africa is where it all started, it is the Wembley, the St Andrews, the Grand Ole Opry of sexually transmitted diseases. Aids has been granted the greatest accolade medical science can accord. It's officially a pandemic. And they got it here first. Actually, Uganda is now the only sub-Saharan country where HIV infection rates are falling, thanks to an open, energetic campaign of public health and precious little help from the rest of us. But Omugo's hospital doesn't deal with any of that good stuff. They see plenty, but this is a monogamous, one-disease institution.

Sleeping sickness. Look, I'm sorry, I know that's not sexy, not very cutting-edge. Nobody asks you to a ball for sleeping sickness, pert celebrities aren't wearing tight 'wake up to sleeping sickness' T-shirts, there's no sleeping-sickness ribbon to pin with pride. Partly that's the fault of the name. You say: 'Oh, do they just get drowsy and catch the zzz's?' It sounds benign, frankly lazy. Perhaps it would be easier if we called it by its grown-up name: human African trypanosomiasis – HAT on the form.

I'm up at dawn because we're going to find some. Up the long, red Ugandan road already busy with the great African herd, more numerous than even the migrating Serengeti wildebeest – the flocks of bicycles. Freedom in Africa is as far as you can pedal, carrying water, wood, maize, manioc, goats, your bed, the mother-in-law. South of the democracy belt it's the bicycle, not the PalmPilot, that's the greatest invention since sliced bread, whatever that is. Everyone waves at the white folk in the white Médecins Sans Frontières Land Cruiser, with the 'No Guns, Thank You' logo on the side. Not just a polite how-do-you-do, but a big teeth-and-eyes hello before they're covered in our dust.

HAT comes in two flavours, *Brucei gambiense* and *Brucei rhodesiense*. *Gambiense* is what's here. It's caused by a parasite, an invisible

worm that flies in the bite of the tsetse fly, in much the same way
as malaria is carried by mosquitoes. First it works its way through
your blood, and you feel a bit rough, a bit dizzy, sort of fluey, and
then the lymph nodes in the back of your neck inflame, trying to
deal with corpuscle corpses. But, seeing as a lot of Africans feel a bit
sick a lot of the time, a bit of a lump is nothing to get on your bike
about. Not many people get treated.

The second stage is when the little wrigglers break into your brain,
and that's when life goes really mango-shaped. You get serious per-
sonality change, become violent, get delirious, hallucinations (always
terrifying). Then you lose the use of your limbs, become limp as a
rag, have to be fed, and finally you slip into a coma. Untreated, it's
100% fatal. With the right treatment, though, even in the final stages
you stand a good chance of making a complete recovery.

Sleeping sickness is back with a vengeance. Across a swathe of
Africa, from Congo and Rwanda, across Uganda and up into Sudan,
it's back because this area has suffered great refugee migrations for
the past 20 years. War, persecution, famine, acts of mahogany-faced
gods, the usual stuff. And here's an interesting thing: it's the tsetse fly
that catches the sleeping sickness from people, only 2% of the little
suckers can carry it, and they have to get it on their first-ever blood
meal. It's a more complicated life cycle than a Tehran transvestite's.
So medical teams have to go out and find the focus for the disease,
the place where a lot of people are infecting a lot of flies, infecting
a lot of people.

Omugo is a focus. You're never immune to sleeping sickness. So
they have to treat entire populations, not individual cases. MSF's
15-year project has been a success in Uganda, numbers are dropping.
It's statistical, empiric, grinding repetitive work, one of the painfully
small medical successes of Africa. But wait a bit, this is not a good-
news story. But then you knew that.

Under a big, broad mango tree in a school playground set about
with tobacco fields and cassava, medical orderlies trained only to find
sleeping sickness have set up their trestle table, car-battery-driven
centrifuge, their boxes of needles and surgical gloves and their
recording ledgers. For a fortnight, men have been bicycling round

the area, telling people to come and be tested. Under colonial rule, all this was easier. Public health could be maintained by coercion, farmers sprayed their water margins with DDT, the most effective and cost-efficient pesticide, and they made sure their workforce was tested for economic reasons. Now it has to be done with coaxing and explanation. It's difficult. It takes African time – why meet trouble halfway?

The medical orderlies are surrounded by a swarming crowd of schoolchildren shoving and laughing. The girls wear garish yellow and purple uniforms and push each other forward to have their fingers pricked. A drop of blood is put into an agent and spun on the little turntable. The white-coated orderlies work rhythmically and fast. The children feign bravado at the needle's jab and tease each other. From the classrooms, that universal tune that lucky kids the world over know and hate drifts across the packed mud playing fields: da da di da. The sound of tables learnt by rote is bizarrely familiar here in the bush.

Boys throw stones into the tree, trying to scrump the last mangoes. One lands on the classroom's tin roof with a percussive clatter. Mr Chalky rushes out shouting, flailing a cartoon cane. The boys scatter, whooping and screeching, and take their swift beating with a stoic, smirking grace. We watch and laugh. Unnoticed on the table, a drop of blood finishes spinning. It looks different from the rest. Not a lot, just a little. Separated like a vinaigrette. It's a sign, an indication that a child is producing the antibodies that fight trypanosomiasis.

The orderly checks his cards and calls a name: 'Helen.' The children twist their heads and a pretty girl with cropped hair steps out from the protection of the group. You can see in her face the dawning that this isn't good. The orderly makes her sit down by herself. The other children stare. She's separate now. No longer one of them. Her eyes are wide. She looks for help. With a prick, this sunny morning has burst into the worst day of her life, perhaps the first day of her slow death. Fingers twisted and knotting in her lap, her shoulders sag. Head bent, tears trickle down her nose onto the yellow and purple uniform.

At the end of the morning there's just one other suspected case, another girl of 14. They sit together but apart, finding no solace in each other, wounded souls hugging a lonely, choking fear to themselves. They have to go back to the hospital for more tests, they have to go now, right this minute. The first, Helen, raggedly crying, mutely refuses to get into the car. She wants her mother. If she doesn't get into the car, maybe they'll just let her run back to the happy, carefree boredom of the classroom. Perhaps they'll just forget all about it, and she's never been in a car before. The nurses gently but immutably stroke away her resistance and we set off back down the long red road to Omugo.

The last of the various tests for sleeping sickness is a lumbar puncture. Sticking a needle into somebody's spine is a serious deal. Back home only doctors can do it. Here, Helen, naked to the waist, sits on a table in a corridor, arms cupping her little breasts. A nurse bends her forward and holds her head with both hands so she can't look round. Behind her a technician runs his fingers gently down her spine, feeling for the point of her hips, swabs a spot on her lower back with rust-coloured disinfectant, then takes a long, fat needle and, with the practised eye of a matador, eases it between vertebrae into the narrow channel of spinal cortex. Too far and Helen's in a world of complications, too shallow and he'll have to do it again. He's yet to make a mistake.

He opens a valve in the shaft of the needle, and viscous, precious drops of spinal fluid glitter into a vial. It's an eerie, almost divine alchemy. This is our most precious bodily fluid. God willing, from birth to death, we never see it. If anything is the essence of who we are, it is these priceless drops. Helen can spare only a few, enough to check for parasites. On the iron beds of the wards, patients lie with a resigned boredom. Everyone comes with a family helper, who cooks their meals in a dark communal shed beside the hospital, fans flies and sits quietly. Mothers come to tend their children, children to tend their mothers. The extended family of Africa is its greatest health service.

The treatment works like this: for the first stage it's a series of seven to ten intramuscular injections of pentamidine taken daily. It's very efficient, has a commendable cure rate and is available throughout

Africa for a reasonable cost. Did I say is? I meant was. The European company that makes it, Aventis Pharma, found that pentamidine could also be used for Aids-related pneumonia (in America, not Africa of course) and it became difficult to find here. The price rose 500%. Due to bad publicity and international pressure, 85,000 vials a year of pentamidine are being donated to the World Health Organization (WHO).

For second-stage sleeping sickness, the treatment is altogether more serious and problematic: melarsoprol. This is one of the oldest drugs still regularly being used, a 51-year-old blunderbuss of a treatment. I watched a nurse preparing it: wearing rubber gloves, she carefully measured a dose into a huge glass syringe, like something from a Hammer horror film. They have to use glass because the drug is so toxic it melts plastic – and she's about to inject it into a woman's vein. The active ingredient is arsenic. The patient gives her arm to the tourniquet, turns her head. She knows what's coming. The injections are given in three sets of three, with a ten-day recuperation period between each. Here's why. The needles find the vein, the tourniquet is loosened, the woman's body stiffens and starts to shake as the plunger is slowly depressed. Her eyes roll up under crocheted brows, nostrils flare and her lips are pulled tight over her teeth in a fierce fighting grimace. She makes small hissing grunts like someone lifting weights. It takes about 30 seconds. The other patients watch and wait. They too know what's coming. They say that it's like having chilli peppers injected into your heart. The woman's small daughter brings a mug of water and sugar with lime juice. It's the only painkiller she'll get.

Melarsoprol is a colonial legacy. It kills outright 1 in 20 patients and because it's been used for so long there's a growing resistance, so something like 30% relapse. Melarsoprol is so poisonous you can't take it again. Nearly half the treated patients die anyway, one way or another, and that's not odds we'd shrug our shoulders at back in Berkshire. Ah, but it's not all bad: there is an alternative. An efficient, shiny-new, pain-free, plastic-syringe high-success drug: DFMO, or eflornithine. It has few side effects and is the best thing for second-stage sleeping sickness. It's the only treatment where melarsoprol has failed.

It should have replaced the arsenic, but it hasn't because, like so many other trickle-down First World gifts, it's been snatched away. Aventis, which also makes DFMO, has stopped making it, and you can guess why – you're ahead of me. It's not worth it. It wasn't invented as a sleeping-sickness drug anyway, they only got stuck with these sick Africans by accident. They were tinkering about looking for an anti-cancer drug (lots of rich cancer patients) and found it wasn't quite the thing for the big C, but, hey, it's just perfect for sleeping sickness. Hell, just bad luck really. Helen up here in the Ugandan bush doesn't see a dollar from one year to the next, so they stopped making it. Supplies ran out in May.

The WHO – which has to keep looking at its headed notepaper to see what its job is supposed to be, and most of the time appears to be suffering from self-induced sleeping sickness – actually stirred itself and asked Aventis nicely if they would reconsider. Well, no, they wouldn't. But they would have a look in the attic, under the stairs, and in the bucket under the sink to see if they could find some more. And they did. And that will run out at the end of the year.

Now, the men at Aventis aren't heartless, money-grubbing ambulance chasers, really. They know what sleeping sickness does, they found a cure for it, for Christ's sake, so out of the goodness of their hearts they gave – not sold, mind you, but gave – the patent to the WHO. Big hand for Aventis. Except that the WHO isn't in the drug-making business. It is looking for another pharmaceutical company who'll make DFMO, but it will cost. Estimates are two or four times as much as it costs now, for what has become for all purposes, if not intents, a bespoke boutique vanity drug.

Back on the ward there's a young man being treated with melarsoprol. It was going well but suddenly he's developed some serious secondary symptoms. He has another parasite. This is quite common, lots of Africans host lots of parasites. This might be river blindness. The arsenic is so powerful it will drive all other infections into the brain. They have to be treated separately first. Originally he came to the hospital with his sick mother. He cycled from Sudan with her on the handlebars. She died. They tested him. He's sick. He speaks halting, quiet English picked up in transit camps. He's been a refugee escaping byzantine civil war and famine most of his life. His ambition is to finish primary school. He's 23. In African terms, that's over half his life gone before he's started. His, and 300,000 other Africans', who are, as you read, feeling a little dizzy with a lump in their necks and worms in their brains.

That's how many people are estimated to have sleeping sickness, but it's really no more than a guess, like trying to guess the weight of the church fête cake or how many cornflakes there are in the box, and that, when you think about it, is even more shocking. Nobody really knows, because mostly Africans suffer and die in remote, mute darkness. I don't know what makes you angry, what induces that tightening of the stomach, the ball of fist, the roar in the ears; being cut up on the motorway maybe, rude waiters, queues at post offices, airline officials. Whatever teaspoon you measure righteous fury in, be prepared to swap it for a bucket.

By 2002 the global pharmaceutical market will be worth $406 billion, and it's growing at a healthy – or should that be unhealthy – 8% a year. Europe will see about $100 billion in sales, the US $170 billion, Africa $5.3 billion. About 1%. Just so you completely understand, that's what the pharmaceutical industry spent on advertising last year. Just so you never forget, how about this? Prozac sales in the US are equivalent to half of Africa's entire drugs bill.

Feeling a little hot under the collar yet? You see it's not just sleeping sickness, it's all of what is known jauntily as tropical medicine. You don't have to be a graduate of the Boston Medical School to know that most of the illness in the world is in the south world and most of the medicine is in the north world. There is more money spent researching a cure for baldness than all tropical diseases. As with DFMO, the pharmaceutical industry says: 'Hold on a minute, we're not the bad guys here, let's keep it rational. We live in a cut-throat commercial world, all that free market and democracy stuff you're so keen to profligatise means that our first call is to shareholders – no shareholders, no research; no research and you're back having your tumour removed with a hacksaw on the kitchen table. You don't go after the motor industry for not making subsidised ambulances, and just think of all the good we do.'

They have a point, up to a point. Which is that this is only a free market for the sellers, not the consumers. Nobody chooses to be their customer. The old vet who looks 70 and is in fact younger than me, his rheumy, tobacco-coloured eyes fearful of the daytime nightmares the worms form in his head, as he shuffles between two sticks up the ward to get some sunlight, didn't look at the brochures and think: 'Shall I get malaria, or river blindness, or sleeping sickness or heartburn?'

Actually, he'd have been better off with river blindness: there's a very good cure and it's donated free to Africa by the pharmaceutical giant Merck (total revenue, $32,714m). It wasn't actually looking for a cure, it discovered by accident that a treatment for de-worming horses did the tic trick. Merck spends 6.3% of its revenue on research, less than most crisp manufacturers, and just over a third of what it spends on marketing and administration.

The vast majority of pharmaceutical research is spent on what they charmingly call 'me-too drugs', commercially tweaked copies of other people's best-sellers, usually for the relief of Western excess, vanity pseudo-sickness and repeat prescriptions, while three-quarters of the world with an average life expectancy under 50 screams: 'Me too, me too.'

Over the past decade there has been a consolidating merger frenzy in the pharmaceutical industry. DFMO was originally invented by a company called Marion Merrill Dow, which became Hoechst, Marion, Roussel, and then Aventis Pharma. I know, they all sound like Andorran advertising agencies. Every merger cuts the overall amount of research and, more importantly, the panorama of research. Less money is spent looking at fewer diseases. Have you ever stopped to think how weird it is that you have to take malaria pills to go to places where the population doesn't take them, or that you get injections for yellow fever, cholera, typhus and hepatitis? None of the locals are immune to these things. They just suffer them. Drug companies can find prophylactics for rich Western holiday-makers, but not for people who live with disease the other 50 weeks of the year.

Malaria, for instance, is not a complicated illness, we've understood its pathology for over a century, it's one of the biggest adult killers in the world, a million people, two, ten, who knows? There have been persistent rumours that there is a vaccine for it, but no pharmaceutical company wants to be caught holding it, heaven forbid, they'd have to make it and that would be a disaster for the stockholders. And when cases of West Nile fever were discovered in New York, they gassed the entire city as if it were the Ho Chi Minh trail, and Third World medical workers cheered: if it takes hold in the US, you can bet your advertising budget there will be a cure in months.

As for the drug-eat-drug free market that the pharmaceutical companies have to survive in . . . well, that's not quite what it seems either. In the US, where most research is done, they get feather-bedded preferential tax breaks on research, and extended 17-year government-granted global patents for drugs which they extend indefinitely by upgrading them to new and improved, like soap powder. And they have the clout to make governments act as their enforcers. Aids treatment as paid for by US insurance companies costs $10,000 per patient per annum. They can do it for $200 in Brazil, but daren't.

Thailand produced a cheap AZT clone. To protect the drug companies, the American government threatened to put huge tariffs on the wooden jewellery and goods that account for 30% of Thailand's foreign income. We're not dealing with bootleg CDs here, how dare anyone apply the morality of the market to dying people? Not just one or two people, but millions and millions. The US drug companies aren't short of a buck, their domestic market was worth $107 billion in 1998–99, up 15% on the year before. They don't even consider Africa a market at all, they sell to international charities and agencies. At the recent Durban Aids conference there was a much press-released move to get AZT to Africa. Companies had said they'd see what they could do about cutting costs. They're really trying to, five of the biggest have said they will have a go, but it's going to take time. You know, it's a jungle out there.

But Bill Clinton had a plan. He'd lend Africa money (at a nominal 7%) to buy the drugs at American prices while at the same time trying to do something about the pressing need to write off Africa's debt. The joke of all this, if you're up to a joke, is that AZT wasn't even discovered by Glaxo Wellcome, which markets it. It was discovered by a Dr Jerome Horowitz of the Michigan Cancer Foundation in 1964, using a publicly funded government grant. Enough, enough. This stuff goes on and on until you're numb with the horror, the venality, the sheer breathtaking unfairness of it.

But you must also consider there may be another deeper, nastier reason that Africa gets left in accident and emergency. Nastier because at least greed is a simple naked motivation. It's in that eye-rolling, feigned sorry smile that comes with the explanation: 'Oh well, that's Africa for you.' It's a beat that runs through all First World talk about Africa's problems. They're somehow qualitatively different, there's misery and then there's African misery. And that somehow they are wilfully or ignorantly complicit in their own troubles – look at the amount they spend on arms. (Uganda's defence budget wouldn't buy you the cockpit of a stealth bomber.) And this is why Africans can't be treated as our medical services treat us, as individuals with needs. They have to be seen as a statistical generic health-care problem. It's as if Africa's problems were so confounded and bleak that they simply couldn't be borne by people like us, so, *ipso facto*, they must be borne by people who aren't quite like us.

It's the same rationale that allowed cultured Christians to trade slaves. Already in the world health community there have been murmurings that the 24.5m Africans infected with HIV will have to be written off, for the good of Africa, of course. Any attempt at individual treatment will inevitably be mere publicity showboating, a waste of resources. And so many resources seem to have been wasted on Africa.

There is an awful, inquisitive fascination at the scope, the depth and the stoically borne horror. Unspoken is the bat-squeak suspicion that they don't feel the same as we do, that a dead child, a mortal illness, a war, a famine, a drought, poverty and loss, mean less in Africa. The currency of mourning has been devalued by glut. Africans seem to have managed to do something that drug companies couldn't manage. They've anaesthetised themselves against Africa.

I went back into the recovery hut where Helen is supposed to be lying flat – lumbar punctures give you a socking migraine – but she's sitting up chatting with her friend. They've had their results and they're like different children, smiling for the photographer. It's good news, no parasites. And it's indeterminate news. In three months, the men on bicycles will go and find them and bring them back for more tests, they're both still high-risk, and that's bad news, because if Helen does have sleeping sickness, chances are there won't be any drugs to treat her and she will die before she reaches 16. But at the moment all she cares about is that in a couple of hours the white truck will come and take her back up the road home; this time she'll enjoy it and wave at the bicycles.

I hope all this makes you angry. I dearly hope you stay angry, because your sustained anger is the last, best hope for Helen and Africa at the moment. Let me leave you with one last fact. Of the 1,223 new medicines developed between 1975 and 1997, just 13 were for tropical diseases. Only four sprang from the pharmaceutical industry's efforts to cure humans. None were found on purpose.

October 2000

Monte Carlo

Odd stuff, money. It doesn't always do what you think it will do. It's like water. Not just as it slips through your fingers but as it finds the path of least resistance. And it's not always pretty. Or clear. Or cool.

Monte Carlo is a money puddle. A cash delta. It is as if all the wealth from the rich northern European pasture has run down the Continent and found its way here, to form a sort of mangrove swamp of avarice before running into the Mediterranean. Maybe swamp is the wrong term. Maybe some of you like swamps. Perhaps sewage outlet would be a better description.

There are two sorts of slum. There are slums that grow out of too little, and slums that grow out of too much. Monte Carlo is the sort of slum that rich people build when they lack for nothing except taste and a sense of the collective good. The one thing a poor slum has over a rich one is dignity. What Monte Carlo has instead of dignity is CCTV cameras and policemen. It's been said that Monte Carlo is the biggest trailer park in the world. An itinerant collection of wasters, drifters and self-delusionists. It's also an example to the rest of us of what money actually does buy you. And the truth of the rubric is that any place that has the appellation 'tax haven' will be a waiting room for purgatory.

It wasn't always that way. Monte Carlo managed to remain an independent principality caught between Italy and France because neither of its neighbours ever wanted to take it on. It simply wasn't worth the effort. After a thousand years of not being anywhere or doing anything much, the wheel of fate spun the ball of chance into Monte Carlo's lucky slot. It got a casino. The South of France became fashionable and invented a new tribe of people who called themselves the Jet Set.

And finally, in a coupling that would have pleased a medieval court, Prince Rainier pulled Grace Kelly. As far as Hollywood was concerned he might well have been short, ugly and boring, but short, ugly and boring was how powerful men were in Hollywood, too. And he was a real prince (who cared if it was only of some Old World Las Vegas?). They agreed he could have Grace mainly because everyone from the Mexican border to Big Sur had already had her.

The new rhinestone royalty produced a family that befitted Monaco. A trailer-trash aristocracy. A princeling who was so characterless he'd get off in a police line-up of one. Princess Caroline, the beautiful public school girl touched with laughable tragedy who ended up marrying a German with more GBH accusations than quarterings on his coat of arms, and the only prince since the Black Death to be accused of pissing in public (he's suing).

And then, of course, there's Stephanie. Where do you start? She's just the Queen of Kitsch, the mother superior of lowbrow, a pin-up princess of pristine trashiness. A real, live, walking, talking, humping and sulking Country and Western lyric. The Grimaldis – bless every one of them – have gone from being highnesses to lownesses. They just are Les Dukes du Hazzard.

After money, Monte is famous for two things. The Monte Carlo Rally and the Monaco Grand Prix. Now, you might justifiably think this shows a distinct frugality of imagination. Well, it's no accident. If you have loads of cash but are technically bankrupt in the taste account, then motorcars come as close to culture as you are likely to get. It's so much easier to boast about a million-pound Bugatti than a Branscusi. 'Oh yeah, the Modigliani. I had one once. Marvellous acceleration, lousy road-holding.' Cars become the imitation of civilisation in a land where no one does anything, or knows anything. The brief history of the motorcar is the High Renaissance Monte Carlo never had. The fact that Princess Grace died in a car crash is symptomatic. It's the equivalent in the rest of Europe of having a Titian fall on your head.

Once a year, Monte Carlo plays it down for the Grand Prix. It is, uniquely, a road race. And where every other European city is desperately trying to get rid of motorcars, Monaco lies on its back in the street like a trucker's prostitute braced for a petrolheads' gang-bang.

The truth is, there's nothing better to do and even if it knew how, it couldn't do anything else, anyway.

Naturally, we arrive by helicopter. The drive from Nice airport along the pretty, barren corniche is tortuous. A refugee column of rich folk and folk who want to stare at rich folk.

From the little heliport, we're whisked round the harbour to our boat. Now, a boat in Monte Carlo sounds glamorous. One of those phrases you throw into the conversation like Ferrari keys: 'Oh, we are just popping down to the bateau in Monte.' Actually, in truth, the harbour is an aquatic favela. A hugger-mugger horizontal tenement of ugly, awkward, moulded plastic bathroom fittings bobbing in cess. Both ex and the other sort.

The boats are built as Portakabins for cocaine, metered sex and competitive lying. They grab the harbour wall with desperate, straining gangplanks. You see, the thing about these waterborne shag pads is that none of them can swim. You know that if they were to be unkindly set adrift, they'd bob and wave until they drowned. The boats in Monte Carlo aren't going anywhere. Which is a good thing because the people on them don't want to go anywhere. Just being here means they've arrived.

Inside, they are designed with all the elegance and savoir-faire of a Swiss proctologist's waiting room. Perhaps someone can explain to me why boats inevitably have pictures of other boats on their walls? It's like being at home on land and decorating your living room with the framed photographs out of estate agents' windows. Anyway, never mind, we are here and we are pleased to be here. And forget the satellite stuff. The most important bit of equipment, the fridge, is working overtime. There's a prostate, emetic dribble of constant champagne.

Boats force intimacy. Whatever you are doing, you are never further than six inches from your neighbour. The next floater's chemical bog is only two sheets of marine plastic from your pillow.

From the sun deck, roof deck thing we can look out over the marina at everyone else looking at us. And everyone else is here. Why motor racing should attract so many people is one of the stupidest mysteries of modern life. Millions and millions of Euro gawpers arrive to be shuffling pedestrian extras and background atmosphere. They shamble along the lines of moored Port-a-loos whose backs are opened up like dolls' houses so that we can be seen. Every ship a little tableaux more Dantesque, a glimpse into a faux-glamorous life. Champagne bucket on table, couple of girls in halter-neck bikinis, steward with botulism on a tray, big bowl of maternity flowers and three or four blokes getting beered up in their devil-may-care shorts and T-shirts, advertising other no-brain holidays that stretch over their fat, hairy, pink bellies which have held more than their fair share of the good things in life.

These boats are living billboards for envy – part matey Budweiser ad, part lap-dancing poster, and a good part recruitment flyer for the Workers Revolutionary Party. Frankly, honestly, hand on heart, we look ridiculous. Not just posy and prattish, not just loud and cheap, but flatulently venal. Repellent. Mostly because we are a big lie. We don't live here. We don't live like this. We're ligging. Or renting. Or being bought and used. It's all a lie.

Monaco isn't a grand place. It isn't a racing track. And none of it is remotely smart and sophisticated. The whole port has a sense of being a *Monty Python* epic recreation of a medieval pilgrimage or crusade. There are flags and banners bearing heraldic symbols, *hoi polloi* sport the livery of their favourite mechanical knights. And it smells like the Middle Ages: of softly decomposing canapés; baking pizzas; ocean-going whores; tan cream; smeary lipstick; baby oil; slippery condoms; clammy G-strings; wrinkled, sodden nylon armpits; frying oil reheated to the consistency of acrid sump sludge. And over it all, the abiding nasal ebb and flow of hot sewage.

Monaco is the lid to its own cavernous, bubbling, torpid septic tank. It's the stink of consumption and corruption. The sun bakes us into a mellifluous bouillabaisse of stewed fat, flesh, gristle and Nike trainers.

I expect you want to know about the birds. Well, there are a lot of them. Ugly, unshaggable ones mostly, holding their German boyfriends' Ferrari flags, lumpy bumbags bobbing on lumpy bums. There are slightly prettier ones. Akimbo le bateau: the famed boat girls. Boat, by the way, is an acronym – Bordering On A Tart. The boat girls have two looks. Unavailable and bored. They look unavailable to strangers and bored to people they've been introduced to, and whose names they don't remember.

They lie on the plastic like anorexic shaved seals and like racing cars they have been chosen for their aerodynamic bodywork. These aren't family saloons or loved, polished classics. They are not reliable or economic, and you wouldn't take one home to meet the family. All they do is go. They are goers. Except, like racing cars, mostly they don't go. They promise to go but they break down. You push their starters and nothing happens.

And then there are the blokes. Photocopier salesmen to a man. Drunk, pee-stained, clingingly insecure, baritone, loud and hideous. Even if they aren't actually photocopier salesmen they have the sounds of photocopier salesmen. And if they are not actually hideous, then their larging-it-with-the-lads kit wraps them in hideousness. The lads make up the majority of this sweaty, champagne-breathing rookery.

And even though the place semaphores sex, reeks of sex, yammers, dribbles and bays for sex, you just know there's very little, actual one-to-one, face-to-face, perky, genital, real-time sex going down. And if it does, it's because there was no way of avoiding it. And, PS: it was very, very unsatisfying.

So, we're all here for the weekend, sniffing out a bit of slippery and an icebox full of San Miguel. What do we actually do?

Well, not much. In fact, very little. We talk about doing tons. Most of it involving getting out of Monaco. We could go to St Paul de Vence and find a restaurant out in the hills. We could visit the Matisse chapel. Go shopping. Do Jacques Cousteau impressions in the Aquarium. But the truth is, doing anything is a Technicolor nightmare. The only people who can get around Monaco with ease are the racing drivers, and they can't get out to do anything either. The town is a labyrinth of crowd control barriers, manned by the sort of policemen that very rich people like. That is, furious head waiters with guns.

If you do decide to make a break for it, the best way is by tender or water taxi. But they can only take you to another bit of shore that you can't move on. Or another boat that's very like the one you're on. So why bother?

The one thing we have to do is go to the Grand Prix Ball, which is touted as being one of the premier social events of the sophisticated Euro season. It's black tie, which on land is a bore but on a boat is ocean-going torture. We all get into the tender in sequins and penguin suits, and are stared at by the surreyed ranks of photocopier salesmen and Finnish petrolheads. I have never been so aware of what it might have felt like to be Captain Bligh, set adrift from the *Bounty*.

The dinner is like every other large corporate bash. Brain-numbing, slow, uncomfortable and organised like a learning difficulties junior school's nativity play, made that soupçon worse because it's supposed to be fun. How is it that, with all this money and experience, you can throw a party that not a single human being can enjoy? That sort of negative enthusiasm takes some doing, as would Caprice on video. She introduces the good cause that has invariably been stapled on to this gala event (which tells you something about the quality of the glittering guests). You've reached some sort of barrel bottom when you clap to a virtual Caprice. A photocopier salesman wins a Harley-Davidson. The Harley contemplates phoning the Samaritans. It's time to go. It was time to go before I got here.

Next door, Monte's premier nightclub has a scrum of furious don't-you-know-who-I-ams and their scrotum-withering rented totty. And there are a lot of young men arguing with moonlighting waiter policemen with wires in their ears trying to park mummy's Porsche.

We take the tender out to see to a party on a boat, which turns out to be not one boat, but two huge ferries stuck back-to-back like vast, mating sea dogs. At a long trestle table, 100 Germans sit and eat Thai-ish school food; our host turns out to be a 40-stone gay Kraut in bespoke cream shorts and jacket with a baseball cap. It's worth the trip just to see him; in this city of utter hideousness he gets the golden apple.

This party is to promote the dotcom business he sunk a Third World debt into. We arrive just ahead of a load of pole dancers who pretend to be lesbians around the pool. The Germans chew Asian cud and stare. On the dance floor, three sorry hookers simulate sex.

It would only take Vincent Price striding out of the dry ice to make this a scene from the Hammer horror movie they didn't dare show.

It's so deeply depressing, so comprehensively devoid of any amusement, expectation or glamour, so utterly tacky, witless, empty and sad that I can't even stand back, wrapped in the pashmina of my hack's cynicism, and laugh at it. Getting off this boat takes on paramount shove-the-women-off-the-life-raft importance. I couldn't want to leave more if it hit an iceberg (and I couldn't wish for an iceberg more). This party is social Ebola. The Blonde wants to try another one on another boat. I can't face it. Not even for the lives of my children.

We return to our floating bidet and Jamie Blandford just happens to be passing. By comparison to the rest of the evening, it's like a visitation from Aristotle.

Monte Carlo is an attack on the senses, the most violent of which is the noise. Our gangplank is ten feet from the racetrack, which sounds great when you say it, but sounds as if your brains are squirting out of your ears like toothpaste when you live it. We spend all day with yellow plastic McNuggets in our ears, every so often raising an eyebrow or shrugging a shoulder by way of conversation.

It's a hurricane of sound. If the racing cars aren't practising then there's something called Formula Three, or go-karts, or racing Porsches. And when they are all done, the local mummy's boys get into their Ferraris and zoom and pretend. It's as pathetic as taking your own football to a Cup Final. And if it's not them, it's the synchronised knockabout street sweepers.

The aptly named pits are a self-contained city of Portakabin cafés and motor homes. They perambulate around the world as the modern equivalent of the circus. Today, naughty boys and girls from nice suburban families run away to join Formula One. The money that it must take to make these little plastic cars go round and round is staggering. Embarrassing. And I'm not someone who naturally spies conspicuous consumption and then thinks of starving black babies or Third World disease. But motor racing is bulimic consumption on a psychotic level. I look over the side of the jetty and lo, there is what pays for most of it. Millions and millions of fag butts. The bay is one huge ashtray. The confetti of a great cancerous wedding.

Waiting for the race to begin, we are entertained by the Swiss Red Arrows. I know that sounds like a joke. Little crimson turboprop trainers buzz and dive-bomb Monte Carlo and on every sun deck every photocopier salesman shouts, 'Tora! Tora! Tora!' high-fives his mates and collapses into self-congratulatory giggles. Switzerland Blitzkrieg-ing Monaco is funny. One fat tax avoider declaring war on another, dropping anti-personnel interest rates. But Switzerland and Monaco are never going to fight a war. You've got to care about something to be prepared to die for it.

As a human being there are many, many things you can feel ashamed of. Things that leave a metallic taste in the mouth, make you promise to do better. Try harder. Reorganise your priorities. And physically or symbolically, every single one of them is here for one weekend a year.

Monte Carlo is a gaudy parable. A speechless Sermon on the Mount. But no one's listening. And they couldn't hear even if they were. The noise has reached concrete-splitting levels. It's the roar of selfishness, greed, vanity, avarice, addiction, lust and pointless stupidity. On the giant screen above the slurping ashtray, shimmering in the petrol haze, the start lights are flashing. Red, amber, green. And they're off.

October 2001

Pakistan

Perhaps the shop could best be described as a sort of Pakistani Evans the Outsize, or Pathan Connection – or Burqas 'R' Us. If you want a burqa, and a surprising number of women do, this hole-in-the-wall swagged salon in Peshawar's Storytellers' Market is where you come. And I want a burqa. Can I have a burqa please? 'Certainly,' replies the manager, an imposing man who's sensibly dressed in a *shalwar kameez* and wool waistcoat with matching white beard. 'Any particular colour?'

Ah, I wasn't prepared for a choice of burqa. The thing seems to imply an absence of choice. But I can see they come in bile green, nappy sienna, sepulchral white and two shades of blue. The blue, I think. 'Ah yes,' nods the manager, 'the most popular choice. And what size?' Oh, about my size. The assistants catch each other's eyes. I feel like an ugly fundamentalist transvestite. It's for my girlfriend, I add lamely. They talk rapidly in Pashtu. A boy at the back titters. I don't need a translation. 'Oh, get her, it's another one of those ridiculous reporters trying to cross the border. You know, we had John Simpson in the shop . . .'

I'm given a blue one. It's beautiful, with needle-sharp pleats and embroidery down the front that stops coquettishly just below the crotch like a teddy. When I finally get it home I'm enchanted to see that it looks very fetching with fishnets and suspenders.

It's made of nylon, the kind that produces enough static to run a short-wave radio. Don't you have anything in cotton? 'Certainly, it's cheaper. The women prefer nylon.' Then he gives me one of those quotes that make you think the world has tripled in size and we're all separated by insurmountable cultural distance. 'Nylon is the modern fashionable choice.' The idea that anything about a burqa could be deemed either fashionable or modern proves that we are singing from very different hymn sheets.

One of the first shocks of getting to Peshawar is seeing so many refugee women wearing burqas. I'd have thought the first thing they'd do at the border was rip the humiliating, hot, sweaty, incapacitating things off and yell for joy. But then I come here with as many pre-conceptions and prejudices as everyone else. In the West we assume the burqa to be a totemic symbol of everything we're using bombs to stop: totalitarianism, fundamentalism. But long before the Taliban made it a uniform of oppression, it was the cultural, not religious, overall of conservative rural tribeswomen, and represented safety, respect, conformity and belonging.

We drove into the city past little piles of khaki rubbish bags in the gutter. Then I realised that refuse sacks would be a laughable extravagance in Peshawar, and that these were widows – burqaed and begging – who had lost their families to spiteful serial wars. To have no family on the frontier is to be nobody; giving to the needy is one of the tenets of Islam; being a recipient, one of its greatest humilia-tions. The burqa may cloche aspiration, intelligence, individuality and beauty, but for these women it hides their shame and makes them anonymous, mute Mother Courages. Stony, stoic war memorials.

You can get to Peshawar from the north down the Khyber Pass, or from the south up the Grand Trunk Road, a fork in the ancient silk route. Dodging the careering lorries, brightly painted like fairground rides, you come to a town called Attock. Here the road meets the confluence of the River Indus, on its way from the high Karakoram mountains, and the River Kabul, which draws down from the high country of Afghanistan.

The Indus is clear mountain water, the Kabul a soup of brown earth. They run for a mile as a striped river. Stalls on the banks serve fish – you can order clear or muddy. Above the gorge of their meeting is a vast, crenellated Mogul fort. Every invader with an eye on the plains of India has had to pass under its shadow. It marks the end of the Punjab and the beginning of the North-West Frontier Province, created by the British as a bulwark against the invasion of the Russians and the raid of the Pathans. For any bookish boy from our wet, green island, this hot, ochre-coloured mountainous place is marinated in the spice of romance. This is where the Great Game was played. It has inspired more rumpty-tumpty poetry than all the globe's pink bits put together.

The frontier scouts that as lead soldiers marched over so many nursery carpets are still here, based in another bastion that towers over Peshawar, no longer manned by C. Aubrey Smith and David Niven with topees and lances, but by tough, moustachioed Punjabis in camouflage with AK-47s. The romance of the frontier tugs at your sleeve at every turn. The city is everything a grandson of the Empire could wish for: dark, odorous and bubbling with intrigue and righteous revenge.

The old town has overgrown its red walls and seeped into broad suburbs, but at its heart it is still dense; an overladen collection of shops, barrows and stalls selling everything from doughnuts and pomegranates to plucked sparrows and broad-spectrum antibiotics. Here there's gold, precious stones and pistols. In the coagulating, slithery streets, donkeys, horse carts, lorries, motorbike taxis, nicked sedans, haughty camels and Korean Land Cruisers play an endless, slow game of chicken with the cyclists, everyone jabbing frantic bursts on their horns. The cyclists boast loud chimes that play tinny tunes, so you're continually shooed aside with a quick stanza of 'Happy Birthday'.

The crowds are dense and varied, and pressed here by the two great movers of mankind: war and trade. The men are all dressed in kurtas. The women sway in various tribal, religious and cultural costumes. There are Punjabis and Afghans, Hazaras (descendants of Genghis Khan's Mongols), Uzbeks, Tamerlane's Tajiks, Persians, Sikhs and the shifting, vengeful tribes of the frontier Waziris, Orakzais, Afridis, Yusufzai, Marwats, Mohmands, Khattaks and Powindahs, the nomadic herdsmen and traders who follow an ancient and circular migration regardless of borders.

In the smoky bazaar I found a tray of coins left behind by Alexander's satraps and Akbar's warriors rubbing their verdigris against the medals of the Queen Empress, given for the forgotten Waziristan campaign that in its day tied up more of Victoria's troops than all the rest of India.

On the outskirts of the old town is the British cemetery. No spick-and-span war-graves committee tends these sentries, who never left their post. There's just an old man in a grubby shirt, sitting on a rickety rope bed outside the English village-style gatehouse. The bleached crosses have tumbled into the dust; parched weeds draw faint life from the graves' sagging earth and form curling wreaths of fading remembrance. You can still make out the avenue of palms, down which the coffins must have been hefted at the slow march, almost hear in the insect hum the dead march played by some red-faced cornetist.

The inscriptions are poignant. One corner is dedicated to children: 'Our little Mavis', born 6 September 1903, died 1 May 1904. And there are the lines of soldiers at eternal ease: 'Edward Henry Le Marchant, Lieutenant Colonel First Battalion the Hampshire Regiment, shot dead by a fanatic 1889, aged forty-five.' 'Bandsman Charles Leighton' also of the Hampshires, aged twenty, assassinated by a ghazi. At the end of their tours, battalions put up stones to the memories that would stay here, on the ragged edge of empire. One poor chap died in an explosion in the soda-water factory, many more of enteric cholera, typhus and nameless fever. I walk round sucking the shire names like dry pebbles and try to explain the bosky characters of Yorkshire and Dorset and Durham to my Pathan guide; he nods politely, feigning interest. It's a salutary reminder, a nudge in the ribs that this sad, sweet wallowing-in-pink nostalgia goes all one way. I'm carrying around the white man's burden of Kipling and Newbolt and Gunga Din.

Afghanistan and the border tribes have suffered more than anyone on earth from the imposed reputations of Empire. They have become Johnny Pathan, your archetypal guerrilla superman, impervious to fear and hardship; dignified chaps who can plug the eye of a butterfly at 1,000 yards with a home-made muzzle loader using their teeth as bullets.

This mythology of multipurpose warrior/trader/bandit with ethics of iron and hospitality of milk and honey creeps as fact into hard-nosed journalism and po-faced military briefing, and it must be said that the Pathans themselves like to talk up their martial CV. Across the border, though, partly through neighbourly fear and respect, Pakistanis like to add the footnote that all Pathans are screaming queens and quote that line of poetry: 'Over the lake there's a shepherd boy with a bum like a peach and he's waiting for me.'

The Pathans stalking the streets of Peshawar all make sure they look the part. Tall and wiry, they move with the loose-limbed grace of mountain men. They're chiselled, handsome people, often with faded blue or green eyes and reddish-blond hair, all swagged in their dusty brown shawls and familiar rolled woollen hats.

They don't look like anyone's victims. But the legends diminish a pitiful truth: Afghans make up the largest displaced population in the world. Daily they arrive in Peshawar starving and sick, with only a few worn-out pots and clothes and their despair. This city had 40,000 inhabitants ten years ago; now there are perhaps 3 million – and the plumbing wasn't great to begin with. Most of these families huddle in the already crowded slums.

To look for refugee camps, though there are plenty, is to mis-understand. The whole city is one vast, squalid, crawling mass of shanty-town camps. Most new, fear-forced immigrants already have extended family here. I visited some who just made it across the closed frontier. They had spent the last of their money renting tiny sties built by speculating Pakistani landlords in a warren-like compound. Mohammed is a mechanic from Kabul. His wife and ten children sit together in a little concrete courtyard staring at brick. She peels a few potatoes for the minute charcoal fire.

They don't have the demeanour of a proud warrior people; they have that faraway, defeated, listless look of the universal brotherhood of refugees, people tossed out by events. The children stare with round, fly-blown eyes and pick their scabby faces, the older girls neurotically twist the ends of their shawls; they don't say much.

Mohammed recounts the litany of his troubles: house blown up, son killed, daughter beaten by the Taliban for extending a naked hand while reaching for fruit, the decision to go, the week-long walk, the hunger, the cold, the children's diarrhoea, his wife's tears, the absent husbands for his daughters, no work, no money, no . . .

His voice trails off; the appalling, undeserved unfairness of his lot has been worried over until it's ragged. It won't even keep his anger warm. There's just the crushing impotence and guilt and his ten hungry children. The future doesn't look good for Mohammed and his family. He says he wants to go home but that doesn't even have the brightness of a dream. He's only been here a week, but many of the boys running round the market trying to cadge a couple of rupees have been here all their lives, and some of the refugee camps have grown into permanent baked-earth suburbs.

I walk round one right on the northern outskirts of the city, a semi-deserted, desperate place where the sewerage ran in thick canals and children formed mud bricks in the street. I sit in the shade of a little stall that sells mould and corruption: the stock is a suppurating mass of decomposing vegetables, the smell as thick as the cloud of flies. The shopkeeper and his sons squat and watch their lives slowly compost.

'This is not a good place,' says my guide. 'These aren't good people.' He is from Kabul, a Dari speaker; these are Pashtu-speaking Pathans from the south. He doesn't trust them, so we make our salaams and go and have lunch in a rooftop restaurant in the Smugglers' Market: kebabs of sweet lamb, skewered alternately with fat, and a salad of radish and lumpy, sour yogurt and flat bread. On the wall is an old tourist poster – 'Come to Sunny Kabul' – turned green and yellow with age and longing.

He stares at it, a city built round a curve in a river cradled by mountains. 'Here's the university where I studied engineering. This is the great mosque. My family lived up here.' What was it like before the Russians? 'It was one of the great cities, all shaded with fruit trees. Kabul, you know, was famous for its fruit trees: apples, oranges, mulberries, grapes, pomegranates, guavas.' He pauses, searching for the right word for home. 'It was beautiful.' He left four years ago: his house was hit by a rocket, his uncle was killed, his brother died on the trek south, and his cousins are still up there somewhere or perhaps dead.

How many people do you know who died in the wars? He thinks thirty, forty, perhaps more. That's an awful lot; is that typical? 'Oh yes, everyone has lost dozens of family and friends. You eat very slowly. Do all English eat slowly?' I tell him that we don't really eat because we're hungry, that meals are social, and that we sit and talk, often for a couple of hours. He laughs at the weird extravagance of the idea.

In Afghanistan's cumulative wars, 1.5 million people have been killed. That's from a population of 25 million, half as many again as the US lost in the whole of the Second World War, but taken from, say, the residents of California. There are 1 million orphans, 1.5 million crippled and limbless, and perhaps 5 million dispossessed refugees scattered around an unsympathetic, distrustful world, most of them here in Pakistan. It says much for the indigenous population and the collegiate charity of Islam that they have, by and large, taken in and accepted this swamp of population with good grace. Refugees will work for starvation wages, and it beggars our own mean-minded, mealy-mouthed immigration policies.

Beyond fruit-growing, banditry and fighting, what the Afghans do best is trade. It's been their business for thousands of years, moving goods at the crossroads of Asia. It was the British who originally allowed them to open the Smugglers' Market at the mouth of the Khyber Pass because Afghanistan is landlocked. This taxless, lawless, no-questions-asked place of buying and selling has over the years crept south until now it lurks on the edge of Peshawar, burgeoning under an official blind eye.

This is the furthest you can legally travel north; lorries wait at the guard post to take relief in and bring goodness knows what back. Between here and the Khyber there is a rough fifty miles of tribal area where Pakistani law only reaches fifteen feet on each side of the road. Here, a foreign traveller in peacetime needs a company of frontier scouts as guards, and the goodwill of the ceaselessly feuding tribesmen. Up there somewhere are the homemade gun market, the hashish exchange and the heroin dealers. Here in the Smugglers' Market the Afghan and Pakistani junkies veg out in alleys and on rubbish wasteland.

A shopkeeper stumbles bellowing into the street, holding a ragged, rubber-limbed addict by the throat. He's been caught stealing a bicycle pump. The shopkeeper offers three or four haymaker punches to the lad's head, but he's feeling no pain and the shopkeeper isn't getting his just satisfaction. The boy is kicked into the gutter. He picks himself up with an exaggerated sloth, and blows his nose between finger and thumb. Heroin is one of Afghanistan's abiding mysteries. If, as we're told, 75 per cent of the world's supply is grown here, how come nobody local has made money out of it? Most Glasgow shooting-gallery tenements are better appointed than an Afghan heroin dealer.

The market's having a bad time at the moment. The shops selling Turkish air-conditioners, Chinese tea sets, Korean microwaves and Taiwanese televisions are virtually empty. In the serried ranks of haberdashery stores, the salesmen squat among their gaudy rolls of bright fabric. Even the fabulously fake M&S, which sells St Michael knickers, shirts and twinsets cheaper than you could find them in Preston, is empty. Likely lads lounge beside their trays of Russian watches and Thai-cloned Disney DVDs, listening to knocked-off Egyptian pop songs and complaining about the war, which has made Peshawar too unstable for the streams of Pakistani brides-to-be and their clucking mothers, who trek up here to stock up on trousseaux.

Back in the centre of the old town, the muezzins compete through loud-hailers for the Friday faithful. The distinctive wail for Allah eddies through the dappled yellow fog of exhaust fumes and charcoal smoke. Outside one of the most fundamentalist mosques, lines of frontier-force policemen lean on their bamboo lathis and iron shields, checking the canisters of their tear-gas guns. In the bright midday street, young zealots stapled to Bin Laden posters try to scream up the zeal, waving Taliban flags and banners helpfully translated into English. 'Oh, sons of Saladin, crusaders fear death as you cherish martyrdom.' Perhaps, but not today. The riot is all air-punching and wind.

The chief of police, a marvellously urbane man, stands in the shade, elegantly smoking and talking cricket with his officers. In a drawling sahib accent he apologises for there not being much of a story yet, but I tell him that I have to dash, I'm late. Bizarrely, I've been asked as a visiting journalist from the vaunted *Sunday Times* – ark of the language of power and success and riches – to judge a junior school's spoken-English competition. I arrive five minutes late, filthy and hot, to be met by a line of governors as still and sombre as Odeon managers at a royal premiere. Inside, an audience of mothers sits willing smooth diphthongs on their neat little children. I'm led to the podium, where I offer my hand to the headmistress, remembering too late that Muslim women don't shake hands. Redder and sweating, I sit with pad and pencil and watch a huge fly drown in my honoured-guest water jug. The children are as bright as children everywhere. I get a stab of missing – they remind me of my own pair, about the same age; a shade or two blonder, but really no different. But then again, how very different.

One by one they stand up, craning for the microphone, flash shy grins at their mothers and gabble in that sing-song rote rhythm you hear in every classroom in the world. The subject they have to speak on for just a minute is 'volunteerism', a word my ignorant dictionary has failed to collate. But then English doesn't belong to me, or books or even *The Times;* it's a gift for anyone who takes the trouble to learn it. So it's not the children's fault I can't understand a word they say, except 'I tunk a-u'. I hand out the prizes and say a few words, which in turn they don't understand. They give me a present of a mujaheddin hat. 'I tunk a-u.' No, I tunk *a-u.*

In all the time I was in Peshawar I was never frightened. I walked everywhere and people argued with me, stopped me in the street and put me right, marvelled with anger and concern at my country's misdeeds, misconceptions, ignorance and wickedness. Their concern, sorrow and anger were heartfelt, but never anything other than respectful and polite. Islam's law of hospitality to strangers was automatic and absolute. I tried to imagine the reverse situation. If Afghan B-52s were dropping cluster bombs and daisycutters on Edinburgh and Glasgow, and I were an Afghan journalist in, say, Newcastle, how would I have been treated?

It's not entirely true that I was never frightened. I was once scared witless. Walking through a dark, crowded bazaar alley, I came upon a Pathan of fearsome aspect. He blocked my path and, as I stepped into the gutter to let him pass, he lunged at me. Grasping my shoulders, he pitched me up against a wall. For a horrifying moment I saw myself lying next to Bandsman Leighton, 'assassinated by a fanatic'. Then, out of the corner of my eye, I glimpsed the iron boss of a heavily bucking cartwheel spinning in the air just where my head had been. The Pathan grinned and then hugged me. Touching his heart with his hand, he said: 'Inshallah.'

East is East and West is West, and 'never the twain shall meet'. Kipling's most famous line was written about these people and this place. But nobody ever quotes the full stanza, which inverts, or at least qualifies, its received meaning. 'Till Earth and Sky stand presently at God's great Judgment Seat; But there is neither East nor West, Border, nor Breed nor Birth. When two strong men stand face to face, though they come from the ends of the earth!'

December 2001

Haiti

The only world leader of any note to turn up for Haiti's bicentenary party, prophetically, was Thabo Mbeki of South Africa. He'd seen the obvious parallels in a black country that had successfully thrown off colonial rule. He took a lot of flak for it in the South African press. He took some in Haiti too. They shot at his helicopter. He can't have foreseen that he might be asked to return the hospitality quite so soon. Jean-Bertrand Aristide begins his exile back in the continent where Haiti's sad story began. He was its best hope in 200 years and its worst disappointment.

The events in this article took place at the beginning of the coup. I flew into Haiti on the day of the largest mass demonstration against Aristide's rule. The Artibonite Resistance Front, aka the Cannibal Army, had taken control of Gonaïves, a city in the north. There was a lot of intimidation by government-sponsored thugs. The chancellor of the university had had his legs smashed in his office; students barricaded themselves on campus; and the Oloffson, the spookily gothic hotel in Port-au-Prince made famous by Graham Greene's *The Comedians*, was empty except for passing tight-lipped evangelical missionaries sipping fruit juice on the veranda, and voodoo covens spitting rum in the tangled garden beneath them. Hanging over the city was an expectation of change. The barometer of anger and retribution was rising; it was insufferably hot, close and dirty. There was drumming and screams in the night, Port-au-Prince was as mad as hell and it was its birthday. Blow out the candles, the petrol bombs and the burning roadblock and make a wish. Haiti.

Two centuries ago the divinely named Toussaint Louverture, a latter-day Spartacus, raised up a black army of slaves and beat Napoleon's grand army, therefore joining that tiny elite club – along with Hannibal, the Zulus and the Ethiopians – of African armies that have beaten Western ones in battle. But the Haitians alone went on to win the war and form a third of the island of Hispaniola into the first and oldest black republic in the world. So why isn't this the biggest global feel-good, politically correct whoopee anniversary of the year? Why isn't there a mini-series and holiday programmes and delegations of Western left-wing politicians parading their collective white-arsed guilt, junketing in solidarity? Well, mostly because it's bloody frightening; really, properly, deeply scary. Haiti is a political and economic dead man walking, and it has been for most of its 200 years. The colonial powers in the Caribbean made sure that no damn slave republic was going to prosper – bad for business. So Haiti has staggered from one corrupt, bankrupt, vainglorious, mad government to another. Poor, friendless Haiti has been cleaved by self-imposed racism between black and mulatto, private armies of thugs and the pervasive influence of voodoo. Ten years ago, Aristide swept to power for a second time – his first crack at the job in 1990, when he was elected in Haiti's first free elections, had been spoilt a bit by a military takeover. A one-time liberation theologist priest, he was going to be the Caribbean's Mandela – part Gandhi, part Eva Perón. He became an embattled, paranoid recluse who suspended parliamentary elections, ruled by increasingly irrational diktat, had his own death squad, and was widely believed to be fundamentally corrupt, steeped in drug money. The anger, the heat of betrayal in the streets, had reached boiling point.

Thirty-three coups and two elections sounds like a political joke. It's Haiti's CV. Politics have always been a seesaw of violent regime change followed by ruthless consolidation that inspires violent change punctuated by occasional foreign intervention. The Americans have tipped up three times, once staying for more than a decade. The French, with a solipsistic vanity, imagine that partially Francophone Haiti is in their sphere of influence. Each new regime scrapes ever more frantically at the empty barrel. Haiti has nothing to offer the outside world except the threat of refugees, and precious little to offer Haitians. There is 70 per cent unemployment and the worst Aids infection in the new world, a problem of sub-Saharan despair.

With nobody to stop them or help them, Haitians take to internecine violence of a Hammer Horror ingenuity.

Haiti is the poorest country in the western hemisphere, and the skintest bit of the poorest country in the western hemisphere is Cité Soleil, a sprawling slum of 250,000 God-and-mammon-forsaken souls on the seashore at the edge of the capital, Port-au-Prince. The one thing everyone who knows about Haiti agrees on, the top piece of advice they all give you, is: don't go near the City of the Sun, it's just too dangerous. Nobody has tried to solve its problems, only exploit them. Even Haitians, who are born living dangerously, say that the city is desperate, its main industry kidnapping, its only law gangs of nihilistic youths. It was advice I was happy to take after a week in this country. And then Louis, my driver and guide, a weary, prematurely aged man with more worries than joys, quietly mentioned, apropos of nothing, that he could take me to Cité Soleil if I wanted to go. 'But wouldn't that be suicidally foolish?' I whimpered. He shrugged: if I wanted to, he'd take me. I so wish he hadn't said that. Leadenly I took the offer to the photographer. We don't want to go, do we? I mean, poverty worldwide has an ugly sameness, a characteristic it shares with uncountable wealth. And, frankly, us going wouldn't make the slightest difference to the inhabitants or anyone else for that matter; no story is worth risking your life for. Being a photographer, Gigi said simply: 'It's what we do; it's not our job to make a difference. We witness and we report.' Damn, damn, damn. I wriggled on the hook for a week, but I knew we were going.

From atop the surrounding hills, Port-au-Prince looks like God aimed the ethereal kitty litter at the sea and missed. It's a pale splatter of mud brick, breeze block and corrugated iron set in a plate of congealed, dried sludge. In passing I should mention that Haiti is a first-rate, Hydra-headed ecological disaster. The richest soil in the Caribbean is being blown into the ocean. The crumpled land is a dusty, dun-coloured, cracked lino. It's easy to pick out the border with the Dominican Republic, because that's where the green starts. That's where the money starts. Picking my way through the streets of Port-au-Prince, I'm prodded by the twin conundrums of late capitalism. Why is it that the poorest travellers have the most luggage, and that the people with the least make the most rubbish? Rubbish is Port-au-Prince's leitmotif; a passing Martian would say that the manufacture and marketing of filth was the city's principal industry. Nowhere has the accumulation and hoarding of garbage reached such obsessive, constipated zeal as in Haiti. Filth flows through the streets and alleys and down the canals and through the squares like slow, slimy magma; rubbish creeps in through doors and windows, absorbing homes and parked cars. People live in and on it, like grubby, glistening surfers. The abiding essence of Port-au-Prince is its smell. Fumes from thousands of exhausted carburettors and the sweet stink of gutter decay and warm piss. Despite all this, they are an astonishingly handsome people. We honk and stutter our way through town past the dock, where market stalls are cut-open sea containers full of contraband. Past the charcoal market, where the barges bring in the charred remains of Haiti's hardwood forest. Past the rolling, smoky rubbish dump that's the size of Rutland, and on to the end of a narrow alley that peters out to nothing. Here, Louis stops the car and we walk across no man's land to the City of the Sun.

In the roofless wreck of a breeze-block hut is a gang of boys, the oldest probably in their twenties, the youngest, five or six. Louis talks quickly and softly in Creole. They stare at us with blank faces; I take off my sunglasses and smile winningly. Two lads in their early teens slide off a wall and walk ahead: our guides and bodyguards. We slither over a field of effluent towards a stand of beaten corrugated huts on the banks of a river of sickly effluvia. We slide and shuffle to the dark side of the sun. I'm something of a passing slum expert – a tourist of poverty, a misery day-tripper – but let me tell you, nothing, nowhere, not the squatter camps of Cape Town, the *favelas* of Rio, the famine centres of Sudan or the hideous Stalinist gulag of Kaliningrad come close to the squalor and deprivation of this place.

This is a city built on shit. That's not a euphemism: it's a stinking, sick dung mire that stretches as far as the eye can see, riven with streams of diarrhoeic runny shite that splatter the beaches and leak out to sea. It's like the battlefield of some gastric Somme, with sunshine. Nothing grows here but shredded plastic and disease. It's so disgusting and inhospitable that there are barely any flies. Naked children sit and play in slimy holes, their houses rusted corrugated lean-tos that teeter and clank; occasional brick sheds squat with black, paneless windows.

The next thing you notice about the City of the Sun is how quiet it is. Slums are generally raucous, energetic places, but there are no roads here, no traffic, no electricity, no generators, nobody to venture out for fun or companionship; no shops, no business. In the shade of a hut, a man with a cleft palate and harelip sits on a brick and bangs a nail into a square of tin, over and over. He's making coconut graters. The boys laugh at him. This place is where Aristide's most ardent support came from. They grasped at him for a saviour. It's from here that he recruited his muscle, but now there's anger and resentment. One of my guides points at the picture of the president on his faded free T-shirt, and searches for an English word, jabbing his chest. 'Fucker,' he says, 'big fucker man, OK.'

There's a saying in Haiti: 'What you see, it's not what you think.' People say it all the time. It explains the inexplicable and makes a mystery of the mundane. I pay a handful of notes to the gang elders. Our guides grin and shake hands. One asks, with a faltering intensity: 'You come back?' We drive into Port-au-Prince on the busy main road behind the little Tap-tap, the brightly painted pick-up truck that serves as public transport. They all have religious exclamations painted on them; this one promises that Jesus is the saviour. A couple of youths are mucking around on the back step, and then they jump off to fight in the road; that rutting grappling that young men casually commit in streets everywhere. We stop and, as if by sleight of hand, now they are fighting over a pistol, holding it high in the air, grabbing each other's wrists. They struggle for the gun, and then one boy seems just to lose interest; he lets go and turns to amble away. There is a pop, pop, pop; guns make such a tinny, silly little noise. The one lad who was firing wildly, I think he's missed, but the other boy, now the victim, stumbles and turns with his hands out, in an imploring but unsurprised, almost bored gesture, and I can see the huge exit wound spreading over his yellow T-shirt. He slumps onto the verge, down on his back. Another lad jogs up; together, with an aggressive, cocky, adrenal strut, they walk into the middle of the road and just stand there, holding their guns, staring into our car.

Louis is shouting: 'See, see, see what it's like here! See, see, how we have to live!' He's livid with fear. The shot boy raises his head from the gutter. His murderer notices the sign of life and trots back: pop pop, pop pop – point-blank, he fires into the yellow shirt. He skips back to his mate, and they amble down the centre of the road. 'For God's sake, let's go!' I shout from the footwell. But Louis is immobile, knuckles white on the wheel. 'We must go,' he repeats, but doesn't move. I shake his shoulder. The car stutters and almost stalls. Back in the hotel, clutching a beer bottle, he recreates the scene, dancing back and forth down the bar, playing the roles. The guns grow: there are two, three, maybe four, more guns in belts, more shots, more boys, more blood, more murder. That night, I can't sleep. I'm childlike scared in the dark. The killing's the secret I can't talk about for fear of tears. It plays over and over in the corners of the room, flickering under the door. Why didn't the dead boy fight harder for his life? How could it all be so banal and awkward, and clumsy? Who'd choose to die in a yellow nylon hockey shirt? Why do I feel this fragile? It was such an amateurly improvised drama. Such brutal bad luck. 'What you see, it's not what you think.'

On our first day in Port-au-Prince, with Aristide still clinging to his rule, we went to the riot. It was the medical students' turn. Somebody demonstrated most days. The government had just announced that it wouldn't put up with any more demonstrations. The police had orders to clear the streets with force. At the medical university, they were patting down visitors for guns. In the courtyard was a display of classroom chairs with bones on them, and placards demanding stuff. On a dais was a coffin with a skeleton in it. It represented the president. There were speeches and pop music. When everyone was shaken up and fizzy enough, they took the coffin round the corner to burn in front of the American embassy, the traditional venue for burnings if you want your picture in the foreign press. Then the police turned up and so did the Chimères. I should perhaps stop here to explain the *dramatis personae*. There are the police, your regular standard banana-republic corrupt cops; then there are Cimo, the riot police – semi-house-trained by the Americans, they come with Action Man body armour, M-16 rifles, pump-action shotguns, pistols, clubs and tear gas. Then there are some paramilitary palace guards. Haiti has no army as such. The army was responsible for so many coups, they got rid of it. It left a hole; there was no ultimate safety net, no forcible full stop.

And then there are the Chimères – they do come up with great names – from 'chimera', the mythical creature: part goat, part snake, part lion, park cockerel. They're the latest version of the ousted dictator 'Papa Doc' Duvalier's secret police, the Tontons Macoute. These are gangs of thugs who drive around in unlicensed SUVs and hang out on street corners and in front of public buildings, intimidating and extorting, drug-dealing, beating, breaking, raping and killing. It's said that most of the money the administration accrued, legal and illegal, went to pay the Chimères. On the other side, the opposition was most people, but by no means all people. Aristide had support: Louis, my driver, for instance, thinks the French were paying the students to riot, which is no dafter than everything else you hear on the street. There hadn't been much of a popular organised alternative to Aristide, just a lot of folk who don't know what they want, but know what they don't want. There's not much press in Haiti, and the TV is state-run. Real politics happens on the radio, everybody listens, and opposition is organised and advertised on pirate stations. Roving journalists report from mobile phones direct into cars and shops and homes. It's impressive. DJ is a high-risk occupation in Haiti, and some of them have enormous influence.

And finally, there's the Artibonite Resistance Front: these are more young gangsters with guns and pick-ups and bits of nicked, cool army kit and American ghetto sports clothes. They're opportunist drug peddlers, extortionists and pimps, and originally they were Aristide's men. But their former leader, Amiot Metayer, was ritualistically murdered, on the president's orders, and the word on the street is his heart was ripped out and put in a jar to go with twenty others for harvest festival. I know that sounds unlikely, but it's what many believe. And if they don't believe it specifically, they believe it's possible. Voodoo is a recognised official religion, practised by 90 per cent of Haitians, most of whom are also Catholic. Aristide was a Catholic priest. Now it's said he was a voodoo priest who had babies pounded in mortars with pestles, like African mealie meal, till they were pulp. Most people believe this is possible, probable.

This mixture of West African animism with a cloak of Catholicism and mystical witchcraft and goblin vendetta, underlies everything in Haiti. It's the spiritual prism that distorts and unifies. Voodoo means that nothing is what it seems. That everything, however obscene or absurd, is believable. I was driven one night out of Port-au-Prince through the pitch-black, potholed roads across the empty fields where the zombies lurk, to the middle of a hissing stand of sugar cane, to see a voodoo ceremony. It was like an evangelical church social, in a barn. There was barbecued jerk chicken and beer. Kids ran around and teenagers flirted. Old women cackled and swayed their hips. The vicar was direct from some hip-hop Ambridge. Nothing was sacrificed: no animals were hurt in the making of this worship. But often they are. Usually it's chickens. Voodoo runs between these hearty rhythmic hoedowns to sacrifices, vendettas, revenge, fear and murder. In the dark corners of markets, you can buy spooky faceless rag dolls with real pubic hair for the pricking of pain and vengeance. Voodoo is one of the few uniting factors in this fragmenting society. It's also the cause and focus of much of its fear.

At the demo, the medical students decided to take the show on the road and march in the general direction of the royal palace. There were about 300 of them; perhaps another 1,000 passively supportive people watching. The riot police in their home-made armoured trucks read their version of the riot act, and the march started off with a lot of heat. The riot cops got out and held their M-16s at high port. There weren't enough of them, a dozen or so, they're nervy and aggressive. And there weren't enough press, only a couple of photographers. In fact, there isn't enough of anyone to offer safety of confidence in numbers. Louis looks round and says: 'This doesn't look good.' He's noticed two truckloads of Chimères who have arrived behind us, blocking an exit. We turn a corner and, no warning, there's a volley of shots. Very loud, very close, all aimed at me. Around me, bodies blur, we're all running, falling, hitting the ground screaming. I haven't been in a riot for thirty years.

Inside I'm Wile E. Coyote: my legs are a whizzing oval blur; I'm motoring on turbo adrenalin. Outside I'm an arthritic tortoise, wheezing and plodding up the desperately exposed street. I'm way, way too old for this. Ahead is a line of very frightened and excited riot cops in balaclavas and American helmets waving their guns at chest height. One of them steps forwards and grabs Gigi's camera; she shouts at him and grips the strap. They tug, both yelling. He's seven-foot-plus in his parachute boots, a highly trained authority figure with guns and a lot of mates; she's a slight girl. I spring into action: 'For Christ's sake, give him the fucking camera!' I can tell by the look she flashes at me that she appreciates my wisdom and tacit support. The cop yanks it out of her hand and chucks it into a truck. Then, in a very Haitian moment, Louis bravely sidles to the cop and gets the camera back, minus the film: 'I recognised him – he's the boyfriend of one of the waitresses in your hotel. I said she'd be angry with him.'

The riot fragments into a series of running fights through the streets. We dodge and chase the police and students for a couple of hours. Within yards of shot and stone and petrol bomb, people get on with their day: shining shoes, selling little bags of drinkable water. We drive to a crossroads and into a cloud of tear gas. It smells like minicab air freshener, and feels like someone scouring your sinuses and eyeballs with a wire brush and Harpic. Over the radio we hear that a protestor has been shot and rushed to hospital. The riot's been reconvened there. On the street, they say a little girl's choked to death on the gas. Outside the hospital are the remains of burning tyres. Inside, the medical students wait. The wounded demonstrator turns out to have been shot with a tear-gas canister. It must have been fired at point-blank range to go into his back. On the operating-theatre table it explodes, killing him and filling the hospital with gas. The police storm the building, shooting one, possibly two students, whose bodies disappear, and they throw one or two others out of second-floor windows. We go back to the hotel. The city quivers with expectant anger, gunfire crackles, radios spill a breathless deluge of exaltation: they have a martyr. Tomorrow there'll be a funeral. Over dinner on the veranda, the photographers commiserate with Gigi over her lost film. They compare tear-gas vintages: not as peppery as Israel 2000, but with a stronger choking aftertaste than Serbia '98.

The next morning, the funeral. It's a long march through Port-au-Prince. The students are here, singing and chanting. There's a bit of a band, there's the riot police, there's a mourning family, and the Chimères hide in ambush up side streets, and there's an atmosphere. But the procession goes off without incident until it reaches the city's rambling walled cemetery. When the coffin goes inside, the rest of us mill about in the street. A rubbish cart turns up; it's state-of-the-art, with hydraulic tippers and pushers, and a postilion team of men in rubber gloves and overalls. It huffs and puffs, trumpets and leaves; it is, I notice, pristinely empty. The Chimères at the entrance stop anyone entering the cemetery. Louis whispers that he knows another way.

It's often a truth that graveyards mimic life in death. This is a chaotic slum, a morbid city of decomposing disorder. The tombs seem to clamber over each other. Thigh bones and spines poke out of cracked catafalques; dead rats rot. Among the Catholic imagery is the smell of rum and the blackened, waxy altars of voodoo. With help, we find the boy's grave, the plaster still wet; there's no name, no flowers. On the way out, Louis points at a mound of broken bricks, shards of plaster, smashed bottles, choked and overgrown with weeds. That is the tomb of Papa Doc Duvalier. 'The people, they came and destroyed it, the body's not here – stolen for magic.'

Aristide came to power promising so much: international recognition, reparations from the French (who took the equivalent of $4 billion in an 1825 divorce settlement). He promised what they all promise: jobs, peace and prosperity, a chicken on every altar. They were never his to give. Haiti's biggest money-earner is expatriate Haitians living in North America, sending home crumpled dollars from their jobs as busboys, maids and drug-dealers. Haiti's depleted soil grows a little sugar, a bit of coffee, some fruit. They used to make baseballs, and those labels that say 'made in' somewhere else, but it's cheaper in China. Aristide's failure was catastrophic: his corruption and cruelty, the heartbreaking trashing of trust and hope – but whatever comes next is unlikely to be much better. It's a nation of guns and protection and fear, which deals in superstition, second-hand drugs and bad horror-movie scripts.

On the road out to the airport, there's a body, bullets in its head, police standing around the long slick of blood, looking pissed off. 'Chimères,' they say. Later we're told he was one of Aristide's bodyguards, killed by the police for some internal infraction. And it turns out that the boy who died in the operating theatre wasn't a martyr after all. He wasn't even a student: he was a docker and Chimère. He was dead, though to beat it all the funeral, it turns out, wasn't even his: it was another kid, killed in a drive-by shooting the week before. In Haiti, 'What you see, it's not what you think.'

March 2004

Iraq

It wasn't a rocket-propelled grenade, a Sam missile or a mortar; it wasn't a bullet or even an infidel Coke bottle full of petrol that did for the helicopter. It was a bird. The aircrew showed us the splat that broke its nose. Welcome to Baghdad, where even the pigeons are suicidal.

The Americans didn't have a Black Hawk to spare for the five-minute hop into the Green Zone, so we were going to have to drive it. This is the bit Jeremy swore he'd never do. When you're asked where you draw the line, this is the place to start drawing. Nobody drives into Baghdad if they've not been given a direct order. Even our minder, Wing Co. Willox, has never done it.

We're definitely not up for this, so we go and have coffee in the Green Bean, the American army's version of Starbucks, in a Porta-kabin that hunkers down behind prefab black walls, 'proud to serve' skinny macchiatos in Iraq, Afghanistan, Uzbekistan and any other stan that needs shock, awe and caffeine. A pair of skinny Iraqis work their way through the fast of Ramadan, serving homesick grunts airlifted blueberry muffins.

An officer from the Irish Fusiliers tips up, all perky green hackle and steely Ulster confidence. 'There's absolutely nothing to worry about,' he says, and instantly you know there's nothing to worry about because worry is too weedy and snivelly a civvy word for what we ought to be feeling. He doesn't mention that they've just shot their way in here or that they sent an unmanned drone down the route to check it out first.

We wear body armour and helmets in the car. This doesn't make you feel safer, just an oven-ready prat. Our folksy briefing boils down to: if by the merest chance anything worrying occurs, close your eyes, put your fingers in your ears and pretend to be a prayer mat.

We travel in a small convoy. Two armour-plated Range Rovers with what they call top cover; Land Rover snatch vehicles in front and behind with a pair of soldiers sticking out the top. Being a human turret is a bad job. 'We do this a bit faster than the Americans,' a lance corporal tells me as we gingerly pull out of the airport perimeter. That's because the Americans do it in tanks. This road is code-named Route Irish. Guinness World Records has just authoritatively announced that Baghdad is the worst place in the world. Presumably in a photo finish with Stow-on-the-Wold. This twenty-five-minute stretch of blasted tarmac from the airport to the Green Zone is, as Jeremy might say, the most dangerous drive – in the world.

Unsurprisingly, there's not much traffic. Surprisingly, there is some. 'It's relative,' says the corporal. 'The worst road in the world is the one the bus runs you over on. The rest are a doddle.'

The fusiliers drive with a practised authority, zigzagging, never contravening each other's line of fire. The top-cover soldiers swivel with their rifles to their shoulders, eyes pressed to the sights. There is a purposeful tension, a tunnel-visioned concentration. Going under bridges and flyovers is the worst: they traverse the parapets with a gaunt expectation and I begin to see everything in hyper-real detail. Every pile of rubbish and burnt-out car waits to jump out at us screaming 'God is great' in a flash of hot light.

The convoy slows down; not a good thing. A car ahead crawls to a stop. The soldiers emphatically signal to it to move on. Maybe it's someone taking a moment to tell God to put the kettle on; maybe it's just a clapped-out motor that's stalled. Army convoys, particularly the American and private-contractor ones, are really dangerous for Iraqis. Lethal force is everyone's first and last option. On a slip road, lopsided purposeful Toyotas packed with grim men seem to race to catch us. Perhaps they just want to get home to break their fast. Perhaps not.

Baghdad looks like it's been beaten senseless, stamped on, bitten, battered and clawed; ugly and dirty, its gouged and grated walls ripped off, windows flapping, ceilings propped on floors. The thudded buildings look like rotten teeth in the receding gums of streets full of twisted flotsam, bent lampposts, tangled railings and pools of slime, all of it coated in ground concrete dust. But it also seems surprisingly familiar, like a hot estate from a suburb of Detroit or Dundee. The journey takes longer than *War and Peace*. So I try and think about other stuff – like what's in it for female suicide bombers? The promise of seventy adolescent virgin blokes all sniggering to give you a premature seeing-to in heaven doesn't seem like much of an incentive. And then I'm back thinking about the increasing sophistication of roadside bombs. The Land Rovers carry secret wizardry that foils radio triggers made from phones or electric car keys, but now the locals are using infrared trips and the bombs are shaped chargers, a cone lined with copper or a metal with a low melting point covered in explosives. When detonated it forms a directed stream of molten shrapnel that'll go through a battle tank. There's no armour that will protect you from being kebabbed.

And then I think about the fact that the biggest helmet available fits on Jeremy's head like a little blue office-party joke hat, and that now he's facing his deepest fear (that he will cry like a girl when they video him having his head cut off with a bread knife to the soundtrack of 'Stairway to Heaven') looking like an unnatural cross between Obelix and the Elephant Man.

The convoy gets to the first of the Green Zone's many checkpoints and the Wing Co. sighs with heartfelt relief. I realise we haven't spoken a word. In the other car, apparently, Jeremy hasn't drawn breath. We deal with fear in different ways. Silently I believe that if I see everything it'll be all right. He has to say everything.

The Green Zone is possibly the most bizarrely peaceful place anywhere, like the eye of a storm. Its peace is a long way from being safe. There are on average twenty-five serious incidents in Baghdad a day. This is when someone gets killed or their future radically re-organised – involving ramps, handrails and incontinence pads. It's an area the size of a small market town drawn around Saddam's *nouveau* Babylon of palaces and monuments. It has a heads-down hush, on the banks of the Tigris, amid date palms and a maze of concrete blast walls that hide government buildings, embassies, command centres, commissariat canteens, car parks and all that the gorgon's head of civil service and ordinance needed to maintain itself. The gauze of normality gives it a hallucinatory atmosphere of science fiction cut with the surreal banality of the suburbs. It's *Desperate Housewives* with guns.

There are a lot of very neatly clipped hedges. Who's tending the privet? The strangest job in the current-affairs world must be apocalypse topiary. We turn into the British military headquarters. A garden cropped like a formation of green guardsmen, with a goat. An Abyssinian goat with droopy ears and a malevolent mien that's called either Dog or Jar Jar Binks. Where would the army be without a Sunday-roast mascot? It can only be a matter of weeks before the *Mirror* and the *Mail* are vying to save it. Maud House is named after a defunct general who passed this way in the previous century. It's instant camping English. There's tea and informality and old copies of *Country Life*. An air of prefects' common-room. Nobody salutes or stands to attention. It's all first names, but the hierarchy is as keen as a pack of hounds. The lieutenant general who is second-in-command of this whole damn shooting match seems to spend a lot of his time half-naked, or perhaps that's half-dressed. He sports no rank badge, but then he doesn't need one. Only a lieutenant general would be walking around headquarters bare to the waist. Apart from the naturism, Birns has more charm than I'd have thought possible to get into a single human being. I imagine the army has a special course for everyone over the rank of colonel that makes them devastatingly good in a room. The polite version of cone-shaped chargers. There is no defence against a blast of molten English niceness.

Maud House is all shiny megalomaniac's marble, mostly bedrooms and bathrooms. It was one of Saddam's private brothels. The army, bless it, always resolutely unaware of its own symbolism, turns a politely blind eye to the fact that the Americans live in Saddam's palaces and the Brits in his knocking shop. So who's the daddy and who's the Yankee bitch?

Saddam's nuclear bunker is the heart of the Green Zone. The first thud of shock and awe, dropped from 15,000 feet, were bunker-busters that crashed through the palace's domed roof and burrowed underground and exploded with maximum prejudice. They barely chipped the corner off the $2 billion safe box. It was built by the Germans and Swiss, who know a thing or two about vaults. One hundred and fifty people could live down here in reinforced concrete catacombs that are sprung on shock-absorbers like a Posturepedic mattress. The air scrubbers and generators, the fixtures and fittings, are all looted and smashed. It smells of damp carpet and panic. There are bullet holes in the airlock doors and bloody handprints picked out on the walls by our leaping flashlights. They look like cave paintings. For something so postmodern, this place is ultimately primitive. A cave, a shaman's secret hole in the ground. Of all the grandiose monuments that Saddam built for himself, this bunker is the most telling, with its flock wallpaper in the dining room, the gold-tapped bidets and the grim 1970s hotel lighting. It is the most complete skin-crawling, silently screaming evocation of hell; the reinforced concrete transubstantiation of sleepless megalomania and hysterical fear. Upstairs, sunlight streams through the two holes in the dome imitating Hadrian's Pantheon.

Saddam had a Tourette's need to graffiti his initials over everything. He was a dreadful size queen. Everything's huge and pantomime-clumsy. It's always the telltale taste of the monomaniac to evoke size without any understanding of scale.

The bunker is guarded by Georgians from the Caucasus. The international nature of the force is crucial to the Americans, who shriek and swoon like the bride's mother trying to do a *placement* when some distant guest sends excuses, mucking up their arrangement of flags and the walls showing the clocks of coalition time.

The vast majority of the soldiers spend the vast majority of their time guarding each other. The truth about the army here in the Green Zone is that their biggest job is protecting themselves. The American soldiers spend a year opening and closing barriers. It's an excoriating cocktail of weeping boredom and gnawing fear. Checkpoints are magnets for suicide bombers, but the work is so repetitively stultifying that the Americans move like zombies, pressing their faces to the car windows with the uncomprehending glazed stare of guppies in an aquarium. We go to Three Head car park, named after the trio of oversized Saddam busts parked next to the tanks. Sweetly, the Americans give Jeremy and me an Abrams battle tank each. We race them between the monumental crossed scimitars at each end of the avenue commemorating the Iran-Iraq war next to the tomb of the unknown soldier, or 'the who-gives-a-shit towel-head' as one of the grunts mutters. I ask my commander what he likes best about his tank. 'Ooh,' he sighs. 'I suppose it's the ability to reach out and touch people.'

Whatever Jeremy says, in the tank I beat him by a barrel. I always beat him. In the bright dusty sunshine we can hear the rockets and mortars land, reaching out and touching people, making someone's day. We chopper back to the airport in the mended helicopter, chugging low over the city. Baghdad is pestilent with rubbish, open streams of sewage and corruption. It's vital and virulent. From the ground someone fires at us. The old helicopter, feeling the heat, launches magnesium flares that splutter and shine like dying suns and fall to earth in trails of white smoke.

At the camp in Basra, the night air glows an ethereal orange from the gas-burning of desert rigs. Until recently the British have had a quietly smug time compared with the Yanks in Baghdad. They've had only half an incident a day, but after we got there things went a bit Rorke's Drift.

Most of my hawk-eyed reporting was reduced to watching Jeremy have his photograph taken with groups of gurning, up-thumbing crack-fighting units. It's like a military Disney World. He stands in huddles of camouflage like a big blue extra from Wallace and Gromit with a Plasticine beam and a teacup on his head.

You can't help liking British servicemen. It's the humour and the banter, the air of gawky competence, the legs-apart, four-square confidence. Our boys do a six-month tour and are trusted to have a couple of beers a day. The Yanks are drier than a desert sandbag. For many of the Brits this is the most exciting posting for years. The best thing they've ever done in their short lives. Many of them catch the old English disease of Arabism. There was a lot of optimism based, it must be said, on very little but wishful thinking and best-case scenarios, but then a war is really no place for a pessimist.

Iraqi policemen are training with Kalashnikovs – at fifty yards most of them have trouble hitting desert, let alone the targets that resemble charging Americans. I ask an instructor what they're like.

He gives me a long, measured look. 'Good lads, most of them, but there are cultural differences.' I'm sorry, but firing a gun is the least culturally differentiated activity in the world. 'It's Arab confetti, sir.' And he looked at his beaming students with something short of pride. And then there are the berets. The Brits spend an obsessive and some might say risibly gay amount of time shaping and positioning their hats. The Iraqis wear them unaware. Plopped like failed soufflés.

We talk to another general, this one surprisingly overdressed, who briefs us off the record. The situation sounds winningly tickety-boo given that I only understand one sentence in fifty. The well-honed military mind runs on TLAs – three-letter abbreviations. These are opaque at the best of times. If you're dyslexic, they are like alphabet spaghetti. He refers to IEDs for improvised explosive devices. I keep calling them IUDs and asking with steely, inquisitive authority why the Shi'ites are attempting to shove contraceptive devices up our warriors. And then there was the lavatory, reserved it said, for D & V, with the warning: 'If you don't want it, don't use it.' I imagine this was military transposition for 'diseases venereal'; Jeremy works out it's diarrhoea and vomiting.

We hitch a lift in a Lynx, the sports car of military helicopters: small, agile and nippy. My feet poke out into the void. We're only held in place by a beefed-up car seat-belt. Jeremy wraps the spare webbing round his hand. Here is another difference in the way we deal with fear. He likes to know hardware stuff, facts, figures, statistics. He wants muzzle velocity and metal thickness. His world is a series of engineering problems, probabilities and solutions. Nuts and bolts are his security bunny. There isn't a metaphysical cloud on his horizon. It's like being strapped in next to a why-ing four-year-old who's taken over the body of old man Steptoe.

On the other hand, I don't care a jot for any of that. It's boring and bogus. The world isn't spun by cogs, it's turned by people. I make my judgement by sizing up the pilot, the driver, the guide. If you decide to trust him, then keep up and shut up. I'd have followed the Lynx's captain any way they fancied. The chap in charge of helicopters was a marvellously urbane floppy-blond Sloane from the Army Air Corps. A bod who was a drawling master of the military mixed metaphor,

'When the wheels come off you need a big punch.' The soldiers called him Flashheart after the character in *Blackadder*. We're off to deliver a parcel to the lifeguards based in Basra.

The Lynx hurtles low, hurdling power lines, sidestepping flocks of suicide pigeons. Basra is another blasted, ugly, sewage-stained city. Every back yard a pile of rotted rubbish. Every car a cannibalised pick'n'mix. And yet most buildings boast a satellite dish pointing expectantly up at the western sky hoping to catch some good news. There isn't any. Neither is there any electricity. We fly down the canal where Saddam's yacht lies on its side, pathetically clogging the waterways.

Then we jink off to see the Marsh Arabs. The one small, really good news story of the war on terrorism. They were persecuted to the point of extinction and their marshes drained. Now the water's back and buffalo splash through the thick reeds that are used to make delicately beautiful huts. Arabs wave from their spindly boats.

The pilot and I talk about Wilfred Thesiger and Jeremy keeps interrupting: 'Who? Who?' Then we turn again to the desert and fly over the battlefield of the Iran-Iraq war. Huge areas of baked tank emplacements and trenches. From 500 feet they are indistinguishable from Bronze-Age archaeology. The wreckage of ancient wars is the dusty vernacular of this, the oldest country in the world.

As we are turning back to camp, the missile snakes out at us. The Lynx spits its glowing rockets and the pilot lurches into a dive. I hang in space, watching the earth tumble and sprint up to grab me; '300, 200, 100'; the staccato voice comes over the headset as we plummet. Thirty seconds later we're flat and level. A dot in the sky.

The machine-gunner in the door says he saw the puff and the flash and the smoke chase after us. Back on the tarmac, we don't mention the missile. Jeremy does, though. For him it's personal. 'I was told the Shi'ites watch *Top Gear*,' he says in a quavering, girly voice. Well, now you know – they obviously do. Back in camp we are mortared and shot at with unnerving regularity. Mortars land with a crump, like a severed head hitting a Persian carpet.

Sitting in a darkened TriStar in full body armour in the middle of the night, waiting to be flown back to Brize Norton, knowing that outside, in the oil-flared dark, helicopters quarter the desert for Sam emplacements – and that the RAF regiment are manning the flight paths for fifty miles but it will take a chest-thudding eight minutes before this ancient airliner is out of missile range – I try and think about something else. I realise that during our time in Iraq I've only spoken to one Iraqi, and that was to say: 'Four mocha frappuccinos, please.'

November 2005

New York

I have written before about the singular fascination of islands and the odd micro-cultures they cultivate. I made a list of the sea-surrounded specks that I particularly liked, but I had the nagging sense I'd missed somewhere, that one of my islands had gone missing. And then, as is the nature of these things, it crashed into me in the middle of the night. Of course. The most cussedly singular of all the self-defining islands is Manhattan. Barely an island at all, cut off by only a mere moat, spanned by great girder bridges, just semi-detached enough for an odd individuality. New York, New York. The only other city apart from Edinburgh and London that I've ever lived in.

For one amazingly happy and self-destructive year, it was my city and I was its citizen. Manhattan is the 19th-century model of how all cities were supposed to look. It was a robber baron's vision of the future. But nothing dates as fast as predictions and futurology. They fix a look that is forever the moment they were conceived in. By the time I got to live there in the '70s, New York had developed the famous look of a stalled archaic thudding grandeur. The emphatic gestures of the skyline were contradicted by the angry filth of the streets. New York was acned with graffiti and rubbish, the roads were potholed and riven with seeping oil and infernal steam. New York was murky. The mafia ran utilities, City Hall was partisan and biddable and the police were notoriously open-handed. It was the time of the great corruption, when Nixon was being dragged, inch by inch, down the long road to impeachment. The stink and guilt and loss of Vietnam hung in the air and, most devastating and depressing of all, disco was at its most noisomely idiotic. The city had gone from being a vision of the future to being a dire dystopian warning. Delegations from European cities gingerly came to see what lay ahead for them – and if they could avoid it.

New York was the urban jungle, a cautionary tale, and New Yorkers rather revelled in their Grimm retelling of it. They talked endlessly and viciously about murder, the more random and salacious the better. Old ladies pushed under subway trains for kicks, joggers gang-raped and brain-damaged in Central Park, junkies found rotting in the basements of Fifth Avenue apartments. New York invented mugging. The word became a constant refrain, the morning complaint like the weather in London or the traffic in Tokyo. Mugging was New York's weather, New York's traffic. So we all learnt to carry nothing, no watch, no ostentatious coat or briefcase, no smart handbag, definitely no jewellery. Everyone walked in the same slumped, determined, aggressive, un-eyecatching way. We all looked the same, millionaires and muggers, students, panhandlers and plutocrats. The midtown socialite and her maid were indistinguishable. New York the über-capitalist city became New York the communist one.

It invented the apocryphal story. New York was a great omnibus of things that had happened to a friend of a cousin of a brother-in-law of a girl at work. The rumours were the morbid pleasure of decay. The favourite was the one about the city worker who bumps into a tough-looking Puerto Rican in the street. Immediately, as all New Yorkers do, he checks for his wallet. It's gone. This one time he's reached the end of his tether, so he turns and, throwing caution to the wind, confronts the thief. Give me the wallet, he shouts. The mugger, shocked at being finally confronted, hands it over. The businessman gets home, and there's his wallet on the bedside table.

The defining film of the moment was *Death Wish*. At night I walked a dog in the park where Charles Bronson meted out summary justice to street thugs. In fact, the park was mostly populated by ancient middle-European men playing floodlit chess. I worked as a janitor's assistant in a Harlem school. My boss was a big Jamaican who carried a revolver in his overalls. I was never frightened in Harlem or on the subway I took there, but I did like the sense of tension, the watchfulness, the worldliness of the naked streets where wits were what you needed. I was in my twenties. I looked like a young punk. I didn't know any better.

Last week I read a short paragraph in the paper: the citizens of

Harlem are signing a petition to stop Columbia University from expanding. In the '70s, Columbia was an island of middle-class aspiration and white liberal hope in the black and Puerto Rican underprivileged sprawl of crime and violence. Harlem was the wicked wood where all the bad people waited before creeping through Central Park to rape and pillage Jews. Harlem was a worldwide byword for robbery, squalor and racial discrimination. Columbia, on the other hand, was secure. Well, apparently we were misinformed. Columbia is now the problem, and Harlem should be protected as a site of cultural and historical significance. The university is an interloper, a conglomerate whose expansion will spoil the atmosphere of the neighbourhood. And that is the final, irrefutable proof that New York, the New York I lived in, no longer exists.

The skyline is more or less the same, but the mean streets are no longer mean. They're just irritable. New Yorkers got what they fervently prayed for: law, order and garbage collection. They got a property boom and a safe island. In terms of murder and robbery, Manhattan is now one of the safest places in the West to live. It's also one of the dullest. More concerned with aspiration and appearances than life, the city that never slept now doesn't go out much past 9.30 pm as it has to get into the office by 6 am. It runs on the spot to CNN, not dances in the dark to Madonna. It just shows you should be careful what you ask for.

I still love the city, though. I go back regularly, walk the old streets. And like all places you return to, it's a mixture of here-and-now and then-and-there. There's a particular bright sunlight you only get in New York, and the buildings look particularly fine and defined against it, as if they're super-hyper-real. It always makes me happy, because it reminds me of being happy.

Manhattan is now a rich middle-class island with bankers' concerns and shopkeepers' worries. It has succeeded in buying off the murderers and muggers, and with them the artists and writers, the social parasites, the lounge lizards, the remittance men and the unforgiving women, the amusing failures and all those who came to the city from all over America and the world to claim social, artistic and sensual asylum from the broad bigotry of small towns and wide suburbs.

They've all gone now, and they've taken the thing that the real-estate sellers, the arbitrage traders and the hedge-fund topiarists all wanted to find here in the first place. New York has once again become a prophecy of the future, a different cautionary tale about the consequences of fear: judicious tedium.

July 2008

Towton

Get on to the B1217 – the Ferrybridge–Tadcaster road – just after the M1 joins the A1M, and you've crossed that unmapped line where the north stops being grim and begins to be bracing. Go through Saxton, past the Crooked Billet pub, and on your left you'll see rising farmland, green corn and copses – and old landscape, untroubled by poets or painters or the hyperbole of tourist boards, but handsome, still and hushed. The road is straight; it knows where it's going, hurrying along, averting its gaze. Through the tonsured hedge you might just notice a big old holly tree on the side of the road. It seems out of place.

Get out of the car, adjust to the hissing silence and step behind the tree. Hidden from the road you'll find a gothic stone cross of some age. Nobody knows who put it here or where it's from. For centuries it lay in the ditch. A date recently inscribed on its base, 28 March 1462, is wrong. It should be the next day: the 29th, Sunday. The movable feast – Palm Sunday.

This oddly lurking crucifix is the only memorial on the site of the largest, longest, bloodiest and most murderous battle ever fought in Britain – Towton. Bloodiest not just by a few hundred, but by thousands. Its closest home-grown mortal rival is Marston Moor, fought two hundred years later with a quarter of the casualties.

By all contemporary accounts, allowing for medieval exaggeration, on this one Sunday between 20,000 and 30,000 men died. Just so that you grasp the magnitude, that's a more grievous massacre of British men than on the first day of the Somme. Without machine guns or shells, young blokes hacked, bludgeoned and trampled, suffocated and drowned. An astonishing 1 per cent of the English population died in this field. The equivalent today would be 600,000.

Walk in the margin of the corn as it is ruffled by the blustering wind. Above, the thick mauve, mordant clouds curdle and thud like bruises, bowling patches of sunlight across the rise and fall of the land. In the distance is a single stunted tree, flattened by the south wind. It marks the corner of this sombre, elegiac place. It would be impossible to walk here and not feel the dread underfoot – the echo of desperate events vibrating just behind the hearing. This is a sad, sad, dumbly eloquent deathscape.

Back down the road at the Crooked Billet, in the car park you'll find a caravan on bricks that is the headquarters of the Towton Society. The pub is happy to have them here; the council has given them temporary permission. Most weekends this is a visitors' centre, if there's someone to volunteer to open up.

I'm met by a band of enthusiasts: an amateur historian, an archae-ologist, a metal detector, a supermarket manager, a chemical engineer, teachers, a printer, a computer technician, a schoolboy and his dad. They are a particularly ordinary English gaggle – the sort of men and occasional woman you'll find in huts and garages or rummaging in car boots and boxes on any weekend. Keen but defensive, proud and embarrassed, inhabiting that mocked attic of England's hobbyists, aware that their interest tiptoes across the line between leisure activ-ity and loopy obsession, they are instantly attractive. Enthusiasm is always likeable. English enthusiasm, so shy and rare, is particularly winning. The men are beginning to wiggle into leggings and jerkins of boiled wool and linen, belting on purses and daggers, stringing bows, filling quivers from the boots of Japanese 4x4s, slipping back across the centuries with apologetic grins. I'm handed a skull. It wears the mocking expression common to all skulls and has long forgotten the fear and agony of its traumatic wound: a double-handed hammer blow to the back of its helmeted head so fearful it split the base of the bone and disengaged it from the spine.

The chances are you've never heard of Towton. The most fatal day in all of English military history has been lost, left to be ploughed under by the seasons of seed time and harvest. It is as if there was a conspiracy never to mention it. There are surprisingly few contem-porary accounts of the battle, and they are sparse, though all agree on the overwhelming size and mortality.

The reason Towton hasn't come down the ages to us may be in part that it was in the middle of the Wars of the Roses, that complex internecine bout of patrician bombast, a hissy fit that stuttered and smouldered through the exhausted fag end of the Middle Ages like a gang feud. The Wars of the Roses have no heroes; there are no good guys and precious little romance. They're as complicated and brain-aching as Russian novels and pigeon-breeding. To begin with every protagonist has at least three names – family, county and title. Their wives and mothers are just as bad, and almost everyone is called Henry or Edward at some point in their lives, and it's all about heredity and family trees. There are feuds and alliances that have precious little to do with the commonweal of peasants and citizens.

The Wars of the Roses aren't taught as history in schools any more, only as literature, as Shakespeare's great canon of regicide and revenge that can be seen as our nation's *Iliad*. And though Harry Hotspur, Warwick the Kingmaker, John of Gaunt and Bolingbroke pass across the stage bawling stentorian English, still bloody Towton is absent, silent as a mass grave. Briefly, just so you get a feel for the threads that come together to weave the shroud of Towton, here are the basics. The Wars of the Roses kick off in 1455, though they're not called the Wars of the Roses (the Victorians made that up). It begins with the eight sons of Edward III, possibly the best king we ever had. One of them's called Lionel – I thought I'd mention that, because I'd have liked us to have a King Lionel. Edward started the Hundred Years War, and his eldest son was the Black Prince.

The problems, the pushing and shoving in the royal queue, arise from here. It's a power struggle between Plantagenets, except they don't call themselves that. They think of themselves as Angevins, descended from Jeffrey of Anjou, whose symbolic flower is the yellow broom, the Latin for which, *Planta genista*, gave us Plantagenet.

After a bit of argy-bargy, happy slapping, black dungeon work and a couple of on-your-toes to the Continent, we get Henry V – cocky sod and, more important, lucky sod – who wins Agincourt but unluckily is then killed by the shits while his son is still a nipper.

Henry VI is a sorry excuse for a monarch. Even by the standards of the inbred, pathetically inept medieval court, Hal Six should never have been put anywhere near a throne. It was said he would have been better suited to sainthood. Obsessively religious and miserable, he probably suffered from catatonic schizophrenia, inherited from his grandfather, the French king. He was incapable of governing a truculent and bitter nation. And he had that other curse of medieval monarchs: a ruthless, scheming and vindictive wife, who produced a very suspect heir, considering Henry had never shown anything other than disgust and incomprehension at the idea of hiding the pink sceptre. For long periods he would retreat into vegetative states. England had a cabbage as a king. That's the Lancastrians.

On the York side we have Edward, Earl of March, who is everything the fairy tale demands: 6ft tall, handsome, dynamic, smart, sensual and brutal. After his father was executed and his head displayed on Micklegate Bar with a mocking paper crown, Edward had himself tentatively proclaimed Edward IV, and the sickly Plantagenet Henry went north to raise an army.

York and Lancaster imply that these wars were a northern spat between round vowels. In fact, they weren't geographically specific; though they were, roughly, North vs South. Edward marched north with his supporters. One of the reasons Towton had such a bloody cast of thousands was that it was one of the few British battles that had two legitimised kings fighting each other. Both Edward and Henry used the decaying system of hierarchical obligation to raise their forces.

By the time Edward had got to Pontefract, Henry and the Lancastrians had moved from York to this broad ridge of farmland. At the dawn of Palm Sunday – the day Christ entered Jerusalem – Edward's army arrived on the rising land above Towton to find the Lancastrian hosts awaiting him. Across a valley, on a ridge, their flanks protected by the River Cock and woodland, things didn't look too good for Edward's Yorkists. If you were a betting man – and he was – you'd put your house on Henry taking the day, rested, fed, with more men. Half the Yorkist army, captained by the Duke of Norfolk, still hadn't arrived, was out there to the south, trudging the muddy arteries of England. And it was snowing – great howling, razoring gusts of snow.

Medieval English battles, like the dirges that commemorate them, tend to follow a set course. The aristocracy dismount; they fight on foot. There are mounted prickers roaming around the rear of the army to discourage the deserters. It is the English way to slug it out, toe to toe, get stuck in, show iron faith. They stand with their men, except for Henry, who is too frail and dotty – he's back in York telling his rosary, chewing his nails, being nagged by the missus.

The armies face each other, an arrow's length apart, perhaps 300 yards. The archers step forward, communion wafers still stuck to the roofs of their mouths, muttering prayers to St Sebastian, patron saint of archers. The order 'Knock, draw, loose' sends a hissing curtain of iron-tipped splinters high into the white air.

English archers have attained a mythic status down the ages because of the showy underdog victories at Crécy and Agincourt. They were nation-specific – only the English and the Welsh took on the discipline, the plebeian odium and the round loathing that came with a bow. None of the continental countries deigned to partake, preferring to be nobly kebabbed. They relied on specialist Genoese crossbowmen – the Polish plumbers of medieval battlefields. Not even the bellicose Scots and Irish could be bothered with bows, but when used in sufficient numbers and with discipline, the longbow was the lethal arbiter of battlefields for three hundred years.

It was slowly replaced by gunpowder. Any terrified peasant could point and pull a trigger, but it took a lifetime of aching, deforming practice to muscle up the 100lb of tug needed to draw a yew bow to dispatch a cloth yard of willow-shafted, goose-feathered, bodkin-tipped arrow 200 yards through plate, through chain, through leather and linen and prayers, into a man's gizzard. The longbow was the most lethally efficient dealer of death on European battlefields until the invention of rifling and the Gatling gun.

The archers stepped forward and together chucked up what they call the 'arrow storm'. An English archer could fire fifteen to twenty arrows in a minute – that's what made the opening moments of battle so horrific. The eclipse of arrows would have crossed high in the frozen air, and in that moment Edward and the House of York had their touch of luck. The thick, stinging curtain of snow slashed the faces of the Lancastrian line, making it difficult to aim or judge

distance, pushing their arrows short. And it carried the arrows of
York further and deeper into the Lancastrian line. God howled and
cracked for Edward that morning, searing the cheeks and freezing
the eyes of Lancaster.

The metal detectors have found the long, broad trench of bodkin
points, showing where the first appalling fusillade was loosed. Empty-
ing their own quivers, they began firing back the arrows wasted by
their enemies. There may have been half a million arrows fired in ten
minutes that day – the largest longbow shafting in history.

Organised ranks of men standing under an arrow storm can do
one of three things. They can take it, the steepling hysteria, the terror,
the incessant keening of the goose feathers, the thud and grunt, the
screaming and pleading, the smell of shit and vomit and split gut;
they can stand with their skin prickling in mortal expectation. Or
they can retreat – get out of the rain, give ground, lose form and
purpose, and run. Or they can attack – move forward, confront the
butcher, the bloody, unmanly, unarmoured, jeering peasant bowmen.
This is what Lancaster did.

Heads down, slipping and sliding down the frozen incline, they
moved across the short valley and crabbed up the other side. All the
while the arrows came, flatter and harder. A glum statistic of medieval
battles is that the host forced to move first usually loses. But Lancaster
had the advantage of numbers; they were on home ground.

As they approached, Edward shouted above the wind to his men
that there was to be no quarter given, no ransoming of fat earls
and mercantile knights. This battle had been a long time coming.
There was a black litany of insults and humiliations, of murder and
summary execution, a debt to be underwritten in blood and tears. As
the army crossed the valley, there will have been the harbinger noise,
the crack and boom of early firearms. York's Burgundian mercenaries
detonate their pieces. The oldest bullet in the world has been found
in this valley.

So the two armies, screaming obscenities or just howling like mad
dogs, slithered together and joined one of the most hellish experiences
of human ingenuity: a medieval battle in the snow.

At the front line there is little room for swashbuckling or dainty footwork. This is a match of thud and stab. The weapons of choice are daggers and maces. Men with iron sallets buckled to the backs of their necks, so they can't be yanked forward to offer a spine stab, stare wide-eyed through slits, straining and flailing with short, maddened blows and ache-tensed muscles into the faces of men inches in front of them.

There was a lot of armour about in 1461. Most men would have had some form of head protection and bits of plate, but the most common protection was a stab vest made from layers of linen sewn together that might deaden the blow, absorb a spent point or a fisted poniard. But this wasn't about killing the opponent. It was about putting the man in front of you down – on the ground. He'd be dead in seconds.

The most common injuries are to the head and neck, and death must often have come by way of suffocation – the air squeezed from your body under the weight of men behind you, jammed in the mangle of battle. The pressure and the impetus came from the army that wasn't yet fighting, shoving and heaving.

Lancaster begins to get the best of it. The battle line expands into a vale now called Bloody Meadow. Most medieval battles have an allotted time. Perhaps because the armies at Towton were uncharacteristically large, and perhaps because for so many of the men this was not their first fight, Towton went on way beyond its span into extra time, gasping and heaving, sick with gore, men expiring of dehydration. On into the afternoon, Edward ever more desperate as his army gave, inch by inch, across the plain. And then, up the B1217, came the banner of the white boar – Norfolk, with the rump of the army. Edward's relief must have been seismic. They wade into the Lancastrian flank. It's the turning point: the line shudders and stalls. And then the movement is back, Lancastrians catch their heels on the bodies of their own dead. The line falters, bends, bunches and breaks. In moments, an army unravels into a rabble, and the rabble runs. And it's time for lunch.

Back at the Crooked Billet we sit in the snug. Some of the Towton Society are dressed in the burgundy and blue of the House of York, with its badge not of a rose but of a sun in splendour; some are kitted in the no less risible leisurewear of Argos. We eat roast beef as tough and tasty as an archer's glove and Yorkshire puddings the size of breastplates. It should seem odd, but it isn't. The rest of the pub barely gives them a second glance. And they talk with glee about this place, this patch of earth, this battle, and the clotted, internecine politics of the Roses. It's easy to mock re-enactors, dressing up and empathising like clairvoyants. We are taught that history comes in books, not fields, to be seen like a court case, with facts and evidence, to be measured against precedent and doubt, to be unemotional, reasonable and forensic. But that's not how it was.

There is another history here. A story handed down that has grown fluent and smooth and rhetorical, that expands and shrinks with the needs of the moment. It is a story of belonging, the events that stitch us into this landscape and in turn sew this landscape into a country. It is the tapestry of us. These are people who can still raise lumps of emotion over the misrepresentation of Richard III, which may well be mildly bonkers but is also endearing and as valid and important as anything done in a university library.

After lunch we troop back to walk the rout of Towton. The wind is up; the clouds spit gusting drizzle. Behind us is Ferrybridge and the massive Drax Power Station. In front, caught in a shaft of sunlight, is York Minster, whose towers were still being built when Towton was fought. We step through the corn that grasps at our legs, sighing and whispering. The retreat was where the real killing happened, the slaughter that put Towton in a league of its own, over and above the Somme.

The Lancastrians ran. The army of York, the fresh men from Norfolk and the prickers on their horses, harried them, whooping with relief and the anger that comes after fear. This was the moment when they made their bounty, the coins and rings and rosaries, the badges and lockets and hidden purses that would pay for the farm, for the cow, for the wife. They moved down into the valley of the River Cock and thousands drowned, their linen jerkins soaking up the frozen water, pulling the desperate men under.

We follow up the old London Road. Before the A1, this rutted, overgrown track was the aorta of the nation. We get to the river, now little more than a stream, dodging rocks and fallen logs. Here, hidden in a swaying copse of ash trees, was the Bridge of Bodies, built of Lancastrian dead to form a dam, the spume running with crimson gore. This was the final horror of Towton. We stare on to the dark water in silence.

'You know, this is the bit I can't imagine,' says the printer, 'what it must have felt like to be hunted down, hundreds of miles from home, to have been through that day, to be wounded, terrified, desperate – what was that like?' And we fall into silence again.

And then, because we've been talking of many things, he says he's got a son all set to join the army, keen as a greyhound for some soldiering. Standing in this awful, overgrown secret morgue, he says he's proud but terribly worried – it frightens him, the thought of his boy. And there, in those words and in that silence, is the thing that history does when you meet it halfway. It bends in on itself and folds the run of years to touch the present, not with a cold hand but with the warm breath of a moment ago.

It snowed all that Palm Sunday. The thick snow deadened the noise of dying whimpers and cawing crows, the shocked and exhausted soldiers too stupefied or disgusted to pursue the rout, the carters and baggage-train servants, the prostitutes and local peasants scuttling up the ridge to harvest the dead, fires being lit for porridge and to mull wine, the breath of the living pluming in the crepuscular white light like small, ardent prayers of gratitude.

Towton gave Edward the throne for a time. Henry fled to Scotland, his wife to France. Ultimately he was imprisoned in the Tower, and finally, ten years after Towton, murdered, possibly by starvation, a means that avoided the sin of regicide. The House of Lancaster died with him. Edward snuffed it in 1483 – of indulgence, obesity and a cold. He left his young sons in the care of his brother Richard. Bad choice. The house of York perished at Bosworth, making way for the Tudors and the New Age.

Towton was the last great explosion of the dark and vicious Middle Ages. It comes at the end of the bleakest of centuries; the war with France, the civil war, the Black Death. It was the last time the old

Saxon-Norman system of obligation would be used to such cata-strophic effect.

The dead of Towton are buried all over here, in mounds and trenches, in pits, in Saxon churchyards and the deserted hamlet of Lead. They are both history and landscape. They make up the most perfectly preserved great battlefield in the country. If Towton were a grand house, it would be nannied by dozens of quangos and charities, patronised by posh interior decorators, fey historians, titled ladies, Anglophile Americans and the Prince of Wales. But it isn't. It's kept by the quiet, respectful community and by this small band, this happy breed of marvellously eccentric enthusiasts, who, as we walk through the corn, I see are the yeomen of England walking back through our history, through Cobbett and Dickens, through Shakespeare to Chaucer and down the years to Domesday. They honour this blessed land, this earth of majesty, this seat of Mars.

August 2008

Essex

You think you know all about Essex: pram-gobby, ponytail face-lifts, Juicy Couture buttcrack, Friday night alco-doner vomit, wheelie-bin doggy shags, Burberry and Chardonnay, effing and bling. We all know about Essex, but that's only the half of it. There's the fat-thighed slags' bottom halves, the metro overspill, the East End outreach. And then, in the north, just past Stansted, yards from the slip roads and interlocking roundabouts, there is another country.

The transformation is as sudden as it is beautiful. The utilitarian Esperanto landscape becomes the soft lilt of ancient fields, thickly edged with poppies and elderflower. The roads bend and drop, following an older topography, the memory of more circuitous journeys.

Twenty minutes from the airport is Thaxted. It crawls up a hill. Georgian and Victorian rural cottages and shops lean on each other for support. The streets are free of the cloned monopolies of building societies and mini-supermarkets. There is an overindulgence of pubs, and a church that is too grand for this market town, and beside it a windmill. It was paid for by the great post-feudal wool boom.

This neat and congenial town, with its greens, a clock mender and merchants' houses, is surrounded by a vale of gently decrepit farmland. It is everything the vile Cotswolds aspire to plagiarise. But it's a little more than it seems. This big church is a cradle of unconventional radicalism. It had a famous vicar, Conrad Noel, who preached Christian socialism, and another, Peter Elers, one of the first openly gay vicars in the Church of England, who blessed a lesbian 'marriage' in 1976 on the understanding that, if the Church blessed battleships and budgerigars, it ought to find it in its heart to bless men and women in love. Gustav Holst lived here, and, a couple of doors away, so did Dick Turpin.

Early on a blissful blue and bright morning, Thaxted is quiet and elegantly somnambulant. Stepping out of the long shadows, I catch sight of two men in white – unusually early cricketers perhaps – and then another man, in a coat of rags, talking to a pantomime dragon. In the distance I can hear the rhythmic timpani of sleigh bells. There are more men lifting their beer-blown faces to the sun. Men in straw hats with ribbons, men with bright waistcoats.

Thaxted's insurgent heretical secret isn't canonical bolshevism or buggery, it's folklore. The glorious weekend is the annual coming together of Britain's morris men. Not just a run-of-the-mill summer ritual line-up of hanky wavers and broomstick bashers, but the seventy-fifth anniversary of the Thaxted Morris Ring – the quango of morris dancing and mumming. This little market town is the heart of the mysterious cult of the morris. This will be the largest get-together of morris men in living memory.

The day starts with various teams going out to Essex villages and doing their jiggy business as a pub crawl before converging on Thaxted high street. We start off in Finchingfield, a village of idiotic prettiness. There's a green, a pond with ducks, a church, cottages, burgeoning flowers, simple yokels leaning on sticks, tow-haired children in smocks delivering wholemeal bread, and an antiques shop with a prominent welcoming message pointing out that this isn't a museum, everything is for sale and if you don't want to buy stuff then sod off. And there's a pub, a real pub-on-the-green called the Fox.

Inside, the moment it opens, there is a gimpy collection of morris men in stripy waistcoats and straw hats with plastic flowers, sinking the first pint like fire engines taking on supplies. They tip out on to the lawn and, after a lot of toing and froing and bad-breath backchat, a team of blokes arrange themselves in a ragged line with a fiddle, an accordion and a penny whistle, and strike up the familiar sound of summer weekends in rural Middle England. Their bright and gaudy costumes make the picture complete as they go after each other like fat, rheumatic game hens, chaffing and puffing and heavily skipping through routines that would bore an infant school. Morris dancers are one of the most riotously risible and despised groups in Britain. Yet they caper on regardless. To be a morris man is to live a regardless life. These are men apart, oblivious of or immune to the mockery and the curled lips. They keep alive an uncared for and unwanted tradition – simply for the pleasure of a thing itself, and their own company, and bladder-deforming quantities of beer. Sir Thomas Beecham's advice to try anything once except incest and folk dancing has wrapped the morris in a received wisdom of disdain. For most people it is bizarre and tasteless Terpsichorean graffiti, like animated garden gnomes.

A pair get up and do a jig with each other. Nobody watches. I notice that one of them is wearing Velcro comfy-fit shoes of the sort advertised in the back of the *Sunday Telegraph*. Behind the dancers there is that eternal punctuation mark of English villages, the comforting war memorial that chimes the knell of passing days, the names resonant of another England; Ernest and Tom Purkiss, Portor Choat, Tom Juniper, Percy Wiffen, T. O. Ruggles-Brice. They seem to belong to the accordion and the tinny roundelay, the clack of wands and the beery 'ya' of bucolic voices. The pub is advertising a Neil Diamond tribute evening.

In the nearby village of Cornish Hall End, the morris men mill about, unclipping their personal tankards from their elasticated belts to sink pints through Lovelace-gaping gullets before forming up in a ragged square and skipping their simple circular pattern. In the beer garden, families lounge, children run in mobs, nobody takes much notice. The Horse and Groom is having a Blues Brothers tribute evening.

The Morris Ring rules the dance. It has been based in Thaxted for all its seventy-five years. This year is its three-quarter century, and promises particularly splendid meetings of the nation's dance troupes. They are all based in villages, and vary in their particulars, but, like football teams, they obey the niceties. Each has a leader, a treasurer and a coach. They dance traditional dances identified by their places of origin. They also have fools who caper with bladders – theirs and pigs'. There are men on hobbyhorses, men who dress up as women, often representing Maid Marian or Queen Victoria, and sometimes they 'go molly' – that is, in blackface.

There are also men who are animals – deer, dragons and horses – and it's always men. There are no women in the Ring. Nobody knows the origins of morris dancing – the name probably comes from

'Moorish'. It may have been born in North Africa or Spain; it may have come back with the Crusades. There was certainly Elizabethan morris dancing. Shakespeare's comic actor Will Kempe famously took nine days to dance from London to Norwich.

Seventy-five years is really not that old for a governing association for an ancient rural folk art. Ping-pong is half a century older, and the Rugby Football Association is nearly twice as old as the Morris Ring. What we see is a recreation – or, perhaps better, a resurrection. The great fire and brimstone, steam and grind of the industrial upheaval of the nineteenth century dislocated, and in many places extinguished, a whole canon of frail, delicate, English rural culture.

Factories and mines broke the legs of the Celtic and Saxon patchwork of time and magic. The mass march of the working classes from hoes to picks, moved from village greens to the satanic mills and smog of back-to-backs. But just as the morris faded to white, so a few urban middle-class musicologists and folklorists stepped out back down the rutted lanes to the extremities of green England and began to piece together the vanished life. Cecil Sharp collected thousands and thousands of folk tunes. They were used by composers such as Elgar, Vaughan Williams, Holst and Britten. The Arts and Crafts movement enthused hundreds of Hampstead socialists to get in touch with their pointy toed roots and to look to a new medievalism of weaving and pottery, husbandry, cottage gardens and vegetarianism. They grew unironic beards and dressed their children in homespun smocks, and occasionally, like Eric Gill (no relation), they lived entirely recreated medieval lives and slept with their children. The folklore of the morris got a worthy and self-conscious kiss of life. It got polite, and a hierarchy, and snobbery, and rules. Like the druid and bardic movements in Wales, a few proselytising enthusiasts became the bottomless butt of jokes for the metropolitan masses.

Writers such as Orwell, Waugh and Betjeman mocked the beer and beards, the lentils and earnestness of the morris. The dance became emblematic of a certain sort of Fabian – humourless and sexless, worthy socialism. But nobody really knew what the original meanings or intentions of the dance had been, and they didn't seem to care much. It was enough that they could make it fit this Hardyesque and patronising vision of a peasant, elfin England.

Anthropologists tend to explain all rural ritual, craft and culture as 'fertility', or harvest thanksgiving. They're the catch-all explanations for rude behaviour that doesn't come with a manual. It seems that there may well be connections with ancient mystical characters and pre-Christian beliefs – the Green Man appears and Herne the Hunter, lord of the forest. There are animistic spirits of flowers and green things, but it never really gets let out from under the tasteful and picturesque hey nonny nonny of pub bores and country tourist posters.

At the next village pub, something quite different happens. They release the beast. In the car park by the wheelie bin, the Saddleworth Morris Men from Yorkshire arrive, trotting like pit ponies, bells on their black clogs, wearing hanging baskets of flowers and feathers on their heads, led by a meaty man with a whip. There is none of the hop, skip and whack about this troupe. They have a muscular, purposeful swagger. Their dance is physical and masculine, and beautifully aggressive under their great flowered hats. They have the gimlet-eyed, tuber-featured faces of the north, and suddenly the morris is captivating. The rhythm stamps out darker motifs and bellicose camaraderie. The patterns they make stay in the mind's eye. You can see them weave spells.

My small boy offers a swan's feather he found to one of the dancers, who takes off his hat to put it in. The boy's mother asks if she can see the hat. 'You mustn't put it on,' the dancer warns like a woodland troll in a fairy story. 'I don't like to say in front of your man, but if a lass wears the hat she has to have ... you know ... go to bed with the morris man. That's the rule.' Nicola thinks about it for a moment, and hands back the hat with an apologetic, maybe-next-time smile.

For all its fecund heritage and its promise of seed time and harvest, morris dancing is incontrovertibly the least sexy jigging in the world. Unlike the folk dances of the rest of Europe, with their silly dressing up and geometric patterns, or the leaping reelers of the Celtic edges of the British Isles, the morris is perversely and defiantly not the vertical expression of a horizontal desire. They not only do not dance with women, but they don't dance for or at women. Indeed, you get the feeling they don't really dance for anyone but themselves.

There is something admirable about this – the absence of showmanship. Nobody could accuse these men of overt displays of vanity. Their vast stomachs held in by sweaty nylon shirts like warm mozzarellas, their blotched faces, the pallor of lives lived on a slow bar stool. They exhibit the stamina and grace of shopping trolleys, with beards that loom like badly eaten Weetabix and hair that has given up under the torture of middle-aged ponytails. Morris dancing never had a golden age. It never grasped the zeitgeist. There was no morris Woodstock or summer of love. It was reborn beyond the aesthetic pale and, contrarily, there is something wonderful about that, something brave and properly, collectively eccentric.

While the bien pensants snigger and change their beliefs and preferences with the season, the morris dancers skip on, knowing that every year will be like the year before, knowing they will always be the back marker of the least 'now' occupations on earth, just ahead of incest, yet continuing, convinced of their own inverted rightness, free of whim or caprice, excused riches, vanity, ambition, celebrity or cachet. And then, as if to prove the utter imperviousness to aesthetics, along come the Britannia Coco-nut Dancers of Bacup.

You've never heard of them, or seen them, unless you're from north Lancashire, and even then you might have given them a wide berth. They rarely travel from their home village – this is the first time they've been to Thaxted, and they only came because the Saddleworth team was here to look after them. They are small, nervous men. And so they might be, for they are wearing white cotton night bonnets of the sort sported by Victorian maids, decorated with sparse ribbons. Then black polo-neck sweaters, like the Milk Tray man, with a white sash, black knee breeches, white stockings and black clogs. As if this weren't enough, someone at some point has said: 'What this outfit really needs is a red and white hooped miniskirt.' 'Are you sure?' the dancers must have replied. And he was. But it doesn't finish there. They have black faces, out of which their little bright eyes shine anxiously. On their hands are strapped single castanets. A single castanet is the definition of uselessness. The corresponding castanet is worn on the knee. To say you couldn't make up the Coco-nutters would be to deny the evidence of your astonished eyes.

The dance begins with each Nutter cocking a hand to his ear to listen to something we human folk can't catch. They then wag a finger at each other, and they're off, stamping and circling, occasionally holding bent wands covered with red, white and blue rosettes that they weave into simple patterns. It's not pretty and it's not clever. It is simply, awe-inspiringly, astonishingly other. Morris men from southern troupes come and watch in slack-jawed silence. Nothing in the civilised world is quite as elementally bizarre and awkwardly compelling as the Coco-nutters of Bacup. What are they for? What were they thinking of? Why do they do these strange, misbegotten, dark little incantations? It's said that they might have originally been Barbary corsairs who worked in Cornish tin mines and travelled to Lancashire, and that the dance is about listening underground, a sign language of miners. And then there's all the usual guff about harvest and spring and fecundity, but that doesn't begin to describe the strangeness of this troupe from the nether folk world.

At teatime in Thaxted, the crowds stumble out of the pubs and line the main street that dips down the steep hill and escapes out into the countryside, which glints with the shimmering gilt of nostalgia, waiting for the return of haystacks and corn dollies and scarecrows. This is distant Albion in the afternoon. From the top of the hill, the morris men parade en masse with their attendant fiddlers and accordionists, drummers and whistlers, hobbyhorses, mystical animals, female impersonators and capering fools. From the bottom of the hill a corresponding group starts up. It's like the final illustration from a compendium of nursery rhymes and cautionary tales. A scene of the Day of Judgement from a half-forgotten, half-recreated lexicon of English folklore and fairy stories. The vivid swag of all the bright pomp and rhythm drags you along, exorcises the ridicule and the patronage, the lifelong received metropolitan wisdom of disdain. This is a lost part of what we once were, and who we still are. The two groups meet and dance their dances, turn swords into pentangles, sticks into eaves and hankies into hankies. They prance and skip and jig, the bells jingle, they shout and clack and cheer and canter, calling up the great lost way of being. The morris twitches like an amputated limb from a body that has been long since buried. It is the last rite of a belief that nobody can recall. The movements and the tune and nonsense, an ancient language that's bereft of the life that formed it.

But as you watch, there is a tingle, a spasm of recognition, a lightness in the stomach, a tightness in the throat, and the faint spark of connection. A distant echo, a folk memory, of what all this once was, what we once were. In the great, Gadarene dash for progress and industry, for the brick and stone and concrete, for the iron and smoke, we broke something vital, severed a link in the chain of ourselves, and there was no going back. There is a realisation that the dislike and the mockery of the morris is not wholly rational or deserved – that if this was some other nation's rural culture we'd watch with polite interest and inquisitive enjoyment. But because it's so close, it comes with the buttock clench of embarrassment, the guilt and the squirm. Like seeing photographs of ourselves in foolish fancy dress at drunken student parties, this is not who we grew up to be.

But the morris men dance on anyway, propitiating they know not what, an awkward family heirloom that doesn't go with anything else and is all we have left of our pre-industrial heritage. The dance is a kiss on the forehead of a skull that has sunk back into the earth and the dappled fields that in turn have become the ring roads, roundabouts, runways, shopping centres and starter-home cul-de-sacs of the postmodern age. They dance anyway. No longer for us, but despite us.

The sun goes down, the accordions play on, the pewter tankards slop, and, at eleven, the clamour and the shouting and the clapping and singing fade away, as if someone has pulled a plug, letting out all the noise. The lights of the town go out, and under the heavy, early summer moon there is a faint sound of a distant violin.

Down a winding cobbled street from the church trips the Abbots Bromley Horn Dance, the most evocative and strangely dramatic of all morris dances, performed for perhaps hundreds of years, conceivably for thousands. They are led by a single fiddler, dressed in a rag coat, playing a tune that is childlike and simple, but also full of sadness and an ethereal, mordant power, like the soundtrack of a dream. Behind him come men carrying antlered fallow-deer heads in front of their faces. Behind them, a man-woman, a hunter and a hobbyhorse. They dance in silence, slowly. The hunt turns and turns, casting patterns in the moonlight. You feel its mossy, shadowed meaning beyond understanding. A ghost dance, a silently keening sadness. The things we misplace always bear a heavier loss than the things we choose to grasp with white knuckles. And in the darkness, quite unexpectedly, I feel tears of mourning on my cheek.

August 2009

Airports

Airports. You've got to love them. No, really. You have got to love them. At least, you must learn to appreciate them. If you don't, life will be a constant dung sarnie of places you want to be sandwiched between termini of frustration and worry, boredom and fury.

I get on with airports. I like the way they look. I appreciate their ergonomics, their thousands of moving parts, the ant-hill logistics of getting everything in and out. You couldn't have come up with something more complicated, thousands of people separated from thousands of pieces of luggage, having to be in a certain seat at a precise time to go up to hundreds of destinations. Add thousands of bits of separated luggage and their people coming the other way, all speaking different languages, some travelling for the first time, some for the umpteenth. And just to make it all more exciting, you have to assume that any one of them might be a self-martyring mass murderer and that they will all want to spend 10 pounds on something they didn't know they needed, and a penny, which they probably suspected they would need.

My love of airports is based on going somewhere, or coming back from somewhere. I'm rarely in airports for any other reason. But last week, I went to Gatwick to meet my daughter. I can't remember the last time I met someone at an airport or indeed was met by anyone who wasn't a driver. But part of the drama of an airport is walking through the exit at the arrivals lounge, the anxiety of luggage and passports and customs behind you, and that audience expectant and attentive. You move through the door, humping your rucksack, rumpled from the flight, still smelling of air freshener and with bits of exploding bread rolls collected in the folds of your sticky shirt and suddenly you're on stage. For a fleeting moment, you think that maybe, just perhaps, there will be someone here for you.

This is an intense and fraught stage, live with expectation, and among the lounging, bored drivers with their scrawled cardboard signs of misspelt names and company logos, there are also the worried faces of family, friends. And as you slide past them, you can see little narratives: a woman waiting for a man she fell in love with over the internet and has never met, an immigrant's child finally given a visa, the divorced parent coming for a brief summer holiday – all the gossamer loose ends of human relationships waiting to be tied up in this concourse.

It's the constant darning of the oldest plot in the world: departures and arrivals, the most ancient saga of travelling and returning. You realise that leaving your clan, your protective family group, is fraught. Our natural genetic impulse is to stay close: our history, our tribal instinct, pulls us back together. Our emotions twist the pressure with homesickness and longing, missing the taste of familiar food, the smell of childhood. All that nostalgia, that awkward nag of belonging, the tug of home, all tell us where we should be.

Still, there is also that itch and excitement of getting away, the adventure, the experience. These are contradictory human urges that are all exposed in the airport. And I'm not used to being here as a non-traveller. I haven't seen Flora for five months. This is the longest absence in her whole 19 years of life, this gap-year thing that is peculiarly Anglo-Saxon. Australians do it all the time, being caught at the far-distant end of Europe's elastic. Every autumn thousands of middle-class kids finish their A-levels, work for a few months and then, in threes and fours, wander out into the world.

What surprised me was my reaction to Flora going. I've always encouraged my children to be inquisitive, to get out there, to see the world. We only pass this way once, I tell them, this globe is where you live, not just this corner of this one city. See your birthright, meet the neighbours, don't just leave your travelling to the TV and glossy magazines. There've always been maps in their rooms and travellers' tales on their bookshelves. When Flora finally hefted my old rucksack and left, I was completely unnerved by it, irritated that she was so insouciant about the journey, so candidly trusting in the goodness of the world, that it would all be all right. I became peevish and nagging with warnings and fears about mosquitoes and bed bugs, mopeds, footpads, jellyfish and amoeba, money belts and etiquette. She was smilingly oblivious and disappeared into the great migration of public school teenagers slogging around the Far East for full-moon parties, inner-tube floating, 12-hour bus rides, huts on beaches, buckets of Red Bull and vodka, flaming limbo dancing, DayGlo face paint and tattoos.

What I felt was the old Velcro rip of affection and connection. My old bore's experienced cautionary instructions were really just displacement for a siren of worry and sadness about the passing of childhood. Of course, it was only a holiday. How much worse would migrating have been? For the past 200 years, so much of Europe moved away.

I've been writing a lot about migration recently. And I'm aware of the great black mere of tears that immigration leaves behind, the terrible mourning and loss and the sadness of economic and political migrants. It marks countries. It marked Ireland and Scotland and it's marked many others. We rarely notice or acknowledge that the greatest gift of being members of the First World club is that we can afford to stay close to our parents and our children and that we can travel with the comfort and assurance of knowing we can get back from anywhere within 24 hours.

While I waited for Flora at the arrivals, I was surprised by the depth and the sharpness of my own anticipation, how much I'd missed her. I watched a trickle of travellers returning. In front of me were a huddle of family: a father and mother and a couple of boys. They were subdued; they had been waiting some time. The children were bored and unhappy, the man kept a protective arm around his wife. Then in through the doors came a woman with a small hurried bag. She was plainly the wife's sister. A called name and the two women ran towards each other and hugged and the connection, the touch, unlocked a dam of tears and they sagged into each other's shoulders and sobbed. The father and children hung back. Without words, you knew that a parent had died. That the immigrant child was returning for the funeral too late to say goodbye or thank you. And as they moved slowly towards the exit, there was a shrill call of 'Daddy!' and Flora in crumpled brightly tie-dyed cotton, with matted hair and barnacled with bangles, dropped her bag and ran to the barrier, a grin like a sickle moon, relieved, I think, to find that I was still here with the living and that, finally, there was someone else to carry her rucksack.

September 2010

The Congo

The broad, brown, bloated Dungu River slips with a clotted lethargy through the silent bush, as if it were too hot and humid to do anything more than roll over and float past the mango trees, where squadrons of bright ibis squabble over nothing. The still air begins to collate clouds for the afternoon deluge; the temperature trudges up with a practised ennui. It is the end of the rainy season. The river rolls on to meet the equally stupefied khaki Kibali, and here is the small town of Dungu. This is close to being the very heart of Africa, the dark heart of the dark, dark continent. The Democratic Republic of the Congo is the byword for everything that is irreparably, congenitally wrong with Africa. All the bleak white fears, the nose-tapping, knowing racism, the comfortable schadenfreude about the ancestor continent, are all comfortingly wrapped in the dark horror of Congo. Of all the places I've travelled, I have never had such dire and unanimous warnings against setting foot in a country.

Six-thirty in the crepuscular morning and the Catholic church fills up for communion. Three priests in Roman finery offer the mass in the fluting local tongue. In place of an organ, there are drums. African voices hymning over their rhythm is one of the great spine-tingling, ear-pricking sounds of this continent. A fresco of the Crucifixion shows a white Christ on the cross; his mother is black, a parable of Africa: the white boy rises again and leaves to take over his father's business. The black woman is left to mourn and make the best of it. There are a lot of bereft mothers in the pews.

This is officially the most dangerous country in the world to be a woman. Up here, in the north-east, there is a war being fought by such a world-winning array of militias, rebel groups, renegade deserters, carpetbaggers and mercenaries that the list reads like the combatants in some slasher computer game: the M23, the Interahamwe, the

Mai-Mai and the Congolese army. This constantly simmering conflict is taken out on the civilian population. No military group is strong enough to hold ground for long, so they rule through projecting terror and inflicting an inflation of creative humiliation.

There is a pandemic of rape, often the most diabolically and physically debilitating type, and proxy-forced rape, where captured boys are made to abuse or murder their neighbours to crush any sense of community and give them nowhere to escape. There are constant kidnappings of children to be taken as slaves and recruits and, therefore, a concomitant increase in despairing domestic violence. In communities that are traumatised and permanently terrified, the true figures can only be guessed at, but they are without parallel. This is effortfully the worst place in the world.

Angélique, a middle-aged woman, says her departing prayers, crosses herself and rises, beaming. She has a smile that belies all other emotions, all anxiety, and transfigures not just her face, but everyone's it bathes. Angélique is a nun, an Augustinian. She doesn't wear the wimple or robes of her order, but the elegant home-tailored costume of local cloth, a turban and DayGlo, acid-green, apple-logoed flip-flops. Her skirt is printed with the face of another nun, a local woman who was martyred in a previous war by the Simba for refusing to marry a colonel, who stabbed her to death for pointing out that she was already betrothed to Christ. Angélique is a singular and powerful force for good in Dungu, which has grown to be the terminus at the end of the line for hundreds of displaced people driven from their homes, not by the ruling factions of power, money and mining, but by that darker embodiment of collective psychopathy, the Lord's Resistance Army (LRA): the oldest and most conceivably sadistic terrorist group in Africa.

When I first came across them a decade ago in northern Uganda, they were known as the Rebels Without a Cause because no one who had met them had lived long enough to discover what it was they wanted. Driven out of their native Uganda, they have bled into the ungoverned badlands where Congo, South Sudan and the Central African Republic meet: these are three remedially dysfunctional nations. The LRA wages a campaign of calculated terror, not with governments or other armies, not for diamonds or gold or political gain, but specifically and systematically for survival. They loot and rape and mutilate and murder and kidnap without aim or motive, just a nihilistic imperative to keep going.

The town is poor, a collection of mud huts that hide themselves in the jungle, a few modest municipal buildings, a street of colonial market shops. Beside the single-lane bridge is a derelict hydroelectric plant. There is no electricity. There was once going to be a railway to take abundant farmed produce to Sudan, now there is barely a road. This is a town, a state, a nation, that isn't just slipping, it's been shoved back into the dark. I'll tell you how poor this is: it's so poor there is no advertising, no painted signs for Coca-Cola or mobile phones; so poor there is no rubbish, no blown plastic bags that litter the rest of Africa; too poor even for beggars: no child or destitute widow or cripple ever asks me for so much as a mouthful of porridge or a biro.

This place was besieged and preyed on by the LRA until the UN set up a small, protective force, a detachment of Moroccan soldiers with their armoured Humvees and blue-bereted boredom. It was enough to offer a cordon of stability, a candle of hope, and refugees ebbed in. The UN Refugee Agency, UNHCR, responsible for the displaced, came to help them. Angélique hadn't meant to become involved; she was a reluctant lifeguard. One day she was in a hospital, and a young woman who had just given birth told her that she knew she was going to die and that someone must look after her infant. Angélique said she would find someone, but there was no one. She saw the dying woman in the street and asked why she wasn't in the hospital. The mother said it was because she was desperate to find someone to save her child.

Angélique, who was preparing to join the refugees herself, said she would go to church and she prayed and agreed to take the baby, and the woman died. Angélique, a middle-aged nun without a family, now had a baby, and for eight months she held it and tended it and then it too died, and people started to bring her babies. She said she couldn't do it again, not after the death of the first, but she did and she found foster parents. She would cajole family members with promises of help and milk and sugar. She got the hospital to give her medicine. Now she lives in her modest hut by the river with six toddlers who clap and gurgle when they see her and climb and hug her legs with beatific expressions like glossy putti, and Angélique's smiles fall on them like a beneficence.

Goodness has a habit of growing in the deficit of its need. Like greatness, some are born to it and achieve it, but the best, like Angélique, have it thrust upon them and reluctantly step up to it. And so, after the orphans came the teenage girls with the children of rape and forced liaisons with soldiers.

Lois is a quiet child with her hair cropped. She's lost two teeth. She was taken from the fields by the LRA when she was just 14 and given to a soldier as his second wife. She speaks of it in a quiet monotone. His other wife hated her, living in the bush was terrible, the constant marches to the Central African Republic and South Sudan, the attacks from the Ugandan army, the brutality of the guerrillas, the executions, the beatings. She bore her rapist husband two children and then, in Sudan, he was scouting for a new camp when he met the Janjaweed, a Muslim militia quite as ruthlessly terrifying as the LRA. They killed him. Lois says she was sad when he died because, she says, 'I would eat sadness.' There was no one to protect her or her infants. The LRA threw her out and she walked through the bush with two tiny children, not much more than a child herself. She doesn't know if her family are alive. She lives in a little camp of refugee women that Angélique has set up. The children play in the hot earth, she constantly watches them, and though she would be accepted back into town life, it won't be so easy for them. I ask what she felt about this man who was their father. She looks up with an expression that is too deep to read and says with a pure, stern finality: 'They are my children and the children of a wild animal from the bush.'

Angélique has formed the women into a collective. They fry doughnuts to sell in the morning, cook catfish lunches for the NGOs, she has charmed and begged and demanded sewing machines so they can start a business, she's opened a school so these young women can take back some of the rudimentary education that was stolen from them along with everything else. They have been given some land to grow food on. Angélique has bought some soya and they plant maize and manioc, pondu – a spinach-like leaf – and peanuts, as a basic protein. The fields around Dungu blend into the jungle with their plantain and palms and mango trees, full of birds and butterflies. They look like Victorian paintings of a savage Eden. This is a miraculously fertile country: they get three harvests a year without fertiliser by rotating crops; no one starves. Children suck on maize cobs contentedly, and why Congo isn't feeding Africa, feeding Europe, isn't so much a mystery as a terrible, sinful shame. But these fields are also the places of most danger. This is where the LRA came to steal women and boys and kill their men.

Here is Pascaline, whose two boys were taken from the fields two years ago. One was killed for being too weak and too young, the other has, against all prayers and odds and hope, returned. He surrendered to the Congolese army, but has been shot and lost a hand. Pascaline is racked with conflicting emotions: ecstatic to have him home, desperately sad for his loss. 'He is 18,' she says. 'I have to dress him. It's not right to be crippled.' Here, where all life is physical and dexterous, it is a sentence to charity and uselessness. She says he has changed – he's dark, it's difficult. But these girls, these women, are not broken reeds. They don't behave like victims, they work together with mutually gleaned strength and energy; they laugh and there is not just a single person bent over a job, there is always company, there is always another hand. The children are looked after by each other and by all. There is one young woman who is obviously severely subnormal. She lives with her sister's family and sits on a small stool while the village works, grinning and counting her fingers, but every other girl takes a moment from their work to wink or to wave, to joke and include her. They fold into each other, like the dough they knead, all rising together. The collective resilience and power of women in this continent is a constant source of speechless admiration.

The UN keeps track of LRA attacks on a map, collated by a friendly and excitable Indian tracker. The red pins cluster in what they call, with a bureaucratic understatement, the Triangle of Death. The village of Ngilima is at the apex of this triangle. Its population has already decamped to Dungu and filled again with ever more desperate refugees from more remote communities in the bush. The UN says the hour-long drive is too dangerous without an escort, so the Moroccans have agreed to accompany me with an armoured car, but I'm woken in the morning to be told there had been a little hiccup. The Moroccans say they can't come after all because it's Ramadan – but never mind, a contingent of Congolese police have agreed to ride shotgun. They are a fabulous force of desperados straight from some Hollywood central casting: dark glasses, berets and bits of uniform, Kalashnikovs and ancient Belgian FN rifles. They all carry looks of obsidian menace and malevolence. We're not entirely sure that they've got actual bullets and I rather hope that they don't, because they keep pointing their guns through our windscreen. You can get a phone signal almost everywhere in Congo, you just can't physically get anywhere. The lack of access makes everything else – government, security, health, news, trade – virtually impossible, so the UN is building roads, which will do more for the country than a squadron of Hercules full of fact-finders and politicians' conferences. Already a little business is being driven in from Uganda on a new safe route and here, on the red-earth road, we pass occasional diggers and crews of navvies protected by Nepalese soldiers opening up the interior. But we leave them behind, and the road that began broad gently narrows until the jungle crowds in, tapping the windows, dousing the light. We drive along a cratered, waterlogged path that looks like tikka masala. The police hunch their shoulders and stare manically into the wall of green, the engines howl and wheels spin, the tension ratchets up, the turned LRA boy soldiers say they watch the trucks from the side of the road. Finally we run into a clearing that is the little village of Ngilima: a row of shops, churches, a smatter of mud huts.

I'm taken to talk to Jean. She bends through the low door shyly, sidling into the room that smells of smoke and damp. She's nervous, weary, she's barefoot in a faded dress, with a headscarf and eyes that reflect a terrible, resigned pain. The bottom half of her face is a coarse lump of wrapped tissue, as if sculpted by a child, with a cloacal hole poked in it. It is the primeval disfigurement of rage. She sits and talks quietly, her mouth opening and closing like a sea creature out of water. She was in the fields with her husband, the LRA came out of the bush and beat him to death in front of her; she knelt on the ground cradling him and they came for her with a machete. But the officer said no, not the machete, not the gun. 'He asked, did I want to live or die? I was crying, holding my husband. "Kill me," I said. He was angry and said, "You're mocking us," so they took a razor and cut off my mouth.' She draws her finger around the lump of scar. 'It fell in my lap like a doughnut.' What? 'It fell in my lap like a doughnut. I went to pick it up. They cut my mouth then each side, cheek to ear. "Go and tell the soldiers," they said. "Tell them to come and get your husband." '

Nobody knows how many LRA soldiers there are: they split and they split and they split into smaller and smaller groups. They have 25 years' practice in inflicting the most atrocious and fearful horror. Terror is a force multiplier: it moves thousands; it paralyses a land the size of Britain. Nothing that the sated imagination of Hollywood or what the trolls on the internet have constructed is as powerful or prehistorically, shriekingly effective as the living nightmares that stalk the hot darkness of Congo. The women come and tell me their stories one after the other. I don't interview them, I just ask them to talk as they see fit, and they speak with a disconnected matter-of-factness as if to distance themselves from the words; they look away from the images they conjure of themselves. Amenisia: her brothers were killed, she escaped into the bush with five children, one died. Marie is 34; her husband, father and uncle were killed in the fields. She is now the second wife of a man who doesn't support her; she misses her father. 'If I say more, I will cry.' She stops. Her 14-year-old daughter is pregnant.

Clementine: Clementine lost her mother and father, fled with six siblings and her four children. Another Marie had a disabled sister and a blind brother; both were murdered. Her husband abandoned her with four children. Florentine doesn't know her age but she was born within the time of the Simba. Her brother was killed on his bicycle; he left nine children, who she looks after; her own marriage is unhappy and barren. Laura is 25; her family name translates as 'I had to go through a lot'. Her fields were burnt, her neighbours slaughtered, she ran with her small children to hide in the jungle, her sister and brother were killed. The Congolese army tried to stop her running away but she persisted, pushing through the roadblocks with her children and an orphan she collected on the way. Vivien, whose surname means 'What's new', has 10 children. Her daughter was kidnapped and is gone, lost; her husband got sick and has died. Now she has 11 children. Another Marie: she escaped from an LRA camp where she had been repeatedly raped.

I walk out of the hut, just for a moment, just to collect myself, because I don't trust my emotions or my face. It isn't the pity that gets you, it's the intense dignity of vulnerable bravery. I come across a family of pygmies, they shake my hand and I suppose them to all be Yoda-ishly wise. Someone points at an ill made, collapsing hut. I duck inside and there, on the floor, a man is dying. He smells faintly of piss, he's wasted away to faded skin rung over a rack of bone; his hands, with their long yellow nails, are crossed on his chest. He opens his malarial eyes and smiles, revealing his last tooth. A niece sits in the shadows to see him on his way. She asks if I could spare a little sugar. It is a surprisingly calm and comforting human meeting. In the square in the heart of Ngilima, the displaced and the bereaved and the lost have all collected together to build a marketplace. Hundreds of people carrying baskets of red earth: they dig trenches, cut posts, carry water for workers; a man with a bullhorn directs the crowd, who sing and clap. This endeavour is an act of immense optimism, like the climax of a Russian realist film: build it and they will come, the market will come, the fear will be banished. I go to see Pascaline's son, who returned from the LRA but lost his hand. He has 11 brothers and sisters; he is the most traumatised of all the victims I see. He has bouts of terrible rage and then periods of silent depression. He sits and talks in whispers and three-word sentences: he was taken with his brother to be porters and given impossibly heavy burdens to carry through the forest. There were hundreds of boys used as slaves. The youngest and weakest were taken away and killed with machetes and sticks. His younger brother complained and was slaughtered. After two years, Felicite was the only one of the boys who'd started who was still alive. Then, one day, they were ambushed by the Congolese army and he surrendered and shouted he'd been kidnapped and was shot in his raised hand – he doesn't know by who. I ask what is the worst thing he's done and he pauses for a long time and his family watch him miserably. 'The looting,' he says quietly. There is no joy in the returned son, there is just a different fear and worry. Later I'm told that without his family there, Felicite has said that the LRA made him kill and rape, and there is the wordless worm of suspicion that this lost boy may have been forced to murder his own brother.

The night before I have to start the long journey back to London, Angélique comes to say goodbye. Hard times in bad places are invariably where you find good people and, over the years of travelling, I have met a bright few, but I can't remember anyone as inspiring as Angélique, an embodiment of Agape, the charitable love of humanity: an exceptional woman, called to a place of exceptional torment. This nun has now been awarded the Nansen humanitarian medal by the UN. Congo is the terror that hides in the jungle at the edge of our world; Congo is the name of the bogeyman, the apocalyptic dark heart of the black continent that has fascinated Europe with its distant horror for centuries. But let me tell you, it is also one of the most moving and beautiful and uplifting places I have been to. Not despite its torments, or our shuddering fascination, but because of them. Angélique gives me a doll that the sewing collective have made for my daughter. She says they thank me for coming all this way to hear their stories. Of course, it's not really me they thank, it's you for listening. She smiles and holds up the rather gimpy thing. 'We don't make dolls for children,' she says. 'But maybe we should start.'

November 2013

Lampedusa

On the morning of 3 October, a fishing boat leaves Tripoli. It is a small wooden boat, like a child's drawing, with a high wheelhouse. It is old, worn out, no one can remember its name. Fish are scarce, and its owner would have been happy to get rid of it for a handful of sticky notes. On board are 520 passengers; they pack every inch of the hold, a biblical human catch, and they stand crammed on deck. Each has paid about $1,600 for the one-way trip. It is a calm, warm day, the tideless Mediterranean is blue, the rickety engine warbles and chokes, slowly pushing north. Its destination is Lampedusa.

This is the last journey, whatever the outcome. The boat is a disposable barque with a disposable cargo: Eritreans, mostly, some Somalis and Syrians, with a couple of Tunisians, men and women and children. There are 41 unaccompanied minors – the youngest is 11. They look back at their last view of Africa. The distinction between an economic migrant and a refugee is simple: are you running from or to? All these souls are escaping.

Lampedusa is a crumb of an island that has fallen off the end of Sicily. It is closer to Africa than it is to mainland Europe. It is our Ellis Island, where the huddled masses – the tired, the poor, the wretched, refugees, hopeless and tempest-tossed – come to be free. On a rocky southern shore above a crumbling coastal gun emplacement there is a modern sculpture, a slab with a door called, grandly, the southern gateway to Europe. It's not a very grand monument; it's not a very big door. Lampedusa is the year-round home of about 5,000 people. Once it lived off fishing, but the fish are all eaten, the coral dead. Now it catches tourists. A baking-hot summer getaway, one and a half hours from Rome, set in the most iridescently clear sea. Someone with nothing better to do has designated one of its beaches as one of the most beautiful in the world. You reach it down a long, rocky path surrounded by wild thyme, marjoram and fennel. A kestrel darts overhead. It's a short curl of soft white sand, where the turtles lay their eggs and the dolphins and whales come up for air. Next to the beach is another bay. This one is surrounded by a steep wall of cliffs and it was here, on the night of 3 October, that the old fishing boat, with its exhausted passengers, ran out of steam and fuel.

They wouldn't normally have expected to get this far: as a practised rule, the Italian coastguard tracks and picks up the trafficking boats at sea and transfers the refugees to the small port in the town. These arks usually call ahead on satellite phones or short-wave radios. It is an organised and familiar run, except not this time. There was no call and somehow no one noticed the blip of 500 Africans on the radar. The boat began to drift towards the cliff. Someone set fire to a blanket to attract help. They could see lights on the shore. The passengers were tired and frightened and so close to the promised land that they panicked and moved to one side of the ship, which swayed, yawed, lost its slippery balance and capsized: 368 Africans drowned.

Giusi Nicolini, the mayor of Lampedusa, spares me a couple of minutes. She's on her way to Rome to talk to the prime minister about the refugee crisis. She smells strongly of nervous cigarette smoke and the frustration of someone who's not been listened to. 'This is not a new crisis. It is not a crisis at all,' she says, emphatically. 'We have been taking in refugees every week for 15 years. They are not the problem. They are not the fault.' Nicolini is exasperated with Rome's maudlin and politically opportunistic reaction to the sinking. 'It's all very well to be moved by nearly 400 coffins,' she says, 'but how do you deal with the survivors? That's what matters. It's not tears for the dead, but tears for the living.'

Lampedusa has a remarkable and surprising relationship with its immigrants. They care about them, they wish them well, they hope for the best. They don't resent them or complain that they don't learn the language or customs. When, at the start of the Arab Spring, in December 2010, around 5,000 Tunisians turned up uninvited, outnumbering the indigenous population, stealing chickens and set-ting fire to the reception centre, the locals called the rocks on which the Tunisians camped the Hill of Shame. Not the Tunisians' shame, mind, but the Italians' shame: the shame of making the desperate and the needy sleep out in the open.

The people of Lampedusa are good – if slightly unusual – Europeans. When the refugees turn up dead, and an awful lot of them do, the locals bury them next to their own fathers and grandmothers in their little cemetery, as unnamed sub-Saharans, with numbered wooden crosses, and year after year, each has flowers laid beside them.

It's not a sentiment that's shared by the Italian authorities in general. When the refugees are brought ashore they're given a medical check and their names are taken, then they're bussed to a camp on the outskirts of town that's been pushed into a thin, dead-end valley: two-storey blocks of dormitories and an administration building, surrounded by a chain-link fence. There are Italian soldiers with side arms and clubs guarding the door and it's patrolled by riot police.

The dormitories are packed, there is barely enough room to walk between the beds, the walls are covered in hopeful, religious graffiti and names, the place smells of sewage and sweat. There are no dining facilities; refugees squat in the open or eat on their beds. There is a small area set aside for nursing mothers, otherwise there is only one lavatory for 100 women.

A Syrian complains that she hasn't been able to go to the loo for days because the door doesn't have a lock and there are always men there. Sanitary towels are difficult to get and are handed out, two at a time, usually by a man. There is no sewerage system on the island and no standing water. A bowser comes daily from the desalination plant. This facility was built for 200 refugees who would spend no more than 48 hours here, but it is now inhabited by more than 700. Most have been here for nearly a month.

The men sleep on sodden foam rubber in caves outside, under shreds of plastic, wrapped in paupers' blankets, dressed in the bright polyester tracksuits that are given to them. They look like a school production of Montagues and Capulets. They also have a coat, a child-sized blanket and cigarettes. The fags are a bribe to forestall arguments. The North Africans seem, in particular, to suffer nicotine withdrawal, according to the camp's bureaucrat. But they don't get detergent. It's wet and it's cold, the wind snaps and flaps at the hastily tied plastic tents. There is nothing to do. Boys cut each other's hair into silly shapes out of a deathly boredom.

Technically, they are not confined, despite the presence of soldiers and the police – they have committed no crime. However, the authorities won't open the gates, so the inmates escape through a convenient hole in the fence, to walk aimlessly around the blustery, paperblown, bordered, pedestrianised, wet town, dreary in the off-season – Margate on the Med, without the slot machines. Little knots of Eritreans and Cameroonians huddle over their mobile phones in the empty streets, or stare at the brown football pitch beside the graveyard of dead and splintered freedom boats piled in a tangled, rusting pyre of flip-flops, life vests, like the sad bones of beached sea creatures.

The Africans stamp their feet and shout and wait without explanation or expectation. This is as bad and ineptly septically organised a camp as I've seen – worse than Syrians can expect in Jordan, worse than the Sudanese camps in Chad, or for Afghans in northern Pakistan. It's not run by the UN, because technically it's not a refugee camp, it's a reception centre. The UN is here, but only to inform the newly arrived of their rights and how to claim political asylum.

The Italian bureaucrat in charge is young, blinking, bad-tempered, self-important and further out of his depth and disorientated than his charges. He insists I sign a waiver agreeing that I will identify no one and nothing, see nothing, say nothing. I refuse. We compromise on something that says I have understood what he is asking.

Newspaper headlines constantly refer to these people as illegal immigrants. They're not, they're refugees. They are already victims, most in ways that sear you with pity and shock. A group of Eritrean boys in their twenties, survivors of the shipwreck, lounge on their beds, flicking lighters, sharing fags, and they tell me how they got here. Natneal Haile carefully writes his name in my notebook. He is a delicate and handsome boy with a bright smile. He speaks good enough English. He left Eritrea, like his friends, to escape the army. The paranoid military dictatorship conscripts all men from the age of 15 up until they're 50. You could spend your entire life in uniform waiting for a war or a coup, for barely $20 a month.

After five years, Natneal deserted, crossed into Sudan and worked his way down to Juba, capital of the new South Sudan, where he laboured for two years. Then he paid traffickers to smuggle him into Libya across the Sahara. In Tripoli, he was jailed for being the wrong person with the wrong religion. 'They are terrible people, the Libyans,' he said. 'So violent. It was very frightening. Everyone has guns. People have guns in their own homes, can you imagine that?' His eyes are wide with astonishment. His friends nod and smile ruefully. 'They have no pity.'

Natneal remained in jail until his family back home paid a £1,000 bribe to have him released. This is a common story. Most of the Eritrean men I spoke to have been imprisoned in Libya or held hostage in the Sahara, all beaten, all tortured. They knew others who had died of thirst, of beatings, of starvation, the girls who'd been raped, whole families abandoned in the desert, disappeared under the sand. They tell the stories with a matter-of-fact fatalism. 'Please,' says Natneal, 'tell the world about our people in Libya. They are dying in prison.'

He got a place on a boat to Lampedusa. The boat sank. All told, the journey from home cost $6,000. This figure is corroborated by others. On average, it takes four years to make this journey. Natneal wants to be a civil engineer. Where would he like to go? 'Norway,' he says. 'Or Switzerland.' He smiles with a shy optimism, as if admitting the name of a girl he fancies. Really? 'Yes,' he beams. Switzerland has taken a high proportion of those escaping military service in Eritrea for asylum, but you have to claim asylum in Switzerland. Norway is the most popular country at the reception centre, deemed by Africans a country of liberal opportunity and safety, if not friendliness. Some say England, because they can speak English, and it's partly, I think, out of politeness to me.

These journeys are far more intrepid and dangerous than climbing a mere mountain or trekking to a pole. They are made by some of the poorest people in the world, who leave their villages, communities, cultures and families knowing, in all likelihood, they will never see them again. They are funded by parents who understand they are sending their children away for ever, that they will never hold their grandchildren, and that they may hear nothing but silence for ever. But still, no one wants to stay in Italy, and that's a problem.

The EU Dublin convention stipulates that people claiming political asylum must remain in the first safe country they land in – you can't pick and choose (although Greece, Spain and Italy claim this is unduly onerous on them). Refugees have to be fingerprinted to be processed, and most of them refuse. Not being criminals, they can't be forced, so there is a stand-off. Some of the refugees have gone on hunger strike, and not all nationalities are treated the same. Syrians are now almost automatically taken in by other countries because the civil war is hot politics. There is a group of Syrians camping in a makeshift tent underneath rocks: they're cold and furious; each buttonholes me with his grievance then shows me a bullet wound. Everyone has been shot. It is left unsaid that they are deserters from Assad's army. France is very keen not to encourage any more North Africans, while Britain doesn't want this UKIP dinner-gong subject on the agenda.

A few years ago, Prime Minister Silvio Berlusconi came to an agreement with Colonel Gaddafi that the Italian coastguard could simply tow migrant boats back to Tripoli, even though this was illegal and deeply immoral. No other European raised a complaint, or even an eyebrow. The reason the refugees don't want to stay in Italy is because this is the most overtly, casually, critically, racist country, given the least opportunity. It is also operatically sentimental. The sinking of the boat was the cause of a hand-wringing bout of pathos in the Italian press. The centre-right Interior Minister, Angelino Alfano, famous for instigating the law that put the holders of the top four government posts above prosecution, decreed a state funeral for the tragedy that had befallen Italy and held it in Agrigento, which happened to be his home town and constituency. But he wouldn't permit the survivors, their families or friends to be there, nor the coffins either. He did, though, invite members of the Eritrean government from which they had fled. It was a state funeral without any bodies or mourners, a photo opportunity for a politician and an allegory for Europe's engagement with its most needful neighbours. The people of Lampedusa were embarrassed, upset. They held their own service with the survivors and the seekers of asylum on a rocky bit of their island, which looks out to sea. Each planted a tiny tree for every drowned soul.

Mohammed is still angry. His delicate Eritrean features are set in a worried frown of sorrow, shock and a sharp, righteous ire. He's come to tell me what happened that night in the bay. He speaks halting but good English, softly. He would like to be a translator. 'When everyone moved to the side of the boat, it went over quite fast,' he says. 'They said on the news we set fire to the boat on purpose, but that's not true. People fell and slipped into the water. They were holding onto each other, grabbing your legs, standing on top of each other. I had to push people away. It was terrible. The noise, the sound of screaming and crying.' He pauses. In the silence, he is hearing it again. 'It went on and on, the shouting, the screaming, for five hours. Five hours. We swam and swam. Parents held up their children till they couldn't hold them any more. We could see the lights in the distance but no one came. It was cold, so cold we were numb. People beside me in the dark said, "I can't swim any more, tell my family." We didn't know them, so they said the name of their villages. "They'll know me," they said. And they would stop swimming and weren't beside me any more. Do you know how hard it is to swim for five hours? You're thinking you can't go on, there is no end. You can't go on so you drown. And then there was a boat. Two boats came and they saw us and went away. One sailed right round us and went away. How could someone do that?' He pauses and looks at me for an answer, as if it might be a European habit. I don't tell him that it is. The identity of these boats is a mystery. There will be an inquiry, but sailors in the Mediterranean are instructed not to stop for refugee boats. There was no call, no message to the coastguard. Mohammed was finally pulled from the sea by a local fisherman. He needs to find the man to thank him.

We are joined by Costantino, 56, a local construction worker, originally from Puglia. He has a pleasure boat, and he went fishing with friends at 7.30 a.m. and he sailed into the bay at about the same time as the coastguard got there and there were bodies everywhere. He picked up 11 survivors and thought there was no one else alive.

'And then I saw this girl in the water, dead, but her hand seemed to move. She was covered in diesel oil. Almost too slippery to pull into the boat ... I cleaned her face with fresh water. She was alive. She was the last person to be saved.'

Costantino is very affected by her; she was very young. He went to the hospital to see how she was. Her name is Luam. He gave her some money and a phone, made sure her parents knew she was alive. She had damaged lungs and was transferred to a hospital in Sicily, from where she discharged herself and slipped away, disappeared into the great diaspora of refugees in Europe. This is what most of them do: vanish to continue their journey illegally in the hands of traffickers and gangs who exploit, enslave, rape and bully. Costantino says he knows where she is, but he won't say. She asked him for one last favour. Her friend, a girl she travelled with, perished in the sea. Could Costantino make sure she was remembered at the service? He took the number recording her death off the small tree and replaced it with the girl's name, Sigerreda.

Mohammed and Costantino make an unlikely couple, sitting side by side, tensely distracted by the unresolved horror and sadness of that night, the bodies floating beside one of the most beautiful beaches in the world. 'Knowing what you know, would you do it again?' I ask Mohammed. Misunderstanding, he says people are doing it now. 'They are at sea right now.' No, would you go through it again? He looks at me with a pitiful disbelief.

'No, no, I couldn't.'

'I can't help thinking about it,' says Costantino. 'You know, we were meant to go out fishing at 6.30 a.m., but I was late, so we went at 7.30. I can't help thinking how many more could have lived if I'd been on time.'

The reason the Lampedusans are kind and good to these desperate visitors is because they can be. They've met them and they see them; the reason we can talk about 'them' as a problem, a plague on our borders, is because we don't see them. If any of these refugees knocked on any of our front doors and asked for help, we would give it. We would insist they be protected and offered a chance to be doctors and civil engineers, nurses and journalists. We would do it because we are also good and kind. It is only by not looking, by turning our backs, that we can sail away and think this is sad, but it is not our sadness.

The divers went down to the deep wreck and the boat revealed its last speechless, shocking gasp of despair. The body of a young African woman with her baby, born to the deep, still joined to her by its umbilical cord. In labour, she drowned. Its first breath the great salt tears of the sea. The sailors who formed a chain to bring the infant to the light, used to the horror of this desperate crossing, sobbed for this nameless child of a nameless mother that was born one of us, a European.

December 2013

Refugee Journey

Kos welcomes migrants. The plane from Gatwick is full of them. The British, back to enjoy the fruits of their professional provincial labours, a second home in the sun for folk who think Spain too cabbie-common but can't afford the Caribbean. Kos is just pretty enough. The beaches are thin and coarse, there's English breakfast and pizza and cheap beer. It's safe, it's lazy and its main commodity, which it doesn't own, the sun, is dependably sultry and shiny. You can see Turkey from the beach. It's just there. The lights of Bodrum flicker in the heat, its khaki hills rising out of the pale, bored, flat water. A fit swimmer could butterfly and backstroke it in a few hours. You wouldn't know it had claimed so many hopeful, thrashing, gasping lives, but that's the thing with the sea, it never looks guilty.

The refugees are arriving in their hundreds every night. The beach is littered with discarded life vests and scuppered rubber dinghies. The pasty, paunchy English, part-time economic migrants, pick their way through the tangled trash of desperation, spilt bags, discarded flip-flops and nappies, and gingerly sag into their sunloungers.

Beside them, the refugees sink onto stained mattresses and beds of flattened cardboard, or cheap festival tents put up along the promenade. Children curl and splay exhausted, or run to play in the sea that they just survived, their parents hunched by sadness and relief. Finally, they're in Europe.

The British tourists wear shorts, T-shirts and trainers. The Syrian refugees wear shorts, T-shirts and trainers. They regard each other without irony. We have paid £50 to get here. It has cost them £900 each. Here on the beach, the myth of evil gangs of traffickers is also abandoned. The facilitators of this crossing are simply opportunistic, just poor people exploiting a pressing need, charging a fortune for a rubber boat. Trips are set up like illegal raves on Facebook. Even the

French honorary consul in Bodrum was doing it. A musclebound blond boy, his VW Camper parked nearby, kitesurfs through the floating detritus of exodus, skipping over the spume of abandoned lives. It's an image of such vain, vaunting solipsism that it defies satire.

The exploitation of the refugees doesn't stop at the shore, where locals scuttle down to nick the outboard motors and oars. Many of the incomers, particularly families, rent cheaper hotel rooms; well, they were cheaper, but prices have doubled for Syrians.

I listen to a BBC reporter say that these are middle-class migrants. The British press continues to call them that, which may seem like semantics, but makes a world of legal difference. They suffer for a name. The United Nations High Commissioner for Refugees (UNHCR) is unequivocal. These are refugees, and to say they're middle-class is laughable. Nothing is as dystopianly egalitarian and classless as a huddle of refugees. Many of them were professional, land-owning, business-running. These were the last people to leave, those with the most reason to stay: professors and engineers, opticians, shopkeepers. When they go, it means the infrastructure has irretrievably collapsed. They're not here to better themselves – the best they can expect is to be a German cab driver or caretaker or shelf-stacker. They go when there is no light left at the end of the tunnel, because the tunnel has been blown up. Offices and shops here have found that they can demand a euro to charge the mobile phones of the homeless. The mobile phone is the one indispensable must-have of the diaspora. Greece has its own troubles. Refugees are an added burden, but they are also an opportunity, a resource. The UNHCR has asked local cafés if, for a down payment of €1,000, they'll let the Syrians use their washrooms and perhaps offer them water; I am told that they've refused. But many people here are actively helping. They hand out food and drink. There are the hastily made-up little NGOs from all over the world, turning up with cars full of eBay clobber. A smiling Dutch family hands out T-shirts with cheery fashion advice. A local physics teacher and his wife have set up a committee to distribute food and organise sanitation. She fears that they're being watched by Golden Dawn, the ultra-right-wing political party, which has a following here. There have been attacks on sleeping refugees. Provocative boys on the back of scooters shout abuse and offer punches and graffiti. The physics teacher says that the mayor and the union of hotel owners are tacitly sympathetic to the right, resisting any infrastructure that might offer the refugees comfort or safety. Temporary camps could, all too easily, become permanent, and the less done to offer succour and encouragement, the better.

Out of town, in a foreclosed, deserted hotel, refugees are being evicted; they're handed fruit and tinned food by a furious pair of French *faire bien*-ers who are trying to impose the democracy of a queue. The air is filled with the smell of peeled oranges. Inside, it's quiet and sad; the walls are covered with children's drawings of families. There's a birthday cake with balloons and candles drawn by a grown-up, in lieu of the real thing, and a simple statement carefully, ornately, written in English: 'I miss you.' The refugees themselves are gentle, quiet and mostly relieved to have made the crossing, to be safe. Yet everyone is also bereft, missing a brother, a son, aunts, parents, grandparents, whole generations. Their stories have the simple, monosyllabic banality of grief. They are polite, sad and hopeful. They smile when you say hello, and are content to repeat the mantra of barrel bombs and crumbled homes, of the viciousness of torture and loss. They'll show you fresh scars, but not a single person begs or asks me for anything but advice. But then all I have to offer is good wishes. The first thing they have to do is register with the police. This is not, underlined not, a registration as a refugee – it is a simple piece of paper that says the authorities in Kos won't exercise their right to arrest and charge the refugees as illegal immigrants for a fortnight. When they have this, they can buy a ticket for the ferry and go to Athens. Refugees queue behind the police station. It's very hot. A British woman with rather mad hair, wearing an odd collection of holiday clothes, says: 'Are you in charge here?' I tell her I'm not. 'Why is there no shade for these people? I put up that tarpaulin.' She points to a limp groundsheet tied to a tree. 'The police won't do anything; it's monstrous. I'm going to chain myself to the railings right here. You're a journalist. Write about that. I'm protesting at the way they treat animals. It's quite disgraceful. I want to get a man arrested for being terribly cruel to a shar pei. I've got photographs.'

The police try to organise the refugees into groups. They are loud, abusive, furious and irrational. Everyone talks in English, which is no one's first language. The chief of police is a fat, incandescent bully who stomps around screaming, shoving and jabbing at the refugees. They, in turn, do their best to placate him, like small grandparents calming a huge, hysterical toddler. I have noticed that, right across Europe, the refugees bring out either the very best in civilians or the very worst in people in uniform. There is a barely contained racism, aimed particularly at black Africans. The powerless and enfeebled state of individual refugees incites or triggers a disgusted intimidation and bullying in policemen, while the obvious power and collective purpose of the crowd frightens them. It's not a combination that is open to rational argument or calm sense, let alone kindness.

A man comes over and asks me to come with him. He's worried about his friend, who has threatened to kill himself. I collect a UNHCR worker and we're led to a young chap I recognise; I saw him the day before in tears. I buy him an orange juice in a café and ask him to tell me his story. His friend has to translate. They're Iraqis from Baghdad. The boy is beautiful, with large, tearful eyes and hands that flutter to his face. The words tumble out in gasps. I had to stop him so the translator could catch up.

'He has – how do you say? – got too many female hormones. In our community the men abuse him very badly, all the time. Whenever he goes out they – how do you say? – the men f*** him and beat him. It's very bad. His family, mother, father, uncles, cousins all sold things so he could get the money to escape. Now he's here, alone.'

'He's not travelled with you?'

'No, we just saw him. I'm with my family.' The UNCHR says it will make sure he gets his papers.

'Will you look after him?' I ask the man. He says yes, but his eyes flicker away.

The boy smiles at me, shakes my hand and walks off with a delicate, swaying gait. He's 22, alone and frail. This isn't how anyone should have to come out. There are noticeably quite a lot of gay men here, fey and camp, displaying small and exuberant flourishes of aesthetic pride: a scarf, glasses, a bit of a hairdo trying not to draw attention but unmistakable. I'm told the owner of the café we're sitting in is a Golden Dawn organiser. I ask the woman who seems to be in charge what she thinks about the refugees filling her town and till.

'Why are you asking me?' she says, with smiling anger.

'I'm asking lots of people.'

'Well, go and talk to them, then. I have nothing to say, nothing.'

We are standing on the little hill where Hippocrates codified medicine 2,400 years ago under the shade of his plane tree, where the Hippocratic oath was first declaimed: 'I will take care that they suffer no hurt or damage...' That night I stand at the door of the docks where the policemen rant and the refugees who have managed to buy tickets file onto the ferry to Athens and the mainland. I see the gay Iraqi boy; he smiles and gives me a shy wave. He's on his own, on his way.

Idomeni station is on the border between Greece and Macedonia. The Greeks, even sensible, liberal, charity-working Greeks, can't say 'Macedonia': it physically sticks in their throats. They have quarrelled over the territory for more than 2,000 years, so they call it FYROM, the Former Yugoslav Republic of Macedonia.

The border runs through sparse farmland. We walk up the railway track. Each side is decorated with plastic bags, bottles, soiled sleeping bags and raggedy shoes. The refugees leave swathes of discarded stuff behind them. They have to carry everything; many men are piggybacking children across Europe. Every unnecessary ounce is a stone within a mile and, at the end of a day, a ton. The refugees are again screamed at, then pressed into groups of 50 so they can be walked across to the unmentionable Macedonia. They wait to be singled out. Here is a young man holding hands with a girl. They are in love. Another boy stands beside them. They are Syrian. He has the confident look of a young intellectual. She looks at him adoringly. She says he's a playwright and a poet and a writer of short stories, all as yet unpublished or performed. He is barely in his twenties, his girlfriend is 17, the boy beside him is 15. He is her best friend and she wouldn't leave him behind. The poet smiles at him. The lad looks shy. At 15 he counts as an unaccompanied minor. The UNHCR could make special provision for him, but they decide he is better off in this makeshift troubadour family. I walk away and I turn to see them standing on the railway line, a tight triangle straight out of a school production of *Romeo and Juliet* with a little Mercutio. At the station there's a broad, confident chap with a couple of his mates. He asks me to sit down for a cup of coffee in a thick Yorkshire accent. They've driven from God's own county to deliver well-meaning, but mostly unnecessary, sleeping bags and more water. He calls himself a philanthropist and shows me a photograph of his Rolls-Royce. He tells Andrew, the photographer, that Andrew's wife can't be a proper Muslim (she's from Kosovo) because she's married a kafir (non-believer). Interestingly, in our trudge across the Balkans, in all of the provocation, the only instance of religious intolerance I hear is from a Pakistani Yorkshireman.

Macedonia is a tense and rugged country, bitter and surrounded by ancient vendettas. It is roughly two-thirds Orthodox Christian and one-third Albanian Muslim, and in 2001 they fought a miserably cruel little conflict against each other. The camp here is basic: tents, a line of stinking vile portable loos. Across fields alongside the railway line, evening creeps up like a premonition. It grows sinister in the darkness. Again, refugees with exhausted, fractious children and with a growing sense of powerless panic are being pushed and bellowed at by Macedonian special-forces troops with handguns and truncheons.

They are lit by searchlights, bleaching the colour from everything. They look grainy and black-and-white. The train pulls in. It's an ancient, battered, European, defeated thing. The pale-yellow light seeps in through the stained and smeared windows, bathing wide-eyed faces. The refugees are marshalled into lines. They have bought tickets for €25 each. Last week they were €6.

The soldiers load the carriages with vile, goading contempt and ferocity. They seem to take pleasure in the lottery of escape. The carriage is filled to crushing until people shout from inside that there is no room, that they can't breathe. The soldiers shout back that it's their fault for sitting in the corridors. One sergeant leans in and grabs a politely remonstrating boy and pulls him roughly out of the train. His family cry in terror. His mother screams with a terrible agony. The loading goes on; the soldiers strut, smirk and joke with each other. There is something about this moment, in this filthy field, with the clutching of children and luggage, that conjures a ghostly remembrance.

Not mine, but ours, the continent's. This was never supposed to happen again. Never. Soldiers cramming frightened and beaten, humiliated and dehumanised others into trains, clutching their mortal goods, to be driven off into the night. The train pulls away, its dirty windows showing bleak, frightened faces. They roll past like newsreel. We're left in the dark and silent field with just the rubbish and their shoes and the distant barking of dogs.

We drive across the border, a cursory glance of passports, and meet the refugees again on the Serbian side of Hungary. The trail is easy to follow: a broad swathe of rubbish, corn taken from fields and roasted on little fires on verges. Straggling groups walking up motorways, exhausted fathers with sleeping toddlers on their shoulders.

At the road crossing, the mood has changed. The Hungarians have built a razor-wire fence that leapfrogs the refugees down their border. They've blocked the railway with a goods wagon and they stand behind it, grim-faced, heavily armed and armoured. The hope and the relief is all gone now, replaced with a stoic determination, salted with despair. There is a spilling-over of anger and the Hungarians spray water cannon and tear gas through the wire like demented cleaning ladies trying to remove stubborn stains. The refugees shout their frustration, children and mothers cry, young men chant: 'Thank you, Serbia, thank you, Serbia.' It is possibly the most unlikely slogan ever heard at a European demonstration. The news reporters, blinking back chemical tears, draw hysterical allusions to the Cold War, the Ottoman invasion of Europe, to Nazis and communists. And the plain truth that, in 1956, the world took in thousands of Hungarian refugees fleeing their own failed and bloodied revolution. Within a day the border is deserted. It's just the rubbish and the lost shoes and a five-mile queue of lorries. The refugees have moved on. They are like water, they find the point of least resistance. The iPhones tell them that that is Croatia, where they'll get shoved onto buses again to Austria, a step closer to somewhere where they can find a bed, be safe and consider nurturing a small new life.

In Budapest's laughably grand station, which is all front and no platform, the thousands of refugees have moved on, leaving piles of mattresses and touching notes stuck to walls and pillars, scribbled in interrupted school English, thanking the locals for their help. The tide has ebbed to find another shore. The truth of this exodus is that those who steeple their fingers and shake their heads and claim to have clear and sensible, firm but fair, arm's-length solutions to all of this have not met a refugee. It is only possible to put up the no-vacancy sign if you don't see who's knocking at the door. For most of us it's simple. We couldn't stand face-to-face with our neighbours and say: 'I feel no obligation to help.' None of you would sit opposite a stricken, bereft, lonely, 22-year-old gay man and say: 'Sorry, son, you're on your own.' Or not take in a young poet and his delicate Juliet and their awkward, gooseberry friend. The one thing the refugees and the Europeans both agree on is that Europe is a place of freedom, fairness and safety. It turns out that one of us is mistaken and the other is lying.

On the banks of the Danube, outside their grandiloquent gothic parliament, there is a small memorial. Jews were lined up here and shot so they would fall and be washed away by the great European river. They weren't killed by German Nazis, but by fascist Hungarians. But first they were told to take off their shoes. And here they are, made in bronze. People come for remembrance and leave stones in them. Hard stones in lost shoes.

October 2015

Victoria Falls

All holidays are invocations of other trips, real and imagined. Past holidays; the promise of holidays; gossip, snaps, Instagrams and advertisements. The tangible realisation of racks of bikinis and sunglasses, the unctions of suntan oil and mosquito spray. 'Dream' is the most wantonly overused word in all holiday brochures, and the heaviest luggage we carry is the weight of expectation.

No destination comes swaddled in so much wish fulfilment and awe assumption as a safari. Safaris are each unique. They are also all the same. There is an assumption on behalf of the purveyors that these are special occasions, perhaps once- or twice-in-a-lifetime experiences. This means that the animals you are almost guaranteed to see on one are retirees cashing in on a lifelong promise, people celebrating significant birthdays and honeymoon couples, for whom the allegory of nature 'red in tooth and claw' seems to be a spur to romance.

The trips are essentially glamping combined with charabanc tours of African parks. They follow a prescribed pattern: an early-morning drive, then breakfast, lion lounging (with lunch) and an afternoon drive where at some point a collapsible table with drinks and canapés will miraculously appear and you can chug champagne or the local beer and watch the sunset, which in Africa is spectacular and short.

You will drive back in the gloaming as the day shift goes off to roost and the night shift starts on its carnivorous business. Dinner will inevitably involve sitting in a circle around a fire, and a buffet of startling generosity and sophistication. You will sleep in some iteration of a tent, with mosquito nets and instructions that on no account are you to unzip the entrance. And you will be escorted by a man with a gun, which for many adds a piquant frisson to the night.

The backstory of safari is hunting, and the big five: lion, leopard, elephant, buffalo, rhino. They are trophy animals and the mood board of Empire adventures. Teddy Roosevelt, Hemingway, Isak Dinesen, Clark Gable, Robert Redford. If you look at the kit that tourists buy to go on safari, it all harks back to those dreams and assumptions: safari jackets and slouch hats. Camouflage is discouraged because of its association with civil wars and terrorism. The look is Edwardian and genteel.

Recently, though, safari companies have been trying to reset the assumptions. Conservation's call is attempting to shift safari away from colonial stuffed heads and white mischief towards more contemporary environmental concerns. It assumes holidaymakers want more, think more – so it's now more David Attenborough and *National Geographic*, where people see animals not as pretty heraldic symbols, but as emblems of existence on a perishable globe.

I have been to a lot of Africa, and on a lot of safaris, but I'd never got to Zimbabwe before. The Blonde and I took our nine-year-old twins to two camps for their first view of African animals. The first was Linkwasha, in Hwange National Park. This is an interesting mixture of woodland and grassland with vleis – seasonal shallow watering holes.

Travelling with children transformed the experience for me. The routine and familiar became new and exciting. My attention was drawn to things I'm usually too blasé to really look at. I asked Beetle, my boy, what he wanted to see, and he immediately said 'warthogs'. They are rarely in the safari top 10, but when we did find them, he was overwhelmed. I watched their staccato gallop, with their tails sticking up like radio aerials, and saw what he meant.

We spent a lot of time tracking. Identifying spoor is a brilliant game with children, and I hadn't noticed before how much dung there is in Africa, and how varied and fascinating it can be. We spent hours following Matabele ants on raids of termite nests. Untainted by adult preconceptions, children see the miniature spectaculars all around – a world in a grain of sand.

Many safari companies are ambivalent about encouraging children. They say it's for safety reasons; I suspect it's equally so as not to break the atmosphere of safaris being sophisticated and romantic. Children are born and grow up and play quite happily all over Africa all the time, and have done for centuries.

We did get to see most of the big five. Elephants are always amazing. Edith, my girl, grew quite overwhelmed by their size, their power; like great actors, they dominate any space they are in.

My particular pleasure is birdwatching, and sharing binoculars with your kids is not to be missed. I'm no twitcher: I have no completist drive to collect every species. I'm perfectly happy to watch any or all birds, but such is the variety here that I did note down more than 50 species in five days, including the purple-crested lourie and the western banded snake eagle in the same afternoon.

Linkwasha Camp was comfortable and beautifully positioned by a vlei. Waterbuck greeted us for breakfast and hyenas giggled outside our tents at night. It's functionally elegant: if Ikea did safaris, this is the safari they'd do. But all the old romance and decoration is absent. There's no taxidermy, no skulls or skins, none of the Edwardian campaign furniture that was once such a feature of tented camps. This one is careful not to compete or detract from the wild. Its minimalism is admirable rather than beautiful.

Ruckomechi, the next camp, on the Mana Pools of the Zambezi River, is more dramatically romantic. The further bank is Zambia, and the camp has the same neat, comfortable austerity, but here we are serenaded by hippopotami, which sound like clubbable old men complaining about the service. There are also crocodiles and waterbirds, fish eagles and varieties of heron and stork.

The game-watching isn't as abundant as in Hwange, but the setting is sensational. There is never nothing to look at. My best day was spent sitting in a boat grounded on a sandbank. The children fixed fishing lines and caught cautious tigerfish, while I watched white-fronted bee-eaters nest in sandbanks and perch excitably in clusters on branches. They have wings like Spitfires and they twist and turn in the air, catching insects – in this case, clouds and clouds of brown-veined white butterflies and African monarchs feeding on purple flowers. Bee-eaters are absurdly handsome, and the combination of the birds, the butterflies, the flowers and the river combined to make one of those moments where nature stuns you with its panache.

That night, Beetle and I slept under a mosquito net up a tree. We looked at the Milky Way, drank a Thermos of exceedingly good Zimbabwean tea and listened to a pride of lions 200 yards away. The noise lions make, particularly in the dark, is far more spine-tinglingly, prehistorically compelling than actually seeing them lounging in clouds of flies in the daylight. Beetle turned over and slept peacefully. I lay awake, listening to the dark. The best thing wild Africa does is make you live on your senses, moment by moment. It was a good, fat-mooned night.

The shame about safari is that so many people imagine it is the real Africa and never take the time or the trouble to observe people – a town or a village. I didn't want my children to go home with only animal memories, so we visited a local school. The children were, as ever, bright and funny. Zimbabwe has been a bad-news place for decades, but there are other stories here, one of which is that these are some of the best-educated people in Africa. This is why Zimbabweans are in such great demand across the continent.

We finished with two days at the Victoria Falls Hotel, a splendid, old-fashioned, comfortable place that reclines into its plush colonialism. I mentioned to the manager that I found all this a little guilt-inducing. He beamed and said, with open palms, that the guilt was all mine: 'This is our shared history and I'm happy that it brings visitors.'

The rolling lawn, with its wicker furniture, has possibly the finest view in the entire world: the border between Zimbabwe and Zambia, and the massive curtain of spume that turns into floating cloud. Early in the morning, we walked down to the Falls and had them to ourselves.

Their monumental power and awe-inducing presence took me by surprise. The Romantic poets made a distinction between beauty, which is made by man out of aesthetics and artifice, and the sublime, which belonged to God or creation and was the product of nature. I really wasn't prepared for such a drenching evocation of the sublime. The thing about the Victoria Falls is that no one can see – or hear – you cry.

Summer 2016

TELEVISION

GMTV

Now, I must admit that I haven't ever seen *GMTV*. I once saw ten minutes of *The Big Breakfast* and it was quite enough to convince me that television in the morning was like drinking in the morning: only real addicts could possibly do it without throwing up.

First thing in the morning is a delicate, softly lilac time. The day needs to be slipped into gingerly, not screamed at by a childish prat with a clipboard and an overworked pituitary gland. But still, with great expectations I crept downstairs to the room where the television sleeps at six o'clock in the morning. That's 6 a.m. real time. Not an hour for grown-ups. I sank on to the sofa, yawned the yawn of the nearly dead, and thought, 'You're a professional. You're being paid for this. Get a grip.' With trepidation, I pushed the button and went over the top into no man's land.

The first thing was Sally, the newsreader, for whom the process of imparting information about world events was obviously entirely novel. She stared at the autocue like a five-year-old watching *The Jungle Book* for the first time. The plot was beyond her, she just liked the colour and movement. When she finished, she smiled brightly and said: 'That's the news at six minutes past five,' but the little clock in the corner said five minutes past six. God, next week she should just stick to 'the big hand's on the six and the little wee hand's on the one'.

Then we had a weather Sloane. Well, frankly, she didn't know whether it was six o'clock or the last trump. She waved a limp hand over the map of Britain – it might just as well have been the Canaries – like a demonstrator trying to flit you with scent in Boots. She was dressed in the sort of hideous suit Harvey Nichols reduced to clear the week after Ascot last year. And for all she knew or cared, it could rain frogs and brimstone all day, because she was going to have a massage.

But these two were mere softening-up for the true ghastliness to follow. This being Bank Holiday Monday, *GMTV* had decided to take the day off. Instead of putting on a really exciting lounge-style cabaret of wit and information, they just did a compilation programme of all their best bits from the last year. They showed a bowel-curdling hour's compilation of family videos. 'We've had some really famous people on this banquette,' said the interlocutor lady, whose name I have scrubbed from my memory.

This was the C-list party from hell. It was like being forced to eat Max Clifford's address book. The lively 'now' people who had sat and plugged their new book, film, TV series, pop song, herbal remedy, comprised Cilla Black, Jim Davidson, Kate Moss with her agent-come-translator, Linda Thorson, the girl from *The Avengers* nobody can remember, Howard Keel. Good grief, Howard Keel. He was the Kaiser's favourite baritone, a sad old has-been even when he was in *Dallas*. Now he's older than God's belly button, but he's still a happening guy for *GMTV*. And, wait for it, Zsa Zsa Gabor's less attractive sister, Eva. How do you think you'd have felt if you'd been woken up at 6 am and found yourself alone in a room with that lot?

And not just that lot, but a him-and-her pair of perky, Celticly lilted morning people who had all the sweet charm of a syrup colonic. It's the same old story. If there's a really dirty job to be done, the English still send in the Scots and the Irish.

Well, that's it for me. Never again. At 7 am I crawled back to bed a broken man. My wife turned over and said: 'Where have you been?' I could just mumble: 'The horror, the horror...' It was the longest day, and it hadn't even begun.

June 1994

Just William

I've got a little list. Like Ko-Ko in *The Mikado*, I've got a little list, and none of them would be missed. It's a bit more than a little list, actually, it's a blueprint for a cultural spring-cleaning. When I'm director-general I'm going to organise a surprise picnic for the most loathed and loathsome TV funsters. The charabanc will jaunt into the country. Brucie will organise the singalong, dozens of great communicators in horrible blazers will sway to 'Tie a Yellow Ribbon'. Gaggles of alternative comedians will keep everybody's ribs tickled until we reach the field. Out they'll scamper, gamboling and communicating happily.

From the edge of the wood, there will come the faint jingling of harnesses. From the shadows, a ragged line of light cavalry will appear. They'll start at the trot, the horses' breath pluming, the tips of the men's sabres catching the light. The ghastly fleshy denizens of the box will look up, startled, meat-paste sandwiches hanging from expensive dental work. The terrible truth will dawn. And as the cavalry breaks into a canter, they'll start running. Esther will be cut down under the steel-shod hoofs, Danny Baker will kneel and beg, Tony Slattery will pretend to be somebody else. But my orders are absolute, no mercy. There will be no survivors. The whole epic will be witnessed by families whom I force to stand and watch. These are the most appalling parents, the ones you meet at PTA meetings, the ones who leave dinner parties early, the ones who pay with book tokens in W. H. Smith. They're the parents who don't have a television for the sake of their children. After the massacre, their kiddies will be forcibly removed and sold into slavery as light-entertainment studio audiences.

Not having a television for the sake of your children is the ultimate brutal smug philistine snobbery. 'We think it's important they should

read books.' 'We think it's important they use their own imagina-
tions.' 'We think it's non-participatory and sedentary.' I think the
argument for not allowing your children to join in the culture of their
contemporaries ought to be grounds for fostering. The sort of parents
who forbid their children to watch television are the type who insist
on speaking French at table, offer carrots as treats and make boys
play with tea sets. It is arrant elitism to suggest that books are better
or more culturally important than television. Or that ten minutes
being imaginative with a cardboard box, a felt-tip pen and a stick
is of more use than Deputy Dawg. Ninety per cent of everything I
ever learnt that was of any interest or use I got from television. The
children who spend their evenings reading might have vocabularies
that impress aunts, but they can't speak the language of their friends.

Generally, I shy from reviewing children's TV because it wasn't
made for me, and if I like it, almost by definition it has missed its
mark. All those weekend pop and slapstick magazine shows leave me
aching with boredom. But then they should. I don't want to read
Paddington Bear for pleasure either, or eat fish fingers for dinner at
5.30 p.m. I can, though, still tell the dread hand of 'worthy children's
television', just as I could when I was six. These are the programmes
that grown-ups thought I ought to like, the ones that were improving.
In my day, they were usually historical adaptations of Edwardian
books or they involved kindly gentlemen on barges who knew about
badgers. I think that pederasty and appalling acting have sunk most
of them.

One hardy perennial of the we-think-this-is-good-for-you children's
television re-emerged last week. William is back. As the last two
Williams inflicted Dennis Waterman and Adrian Dannatt on us,
you'd have thought they would have put a stake through the little
scamp's blazer and buried him at a crossroads, but no. I watched
in amazement as naughty ancient William went through the frogs,
mud-on-the-carpet, vicars, toffs-in-toppers, stinky-girls and soppy-
old-tongue-sarnies routine yet again. Who is *Just William* made for?
Who is supposed to be watching? Real kids have just plugged into
The Bill and MTV, so what are they supposed to make of pre-decimal
pocket money? 'I've just bought a tub of Ecstasy for half a crown.'

'What's half a crown?' I imagine that a lot of people at the BBC are very pleased with William. It's quality television. Yet Richmal Crompton was a second-rate, patronising, humourless writer fifty years ago; all the television adaptations of her *oeuvre* have been well up to that standard.

The line between what is, and is not, children's television is far vaguer than it was when I settled in front of *Picture Book* and *Twizzle*. The most popular children's programme now is *Neighbours*; I would imagine that within twenty years there will be no children's television aimed specifically at kids between five and eleven. They will go straight from cartoons to soaps (and barely notice the difference). The big should-we-let-them-watch-it? programme at the moment is an American import called *Mighty Morphin Power Rangers*. Flora Gill, aged three (well, very nearly four), adores it. I watched an episode last week. I'd love to be able to tell you what happened, but translating cuneiform would be easier. There were these kids who miraculously turned into superheroes, yet were also somehow dinosaurs and sometimes one large robot. They had powers that sometimes worked and there was a bit of a love story and some comedy and some singing. I know this sounds unlikely, but the villain was called Oyster Man. How do you make a villain out of an oyster? Well, you give him two large nipples that squirt plastic acid. And that's as much as I could glean. There obviously was a plot, but the programme is cut so fast and so much is assumed to be known that it was way over my head. I'm not being ingenuous. I really couldn't follow it. But it made perfect sense to Flora, so I asked her to do the review: 'It's really good because they fight the baddies who want to break the world and they always win.' Then she karate-chopped me. Well, as a parent, that's a comforting moral message. Far better than William, which is all about bribery, burglary and lying. Being able to karate-chop is quite an achievement at three, nearly four.

November 1994

Prime Suspect

When I got this job, they said, what do you think you need to be a good, insightful, even-handed, tough but fair television critic? Oh, passion, I said. Passion and commitment, insight and love, and a lively interest in popular culture. A working knowledge of the history of the medium, a pretty shabby social life and a sofa.

If they asked me now, I would say the first requirement was a bottomless bucket of facile things to say about policemen. Review television and you will meet more policemen than the Krays. By the time you get to your thousandth bending the rules, trouble at home, sex in the office, prematurely balding, cynical but sentimental, go-go-go merchant, you really start earning your wages. What else is there to say about policemen? 'Hold on, Alpha Alpha Garbo, I am just checking. The answer is negative, over.' There is nothing. Not a single original amusing thing left to add to the long march of coppers, and that is because there is not a single amusing, new or original thing being made about them on television.

We've done comedy cops, realistic cops, social philosophy cops, parody cops; we've done parody of parody cops. But policemen stopped being individual in about 1982. Since then, it has been like watching classical kabuki. The sets are the same, the costumes are the same, the dialogue is the same, and there are only three plots. It is comparing like with like and giving marks for handbrake turns. There is only one thing left that can deal with policemen: allegory. I am going to finish this once and for all, in a metaphorical sense of course. No more Mr Simile Guy.

Prime Suspect last week was the fifth *Prime Suspect*. Five. They've done this story five times. The cast changes, the crime varies slightly, but the story is just the same. Allegorically, *Prime Suspect* is not about a leathery senior policewoman fighting misogyny, her own sexuality and obsessive tunnel-visioned ambition. It is really about a leathery prime minister fighting misogyny, her own sexuality and excessive tunnel-visioned ambition. It is the biography of Margaret Thatcher. Helen Mirren is Margaret Thatcher. Prime suspect, prime minister, geddit?

The first *Prime Suspect* was so successful because we were living in the middle of the Thatcher years. Nobody had ever made a drama that explained why we both loathed but were entranced by this dictatorial, barmy, sexually radiant woman. All the political satirists went head-to-head with her, threw cartoon ridicule, hurled insults at her and went down like plastic *Belgranos* in her wake. The name-calling and mud-slinging made her more mysterious and enigmatic, added to the sense of Thatcher as unstoppable force of nature. Only a silver ballot would do it.

Prime Suspect used the allegory of a police station – what better for the Thatcher Cabinet? And a Britain populated with child abusers, prostitutes and deviants – how very much like Thatcher's view of us. Mirren got closer to explaining what Thatcherism really was than a decade of *Newsnights* and *Spitting Images*. And when she got her kit off, there was that same creepy-crawly horror that you would feel if *Hello!* printed photographs of Margaret having her toes sucked by David Mellor.

Now, five series and one and a half administrations later, the Thatcher years have an uncomfortable poignancy. *Prime Suspect* has followed the Iron Lady into a peripheral dark limbo – for the sake of allegory, appropriately called Manchester. Mirren, like Thatcher, has lost it. She is a shadow of her former self, she has gone off like a Catherine wheel that spun off its nail. It was a sad end to the longest-serving policewoman this century. Next week, class, we are doing Pets Win Prizes, the allegorical dissection of John Major and which giant centipede will make it over the obstacles to join the ERM.

October 1996

Jane Austen

Three hundred years after the sack of the Roman Empire, when Europe was well into its dark age, people who lived near Roman ruins imagined that they had been built by an extinct race of giants, superhumans. I know how they felt. I feel the same way about the Georgians. I mean, how did they make all that furniture, all those tables and chairs and sideboards and stuff? When they were bored with ordinary furniture, they made gear that had no known or conceivable use – davenports, pembrokes, break-fronted side cabinets, secretaires, folding commodes, reading stands with concealed card tables, and whatnots. 'What you making, Jude?' 'Dunno, it's just a sort of whatnot.' They ran out of names before they ran out of furniture.

Where the ancient Egyptians are remembered as being a civilisation obsessed with death – 60 per cent of the population were employed in sarcophagus- and pyramid-selling – the Georgians were a people with a furniture fetish. When they weren't turning out linen presses, they were dancing – stupid, insipid, childish hop, skip and jump dancing – or they sat on the chairs they'd just varnished, boring each other rigid. I know all this because I've seen it on television.

This is how the Georgians will be remembered: as tedious, skipping joiners, and Jane Austen's *Emma* was the most trippingly tedious Georgian of the lot. Her *raison d'être* was social woodwork. She was a nuptial joiner, and I desperately – more desperately than I've ever felt anything for a long time – wanted to screw her into a mahogany coffin with scrolled finials, fluted pilasters, bas-relief acanthus and a fold-out bureau plas. And bury her. In all the fiery, clamorous, pounding, ferrous Industrial Revolution that finally drove a steel spike through the marquetry heart of the awful Georgians there is not a single engine powerful enough to dig a pit deep enough to bury bloody Emma in, for still she stalks the earth. She is horrible. The television film was utter purgatory, like watching a dramatisation of the *Antiques Roadshow* written by Hugh Scully. If you want to know what the Georgians were really like, just watch the furniture experts on the *Roadshow*, those sprmaunced and pinched plonkers with marbled hair and patinated jowls pulling ancient drawers off old widows' ball-and-claw feet and getting all arch about their lovely dovetails. That's the true voice of Georgiana.

Back to *Emma*. The production was as predictable as a church service: the Christmas-card carriages, the lingering establishing shots, the fifteen reaction cutaways for every one bit of twee declamatory reception-room wit, the reverential editing and more dolly track than Intercity for the obligatory walk in the gardens. Here were all the careful National Trust accoutrements and clutter. You could imagine the museum handlers waiting just out of shot to rush in and rescue hairbrushes and cake stands.

The story of Emma is, of course, vomitously dire, a moral husk of a tale larded with empty snobbery and vain civility. Emma is a role model for girls as Oliver Reed is for boys. The original It girl whose crass attempts at genetic engineering fall apart when everybody settles happily into their allotted social strata, a result that is pitifully obvious even before the opening credits have faded into a swoon of Barbara Cartland watery silk. I managed to stay through to the bitter saccharine end only by imagining complicated and explicit humiliations for each member of the cast.

All my life I thought it was a good thing that we won the Napoleonic Wars. Now, I have doubts. In fact, I'm beginning to wish that the Mongol hordes hadn't been stopped at the gates of Vienna and had rushed on across Europe to ravage and lay waste Bath, Cirencester and Swindon for five hundred years.

December 1996

Teletubbies

Last week there was an episode of *Teletubbies* called *Naughty Lady, Yellow Cow*, which sounds like a Russ Meyer film. I'm assuming you won't have seen *Teletubbies*, and trying to make its truly spooky weirdness live for you is difficult. But here goes. The *Teletubbies* are small dancers dressed up as coloured fluffy aliens with blank, deeply frightening plastic faces that blink. They live in hyper-reality, a grassy landscape that vaguely resembles pit-village land reclamation, with real rabbits and plastic flowers. They meow and giggle, with candy-floss voices. Oh, and they have a television in their tummies which is switched on by a big windmill.

The Teletubbies live in a bunker underground, with a metal rott-weiler Hoover and a crematorium-sized toaster. The naughty lady was real-ish – she appeared on the gut-television, speaking to a group of ethnically correct children: 'I'm going to be naughty, now.' She then apparently suffered a short epileptic fit before telling a story about a naughty yellow cow which was her favourite friend. It was a story only in the loosest sense, as it was bereft of beginning, middle or end, and utterly plotless. The cow was yanked off on a piece of fishing gut and reappeared in a hideously badly made prop teapot.

This is only scratching the surface of this truly bizarre programme. Overall, it was, well, like . . . Imagine not sleeping for three days and then taking acid in a Japanese toy shop with Virginia Bottomley. Who knows what children make of it – but they don't pay the licence fee or whine to the *Daily Mail*. What is truly awe-inspiring about *Teletubbies* is that it was made not just by people who are apparently drug-free but who have done research, questioned study groups, actu-ally thought about it. The question we should be asking isn't what effect does children's television have on our children, but what effect does it have on the people who produce it?

At last week's international convention on children's television, a Scandinavian kiddies TV producer laid into the Teletubbies' deconsonanted, monosyllabic muttering for impeding children's language development. Oh, righto. But what I want to know is: in Norwegian, how could they possibly tell? It begged the question: what has Scandinavia ever done for children's television? Sorry, my mistake, there was *Noggin the Nog*. And it raised the blissful image of the Teletubbies made by Ingmar Bergman.

TINKY WINKY: The sun is smiling. It mocks me.

LAA-LAA: Have toast.

TINKY WINKY: How can I eat? It is sad.

LAA-LAA: Where's Po?

TINKY WINKY: Black death.

LAA-LAA (wailing): The rabbits, the rabbits have black death!

TINKY WINKY: Now I have to play chess with the vacuum cleaner for my soul.

DIPSY (comes in covered in snow and sacking bandages): Teletubbies say there is no God. Life is a meaningless treadmill of misery and hugs.

Closing shot. Teletubbies silhouetted against blasted skyline, dancing with a man carrying a scythe to tune of 'Have You Seen the Muffin Man'?

An American producer defended the Tubbies by calling the Scanda broad 'an ignorant slut'. He then went on to explain that slut didn't mean the same in America as it does here. (Ignorant is presumably pretty international.) All of which rather proves the point that being brought up on a televisual diet of *Blue Peter* and *Sesame Street* doesn't necessarily mean you're a well-rounded human being who can talk peace and love to the rest of the world, although you can probably make a slut out of an old loo roll and sticky-back plastic.

Overall, the international convention on children's television has been gloriously bad-tempered and intemperate when compared with, say, the international sales conference of pornography producers, which is a vicars' tea party – often quite literally. And it proved a point that can't be stated too often: it is not television's job to turn children into wholesome adults, and getting educated doesn't necessarily make you a nice person. Just because you knew what was through the round window when you were four doesn't mean you won't break into someone else's when you're fourteen. Watching television doesn't necessarily make you anything.

May 1997/March 1998

Brideshead. Revisited.

You remember the bit in *Crocodile Dundee* when the great antipodean is transported to a hotel room in New York and his girlfriend points at the television and says: 'That's a television, magic box, conjures Dreamtime out of thin air. It's what we do instead of abusing wallabies'? And Croc says: 'Oh yes, I saw one once,' switches on and there's *I Love Lucy*. 'Yep, that was it.' Well, I've just had a Dundee moment. I turned on the set and there was *Brideshead Revisited*. 'Yep, that was it.' Seeing *Brideshead* for the first time was one of those dead-Kennedy moments.

Cue colon-knotting music . . .

I remember my first sight of Brideshead, glittering in the yellow evening sunlight, timeless and remote, yet somehow completely present and prescient. We none of us knew quite how important it would become, or with what nostalgia in the years to follow we would, each in our own ways, return to that honey-coloured memory, and think: did this really happen? Was I really here? For it was perhaps in that endless summer that I was perhaps first really happy and yet with the unknowing knowingness of youthful knowledge we rolled up the long drive, that insatiable, irresistible tune thumping in each of our breasts. The siren call of languor that was to mean so much to so many of us in our own private ways. Was I perhaps in some way aware of the shrill bat squeak of a kind of love? Probably. Was this then the enchanted sight of a kind of heaven, what we would perhaps in time call a golden age or simply perhaps gilded Thatcherism? Perhaps.

Brideshead is one of the twin totems of television drama, the binary shibboleths, if you will, or perhaps the iconic brace. The other pillar of excellence, the alternate jewel in the crown was, of course, *The Jewel in the Crown*. These were the Pelion and Ossa of hindsight television that are always being held up as examples of the sort of thing we have lost for ever, a honey-coloured Gale's golden age of drama that will never come again, now made impossible by Producer Choice or satellite or digital or just general all-purpose dumbing-down.

Well, they've both been reshown recently, and *Jewel* has grown in stature. Its largo pace and staggering performances, its expansive script and encompassing vision confirm it as a true masterpiece. But *Brideshead...* I watched with growing disbelief. The series that sold a million teddy bears, that sent a thousand people to the property ads of *Country Life* looking for a rustic pile, that reduced a thousand thousand dinner-party hostesses to dementia searching for plovers' eggs. Oh my God, it's so awful, so utterly, risibly naff, so arch and mannered, so stuffed with appalling performances, with a script that needed an intravenous dose of syrup of figs or just a bullet.

The first thing that screamingly stuck its hand down the front of my Oxford bags was that it was so gay – howlingly, retentively, fumblingly, Dorothy-friendly homoerotic. I mean, we all knew it was a little fey, but I'd always imagined it was just a sensitive phase. This was as if someone had called a casting director and said, 'Look, we need a pair of irons.' 'Well, I can do you one – will you take an Anthony Andrews instead?' I just wanted to chuck a tapestry scatter cushion at the screen and bellow: 'For Christ's sake, snog him, and save us having to sit through another umpteen episodes!'

The acting is utter dross, with the towering exceptions of Nickolas Grace as Anthony Blanche and John Gielgud as Irons's father. In fairness, I can't really say that Irons himself acts badly, because he doesn't perceptibly act at all. He strolls and smiles, but I can say with even-handedness that he strolls badly and smiles horribly and that Marcel Marceau was his speech coach – his part could have been written on the back of a postcard in lemon juice. All the post-synch narration is so embarrassing, I nearly ate the sofa. Anthony Andrews, on the other hand, is just plain lost. He never shows the remotest sense that he's aware of what programme he's in, let alone which scene. His confused torment comes across as idiot stupidity. He's not struggling with demons, he's simply a struggling imbecile.

The straitening question is: why on earth did we fall for this so heavily first time round? Well, the camerawork is solidly adequate, and there's that music, which is potent in a Noël Cowardish cheap way. But that's no excuse. I can only put it down to mass-hysterical avarice. *Brideshead* wasn't redolent of the 1920s, it was the zeitgeist of the 1980s. We were all going for the burn, feeling the pain, filling our Filofaxes, passing on wimpy lunch so that eventually we could aspire to this ghastly, snobbish, cultureless, tipsy, ivy-clad repressed nirvana without a working class, all claret and cufflinks and cardies and a nanny in every attic.

But we're over all that now, thank God. Every generation has to see things through the veil of its own time, and today *Brideshead* looks disturbingly like syrup-coloured perspiring dreams.

February 1998

Sportsmen

There's a Harold Nicolson story I dimly and inaccurately remember. Nicolson meets a chap with whom he was at school. A gilded youth, captain of the XV, XI, VIII, IV – probably the whole lottery card – firm of wind and limb, square of jaw. This Athenian paragon would exhort the runtish Nicolson to strive for the simple imperial virtues of fair play, teamwork, self-sacrifice and Christian exhaustion. Now, twenty years on, Adonis has become a down-at-heel lonely bore, travelling in ladies' underwear, who clasps Nicolson with a needy urgency, romancing over under-fifteen inter-house semi-finals and deathless hushes in forgotten closes, pulling out faded cuttings of match reports and litanising team-mates.

Although, as I say, I don't remember much of the story, the moral and Nicolson's steely, embarrassed disdain have the clarity of absolute truth. You should, he said, feel nothing but pity for the schoolboy hero, laurelled and harlequined in the colours of physical excellence. For his life has peaked before he's barely stepped on to the field. Everything for ever after will be anticlimax and a slow descent into disappointment and comparative failure.

As someone who had all the natural grace, ball control and co-ordination of a supermarket trolley, I draw great pleasure and comfort from all this. I will with a lofty sneer do almost anything to avoid sport on television; but I wouldn't miss *Sports Personality of the Year* for the world. Here the sneer grows into a grin and then a guffaw. It's the audience, you see. The collected jowly, puce-faced, vigorously shorn has-beens, the gala-event, round-of-applause anecdotalists who so warm the cockles of my sedentary heart. There is nothing so risible as set-aside sportsmen, their beefy hands clasping Sta-Prest knees, as they mumble pat-on-the-back bonhomie through crumpled septums for everyone and anyone. All that old animosity, the desire to grind the other fellow into the dust, emulsifies into a sweet yoghurt of mutual admiration.

They all have the same microbic vocabulary of excellence, like politicians trying to find the correct phrase for a disaster. But their achievements now wiped from the record books by younger mono-syllabic muscle, the one-time heroes will turn up in any room with a plate of crisps and a microphone to polish again that moment when the ball did what balls do or the chin did what chins do. Wistfully, they mention that the game has changed. They only got paid three-and-fourpence, but the giants were more gigantic, not of course to detract from the brilliant lads of today. In every eye (except Jackie Stewart's, who doesn't have one – hence the execrable cap and windcheater), you catch the glint of jealousy and rage and more: of anger at business finished too soon. The actual moment of glory, the validation of their whole lives, was so fleeting, often just the stutter of a shutter, the ball in a hole, pocket, net, the raised cup, the tear; over so quickly that it can only be experienced in retrospect, an endless looped tape, your life stalled on permanent replay, turned into a thirty-second story that becomes as familiar and banal as a door key.

Every year, the *Sports Personality of the Year* is the one British sport-ing event that doesn't disappoint. It reiterates the great truth that all physical triumph is really a cruel practical joke on the road to failure. This being the *Sports Personality of the Century* they had to make it something special. And didn't they just. It was no surprise that Muhammad Ali won. We knew Jesse Owens wouldn't. He couldn't turn up to collect the prize. It had to be Ali's, because despite being hated, cursed and reviled as an 'uppity negro', a pinko, Muslim, unpatriotic loudmouth in his active years, Ali would elicit the greatest outpouring of toe-curling sentimentality, which when all is said and done is the most truly profound pleasure for the sportsman. Nowhere else in a zipped-up life can the adult male feel such unchecked, infant-ile, thumb-sucking emotion as during the great-moments-set-to-arias montage.

But the bathos turned to pitiful, mewing embarrassment. Not even through the rosy, uncritical, Kleenex-clogged eyes of television sport could Ali be seen as anything other than a monumental disaster of

a man. Some say it's Parkinson's disease and unrelated to boxing. I
don't believe that. Shambles like a drugged bear, shakes like a leaf.
The reiteration of his brilliance and the old footage only underlined
how truly, awesomely pathetic he is, sitting speechless and confused,
punched into a twitching simplicity, surrounded by boxers all talking
about what an inspiration he was, for all the world as if the award
were posthumous.

Ali was the best worst advertisement for sports and sportsmen.
Please, whose role model is he supposed to be? Who could say
to children: eat up your greens, or you won't grow up to be like
Muhammad Ali? The director live in his box lost his nerve and pro-
duced a memorably shambolic confusion of pictures. It was as if the
camera wanted to get out of the room and away from this desperate
mocking of a sick man. Personally, I was stunned. I was amazed,
Brian, gobsmacked and speechless. So this, then, is the great symbol
of physical achievement in the twentieth century. No theatre of the
absurd could have come up with a blacker or bleaker irony.

The rest of it paled beside it. The compilation best-of-the-century
clips were pretty dreadful, no top ten goals or putts, etc. Now the
BBC has hardly any sport of its own to show – it's presumably too
expensive to buy, say, motor-racing film from Bernie Ecclestone or
the Labour Party or whoever owns it – it all looked very thin and
half-hearted. What shone through was that Britain's sporting decline
has been a swan dive over the past century, and that at least is a
hopeful sign. When we can finally boast that we no longer qualify for
anything and that we're beaten at quoits by small Pacific atolls and
that we've reverted to calling sport by its proper name – games – only
then can we claim to be the most civilised and sensible modern
country in the world. Encouraging youngsters to punch each other's
heads, chase balls or run in circles for money is really qualitatively
and socially no different from urchins diving for coins. The fact that
you think you're an altogether more sophisticated and knowledgeable
manner of fan changes nothing. It just says a lot about you and
delusions.

Finally, in the audience of flabby has-beens were Alan Yentob and
Greg Dyke. What on earth were they doing there? Handing out

oranges, perhaps? Between them sat a small boy – I hope the evening was a salutary warning for him to swap his season ticket for a library card. With luck he'd have seen enough of sportsmen and television executives not to touch either with a vaulting pole. I hope the poor lad's name wasn't Tristram. Come and be a journalist, son, it's a man's life and there's all the balls you could wish for.

December 1999

David Attenborough

It's obvious, isn't it? David Attenborough is God.

Consider the evidence. He is omnipresent. There is no corner of rainforest or tundra where Attenborough is not. He is omnipotent. He says come, and the elements come. He says go, and yea, even the waters of the deep recede. All elements are as one to Attenborough. All creatures great and small do his bidding, pose and prance, mate and die. He is timeless. He has been the still, small voice of calm at the heart of your life cycle since before you can remember. He was here before JC – Judith Chalmers. He has followed the course of all true deities: once he was corporeal, he strode and lurked with the furry denizens of the world, but now he has ascended into the ether, and is just a voice of unutterable wisdom and love that resonates from horizon to horizon around the world, echoing from snowy peaks, whispering in the smallest burrow.

But most important of all, dearly beloved, you and I know that when Attenborough says something, it's the truth. In a world of hype and puff and spin, his is the voice of absolute veracity. Attenborough is the word, and the word is Attenborough. *The Blue Planet*, it must be said, is among the greatest creations of a beneficent small-screen god. It didn't quite take seven days to make, but the modern equivalent, £7 million, which, all things considered – and all things watery are considered – is, frankly, a miracle. That's the same as a Sunday-night costume drama. It makes you realise what overrated creatures actors are when one small fish with a brain the size of an aspirin can fill you with more real, ragged emotion than the RSC.

The filming and editing and sound on this series is staggering. The awe of the visuals never lets up for a moment. Whether it's killer whales hunting grey whales, or the underwater smorgasbord that is a shoal of sardines, we are left on the edge of our seats, jaws hanging, simply stunned at the complex, sleek beauty of the world out there. I had no idea, we all say, that I shared this small, spinning, drenched globe with so much beauty and wonder.

And here, we come to my personal purveyance of dissent. Because we don't. This is not the real world. This is Unnatural History, life cut together with the niftiness of a Guinness commercial. This vast place only exists, Tardis-like, in the small glass box. The sea isn't like this. Nature isn't like this. *The Blue Planet* is like being in a vast baroque cathedral. It's an idealised, hyper-realistic lie told on behalf of a deeper truth. You must remember that all nature films are shot silent. All the deliciously *Star Wars* sound effects are added later, by a man with a bucket, a pair of rubber gloves and a synthesiser. But most unnaturally of all, Attenborough gives nature a narrative, a story, a series of short parables. This imposes a human linear order and design on the instinctual chaos of natural selection. He does what all religions try to do: make sense of the random.

Attenborough's view of the world is all-pervasive. There are at least four acolyte channels solely devoted to its propagation. We all know, absolutely know, the truth about hundreds of natural things that only exist in our small box in the living room. We have never experienced them, and nobody ever will. Well, it's fine if the greater good that this soundtracked, edited, masterfully filmed vision provokes is a greater awareness of the fragility and privilege of life. But I also happen to think it can lead to the heresy of a sort of self-hating, utopian intolerance. Nature films such as *The Blue Planet* may also provoke a dysfunctional and twisted misunderstanding of mankind that ends up in the wackier and more violent nihilism of the extreme alternative eco-green movement. The species we should really be in awe of is not the one in front of the camera, but the one behind it.

September 2001

D-Day

It suddenly struck me, on D-Day, that all those old men are going to leave me. Having heard 'They shall not grow old as we that are left grow old' for nigh on half a century without ever really listening, the truth of the matter finally dawned: they were all going to die, and quite soon. My dad's generation was going to leave me all alone, undefended. I suppose I ought to apologise for being quite so monumentally solipsistic about Operation Overlord. 'It really wasn't all about you,' my mother pointed out. But I'm not going to, because the act of remembrance is profoundly personal, and it is all about me. I think my dad and all of them wanted it to be about me, just as I want it all to be about my son.

All my life I've been aware of the war humming in the background. I was born ten years after it was finished, and without ever seeing it. It formed my generation and the world we lived in. I played Hurricanes and Spitfires in the playground, and war films still form the basis of all my moral philosophy. All the men I've ever got to my feet for or called Sir had been in the war, just as all the men from my grandfather's age had been in the Great War. They're down to a handful, and soon the veterans of the Second World War will be too. What will I do without them? It was the event whose gravity has informed the orbit of everything in public life, politics, diplomacy, social science, culture; it made the United Nations, the welfare state and the European Union; and it ended the age of empire. It'll be odd and sad not to have these men as a touchstone, a fixed point of reference.

I watched parts of the coverage of D-Day on CNN, whose broadcast and commentary was incredibly good, though I should admit to having a lusty fondness for Christiane Amanpour. It was particularly nice to have a woman's voice, rather than those over-sonorous

men who invariably get wheeled out to do dead soldiers, with that
memorial rhythm that sounds like a rolling gun carriage with one
oval wheel. I'm sure this is how epic poetry was born: men tumpity-
tumping old battle honours.

For me, the highlight was President Bush's rattling good speech.
The band of brothers who wrote it for him had obviously imbibed
every episode of *The West Wing*, and it made the French chappie
sound like a cheese-eating surrender monkey. By contrast, our own
dear monarch sounded as if she was winding up a dog show. She
was, though, the only head of state who had actually lived through
D-Day and served in uniform, so I suppose she had the right to
say whatever she wanted. But it is a feature of our royal family to
perfectly judge an occasion, then quite purposely understate it. There
is a certain type of blimpish, smug bar bore who imagines that this
is the very height of eloquence and oratory; that the finest thing
you can say is a muttered, embarrassed platitude. It's such a dull
English affectation.

I must say I was dreading the BBC's big drama, *D-Day*: it sounded
like a buffet of cringeworthy first-hand reminiscence, dramatised.
Television really shouldn't attempt large-scale action; film does it
far better. And the dramatising spoken narrative is all too David
Starkey and his blessed Queenie Elizabethans. But, as so often in
this game, I was wrong. It was a marvellous combination of remem-
brance and drama. The action scenes were kept micro-focused, and
the cutting of original film with dramatisation was neatly done. It
was compelling both as history and a memorial to the day, and no
other television network or platform could, or would, have made it.
This was an example of the best sort of public-service broadcasting:
popular, intelligent, informative and gripping, without being remotely
patronising or intellectually compromised. Get rid of the licence fee
and you'll never see its like again.

A broadsheet obituarist once pointed out to me that veteran
soldiers die by rank. First to go are the generals, admirals and air
marshals, then the brigadiers, then a bit of a gap and the colonels and
wing commanders and passed-over majors, then a steady trickle of
captains and lieutenants. As they get older and rarer, so the soldiers

are mythologised and grow ever more heroic, until finally drummer boys and under-age privates are venerated and laurelled with honours like ancient field marshals. There is something touching about that.

June 2004

The Queen

Into every reign, a little life must fall. It's the Queen's eightieth year, the fifty-fourth of her reign over us. What was most obvious in the birthday-card documentary *The Queen at 80* was that she has enjoyed the meagrest drizzle of real life in an existence of duty. Even the poorest of her subjects is free to flick two fingers at the sort of men who belong to the Aston Martin Owners' Club. But Elizabeth's bizarrely self-imposed, self-denying definition of duty keeps her on her feet in the rain watching them for an hour and a half. Hers is a world set about with cliché and small talk, shared with the dullest people in existence, or interesting people rendered stupid by the nature of their meeting.

Royal documentaries are now a sub-genre with its own conventions and traditions and an agreed tone of toadying insider gossip that invariably stresses the hard work and the value for money. They have both that courteous cringe and nerdy statistics that always remind me of Raymond Baxter doing air shows. The first royal documentary, made in 1969, was a huge international event. Now they seem to be just another fly-on-the-wall, slice-of-real-life TV fitted in between airlines and cruise ships.

For the eightieth-birthday grovel, the role of Gold-Microphone-in-Waiting – traditionally the hereditary job of members of the Dimbleby family – was given to Andrew Marr, who happily slipped into the hushed tones of reverence, with just that splash of supine familiarity that manages to make the monarch sound like a cross between a steam engine and a public park. That, coupled with the vox pops from politicians – who always have that particularly infant-school tone when talking about the Queen, as if she were some gallant little special-needs pupil – made me think, not for the first time, what a ridiculous and disingenuous excuse for a head of state the hereditary principle provides.

Royal television has made me a convinced republican, not because I yearn for a President Roy Hattersley or Bobby Charlton, but because, through no fault of its own, the royal family now represents everything that is tacky, obsolete, corrupt and servile in the country. It's a magnet for lickspittle special pleaders, nostalgia snobs and men who have ties that say secret things to other men. I think that what we do to the Queen and her family is inhumane. What other eighty-year-old woman would we force to do what Elizabeth Windsor does? We should stop being humiliated as a nation by the exploitation of this over-functioned family. We stopped chimpanzees having to perform tea parties in captivity years ago – why do we still expect it of these humans? Like Elsa, the Queen and her cubs should be set free. Why don't we just have nobody at all? If the ambassador from Tuvalu or the Aston Martin Owners' Club turns up, just tell them she's out, running wild in the heather.

April 2006

Sex and the City

'Now, ladies, there is a washroom on the bus, there is a toi-*lette*.
It is, though, a toilet on a bus, you know what I'm saying? So . . .
no twosies, if you're with me. No twosies.' There is a murmur of
sisterly understanding. Welcome to the *Sex and the City* bus tour of
New York. 'We've all seen the film? OK-ee!' Of course we have. The
high humour point is a woman twosie-ing in her pants. So we're
all bonded over twosies. We're getting the twosie motif. 'OK! Let's
begin with who thinks they're a Charlotte?' A few hands go up. 'Yay,
all right! OK, who identifies with Miranda?' No hands go up. 'OK,
who's a Carrie?' There's a collective sigh of doppelgänger-identification
angst, and a yearning forest of arms. 'OK, who's a Samantha?' There
are giggles, and a couple of birds at the back raise their hands. They
might just as well have spread their legs. 'Ooh! Sluts! My sort of girls!'
The tour guide breathes into the microphone suggestively, and this
huge intercontinental tour bus pneumatically, and empathetically,
jerks itself into the traffic. I watch the driver negotiate the loathing
from the New York streets. He could be a special-rendition taxi driver.

Nothing is as instantly and comfortably hateable as tourists,
particularly large, loose, lost crowds of tourists. A bus full of them
navigating New York's residential side streets is an invitation to some
of the worst karma available in the Western world. Our tour-guide
compère starts by telling us something about herself. She's not from
around here. 'I do stand-up and improv and moved to New York five
years ago, and I've been doing the *Sex and the City* tour for more
than a year.' The bright and brilliant cliché of this life shines down
the central aisle. It isn't just an introduction. It's a pathetic character
scenario. With her bad haircut and designer bag spilling tissues and
drug-store receipts, she has made herself into an episode of the show,
and the bus sends back its unconditional pity.

The tour is a rambling, exhausting, discursive, self-reverential troll through downtown, and it's rather like being trapped on a large white bus with a lot of women talking about *Sex and the City*. So it goes: 'You remember the episode where Carrie spills the cappuccino because she's looking after the dog and has lost the manuscript with a description of oral sex with the Russian and then oh my God she bumps into Big who she hasn't seen since that time with the martini olives and the haemorrhoids? Well, if you look to the right, that's the café, and it's like oh my God bad-hair dog blow-job cappuccino hell. You remember that of course.' Of course they remember that. It's like asking Taliban summer-school students if they remember the bit where Muhammad smote the gay Jews. 'And if you want brunch or something, I can recommend it.'

'Now here on the left is the restaurant where Samantha found out she was pregnant with cocker spaniels and then swallowed her contact lenses and the hot doctor at the next table offered to get them all out for her. You remember that?' They remember that. Corresponding clips from the series are played on the tiny, milky overhead screens. It's an oddly disembodied sensation of travelling in a magic-realist bus, or coming around from an anaesthetic. After an age, we stop. 'Ladies, I'm very particular about time. If you're not back in 17 minutes' – she checks her watch – 'we will leave you behind.' And for a moment we all consider this. We could be left behind in the parallel land of *Sex and the City*, like an episode of *Star Trek*, to live forever in this mythical New York of endless brunch and always fornicating on top wearing a black bra. We've pulled up next to a sex shop. Apparently, we all remember that someone once bought a Rabbit vibrator here. We get off the bus and file into the shop, which is odd. Sex shops are generally solitary, furtive, and male. The Rabbits are piled high. That is the nature of rabbits. There's a buzz of anticipation. They were expecting us with a discount, and a couple of women get out their credit cards. I suppose a vibrator might be an impulse buy, and buying yourself one in front of 50 strangers with whom you then have to share a bus journey might be considered the height of liberated insouciance. But buying a sex aid because some actress has faked an orgasm on TV with it is evidence that there's more wrong with your social life than can be fixed by a dildo. We get back on the bus. I can't tell if anyone's chosen to stay behind and live on Mr. Big Island forever: 'No, you all go on. My place is here.'

Looking around at the women, I try to discern some defining characteristic. Surely girls who come to New York to spend a day on a bus looking at fleeting backgrounds from a defunct TV series in the company of other like-minded girls should have some deforming mark so we can recognise them on the street or at the bar or in the dark. But they aren't tattooed, or particularly fat, or lopsided with walleyes. They aren't carrying oxygen tanks or wearing padded safety helmets. They aren't noticeably over- or underdressed. There isn't a winking absence of underwear or overindulgence of cleavage. They are a relatively plain cross section of women from across the States and beyond. Most of them won't see 25 again. They are all gamely fighting a losing battle against comfort carbs, gravity, and the capricious idiocy of fashion. One has brought along her boyfriend, like a large, sulky handbag, which was, I think, an act of overt hostility and humiliation. I assume he'd been caught humping a short-order waitress, and this was part of his punishment. The other girls regard him and me with barely disguised disgust. Mr Big wouldn't be caught dead on a *Sex and the City* bus tour. What sort of demi-man would? Well, the three English poofs at the back would. They started out screechy and hyperventilatingly *Cage aux Folles*, but they got quieter and shiftier as we went on; there wasn't anything like enough camp irony. This was all way too real.

We crawl into the Meatpacking District. Our conspiratorial and cozily gossipy stand-up tour guide tells us that this is where the girls did a lot of their shopping, and that it's a sort of secret place that only really savvy New Yorkers know about. She reels off a list of shops and what each character bought in them. We're chucked off for 20-minute retail reruns. I hide in Diane von Furstenberg's changing room. And just in case you're from Alaska, the Meatpacking District is New York's secret like the Vatican is Rome's.

We're taken to the Magnolia Bakery, where queues of weirdly excited and messianic women wait impatiently to eat the teeth-meltingly sweet, infantile cupcakes like a votive Communion promising a blessed afterwork life of copious, cool sex, witty friendship, miraculously available taxis, Manolos, Cosmos, and happy-ending aphorisms. We don't have to line up. Our cakes come with the ticket. Massive trays of cupcakes appear and are offered to us in a tramp's *pissoir* alley on slimy benches beside a children's recreational park. Feeding cake to yearningly single women beside a playground with happy West Village moms and their gilded tots was an act of sadistic patronage. We guiltily stuff our faces, begging the refined calories to transport us into closer connection with the fabled story arc.

If I were a French philosopher, *un philosophe français* (and it's certainly a request I'm putting on the form for reincarnation), I'd say that perhaps the *Sex and the City* bus tour is really how postmodern epic sagas are conceived: popular prose poetry, stories of wish fulfillment and inspiration, shaped by the repetition of gossip and the lives of heroes. It's probably what Homer did. You could see this bus as an air-conditioned *Odyssey* workshop, and it's only a cultural snobbery that makes us regard it as any more risible than guided tours around Brontë country or the classic ruins of North Africa, invigilated by some bitter, tight, redundant academic. But then, if I'm going to be a French philosopher, I'm going to have to inflate my cultural snobbery, and not by any stretch of the zeitgeist, or Homeric blindness, is Carrie Bradshaw Helen of Troy. And *Sex and the City* ain't a chic, ironic take on *Wuthering Heights*. These women on the bus are missing the point. The storyville they're looking for doesn't exist and never did, and trying to search for the literal in literature inevitably kills the object of affection, murders the fiction stone-dead.

After four hours, we're dropped off in Midtown. The bus is strangely subdued. The women file out swiftly, each tipping our stand-up guide a grudged, crumpled ten without making eye contact. We all realise what an obsessively ridiculous, embarrassing, empty, and needy exercise this has been. I can't imagine anyone here would repeat the trip, or recommend it to a friend. And I guess that a good many of us will keep it as a guilty secret, like drunkenly snogging the doorman. As if to underline our gullibility, they deposit us beside the HBO store. As I step out onto the sidewalk, I notice with surprise that the real New York is looking beautiful. It's a sunny, clear day.

People are loaded down with shopping bags and thinking about a late lunch. We're in the last days before recession will hit, and the light seems particularly golden, the mood glossy and sybaritic. New York as seen through the fish-eye lens of *Sex and the City* will be buried under an avalanche of stinking credit. And, as ever, the reality of New York, good and bad, rich and poor, in credit or in hock, is so much more exciting than any fiction.

January 2009

Peppa Pig

Having a second family – or, rather, a family with an interregnum between siblings – brings back things I'd forgotten. Some return with an intense pleasure: having a toddler fall asleep on your shoulder; making animal noises; dancing to 'Single Ladies'. One of the things that returns like milk sick in the back of the car is children's television. I'd forgotten the true, grim, brain-melting, smiley awfulness of toddler TV. I always say that television gets better and better, that the quality improves year on year, but children's television is the exception.

At the moment I'm being brain-bludgeoned by *Peppa Pig*. A normal healthy adult life should never be afflicted by Peppa Pig and her foul porcine family. Miserably, my household has got it like heroin addiction; the twins can't ingest enough of it. It begins at seven in the morning. The Sky box is overrun with pigs; even Jack Bauer couldn't hold his own against Peppa and her family.

They are peculiarly unattractively realised cartoons, ugly hog-blobs with distressing stick arms. They do things like eat picnics, fly kites and massacre lambs with chainsaws. I made the last one up. Their voices are insistently annoying, in the manner of infant-school teachers telling stories. What I find particularly tiresome is that daddy pig, who wears glasses, as do I, is a functioning cretin. Most of the stories revolve around this fat, lazy, stupid, lying, feckless sack of sausages.

As far as I can tell, which isn't very far, all children's television is now policed by committees of single-parent lesbians, nursery assistants, social workers, outreach-policy face communicators and possibly Esther Rantzen. Everything is made to inculcate simple, short messages about honesty, kindness, inclusivity, cosiness and sensible eating of organic, unprocessed food. The fun is merely there as a coating for the message; the entertainment quality is pretty remedial.

With *Peppa Pig*, it's barely noticeable. I'm all for moral television; I want The Goodies to be machine-gunned and thrown into a pit of lime. But kids' TV now isn't about good and evil, it's about constructing the image of a world where there is no evil at all, no sharp edges, nothing but cute lessons without blame, a bland conformity and lots of hugs. And what children learn, I suspect, is nothing at all. Any moment the twins will realise they're being preached to in a spookily Orwellian way by talking pigs.

By chance I caught a *Tom and Jerry* cartoon this week, and by comparison it was astonishing. Sixty years old, the production and the drawings were beautiful, the animation fluid and sophisticated and articulate. It seemed so fabulously anarchic and naughty, a world made up entirely of danger and death. The violence... there was so much violence, so much agony! And it was all so funny. Nothing that happens after the watershed, nothing Jonathan Ross could possibly say, is as spectacularly, wonderfully wrong as a *Tom and Jerry* cartoon.

Entertainment isn't the servant of the moral or the message. It is the moral and the message. More important than learning table manners, racial courtesy and not to play with matches, kids need television to show them plot development, suspense, narrative arts, the mechanics of humour. Television is part of their culture, not their classroom.

March 2009

Big Brother

I was lying in bed, havering between the choice of home-made dreams, a few pages of a book (*The White War*, an evocative study of the little-known Italian/Austrian front, 1915–19) or 15 minutes of the telly. As usual, I succumbed to the siren of the box. This, I suspect, is the most common of night rituals in the Western world: the search for something to bathe the frontal lobes and send us to sleep. In America, they put on chat shows specifically to waft viewers into the embrace of Morpheus. As many of us die in our sleep, the last images of a bright glorious and complex world, the staggering edifice of civilisation, the riveting tapestry of human emotion, may well be David Letterman swapping pizza recipes with Richard Dreyfuss. This is a sanguine and humbling reflection on our shared humanity.

So I was shuffling the images like a game of patience, searching for the comforting narcotic of a multi-cadaver *CSI* or perhaps a virulently pustular *House*, when I was arrested by a black-and-white image of a bed. It was a tangle of sheets, under which a body, perchance asleep, perchance two bodies, lay. It reminded me of the time when television broadcast really good films in black and white. I thought perhaps I recognised this – it was one of those middle-order Truffauts about the inexorable break-up of a marriage. There was a French new-wave atmosphere, the ambient sound, the fixed, incisive camera, the knowing nod to American cinema noir. The shot lingered, with an auteur's indulgence, and then cut precipitously to another image of the bed. There was movement under the covers. This wasn't French. Too dark, too doom-laden – this was Scandinavian, one of those Bergmans when he was between marriages, living on some blasted island and had producers who cared only about art, truth and European film festivals, not Yankee box offices. An arm appeared from under the sheet, a female hand, supplicant, yearning. What was this film? I flicked to the index – *Big Brother Live*.

Big Brother: I'd completely forgotten it was on. So had everyone else, it seems. No surprise to hear that the show has only one more series to run. A girl once told me of a dreadful female condition called *la répulsion*. It's that moment when you wake and look down at your sleeping partner of many years and are suddenly overwhelmed with revulsion. The thought of touching them, or being touched, is shudderingly repugnant. The repulsion is irrevocable and irreconcilable, and it was what I felt about *Big Brother*. Not that I was ever very lustful for it. I think we all share the same feeling. We look at it and wonder, what on earth were we thinking of? How could we have been taken in? How did it ever exert such a grip? The next day, I watched some more: 'Will the contestants please come to the garden for more oil wrestling.' The children were doused in baby oil, wearing their swimsuits, tattoos and grins of entitlement. They squirmed at each other without purpose, effort or expectation. Back on the sofa, I squirmed with them. It looked like the worst of a student YouTube download. It comes as a surprise how instantly and completely the audience goes off programmes they thought they'd love for ever.

Which brings us neatly to *The X Factor*, which began its long vaudevillian parade of money boys, fat loud girls, last-chance widows and duos with sob stories last weekend. The stipulation for a contestant on *The X Factor* is an uncontrollable vibrato and a great deal of cancer in the family. The show will drag its sugary slug trail of sentimentality from now until the traditional Christmas single of an overproduced 1980s ballad doused with a lachrymose orchestra. Not so much a wall of sound as a shroud of sound, dedicated to some carcinogenically defunct auntie. As Oscar Wilde so perceptively put it, it would take a heart of stone not to laugh out loud.

What struck me about this year's incarnation is a truth about television: the medium manipulates the manipulators. The judges are getting to be more and more like the strange, emotionally inflated, vainly insecure, critically tone-deaf contestants. They have gone from being warders to inmates. You look at that line of faces, bereft of a natural expression, the body language tortured into a physical

Tourette's by a thousand paparazzi, and you have to think: these are very, very bizarre, truncated human beings. Television is not a natural habitat. Those who stay on it too long or have nowhere else to go are irreparably deformed by it.

I watched *The X Factor* and thought about the marathon to come. The predictable so-naive kids. The predictable exclamations of joy and despair. The predictable tears, the predictable and cynical guest appearances to boost plummeting record sales. The predictable scrabble for some corner of the power ballad, the greatest hit that hasn't already been plundered. And I was filled with a yawning ennui. Already I can sense the first cold twinges of falling out of love. When it happens, it will come with the suddenness of the guillotine.

August 2009

Alan Bennett

Alan Bennett: if he didn't exist, we'd have to invent him. But who would we get to do it? Can you imagine Alan Bennett made up by David Hare? Or J.K. Rowling's Alan Bennett? Stephen Fry might be able to knock one up. They'd all be interesting, but none would be quite as wonderful as the Alan Bennett created by Alan Bennett.

Creative people generally don't care much about their personal performances, their own theatre; they are happy as an unfinished work in progress. But Bennett is a fully polished, one-man, three-act classic. Indeed, for all the brilliance of his oeuvre, he may well be his own masterwork: a cunning and intriguing conflation of *Wind in the Willows* creature and the emcee from *Cabaret*, all done up in the conventional donnish costume of a jacket a size too large, a pullie and tie. Never varying, with that precise Yorkshire accent delivered in a slightly plaintive minor key, but behind it a Robespierre of social mayhem. Beneath the thin ice of homespun humour rages a Brechtian fury at injustice and cant, cruelty, cynicism, modernity and railway milk cartons. His anger is so hot, it can turn granite to toffee. I reckon Bennett is one of those rare people who can appear on TV and still be universally loved.

Watching him in *Being Alan Bennett*, I was, as ever, amazed at how remarkably unchanged he is, the Mount Rushmore of British theatre. There was a clip of him doing the peerless vicar sketch from *Beyond the Fringe* 50 years ago, looking exactly as he does today: same hair, same spectacles, same demeanour, same schtick. Bennett arrived fully formed; there has been no need to modify or modernise. He has taken the meagre raw material of his lower-middle-class origins in Leeds and spun them into a cloth of gold that is now large enough to swag St Paul's. He is a camp Rumpelstiltskin. Very little makes me laugh on television, but Bennett always does. Every line perfectly weighted, every long pause hanging over a chasm of pathos and pity, sadness and irritation.

This *South Bank Show*-style programme was a puff for his new play at the National Theatre. But really it is a homage to him as a performer, a character, the Bennett of Bennetts. He walks through a real world, making small dramas in the Women's Institute, a doctor's waiting room; and one of the things he does particularly brilliantly is swear. He is a masterclass in profanity. Compare his f-word with Gordon Ramsay's. For Ramsay, it's punctuation, a meaningless bark, but the word that emerges from Bennett's cat's-arse lips is glistening, semi-precious. He sucks at the word, with its soft-centred vowel, like a humbug. It is memorably beautiful. His dissection of Philip Larkin's poem 'This Be the Verse' and then setting it to the theme tune of *Last of the Summer Wine* left me agape and gasping.

December 2009

Alan Whicker

Alan Whicker, who has just died at the age of 87, or 91, depending on whose *Who's Who* you believe, was one of the first and best television journalists. He didn't come to the newly popular small screen from print or acting or academe, like most of his contemporaries; his style and form of reporting were made for and by the camera and the sitting-room sofa. In the Second World War, he was part of the army film unit: he reported the invasion of Italy and was one of the first men in liberated Milan.

At the BBC, he joined the new magazine programme *Tonight*, which came after the evening news and replaced the toddlers' truce – an hour where the BBC went off the air to allow parents to put their children to bed. It's now almost impossible to imagine a corporation, or a society, where that sort of paternalism and cosy collective assumption would seem normal, or desirable.

From *Tonight*, he went on to *Whicker's World*, which ran for 30 years – half of popular television's lifespan. It made Whicker one of the most instantly recognisable and famous men in the country. His particular skill was to interview people in a chatty, unconfrontational way, managing to elicit astonishingly revealing confidences while imparting a sort of editorial semaphore of irony and disbelief to the audience just by the way he stood and with his tiny inflections and mannerisms. The barely raised eyebrow was picked up by the camera, but was invisible to the person standing next to him. Jeremy Clarkson once said to me that Whicker could say more by folding his arms than most presenters can with an autocue, Rada training and four scriptwriters.

His persona of moustache and blazer, thick glasses and clubbable ties reeked of golf-club provincial probity and became a sort of camouflage that gave him access to Papa Doc Duvalier, the rich and famous of California, the entitled and titled of old Europe, the head-hunters of Borneo and day-trippers to Blackpool. He spoke with a much-mimicked enunciation, with a dying fall at the end of sentences that seemed to be punctuated with dashes. But his observations were always incisive, often witty and, most important, clear. He spoke straight at this new audience, never down to them, and never with overfamiliarity. They trusted him to show them the world. Whicker was so famous that he became rhyming slang, twice: a whicker was a pound, a 'nicker'; it was also underpants.

Most people reading this won't have seen him or the other present-ers on the *Tonight* programme: Kenneth Allsop, Julian Pettifer, Chris Brasher, Fyfe Robertson, Trevor Philpott, Cliff Michelmore. All of them titans of TV, a dream team who, between them, invented a style of magazine programme comprising light news, consumer affairs, travelogue and local interest that set the pattern and the parameters for almost everything you now watch between the 6 pm news and the watershed.

You think *The One Show* came out of thin air? I know it is mostly thin air, but it is the anaemic end of an older tale. As television enters its third generation, it's difficult not to think of its themes and genres as being immutable, eternal. But the box wasn't born with an instruction book; the plots all had to be created and honed. And Whicker was one of the first on-screen presenters to do features journalism that showed there was more to the world than events and nature, and more to TV than news and entertainment. This is a medium that childishly still has a wilfully short memory, that is mesmerised by youth and newness. As we speak, a dozen trendy Tristrams are desperately searching for the new Alan Whicker, quite unaware that there was ever an old Alan Whicker.

July 2013

Rev.

The BBC's guiding principles came from eye-rolling dark passages of the black book. Lord Reith, the son of a Presbyterian free-church minister from Kincardineshire, was television's Moses, who led the chosen presenters to the promised land of your front room, never imagining that one day they'd be in your bedroom. Be ever mindful that television's default morality is Scottish low church. It believes in education and information, and that the entertainment bit is a feeble joke at the end of the sermon. It believes in hard work, accountability, responsibility, charity and righteous outrage; also, that you are your brother's keeper; and, most of all, it believes in judgment.

You can find elements of all that in almost every programme on the box, from *Countryfile* to *Britain's Got Talent*; from the relentless justice of police series to the pulpit judgments of *Question Time* and *Loose Women*. Television never wanders far from the kirkyard.

Many atheist liberals were pleased when broadcasting discarded its obligation to set aside time for religious content, imagining that it showed a modern, humanistic approach. Of course, the revealed truth is quite the opposite. Television would do without overtly devotional programmes because everything else was already larded and blessed with theology. It did keep the vestigial evensong of *Songs of Praise*, but Channel 4 now seems to have secularised its ethical early-evening slot, the awkwardly self-conscious three minutes where polyandrous God-botherers could explain how they found time to nag three husbands.

The assumption among people who make television that the nation is no longer deistic is a piece of solipsistic reasoning made while looking in the mirror. Fewer folk may go to the Church of England, but people believe more varied things than they ever did. Atheists, as ever, are an odd minority. And religion has never been more tangible in world affairs and public life. Not having more sensible and serious religious broadcasting isn't modern, it's a failure to face modernity.

Which brings us to *Rev*, Tom Hollander's winning creation of the harassed but well-meaning inner-city vicar in charge of the parable of the crumbling church. There is a litany of religious comedy on television: like the books of the Old Testament, how many can you remember? *All Gas & Gaiters*, *Oh Brother!*, *Father Ted*, *The Vicar of Dibley* and the chuckles with gore and tits that was *The Borgias*. We have a long tradition of apparently ineffectual, apologetic, meek and nerdy priests who turn out, when push comes to shove, to have spines made out of the rood. Hollander's Rev. falls comfortably into the stereotype. It's a character that reflects how the English like to see their own spirituality – as something slightly embarrassing, a bit homemade; woolly, accommodating, but ultimately immutable.

Rev.'s humour is so slight and polite that it knocks before telling a joke. That's not a criticism. There is a dearth of comfortingly cosy humour on television, which is possibly one of the reasons for *Rev.*'s success. The first episode of the new series dealt with the church's relationship with the local mosque, and while the general tone was ecumenical and happy, there was an underlying belief, maybe faith, that drama needs to take the practical truths and hard edges of religion more seriously. And that would be a good thing, because nobody else on television is – mostly for fear of upsetting Muslims, which in itself is insulting to Islam.

Hollander, as ever, is the most subtly detailed comic actor. He doesn't wear his part like fancy dress, and manages to reveal a quiet pathos under the slapstick. And, mentioning polyandry, Olivia Colman must have been married to just about every actor on the box at some time or other. She is a one-size-fits-all family service.

March 2014

Doctor Who

We start with a shot of a dinosaur, lost outside the Palace of Westminster, being gawped at by a lot of extras from *Sherlock*. I wasn't expecting much from *Doctor Who*, but perhaps, at last, they've got a sense of irony. Here was this ancient, clunking special-effects monster, with a brain the size of a walnut, that ought to be extinct, eating up an absurd amount of the licence-fee drama budget, and it only goes and coughs up a police box: perfect, what a clever illustration of the whole sorry franchise. *T. Rex* spit. Then the door opened and it was back to monkey business as usual.

Peter Capaldi, the new Doctor, stumbled out and gurned, then mimed and posed and postured and gasped and growled and flayed and pranced and lolled and gaped and sighed and shrugged his way into the role. He looked like nothing so much as Malvolio doing his impression of Falstaff, who'd been cutting chillies and had a pee without washing his hands first. It wasn't an audition for a new part, rather a postmortem for a venerable career: a perfectly good comic actor with dramatic power and insight measuring himself for his own coffin, which will need to be bigger on the inside than it appears. He put everything in it from every part he's ever had, including random kitchen-sink, and the anecdotes he used to tell when drunk on holiday. Rarely have we been shown quite so much for quite so little: 37 Characters in Search of an Actor.

But then, who can blame him? Well, apart from me, and Melpomene (muse of the theatre: do keep up). He's seen past Doctors vacuuming up the big theatrical roles and interesting films, modelling Edwardian coats in men's magazines, getting propositioned. His agent will be happy, the kids will be proud, the bank will smile. Mind you, it doesn't apply to all former Doctor Whos. I suspect Sylvester McCoy is still available for pantos; he made a brief appearance as an injured ventriloquist on *Casualty* in 2008.

Capaldi is all set to be a bad Doctor Who, because Doctor Who is a dumb, characterless part; he's always bad, they've all been bad, the good actors just as bad as the bad actors. Just regress the silly man back to his first iteration in the 1960s. The idea was a straight steal from H.G. Wells, and the character was Nemo from Jules Verne – the two inventors of science fantasy. Since then, the Doctor has been a collection of discardable tricks and gestures and Edwardian boarding school dressing-up. It was never meant to get this big, but it is now really important for the BBC, and in their panic, it has lost even the modicum of gauche, hokey charm it once had. Now *Doctor Who* looks and sounds like a desperate cash cow being milked by committee; you can hear the nervous coterie of Tristrams second-guessing and memo-ising every aspect of the script.

This is a post-Savile Doctor. There was obviously a concern about the character going from being the romantic interest of his young companion to a chap old enough to be her grandfather. So there's rather too much sweaty-palmed denial of any erotic intent, which is weird and ageist. The rest of it, as ever, is a dismally weak plot, sorted out with the MacGuffin of a magic screwdriver, implausible coincidence, happenstance and just-in-time-ism. The special effects come on like objects in The Antique Steampunk Roadshow, and the prosthetics – a lizard lesbian and a servant who is apparently made out of a polished turd – reminded me of Shatner-era *Star Trek*.

The Doctor turns out to be not unlike Richard Dawkins, madly science-fictive and theophobic, with selective amnesia and vague, formless feelings of charity, which is possibly also an irony, because Dawkins married one of Doctor Who's former girl companions. Mostly, though, this is a damnable waste of drama, money and Capaldi. I suppose we'll have to wait a couple of years before he's released back into the community and can give us his Macbeth, sold out to fans who'll be disappointed that the Thane of Cawdor isn't a bowel movement, Lady M isn't a newt and the blasted heath isn't actually blasted by Daleks.

August 2014

Strictly Come Dancing

You know that summer's over when the shadows are growing longer and *Strictly* and *The X Factor* come round again, a harvest festival of variety and light entertainment. This might fill you with a secure sense of the comforting, spinning Hobnob of time, a confirmation that all is right with the world, and that, despite the weather forecast and the news, God really does hold us in the palm of his living hand. Or it might make you want to join an extremist organisation and strive suicidally for the destruction of Western civilisation.

Personally, I waver somewhere in the middle. I like the idea of light entertainment. It was the oeuvre that launched commercial television and prevented the BBC from growing into a whiskery, good-for-you tool of improvement and common-room sense. Light entertainment is amusement without apology or ambition. It faces the audience and says, I know what you like, my love – not, I know what you ought to like, dear. (Or, I can take what you like and subvert it.) And there is very little light entertainment left; like sphagnum moss, it's endangered. There's tons of dark entertainment, masses of murder and misery, suspense and treachery, loads and loads of embarrassment and schadenfreude.

Yet liking the idea of light entertainment is not the same as actually liking light entertainment, which I don't, because I'm a cultural snob. It's always predictable and repetitive and cheap. Its *mot juste* is, we're just in it for a bit of fun, a bit of glam and glitz and carefree amusement – we're just what the ordinary working family wants at the end of the day. Which assumes that my and your daily lives are dull, monotone grinds, bereft of colour, chiaroscuro, interest or gaiety. Well, that's not the case for me and, I like to imagine, most of you. Actually, almost all of my weekday evenings are far more exciting, witty, glamorous and entertaining than watching *The X Factor*.

So it was with mixed emotions that I sat down to the first preview episode of *Strictly Come Dancing,* which kicked off, both physically and metaphorically, with the public sacking of Bruce Forsyth, a sad, embarrassing and chronic piece of Stalinist stagecraft that was an unhappy reminder of the bit in *Animal Farm* where they take Boxer, the old carthorse, off to the glue factory. They might have given him a gold watch – Bruce, not Boxer – and a card signed by everyone in the office, except he wouldn't know who they were, or what to do with a watch: his timing's been off the wall for years.

I understand that some of you will be thinking that being unkind to an old man at the end of a long career is tasteless, but, pray tell me, which bit of Bruce Forsyth isn't tasteless? The week's most bum-squeaky, chew-your-knuckles moment of turbo-embarrassment was watching him do his little tap dance. There was nothing light or entertaining about that. But then he was led out by Claudia and Tess, his Goneril and Regan, to a blasted heath of bunkers, Velcro shoes, baseball caps and permanent sunshine.

So now there is a brace of female presenters, because Danny Cohen has deemed it so. The director of BBC Television is a zealot for political correctness and gender equality, which he seems to think can be judged by weighing men and women like a recipe. The idea that having two coiffed-up, suggestive girls in sparkly frocks instead of one is a blow for women's lib is absurd, as is the notion that losing Bruce and adding an extra push-up bra makes a programme somehow politically correct. This is a show all about sexual stereotypes – has he ever watched a paso doble? – and getting women into tiny costumes so they can be led around a dance floor, all with an added sprinkle of pre-Larry Grayson gay double entendre.

September 2014

World War One

We are now as far from the Somme as the soldiers who fought there were from Waterloo; but the Great War has a muddy hold on us, in a way the equally decisive Napoleonic wars never had for the Edwardians. This might not be the right moment to call for a deconstruction of the meaning and semiotics of the Great War. But we are past the point of being able to ask anyone who was there what it meant. We are left with a confused and often mawkishly repellent, reductive and saccharine sense of it – as evident in the mire of concepts that struggled to make it current and relevant last week.

The Tristrams are, at best, pacifists about commemorating wars. They'd rather not fight them at all. They don't want to do more hagiographies of soldiers, and the old understated narrative of pride and sadness is not a recipe the BBC can now make with conviction. So they do what Tristrams do when they're stuck with brain ache: they change concepts. They go to the format drawer and see if they can fit an old problem into a new shape.

Bizarrely – though, I grudgingly have to add, bravely – they thought the best way to commemorate a century of European wars was to pretend it was *Autumnwatch*. In place of a weirdly onanistic shed that looks like a boy scouts' camp, they went to the Imperial War Museum and treated it as if it were a wetland bird reserve.

The People Remember was presented by Sophie Raworth, who I see is called 'main relief presenter'. One dreads to think what that entails. Raworth is one of the passing roundabout of competent autocue readers and empathy-dispensers that television thinks it needs to front dull but worthy special events. She was joined (there had to be a man to create the all-important chemistry) by Andy Torbet, who you might have missed. He is an escapist outdoors presenter – like Bear Grylls, but without the sense of having escaped from a locked ward. The BBC call him their 'action man' – what's better than to get Action Man to present a memorial for real soldiers?

The aim was feel-good news: the trenches, like nature, may have been red in tooth and claw, but that doesn't mean we can't glean some Disneyesque tale of pluck, fortitude and a happy ending from them.

The Imperial War Museum is built on the old Bedlam. It was planned as a sarcophagus of remembrance where the detritus of war could bear silent witness. It has now become a Horrible Histories interactive adventure. Oh, oh, oh, what a pathetically poor show this was. Its intentions and ambitions were so small-minded and polite; its format was designed to be ever lively, never deathly.

Then there was *The Passing Bells*, five half-hour episodes that took German and English lads, and followed their 'journey' through conflict. I haven't got to the end yet, but I suspect from the title (a slightly misquoted bit of Wilfred Owen) that this doesn't ring well for them. I caught an interview on morning television with its writer, Tony Jordan; he does scripts for *EastEnders*, and wrote *Hustle* and *Life on Mars*. He is a Tristram's dream. You may have noticed that everything he's written sounds pretty much the same. He has a tone and rhythm, with a limited emotional palette that is dandy for early-evening viewing. It offers short, intense, dramatic pulls and pushes. Every scene is either a crisis or a resolution.

The Passing Bells was a period version of *EastEnders*, with the Fowlers and the Von Beales at opposite sides of the European square, having their sons go off for a barney. The context was delivered with headline-reading brevity, and was absurd. Jordan said what he wanted was to make the war relevant to youth today. As he authoritatively claimed, they didn't feel engaged with this old history stuff. Jordan is 57. What peculiar hotline does he have to the youth of today and their feelings for the Great War? I expect it is the general TV belief that if you dress like a kidult and keep up with YouTube, you will stay down with the kids.

The Passing Bells wasn't awful, it just wasn't about the First World War. It could have been set in the Seven Years' War or the Korean War. It was simple and sentimental, and demanded only that you had a passing understanding of soap operas.

Our collective view of the Great War is shaped by a few writers, mostly poets, and a popular re-evaluation that was made in the 1960s. It's not necessarily accurate, or complete, but at least it is coherent and purposeful. So perhaps it was fitting that by far the best memorial programme of the week was Simon Armitage's *The Great War: An Elegy*, a poet's reaction to a handful of real-life stories, unmediated by drama or fancy formats; simply the stories of people who were caught up in the conflict, remembered by their children and grandchildren.

Armitage wrote a poem for each life. You might have thought the last thing the Great War needed was more poetry, and that it would be a brave poet who ventured into that over-poppied field. But Armitage is a brave poet. And, in a way, while historians squabble and commentators nitpick, poets have become the arbiters and experts of war. This was a touching, delicately profound and poetic programme.

The BBC already has the definitive history of the war, written by Correlli Barnett and John Terraine. *The Great War* was the first significant factual series on TV, full of interviews not with the children and grandchildren of the war, but with the eyewitnesses. It is an irreplaceable and unrepeatable archive, and a defining piece of television. You can get it as a box set, and if you would like your children to be more engaged with the Great War, you could sit and watch it with them, without having to call anyone dude, bump fists or wear a 'This Is What a Tristram Looks Like' T-shirt.

November 2014

Autumnwatch

Let's start with the return of *Autumnwatch*. This has become a telling date in the warp and weft of urban life, like Halloween and Remembrance Sunday. The start of *Autumnwatch* is a reminder to turn up the thermostat, get down to the chemists with a repeat prescription for antidepressants and give thanks that every barnacle goose in the world goes to the Solway Firth and not your local park. Of all the dung invented by Dame Nature, goose crap is one of the worst.

Tristrams put a great deal of time and money into *Autumnwatch*, believing it to be the faerie Celtic green man through the wardrobe and carved heart of BBC1 viewers. A window into the soul of rolling green Albion that is held in perpetuity in the mind's eye of every suburban Englishman who buys calendars with pictures of rapey stags in the Cairngorms on them. (Why do people still buy calendars?)

I can't quite get over how fundamentally weird the live wildlife programme is. It's like being shown round your own home by a team of born-again estate agents. Look, here's the ensuite bathroom, not much happening here at the moment – is that a duck there? Yes, it is definitely a duck, a yellow plastic duck, the first yellow plastic duck of autumn. Marvellous! We'll come back a little later; perhaps there'll be somebody shaving their legs. Now over to Chris, in one of those coats you only ever see in motorway service stations, and always wonder who buys them.

After five minutes of this, I am shouting at the screen: 'I actually live here. I have lived here for twice as long as you've been alive! I know what Outside looks like.'

Autumnwatch is the astonishing patronage of being sold something you already own by somebody you wouldn't let through the door. One of the overemphatic presenters last week said nature programmes on television hadn't done what they were meant to do, improve our relationship with wild stuff. After half a century of Attenborough, species are still disappearing like the sweets of your childhood. And that, apparently, was a terrible failure and a crying shame.

Well, it isn't either of those. The point of nature shows from the audience's perspective is that they are uncomplicated, undemanding, pretty and emotionally winsome, a pleasant way to relax in the evening. It doesn't have anything to do with real life. Nature films are as unlike the experience of being outside as *EastEnders* is of living in the East End.

November 2015

Ageing

Television has a problem with old people. Like a sulky teenager, it doesn't want to be seen out with them, but they pay for everything. Terrestrial television's audience would call itself 'middle-aged'; anyone under the age of 30 would call them 'ancient'. Most BBC customers are in their sixties. And that is the bane of Tristrams' lives. They are desperate to be seen as zeitgeisty and postmillennial. But every time they look at the sofa, it's occupied by dozing folk with plastic teeth and inconti knickers. It's a bummer.

So they make programmes that are about subjects that will interest the elasticated waist and Velcro shoe folk – about history and rural murders and property makeovers (only pensioners can afford a house or an extension) – but then give them younger, trendier presenters. So, rather in the manner of Simon Cowell, they look preternaturally youthful but sound geriatric. TV isn't ready to face up to old age in an adult way.

Take *A Granny's Guide to the Modern World*. This was a bizarre compilation of genres familiar to the old – a bit of infotainment, a snatch of *That's Life*, a touch of vox pop and gentle practical-joke comedy. The premise was that old people don't have any idea how the 21st century works, or indeed what it's for, so they need to be taught, in a larky and patronising way, what's what.

For instance, they are all strangers to political correctness, so we were shown old gits asking young Afro-Caribbean persons of self-divined gender if it's still acceptable to call people 'nignogs'. And the young giggled and said, no, not really. They giggled because you can't take old people seriously: you can't be offended by them – it would be like being offended by a pet. Then an old lady asked a couple of hi-vis builders to teach her how to swear. 'Wanker usually comes with a hand gesture – like this, love,' she is helpfully told. Three old ladies were taken to Amsterdam, to be shown how to roll joints and smoke bongs, and were then dumped in a playground to play on the swings.

The first thing I noticed about all of this is that the setups were all wholly unconvincing, not least because they were so unlikely. Could you actually believe that anybody born during the war, who grew up with National Service, lived through punk and the old football terraces, would be a stranger to swearing? And how likely was it that anyone could have lived through the 1960s and 1970s, heard Enoch Powell and Martin Luther King and not understood racism? Or, indeed, how to roll a joint? The programme's premise was that old people were simpletons, unobservant, gullible and increasingly ignorant. The precise opposite of the truth. But it is somehow necessary to reduce them to being innocents with rheumatism, so they can be pitied and passed over.

The programme was presented by Barry Humphries, who seemed to have little to do with the content. He offered the only amusing, indeed germane, part of the programme, and it made you want to see more of him on TV as himself, rather than his alter egos. It's worth noting that Humphries is 82. He was born during the Great Depression and was 11 when the war finished. Nobody would suggest he is a stranger to swearing or unaware of political correctness or which end of a joint is which. Age and experience have made him witty, dry (apparently), urbane and clever, in ways that only come with age. So how young and foolish do you have to be to make a programme that purports to prove one thing, presented by somebody who is living proof that it isn't true?

There were two documentaries last week that showed us how very weird and awkward the past was, one on the 1980s, the other on 1966. In *The 8os*, Dominic Sandbrook continued his thoughtful search through the rags and bones of popular culture on the still warm rubbish heap of history. Most of the BBC's audience still remember the 1980s; even so, Sandbrook introduced the era as if it were archaeology, with the headline-grabbing assertion that the prime mover of the decade was a strong, determined housewife. No, not Margaret Thatcher, but Delia Smith. Apparently, it wasn't breaking the miners, mothballing the docks, selling off council houses, invading the Falklands and massaging Ronald Reagan's prostate that defined the decade. They were as nothing compared to teaching the nation how to bake lasagne.

Sandbrook's thesis is that history is made by unorchestrated mass movements, serendipity, technology and fashion. So it was the Treaty of Versailles, hyperinflation, the rise of communism and Lotte Lenya that brought about the Second World War, not Hitler. Well, I'm all for the social, technological and cultural recipe for history, but I also remember (most of) the 1980s and must point out that at the time it did seem to be Margaret Thatcher's fault. Certainly more than Delia's. And Sandbrook got the food thing wrong: it wasn't all about home cooking, aspiration, microwaves and pesto. This was the decade of fast food, cheap fat and sugar. It was when the old caff got rolled over by Macky Ds, KFC, pizzas and doners. This was the great farting dawn of the takeaway.

It was also the decade when the people, after 20 years of activism and raised fists, seemed to be at their most powerless. It was the decade of bad music and good films; of the rise of multinationals, big government and international bankers. So I disagreed with a lot of Sandbrook's marketing and PR conclusions, but he made a good argument that I wanted to engage in. He is a winning and smartly agreeable presenter, though with a bit too much smug walking out of shot, having delivered a killer line. And the parka with the fur collar was a bad style choice for a bald, middle-aged man.

I also remember 1966; indeed, I watched the World Cup as it happened, on our small fuzzy set in its Regency-style cabinet. It was exciting, but not ecstatic. The mythologising of 1966 has grown exponentially in retrospect. At the time there wasn't a lot of football on TV; it was a game followed by old men in caps with embarrassing rattles. It seemed deeply uncool, un-now. That year was all about the Beatles and the Stones and Wilson's government, the Rhodesian crisis, nuclear disarmament and, above all, Vietnam.

Generation 66, though, was thuddingly dull, concentrating instead on all the weird and inexplicable things humans had to put up with, or didn't have, back in black-and-white. It is a rule of historical documentaries that the denizens of the past must all be naive, simple and ignorant. The universal given of all history is that it's a one-way ratchet: stuff gets inexorably better, more comfortable and sophisticated. So kids today must be altogether an improvement on yesterday's kids.

After *Generation 66*, they showed *Cathy Come Home*, one of the most important and influential TV programmes of all time. I hadn't seen it since 1966, so I sat tensely waiting to be disappointed. But from the first shot I was again enthralled. It is still brilliant, perhaps even more gripping and compelling than I remembered. The montaging of real footage with the story of this young family trying to find a home; the voiceover delivering dry political and economic fact; the tight, intimate camerawork; the naturalistic script – still unspeakably moving. What was so freshly shocking was how current it still is: home ownership at the lowest it's been for decades, the housing deficit critical and young families still bearing the worst of it.

So there we have it: the best programme on TV last week was made in 1966. In black-and-white. Not everything gets better.

August 2016

LIFE

Clouds House

The house is large, too large to be a family home but not big enough to be a country hotel. It is pretty but not exceptional, meriting only a dismissive sentence in Pevsner. You approach it down a dark drive of leggy rhododendrons and laurels; the view at the bottom is wonderful, beyond the ha-ha stretches and folded chalk of Wiltshire.

I saw it first six years ago on 1 April. The bluebells were just finishing and the daffodils starting, or maybe the bluebells were starting and the daffodils were finishing. My grip on the natural rhythm of things was shaky. My grip on most things was shaky. I stood in the spring sunshine, pigeons cooed, flowers nodded, the clouds scudded and I swallowed hard on the rising foam of tears and vomit. How unfair that I should have been reduced to this. At the age of 30, my best endeavours, a river of booze and a desert of chemicals had brought me to the bon viveurs' Lubyanka – a drying-out clinic.

'Well, I'm afraid you're an alcoholic; there really isn't any doubt about it.' Two weeks earlier I had been sitting in a tasteful private doctor's consulting room and a tasteful private doctor had told me that I was an alcoholic. 'Fine.' I tried to make it sound mildly in-convenient, but not worrying. 'What can you give me for it?' 'It doesn't work like that. I can't prescribe you any drugs. You would simply abuse them and drink. Anyway, you should go to a treatment centre. I can book you in now. It's expensive, but I strongly recom-mend you go.' 'Fine, but not right now. I'll go in two weeks.' 'Two weeks . . . that's 1 April then.' He smiled at a tasteful private joke.

It is 2 April and I am sitting in my first group-therapy session. I have just spent my first night in treatment. This is the first day in 10 years that I haven't started with a drink. This is not what I expected. This is hell. I don't know quite what I did expect – fruit juice and brisk walks, housey-housey and stern lectures from low-church ministers, but not this. This is like some awful parody of boarding school, the same smells, the same gloss paint and tatty furniture; inmates being sent and summoned by bells, books to read, homework and, worst of all, dormitories. I am sharing a room with five other poor bastards, ranging from a scholarly-looking heroin dealer who has just had his leg amputated, to a cacophonously flatulent transcontinental lorry driver who couldn't stop having one for the road. I'm put in the bed by the door. Later I learn that alcohol withdrawal can be fatal. They put new boys next to the door just in case. I have my blood pressure taken every 20 minutes. All night.

By the time the bell goes at 7 am I want to die. The nurse gives me a Heminevrin, a sort of shandy in a pill that takes the edge off the shakes. I can't face breakfast. The morning is spent filling in multiple-choice forms. Have you ever stolen money to buy drink? Yes. Have you ever manufactured an argument so that you could go out for a drink? Yes. Have you ever gone to bed with an inappropriate partner because you were drunk? Oh my God, yes. Have you ever had blackouts, shakes, hepatitis, DTs, partial paralysis, peripheral neuritis? Yes, yes, yes. Page after page of little ticks. I can't face lunch.

'Group' is the central core of treatment, 10 chairs ranged in a circle. The meeting is facilitated by a counsellor who is a recovering addict and alcoholic. He is an unappetising little chap who chainsmokes, has bitten fingernails and appalling shoes. I, on the other hand, smoke a different brand, have long filthy nails and am wearing someone else's appalling shoes.

The group is the engine that drives treatment; if the group doesn't work, treatment doesn't work. There is no particular magic involved, just a lot of talking. Why this should work when so many other more complicated therapies fail is a mystery. But work it does. Most alcoholics have tried dozens of different strategies to halt the steady decline from social drinking to park bench: going to psychiatrists, changing jobs, changing homes, changing drinks, changing partners, only drinking at weekends, never drinking before 6 pm, going to health clubs, reading self-help books, taking prescribed drugs, aversion therapy, acupuncture and good old-fashioned willpower. The list is endless. The vast majority die trying to contain an increasingly chronic condition. The lucky few make it to AA via a treatment centre or on their own.

Sitting in my first group feeling sad and sick and lonely, I didn't feel in the slightest bit lucky. The next hour convinced me that I had been handed over to the Moonies' Gestapo. 'So, tell us a little bit about yourself and why you're here.' I mutter a few anodyne platitudes: 'Bit of a drink problem ... life somewhat at sixes and sevens ... need time to re-evaluate ... bit of a breather – glad for any help you can offer ...' and finish with a winning smile. The group stares at me. A girl sitting opposite leans forward and shouts, literally shouts, 'What a fucking crock of shit. You're just a snotty sick alcoholic. Christ, get fucking real.'

I am so horrified I can't reply. I can feel tears pricking my eyes. I turn helplessly to the counsellor. He just looks at me with a seen-it-all-before expression, and says, 'Sarah's right. You must be scrupulously honest with the group. We all know what it's like. We've all been there; just sit back and listen. Try to hear the similarities to your life. Don't concentrate on the differences.' The group continues, with everyone taking a turn to talk, some mumbling evasively, some garrulous with born-again enthusiasm, but all recounting sad, horrifying, funny episodes, laced with the sort of words I associated with polytechnic psychologists or Californian gurus. I concentrate on feeling sorry for myself and thinking of a ghastly revenge for Sarah. Sarah, I later learn, is a one-time model and social gad. Her family live in a house on Cheyne Walk and she went to St Mary's Ascot. She is also a junkie whose family have changed the locks to stop her selling any more of their possessions. She has borrowed or stolen money from everyone she knows. Before coming here she was working as a prostitute on the Earl's Court Road.

There is a point when all alcoholics or addicts in treatment reach a crossroads. They either believe that their lives can be rescued from the brink with the help of others, or they don't. If they do, things start to change quite fast. If they don't, they usually discharge themselves, trusting in some personal scheme to save their lives. Realistically, their chances are almost nil. I saw a glimmer of hope quite early. After about a week the worst of the withdrawals had abated. I grew to enjoy the boarding-school life of chores and walks, groups and tutorials with a counsellor – a nice old gent who had been sober as long as I'd been alive. I had a small covey of friends: Cathy, a sometime stylist; Sabrina, a manqué actress, and Dickie, a City banker with a bright red face to match his bright red braces and an endless, excruciating fund of cricketing metaphors.

The moment I saw that the promises of a new life might just perhaps apply to me was late one night in the dorm after lights out. We were talking quietly. I felt pleasantly sleepy and the voices coming out of the dark made me feel safe. The chap who now slept in the bed by the door was a young tramp from the Midlands. He spoke with a slow Brummie accent. He was in a terrible state, very close to death. He started telling us his story. Until two years previously he had lived with his widowed mother, drinking whatever he could get his hands on. He ran out of money and his mother refused to give him another penny. One Monday morning, Mother took her widow's mite to the cash-and-carry, leaving her son desperate and thirsty. He called a local junk shop and told them his mother had just died and could they please take away her belongings for cash. With £200 in his pocket he left a home containing nothing except a brief note saying sorry. The money was soon exhausted. He ended up living in a public lavatory in the centre of Birmingham, begging and stealing. Finally, he arrived in treatment via a casualty ward. Why, I asked, if he had no commitments, had he decided to live in a public loo in Birmingham? 'Oh. I did manage to get away at the weekends,' he said. 'I had a little place in the country – a telephone box outside Milton Keynes.'

I laughed until the tears ran down my face and my sides ached. In the darkness the others choked and sobbed with laughter, bedsteads squeaking, mattresses groaning – every time we stopped to catch our breath someone would wheeze 'Milton Keynes' or 'telephone box' and we'd be off again, shrieking like schoolboys. It wasn't as if it was that funny. I had smiled wanly at far better jokes in bars any day of the week. This was different. It was the companionship, the camaraderie. We were all in it together; sad and frightened, we had all recognised a small piece of ourselves in the story. The chain of events, the feelings, all had a ghastly familiarity. It was the laughter of relief. We had stepped out of the chamber of horrors and if we stayed away from the first drink, we wouldn't have to go back.

The next morning I felt lighter. The pall of nameless doom that alcoholics wake up to had lifted, as had the desire to sink a can of Special Brew. That wasn't the end, of course. I wasn't cured – there isn't a cure, just a remission. Neither was it all plain sailing from then on, but I had seen the point and I did have hope. Treatment continued. I learnt to listen to other drunks and identify with them. Alcoholics aren't all tramps. In fact very few of them are. They come from every conceivable walk of life and their stories are all as unique as snowflakes, but within them there are patterns that are common to all. The identification of these patterns forms a special bond.

I left treatment six weeks later. In a practical sense, that is when my recovery began. It is one thing to stay sober in a protective, closed environment where no one drinks, and quite another to try it in the real world, where everyone does. I had learnt, however, that by talking to other drunks and junkies I could survive; more than just survive, I could live with gusto. As Dickie had put it, 'If life's still bowling you bouncers, then what's the point?'

Dickie himself never got the point. He never stopped drinking. Six months later he died in a hotel room in Spain, out of a family and out of his head. Sarah didn't make it either. She spent the next three years in and out of treatment centres, never managing more than a few clean months each time. Finally an overdose ended it. Cathy made it. So did Sabrina. No one really knows in percentage terms how successful treatment centres are. Of the handful of patients that I was with, maybe half of them are still happily living sober. Fifty per cent may not seem like terribly good odds, but they are a damn sight better than you can find elsewhere.

Anyone who has had a couple of drinks thinks they understand what it is like to be an alcoholic. We have all been drunk, we have all had a hangover, we have all done something a bit silly, all had one too many. But the difference is not just one of degree – it's like comparing having a bath to swimming the Channel. The Channel is longer, lonelier, far more dangerous and a whole lot wetter.

September 1991

Fashion

The Galleria Vittorio Emanuele is a shopping arcade. At one end is La Scala and at the other the Milan Duomo, the second largest church in Christendom. The galleria is no ordinary mall. It is to Burlington Arcade in London what Gianni Versace is to Jeff Banks. This is the biggest, most histrionic promenade in Italy. And this week, Milan Fashion Week, the world has come to see and be seen.

The old men of Milan, too, come here to talk, all year round. They move in little gaggles, very slowly with great gravitas. I sat and watched a group outside Prada, the handbag shop where you can on impulse buy a very thin, very discreet crocodile wallet for the price of an airline ticket to Sydney.

This year, ancient Italian men are wearing generously cut worsted suits, either with waistcoat or cardigan, in natural earth colours with muted checks. Ties are carelessly knotted and discreet, and collar sizes are too big for the neck. Hats are in, shoes are brown and highly polished, and elasticated clip-on braces seem to be making a comeback. The whole look is rather like Quasimodo Medici meets Jimmy Hoffa.

The show eddies and shimmers around these little islands of ruminating retired burghers. A crocodile of tiny matt-black Japanese girls files past, questing labels like polite, smiley soldier ants. German fashion editors in short skirts with bulldozer knees and steel-tipped blitzkrieg pumps hurry to their next show. Impossibly tasteful New York editors carrying vast sea-snake Filofaxes try to look European, their hair as glossy as mink, cut in that dramatically understated I've-no-time-for-all-this, working-girl way that needs only two visits to the hairdresser a week. Navigating down the middle of the walk is a woman who looks like an indecisive Ivana Trump who, because she was unable to make up her mind, decided to wear everything in the steamer trunk. She's sweating and glowing because she's pushing her daughter in a wheelchair. The girl is about 16, pretty and embarrassed. She has been dressed in an expensive silk two-piece suit with gold Chanel earrings, and a quilted bag hangs by a chain from the armrest. On her feet are black patent leather court shoes with clean soles. Her atrophied legs are swagged in black silk stockings. The skirt is very short. The elaborate lacy tops show against her white thighs. Her mother's having difficulty getting the chair into Prada. The door is heavy and there are steps. The assistants with the Novocaine expressions watch without helping. Milan Fashion Week isn't designed for the disabled. Not the physically disabled, anyway.

You can't pick up a newspaper these days without thinking that the world has gone mad. Well, nothing will more convince you that the whole of western civilisation is utterly, howlingly, stark-staringly, foamingly doolally than the collections will. If they finished the shows with a grand catwalk parade of Naomi, Kate, Helena and Claudia wearing spangly straitjackets, I wouldn't be in the slightest bit surprised, and neither would the fashion editors. They would just go and blow a week's rent on one and tell you to do the same.

I've never been to a fashion show before, but I've seen so many on television and in magazines that I thought I knew what they were like. No image can prepare you for the truly disturbing 3-D reality. First you get to a doorway in a side street that's blocked with crash barriers and riot police and badly parked winking Mercedes with lounging, winking drivers. There's a huge scrum of fashion victims all shouting and waving their hands, breaking off every so often to kiss each other and make foreplay noises. On the door are squads of camp couture Stasi in suits and hatchet-faced girls with long legs and lists. When you've finally shoved your way in past a dozen impeccably rude bouncers there is a dark room with a raised catwalk, a backdrop and ranks of tiny chairs. At the end of the catwalk there is a bank of photographers packed so tightly that their vast lenses mould into one and look like a single huge composite bluebottle eye. The smudgers and the camera crews argue and snap at each other like starlings on a town hall. A Stasi in a suit unceremoniously evicts the Korean gatecrasher who is in my chair. She looks unconcerned and moves down two seats.

In the gloaming I watch the audience scramble in, middle-aged women with puffy legs wearing tiny dresses, and see-through black silk shirts over cretonne bosoms propped up on bony rolling lacy corsets. Fortysomething ladies with leather skin and leopard-fur hair the texture of guinea pigs' beds stumble over the furniture because they're too vain to take off their dark glasses in a room where you really need a torch. An ancient crone sits beside me. She's got hands like carmine-tipped liver-spotted claws and her lips have so much collagen in them that her mouth won't close properly. If the women are bad, then the men are worse. The woman who is dressed ten years younger than her passport is sad but understandable. A balding American fashion editor with a pigtail, a Johnny Depp beard, a paunchy male version of the Elizabeth Hurley dress, all safety pins down the side, and a cravat is beyond pity. Nobody looks normal, nobody here could walk down the aisle at Sainsbury's without accompanying laughter. These are professional fashion watchers, men and women whose whole lives are dedicated to knowing what looks good, what is chic; they spend hours dressing models for photographs and then poring over the transparencies. You wonder what happens to their eyes when they look in the mirror. Fashion professionals don't see things like you or I. The whole room is a zebra pelt of black and white and that colour that has been the fashion staple for so long they've invented a dozen names for it – taupe, camel, fawn, buff. Frankly, it's beige. Suzy Menkes hurries in and takes her seat, front and centre. She is the fashion correspondent for the *International Herald Tribune* and by the lights of the arcane pecking order of this bizarre business is accepted as the queen bee. Her hair looks as though she has forgotten to take out one of the curlers, but it's not funny. It's her personal fashion statement. The show can begin. Music, lights, models.

If the fashion writers look odd, they at least have recognisable human shapes. The models are from another planet. No photograph prepares you for the way they look in the absence of flesh. A photograph adds a stone to everybody's image. These girls are fuse-wire thin and unbelievably tall. Their legs are like grissini, barely capable of taking the weight of their etiolated bodies. They move in an odd, careful, swaying way that is newborn and uncoordinated, like creatures who would be happier slithering on their tummies and have just been made to walk upright. Their shoulders look like universal spanners, their chests like xylophones, their tendoned necks sway and jerk their bony heads with ears that look like folded bats' wings. They have glazed, sedated eyes, and the ones who don't seem terrified look to me to be psychotic. Nobody normal could aspire to look this way.

The models teeter and sway down the catwalk, pause momentarily and grimace at the giant flashing bug eye. It's impossible to say how many girls are in a collection because so many of them look the same. At the Dolce e Gabbana show I thought there were only eight girls. At the end, about 30 came out and clapped and took a bow. One who is instantly recognisable is Nadja Auermann, a terrifying-looking specimen with hair like the chrome bumper on a Chevy and eyes the colour of mineral water. She's not the sort of person you want to meet in a dark alley. All the models have minders who run them from show to show on the back of scooters. Nadja looks as though she probably has a trainer and travels in a circus cage. The minute the show finishes there's a smattering of applause from the planted claque and we all crowd for the door, ten steps behind Menkes whose bobbing quiff hits the street at a sprint.

This scenario is repeated every half-hour from nine in the morning to eight at night for five days. The models do it over and over again, always late, always uncomfortable, shouted at, gay-manhandled, bullied and permanently starving. The top two or three might get a couple of thousand a show, but most of these poor creatures count their earnings in hundreds and a few free shirts. I stumbled out of my first collection feeling as if I'd taken part in something degrading. The closest thing I'd ever seen to this was a pub strip show. This is striptease for fetishists who want sexless girls to put clothes on. By the fourth show I was talking hem lengths and pastel shades with the best of them.

At lunch a shrill posse of London fashion editors are talking with blasé excitement over the mozzarella and rocket: 'Oh my God, blusher's back.' 'And more corsets!' 'Is smoking in again?' I ask whether they don't think the models look, well, sort of strange. 'Oh, yes, Helena's got so fat. Did you see her tummy!' (Helena Christensen is about 5ft 11in. She's reported to be size 6-ish.) Has the fact that so many of the design houses have been accused of fraud and bribery affected the shows? Six pairs of hard chic eyes stare at me uncomprehending. Am I mad? Versace, Armani and the rest are above the law; the law is for people who shop at Next. They could have accused Messrs Dolce and Gabbana of having dead puppies in their fridges, but they'd still have excellent tailoring and do wonderful things with ostrich feathers.

At night, after the shows, there's dinner, and parties for those who've still got the energy. I went to the bash for 30 years of Italian *Vogue* in an architecturally fascist gallery. It was full of black and white and beige people, silly cocktail frocks worn with gumboots. I doubt if there was a room anywhere in the world that night with more titanically lusted-after people in it. It was so, so utterly sexless. Everyone looked as if, given the choice between a demon lover and the perfect handbag, they'd go for the bag. They were so bored, so miserable, so slidey-eyed and self-conscious. It was as if every invitation had come with an RSVP suicide note. This was one of the top ten industries in the world having a good time, letting its lacquered hair down, and I couldn't fathom why it was all so joyless. Fashion is, after all, great fun; shopping is the second of life's great pleasures. How come, here at the centre of it all, they're bonkers and gloomy? We, you and I, wear clothes as outward and visible signs of our internal desires, aspirations and characters. We bring our lives to our wardrobes, but here on the catwalk and in the Stygian auditoria, the clothes are the people. What's outside is also what's inside.

In the arcade, the small, solemn huddles of old men continue their peregrinations. 'So, signor. I hear that blusher is back?' 'Si, si, and more corsetry.' 'More corsetry, you say, good, good.'

October 1995

Pornography

'Dead puppies,' shouts a barely controlled voice from the dark. Dead puppies. I'm laughing so hard I think I'm going to strain something. We're all laughing that whooping, rip-roaring laughter that comes along all too rarely after you're old enough to have your own overdraft. Back-of-the-school-bus, infectious hysteria. We're all laughing here in the dark. Five feet away in a bright pool of light, a man wearing only a chef's hat at a rakish angle is manipulating the end of a vast penis as if it had a childproof cap. A naked woman with breasts the size and texture of pink bowling balls is lying, legs akimbo, in a wedding cake. They're not laughing. 'Dead puppies' is the technical term for 'shut the fuck up and concentrate'.

'Sex, please,' shouts another voice from the hot blackness. 'Rolling, speed, action,' and the chef heaves the penis like a sock of billiard balls at the girl's frosted sphincter. It nuzzles the puckered blind eye like a physics problem – how do you get a quart into a shot glass? How do you get an elephant into a telephone box? How in God's name do you get that monstrous willy up a bum? The chef spreads his feet on the sticky floor for purchase, places a hand on his own muscular buttock for leverage, and pushes. A single marine raising the flag on Iwo Jima, the staff bends then takes the strain. The girl's dead-tarantula eyelashes flutter, her pink-taloned fingers grip her own hock and the knob begins to disappear. Inch by truncheon-inch. The breasts, two true troopers, never move – they don't even shudder. In the darkness there is a faint drawing-in of breath. Let me tell you, nothing Paul Daniels ever made vanish was remotely as awe-inspiring or captivatingly magic as this.

It's halfway through the second and final day of shooting *Hot House Tales,* my debut as a director – my debut as a film writer also, actually – and I've spent most of it helpless with mirth or transfixed with admiration. I'm in Hollywood, well, Hollywood Lite, and I'm an author. I'm a player. I'm a name. I'm a call-back. I'm a table-hopping destination. I'm in movies. This is the dream, my dream, that I've had since my mother took me to see my first porn movie, *The Devil In Miss Jones,* in Times Square when I was 19. The idea that you could realise your hot, sweaty-fisted fantasies and make them happen, show them in Technicolor, is the ultimate boys' fantasy. All my adult life I've wanted to have a pneumatic woman buggered on a wedding cake by a cartoonishly hung black man. Who hasn't? It was surprisingly easy to make it happen. This is America, after all. A country addicted to making dreams come true and pneumatic breasts.

Metro, one of the biggest adult entertainment companies, with a multimillion-pound turnover and a listing on the Nasdaq, was only too happy to have an unknown hack write and direct a movie and do a feature on it. In fact they had a free slot in a month. Could they possibly have an 80-minute script by Monday? (It was Friday.) For the next two days I asked everyone I knew what they wanted to see in a porn movie. Is there a consensus as to what's sexy? I particularly wanted to know what women found erotic. Men's fantasies are all either desperately predictable – naughty underwater nurses, surprised maids, bored housewives – or solitary-user specific, as in: 'I've always wanted to see really elegant girls in evening gowns scrabbling through piles of manure for diamonds.' I'd imagined that women would want a story, a context and, above all, romance. In fact, all the women I spoke to had the same fantasy: anonymous sex. Fucking a stranger. Just eye-contact and then down to it. Well I never, I must have brushed past a million women since I was 16 and never once have I been propositioned. I thought you had to make them laugh first, at least.

I started off with a list of things that didn't turn me on – spotty bums; socks (porn stars wear them because they think dirty feet are even less sexy); clichéd, aggressive swearing of the 'you know you want it, you dirty bitch' type; snarling; cheap jewellery; stick-on nails, and most of all, the violent domination and humiliation that's so often a feature in pornography. Metro had its own requirements. It faxed a list of movie must-haves: six to eight females and four to six males.

One female will be the star, be featured on the video box and do two scenes. There should be seven scenes in total, of the following types: boy-girl; girl-girl; girl-girl-boy; girl-boy-boy; girl-anal; boy-girl oral; and solo girl masturbation. However, girls wanking is something else that doesn't do it for me, so I ditched that and started typing with my other hand. The plot had to be simple, the dialogue simpler. 'They don't do talking,' Susan Yanetti, Metro's sardonic and amused PR, told me. 'Really. They won't read the script and they can't act. It's not what they do.'

After some thought, I decided to set my vignettes in the rooms of a cheap boarding house, and have them all link up, like *La Ronde*. Some would be funny, some deeply erotic. In all of them, the power would be with the women. Initially, I wanted each scene to be surprising – something I hadn't seen before. But as I started writing, I realised that many of my fantasies were second-hand, formed by erotic films I'd seen or books I'd read. And much eroticism is in a nuance – the sway of a hip, the look in an eye – something intangible that fires a spark between the screen and the viewer. Still, the plot came fast and I started to have a ball. (It's impossible to talk about pornography in anything but *double entendres*. Just ignore them.) I plagiarised the *Decameron*, the *Canterbury Tales* and Greek myths for storylines. I'm telling you – writing a porn film is the best fun.

At 4 am on Sunday, I faxed the script to Metro and waited for the call. Susan Yanetti called me back within a few hours. 'I reckon we've got a porno movie here,' she said. 'It's very good. Really, you have a talent for this. It's much better than the stuff we normally get.'

Let me tell you, I have won more than my fair share of press awards. I have been paid disgusting amounts of money to write for prestigious magazines. I have had fan mail from Elizabeth Hurley, and been kissed by Michael Winner. But nothing – no gong or compliment – had ever filled me with such pride.

However, Susan had some changes. 'A lot of this is way over the customers' heads, let alone the actors'. And this boy-on-boy scene has got to go or they won't stock it in the shops. The merest hint of homosexuality and the poor dears lose their erections. Remember, what we're making is a masturbation aid; the wankers can't handle a hint of gayness. And I think we have to drop the scene where the Chinese girl smokes a joint in her vagina and says, "My pussy's got the munchies for you."

'Why?' I asked. 'Can't you find a girl who can do pelvic floor-exercises?'

'It's not that – it's drugs. They're real strict about that.'

'So you can have a girl gang-banged by twenty strangers in ways which are illegal in eighteen states, but smoking grass is immoral?'

'Adrian, this is America.'

This is Van Nuys. It is 40 minutes outside Beverly Hills and 208 hotter. It has a baked-on, low-level grimness which should make it illegal to buy razor blades here without a prescription. The Metro office is situated in a prefab hangar in a street of hangars beside a military airport. The Tomcats howl orgasmically up the runway, but everything else is eerily silent. You'd never know what they did here.

Inside the offices, there is a matter-of-fact air. There is not an inflated breast in sight – the pictures on the walls are, bizarrely, Disney animation drawings. Susan greets us and gives me my re-written script. To say that it had been emasculated wouldn't be entirely accurate. Everything that isn't masculation has been filleted; a plot and dialogue that I'd thought *Sesame Street*-simple is now Care in the Community remedial.

But never mind. It's a movie script, it's got my name on it, and we're in production. We have our first production meeting with the producer and cameraman – two young dudes in shorts and band T-shirts with futuristic facial hair, both called Michael (though the cameraman calls himself 'Quasar Man'). They are a team. They make 20-odd movies a year and they talk like a double-act, finishing each other's sentences, sliding into pop-song riffs, and making each other snigger. Quasar Man is Canadian and has a Tourette's-like obsession with talking in an Austin Powers accent and clicking the air with inverted commas. Ironically, of course. They are like the Valley version of Beavis and Butt-head and I like them immediately. The production meeting is brief.

'Have you got any questions?'

'No.'

'Good. We'll see you on the set.'

Before we begin filming, Susan shows me round the warehouse at the back of the hangar. Racks of VCRs are continuously making copies, while thousands of videos lie waiting to be packed and shipped. The films are arranged by subject: black men; white girls; gang-bangs; nurses; gay men; transsexuals; and anal (or 'A', as it's known). There is also a section devoted to double-A – two penises in one bottom – a thought which makes the mind boggle and the cheeks clench.

Porn is one of the biggest businesses in the world. In America alone it turns over $7–10bn a year – that's more than Hollywood. Worldwide, it grosses half a trillion. The cosy, liberal assumption that pornography is a sad, solitary, under-the-mattress toss-aid for socially inept, underclass old men is patently untrue. A few low-rent, dirty old wankers and some hairy-palmed students simply don't generate that sort of money. But then, no one does know actually who's watching this stuff – although we all assume we know why.

'Nobody has ever done any real market research,' says Susan. 'There is no demographic picture because people just lie about sex. It's stiff with hypocrisy, guilt and shame. But, essentially, pornography is bought by men. Women may watch it and enjoy it, but no woman rents a video to watch on her own with her hand down her knickers.'

I asked how many films Metro had in its catalogue. 'No one's counting,' says Susan, 'but it must be 25,000 at least. They get re-edited and made into compilations.' That's just one company and it's all been made in the last 15 years.

Porn's boom came with video. It is said that it was the porn industry that killed Betamax by choosing VHS. Certainly, it is the porn industry that is driving DVD – for every mainstream video title there are 12 porn titles available. An American computer company wanted to advertise the power of the Internet by listing the top ten most popular sites. It gave up, because all of them were porn. In fact, the top 20 sites are porn with the singular exception of the Mormons' Doomsday Census.

*

The studio is low-rent and decrepit, but fantastically exciting to me because my boarding house has finally come to life. Each room has been built and dressed with remarkable care and authenticity. They all look deeply seedy.

Among the collateral pleasures of porn are the stunningly hideous bedspreads, coffee tables and pictures in the backgrounds. If you ever wondered where they come from, I can tell you there's a props room in the Valley that is the British Museum of solitary ejaculation. Hundreds of horrendous beds, sofas, lamps, statues, rhinestone-covered telephones, soft toys, kitchens and operating theatres. It's an X-rated style obscenity all of its own.

Upstairs in make-up, Clarissa is being plastered for the first scene. My story called for a Vietnamese girl. Clarissa is half-Mexican – close – and also very young and exceedingly nervous. I try to talk to her about motivation and the Method.

'Have you actually read the script?'

'Yes.' She's such a bad actress she can't even lie in a single affirmative believably. This is only her second movie and she's terrified of being recognised, so has insisted on a wig. Unfortunately, the wig is exactly the same colour, cut and length as her own hair (she's not bright). 'It'll be fine,' I say. 'You look wonderful.' She smiles gratefully, proving I'm a better actor than she is. She has every reason to be nervous. Her scene is with Ron Jeremy and she's never seen him.

Ron Jeremy is a god, there's no two ways about it. He is the most famous male porn star in America and he's hideous. Truly, madly, deeply hideous. Fat, short, balding – he is a soft, dank, hairy fast-food bin with a greasy Village People moustache. Ron is the Mickey Rooney of porn: he's been around since naughty postcards and has had everyone. They all love Ron. He's funny and he can act. Trouble is, no one wants to fuck him any more. Clarissa is getting a $200 premium to do it with Ron.

When Ron arrives, he's wearing a filthy red T-shirt and shorts that do nothing for him. 'Hey,' he yells, 'great script!'

'Don't take any notice,' whispers Mike the producer. 'He says that every time.'

Ron wants to talk about motivation. He knows his lines and he takes it all very seriously. 'Hey, I've done legit work, you know. I've done England. I've been on Ruby Wax twice.' (My, there aren't a lot of men who can say that.) 'Look, I brought some costumes along. See what you think.' He produces a plastic bag containing three T-shirts and three pairs of shorts – all grubby, identical variations on the vile things he's already wearing.

I get my first bad set of giggles.

The scene doesn't go well. Clarissa sees Ron and goes as stiff as a board. She's the only thing that does. Ron, once famous for being able to auto-fellate, come on cue and hit a nostril at five paces, can't get it up. He has to use what is technically known as the 'kung fu death grip' – pinching the base of his penis so hard the blood can't get out. Clarissa is horrified.

'Just a minute,' Ron pants. Gunther, the video tech, groans. 'The three words you never want to hear on a set are: "Just a minute." It means the talent can't get wood.' In the end, the scene is cut down to a facial. That is, Ron wanks on to Clarissa's cheek. It's not pretty, it's not erotic and it's not a good start. I follow her out into the sunlight. 'Are you all right?' I ask. She says she's fine – she's grateful for the money but isn't sure she's going to do it again.

Being able to achieve and sustain an erection to order is the great improbable at the heart of porn movies. Very few men can do it. Lots think they can, but in the business there are only about 25 men who work regularly. Viagra is changing that, but no one with an ounce of professional pride will admit they use it.

The next scene – boy-girl-girl – has the best, most sought-after erection in the business. It's British and (wouldn't you know?) it's from Essex. Stephen Scott – whose stage name is, incomprehensibly, Mark Davies – has been voted Best Male Porn Star three times at Cannes. The crew love him. 'Woody' is his middle name. He gets it up, goes grinding on and on like the good ship *Venus* and then ejaculates in a blur of fist. Most importantly, the girls love doing it with him. One of the many myths about porn films is that they exploit women. Philosophically, we can argue about it but, practically, it's quite the reverse. The girls get paid up to three times more than the men, can choose their male partners and their positions. Mark is in demand, sometimes making two films a day. He's been in the sex business since he was 17, first as a stripper and then as a Chippendale. He's also easy-going and charming. As we chat about England and California, I quite forget that I'm making small-talk with a naked man who's licking his fingers and manipulating the bell-end of a very big penis. He's also the proud owner of a 'convertible' – he's got a foreskin, most Americans don't – though he's fucked so much that he has torn it twice. Stress fractures in a cavalier's bonnet – you couldn't make it up.

Mark does everything. 'What about double-A?' I ask him.

'Sure. Some guys won't do it, they think it's sort of gay. You know, touching another guy's cock. It doesn't bother me.'

'But what about the girls?'

'Well, they're big, you know? You could drop a golf ball down them and it wouldn't touch the sides. There's one girl who can stick a pineapple up her ass.'

It's not just being able to do it, it's considering it in the first place. Anal sex used to be rare in porn movies but now it's *de rigueur*. Every show has to have it. Susan thinks it is because punters want to see what they can't get at home. Mostly, the male actors don't like it – it's not as nice or as well-appointed as a vagina – but the women do. Johnny Black, a female ex-paratrooper captain who's starring in a later scene, asks specifically if she can do A. (I tell her that if she feels it's in keeping with the motivation of her character to go for it by all means.)

In the make-up room, naked bodies are being primped and patted and plucked. The producer comes in and shouts, 'Time to blow the pipes!' The couple for the next scene go off to the loo with vinegar douches and enema pipes. It's a little touch of hygienic good manners – like brushing your teeth before kissing Michelle Pfeiffer.

Mark's scene is with Claudia Chase and Temptress, who begin with girl-on-girl and move on to a boy-girl-girl number. There is a definite frisson on the set; both the girls are truly beautiful and Temptress is doing a man on screen for the first time in ages. Up until now she has mainly been doing lesbian work and stripping (she takes dollar

bills from punters' mouths by clasping them between her buttocks).
Mark's trick is to turn the girls on for real.

Temptress is a pushover. Between takes they don't stop – his head
stays butted between her thighs.

'What makes him so good?' I shout.

'Oh, he's really good at going down on us,' giggles Claudia. 'He's
the best.'

Mark comes up for air. 'I've got a really short tongue,' he smiles.

'Oh, I've got a really short tongue as well,' I mutter. 'What a
coincidence.' The crew dissolves into fits.

Real female orgasms aren't as rare as you'd imagine on set. Some
girls hold back because they think orgasms should only be with their
boyfriends, but most just go with it. Temptress comes at the top of
her voice. With great professionalism, Mark gives both girls a simul-
taneous facial. 'I'll come from here to here, and I won't get it in your
eyes.' He's the Tiger Woods of sperm. As we pack up the scene, Mark
asks Temptress if she has a boyfriend. 'Not any more,' she replies.

'Well, if you'd like some uncomplicated fucking, let's get together.'
It's rather touching, if a little bizarre. You have troilistic sex, *then* ask
the girl for a date. And so it goes on.

That afternoon, a German TV crew turn up, then a Dutch one.
There's a seedy little guy making a documentary to go on the backside
of the DVD. At any one time there are five cameras on the set all
trying to keep out of each others' way. Quasar Man keeps up a steady
stream of Austin Powers jokes and teases the naked talent remorse-
lessly. 'OK, time to stick the Johnson up the colon.'

We're actually shooting two films simultaneously – the hardcore
video version and a soft *Playboy* channel one, so every shot has to be
duplicated ('Legs together, I'm getting ball sack'). Johnson-touching-
sphincter is definitely hardcore.

Quasar Man is terrified of penises touching him. Has he ever been
hit?

'Once I got a ricochet on my shoes. This job really puts you off
sex.' Continuity is also a problem. 'Was that duvet cover on the bed?'
he shouts.

'Who cares, for Chrissakes?' cries the producer. 'If the masturbators are stopping to say, "Oh look, that duvet cover is a different colour," they must be gay.'

'I know it's just porn, but I want to get it right,' replies Quasar Man. 'I don't want to be back handing out the lube.' The assistant responsible for the condoms, KY and tissues has the lowliest job on the lot.

I quickly learn the language of pornography. The come shot is a 'pop'; an FIP is a 'faked internal pop' for the soft version. All the positions have names. The 'cowgirl' (her on top) is good for bum shots. 'Reverse cow' (her on top facing the other way) is good for close-up plumbing shots. 'Monkey-fucking' is a position never seen in real life, where the man squats over the girl in a sort of simian doggy fashion. Between takes, a stills photographer known as Creepy Drew takes publicity and magazine shots in quick succession – hard, soft and ultra-light. All day, the most disgusting chef I've ever seen, a man who looks like the wagon-train cook from a John Wayne film, scuttles round the set handing out canapés. Prawns and guacamole on tortilla chips; tuna and onion sandwiches; chicken and mango salsa. As the cameras are moved or videos changed, the girls look after the male talent, helping them keep their erections. They ask them, 'What do you need, honey?' and kiss or give blow jobs, fondle scrotums or just lie with their legs apart 'showing pink'. All day there is a masturbating man somewhere in my peripheral vision, until the last pop is shot at 2 am. I go back to my Beverly Hills hotel and watch a porn movie, too tired to sleep. It's an 8 am start tomorrow.

Houston is currently the hottest thing in porn movies. She became a major star by lying on a turntable and having sex with more men in one day than anyone else in the world, ever – 620. Climbing Mount Everest in a sandpaper bikini would have been an easier route to stardom.

Houston is our featured talent. I meet her in the make-up room (her make-up takes longer than Chewbacca's), where she is trimming what's left of her pubic hair, gingerly circumnavigating a pudendum that looks like a badly made pastrami sandwich. She grabs a clump of clippings. 'I should sell this stuff, you know.'

Ah, a true diva.

We talk about her role. 'I really like this scene with all the cakes,' she says. 'I do something like this in my act.' A lot of the girls make serious money dancing in strip clubs, using the videos to promote themselves. Houston has a body that's built for pornography. Built with care and attention by real craftsmen. She's tough and very professional, going over and over her lines. 'I don't think I can say, "Oh bugger me" here. It doesn't sound right. Can I say, "Hey, fuck me in the ass" instead?'

Houston's first scene is a blow job. She makes it look incredibly exciting. 'The trick is that you've got to really enjoy it.' Her second scene is the wedding-cake buggery. It's complicated. She has to talk, eat cake and have sex in a number of camera-pleasing but precarious positions with a man who should have 'Not for internal use' tattooed on his cock. Here we hit a glitch. Houston, we have a problem. While the actor is willing to have his equipment varnished and to mime reciprocation for the softcore version, he won't actually go down on Houston. 'I've got an allergy to sugar,' he mumbles, 'and she's covered in cake.' Great. We get the only porn star in the world who's allergic to icing. The producer has his own theory, however. 'It's a cultural thing. He doesn't want to put his mouth where 619 guys and Ron Jeremy have been.' Quite.

Eventually, Quasar Man shoots around the problem with a string of obscene jokes. 'Time for Johnson to probe colon. Park the Cadillac in the cul-de-sac...' The buggery scene comes to an abrupt end, however, when the Caddie hits creosote. Now, imagine the most embarrassing thing in the world, and then compare it to being covered in cake, having anal sex with a stranger, being filmed up-close by three camera crews, and then shitting yourself. That's top-of-the-range humiliation, but Houston never blinked. She didn't blush or even smile apologetically. She just called the lube guy for a paper towel, cleaned herself up and went for the pop shot. It was the most damnably cool thing I ever saw. Houston is a true, 18-carat star.

The next problem we had was the Catholic girl and the two strangers. This set-up had been utterly mangled from my original. All that was left was an unexplained Catholic shrine and a girl who took the double-pop shot like communion.

She was to start off by praying. Melody Love, a small but perkily formed Hispanic girl, throws a fit. 'Oh my God, I can't do that. I'm Catholic. Not in front of Jesus.' I try to reason with her. 'You're going to have sex simultaneously with two strange men for money as an aid to masturbation (a sin). Do you think God's going to mind more because you're pretending to pray?' We compromise by removing the picture of Christ. What He can't see won't bother Him. I just hope He doesn't watch the *Playboy* channel.

One of the men, Tyce Bune, comes in for a lot of ribbing from Quasar Man about the size of his penis. 'God, here it comes – the smallest dick in movies, cock in a sock. Hey Tyce, you going to get an erection? Oh, that *is* an erection. I'll get in close, then.' Frankly, if I had a willy his size, I'd wear it on the outside with a blue rosette saying 'Best In Show'.

I watch the scene from a redundant sofa. Beside me is the porn-star wife of the other exorbitantly hung man in this threesome. After a couple of minutes, I look round. She's concentrating intently and masturbating. Catching my eye, she smiles politely. 'Isn't he great? We've been married for ten years. I wish you'd asked me to do this scene, I'd have been much better.' Actually, the producer tries not to cast husbands and wives together – their familiarity transmits to the screen.

'You still find this exciting even though it's work?' I ask her, totally bemused. 'Oh yeah, honey, you've got to love sex if you want to survive in this business. If you don't really enjoy it, well, it hurts for a start. You can be rubbed raw. You've got to be into it. Here,' she continues, 'you want to see the best natural bosoms in the business?' Oh, if you must. She shows me. They would be the best natural bosoms in any business you care to mention.

At 2 am, we get to the last set-up. The lesbian scene. Two excessively exuberant girls – one blonde, one dark with thin, parched, recreation area pubic hair – play a cop and an illegal immigrant. The cop pulls on a surgical glove and, in a Texan accent says: 'I'm going to have to search you, Maria. Bend over.'

'No, no! Not that!' For a moment, I have an image of her as Rod Steiger with implants and think that perhaps we should call the movie *On Heat In The Night*. Though the crew are exhausted and have been watching sex for 16 hours straight, they really like this bit. Outside the pool of light, they squat in the shadows and silently watch the girls slither about on the bed, howling like vixens. But then I notice something odd. The gaffers and grips and runners and sparks and the lube boy have all turned from the action to stare at the monitor. Five feet away from them two live girls are having sex, but they'd rather watch it on the screen. Pornography is something that happens on a screen. This is its familiar, omnipotent voyeurism; its erotic charge comes from being disengaged.

The last-gasp close-up is caught. It's a wrap. The girls roll off the bed giggling, kiss and say, 'Thanks, we should do this again.' The studio lights go on and the crew divvy up the few remaining cigarettes. Plugs are pulled. The miles of cable are wound round thumb and elbow and that's it. We say goodbye in that intense way you do when you've shared a common task, and exhaustion, with a team. Manly bear hugs. Many a 'Hey, keep in touch'. Michael the producer says, 'You ever want to do this again, just call. We should make one a year.'

And that's it. Exit, roll credits. I walk into the cool darkness of the Valley, get into the black limo and sleep, dreamlessly.

No story I have ever covered has elicited such fantastic interest as the making of a porn movie. Not war, pestilence, politics or celebrity. People come up to me in restaurants, at parties. They call me, wanting to know what it's really like. 'What are the stars really like?' 'Do they really...?' 'Is it actually...?' Everyone wants to see it. There is a vast, intense interest in seeing people have sex on screen.

This may be because we live in the only theocratically censorious state in Europe, where hardcore pornography is illegal. The first film was produced in 1896 in this country. The first act of censorship was in 1898 when the British cheesemaking industry had a shot of blue-veined cheese withdrawn. Censoring cheese is no less absurd than censoring an erect penis. All the pseudo-social-scientific arguments about pornography encouraging rape and violence and sexual dysfunction have been made patently bogus by the 15-year experiment of us having no pornography while the rest of Europe has as much as it likes. The sexual-crime rates in Switzerland and Denmark are not notably soaring compared with ours. The things that most of us think should be banned – underage sex, violence – are already covered by the law whether you have a camera there or not.

But although everyone who has spoken to me wants to see the movie and wants to know every sweaty detail, so they have all wanted the sex stars to be dysfunctional, unhappy and exploited. 'Well, of course they're all on drugs, aren't they?' 'They're pretty sick people, aren't they?' 'It's a very sleazy business, isn't it?' There is a need to have received wisdom confirmed. The bottom line is that we want filmed sex to have a riotous comeuppance for the actors because sex is the intimate act that proves the invisible truth of love and love is the most precious and powerful thing our species owns. But again, this doesn't make sense. Why don't we censor or become outraged at actors faking all the other facets of love? Why aren't two strangers who say, 'I'll love you for ever' on screen far more wholly immoral? Why isn't *Romeo and Juliet* by common consent the most disgustingly depraved play ever written and only performed in seedy clubs on the Rieperbahn? It doesn't make sense, but then, nothing about sex makes sense. Why should it? The wiring in our heads that connects desires, lust, jealousy, passion, devotion, frustration and biology is so complex and irrational, that to even consider a rational debate about sex and pornography is absurd.

Making *Hot House Tales* I learnt that these are not exploited people. The set is matriarchal, with the women choosing what they'll do and with whom. Only the film crew are cynical about the act – but then, all film crews are cynical. The stars are surprisingly innocent. I mean that in a fundamental not a physical sense. They are incredibly kind to each other. Each scene would start with the girl saying, 'OK, what are your do's and don'ts? I don't like fingers up my arse or my hair being pulled, but slapping's good. Do you mind me biting your balls?' They would help the guys keep their erections between shots in a fond, almost loving, way. And the sex is real. It's real in the sense that running round a track is as real as running for a bus. I discovered that to compare porn stars with actors is a misinterpretation of what they do. They're much closer to being athletes. They physically perform for public pleasure. They are an elite. Very few people can do what they do. You may play tennis but you're a million miles away from winning Wimbledon. You have sex but it's not in the same ballpark as these people. They take it seriously. They train, they're focused and they're very, very good. Is a girl with breast implants who'll take two penises up her backside any weirder than a shot-putter who'll take male hormones to throw a cannonball? There's no question which gives the most pleasure to watch. But one is a national hero and the other a seedy pariah. It doesn't make sense.

Are the stars exploited? Well, a lot of the women have what are known as 'suitcase pimps' – parasite boyfriends who carry their bags and take their money, and there are some pretty seedy agents on the periphery of the business. Is there a lot of disease? Everyone has to produce a DNA test every 30 days. It's an unbreakable rule. A porn film has safer sex than a lot of you have with your own spouses. Are they happy? Well, that's a piece of string. They have the same run of broken marriages and fractured lives that you'd find anywhere in LA. Certainly they're far less miserably abused, abusive and disposable than their equivalents in Hollywood.

What I found, though, was a sincere sense of awe and envy for their ability to be straightforward about sex and still get pleasure from it. I have never met a group of people who were so relaxed about their bodies and their function. They've shed the straitjacket of insecurity that the rest of us lug into bed. In the pool of bright light, I watched a remarkable fraternity of nice, attractive and amusing people doing what the rest of us cool libertarian liberals have been talking about since the Sixties. That is, be honest, relaxed and open about sex. I also learnt that we look for truths that will confirm and bolster our own complicated social, political and moral dilemmas about sex. We see and understand what we want, what we need, to see. And if you are reading this with a disbelieving sneer on your face, well, join everyone else I've said it to.

What *Hot House Tales* will look like, heaven only knows. I'm pretty sure it is not going to be the *Citizen Kane* of adult entertainment

– probably more like the *Chitty Chitty Bang Bang* of skin flicks. But I do now see what a vaunting piece of hubris and self-delusion it was to ever imagine you could direct sex. I might as well have tried to pole a punt with my penis.

November 1999

Stalking

A house with no road. That's odd for a start when you think about it. Not just a practical business, but the metaphysical questions it implies. Letterewe, it's quite a big house. Seven or eight bedrooms, billiards room, dining room, study, sitting rooms, wash-rooms, drying rooms, walled garden and a gunroom. It has that turrety, crenellated, white-and-grey, hunched look of a place that's turned up its granite collar and is keeping a weather eye. It's typically Scots, a home for boots and tweed and tappety barometers; with deep, gimlet windows and blind corridors. A place that rubs its knuckles over smoky fires. From the eaves, glassy, dust-lidded eyes catch the firelight and follow you with a mournful, flickering disinterest.

You get to Letterewe by boat, from a little jetty on Loch Maree. A long, Stygian, black lake that's separated from the green, Hebridian sea by a strip of battered land, Maree was once famous for its salmon but the fish have grown shy. There are islands where the Vikings briefly forced an uneasy steading. They say a Norse princess is buried here under a strand of storm-gnarled pines, the victim of some improbably operatic love-tryst.

The house is not on an island. It squats on the further shore. It has no road because there's nothing to tether the other end of a road to. Here is an A but there is no B. Behind it rise thousands of acres of wilderness, traversable only by foot or hoof. Long, crumpled miles of crag and gully, hump-backed mountains, springy, sodden moor, burns and cataracts, high lochans and mossy corries inhabited only by ptarmigan, raven, hawk, the wind and the deer.

I'm not sure quite what this story is about. On the face of it, it's about stalking. Here we are in Letterewe, a stalking lodge. Shortly, we'll go out, walk a lot, crawl a bit, spy a stag, kill it, hump it down the hill and sell it to Germany. That's stalking. But that's not the half of it.

I know what this story isn't. And you should know before you pull on the waterproofs and yomp through miles of heathery prose. It's not funny and I don't think it's terribly exciting. It's not postmodern Hemingway. Or nature notes. I think it's about smoking. And typing. And my grandfather.

My mother's father died before I was born. He was a dentist. He wanted to be an engineer but took to teeth – which must have been a worry for his patients. I have his First World War dog-tags and a photograph of him in a swaggery officer's uniform. His tag shows that he was a non-commissioned motorbike messenger. He has a slightly buck-toothed smile (that must have been another worry for his patients). All I know of him is that he loved to shoot. To stalk.

He would spend all his spare time up here on the hill and he wanted his only child to be a boy. When she failed to grow into one, he lost interest. When he dropped dead in an Edinburgh street, his hunting friends took his ashes away to the Highlands, failing to tell his widow or child precisely where.

My grandfather was French and very proud. After he died, they discovered he was actually half-Indian and plainly not so proud. That's my grandfather: a Frenchman who was an Indian; an engineer who was a dentist; an officer who was a private; a sporting gent who lived in a lower-middle-class suburban bungalow. I never think about him. I didn't know him. Apparently, no one did.

I shot my first stag nearly twenty years ago. A bloke I was staying with came down to breakfast, forked a wheel of black pudding and said, 'Do you fancy shooting a stag today?' And I said, 'Why not?' And I did without thinking. It was August, hot and sunny. The stags were still in velvet, and as the stalker gutted him, for the first time I caught that smell, that heavy, delicious, repellent scent of cud and blood and through it, wrapped in it, came this image, a feeling of my grandfather. It was so intense, so insistently present that it made me start.

I'm not really that sort. The sort who gets vibes and feels things. I don't do 'otherworldly'. I've never been in touch with all that stuff that people always tell you you should get in touch with. But there he was, as plain as the scent on the wind in my face. I didn't talk to him. Nothing weird and wicca-y. But I took to stalking. I'd go every autumn and shoot a stag and sometimes grandfather would be there and sometimes he wouldn't. And then, one year, I couldn't get up a hill. Well I could, but it took me so long, boys had grown beards. By the time I reached the top, making a noise like a boarding-house Ascot, feeling worse than Florence Nightingale's in-tray, I couldn't breathe. I was drowning 2,000 feet above sea level. It was the fags or the stags. I couldn't do both.

So I retired from stalking. Occasionally, I'd look out of the window at the questing metropolitan traffic wardens and hum, 'My heart's in the Highlands, my heart is not here. My heart's in the Highlands, a-chasing the deer.' But I'd take a drag and think that I'd made the right choice, that urban, cultivated choice, and go back to typing.

And then the damnedest thing happened. I gave up smoking. Just like that. I've loved cigarettes with an unquestioning adoration since I was fifteen, bum-sucked fifty of the little darlings down to their tight brown bottoms every day for thirty years. And I fell out of love just like that. I was shocked. It was borderline psychopathic. Here's the thing with giving up smoking. Everyone tells you how good you are, how strong-willed, how sensible and decent. But it's nonsense. It's not like that. Giving up on fags is giving up on immortality. It's not strong will. It's the spirit submitting to the body. It's the triumph of fear. It's middle age. Stopping smoking is a milestone on the road away from golden, fire-breathing youth towards Crown Green bowls. And I knew it. I felt bad. I could breathe but that's small recompense. So I gave myself a consolation prize. I'd go back to the hill and the stags, which is how I came to Letterewe.

The first rule of stalking is the first rule of life. It's all in the kit. And of all the kit, in all the world, Scots outdoor kit is the bonniest. Stalking actually begins weeks and miles before the Highlands with an intense track round the gun shops and Outward Bound fantasy-mongers of the metropolis, where you can frot waterproof, breathable fabric with labels that are short novels; leer over inflatable stoves and mosquito-repelling wristwatches, while all around you is the siren call of the wild, the slow rending of Velcro. There are boots and gaiters and belts and knives and jackets and fleeces and plus twos, plus fours and the delightful anticipation of new hats. All essential.

The most imperative bit of kit, though, is a cook. A good Scots cook; no snorting, gummy chalet girls with hips like sandbags and 37 Saucy Things To Do With Pasta. We want porridge made with pinhead oats and salt. We need oatcake farls and underage grouse and plump partridge and fat-backed bacon and barley for broth and scones for tea and mutton and rowan jelly and venison and claret and whisky. And Mars Bars. We demand The Full McMonty.

And then all of a sudden it's the airport and Inverness and Jackie from – would you believe – 'Hy Jack Cabs' (the plural is an exaggeration). And the drive across country to Wester Ross and Loch Maree. Which is where we came in. Suddenly, after all the fluster and humping and tickets and lists is just the dying light, the silence and the cool, clean air.

I've shot at lots of things in lots of places. But nothing is like stalking. I can't remember a single pheasant drive with any clarity. I can, though, remember every stag I ever stalked. I can place each one with minute detail. Each is a story, a coherent narrative complete and different. But they all start with the box.

'Do you mind having a go at the box straight away?' asks the stalker. The box is cardboard, placed a hundred yards off with the target Sellotaped to its side. There's a bit of grotty carpet on the grass 'for your nice clothes'.

'OK. In your own time, just to get a feel of the gun. Take it easy, no pressure.' I lie on the damp lawn outside the gunroom, still in my London clothes. The stalkers stand back with their fingers in their ears; a brace of pony boys feign indifference. One rests a telescope in the doorjamb and squints. *No pressure.* The telescopic sight isn't the crosshair type of spy films and book jackets. It's the more difficult post site. A blunt, black arrow points up from the bottom of the circle. Where it touches space is where the shot will fall. The stick quests across the tree line, the box bobs as if it were at sea; the target's an indistinguishable dot, a full stop in search of a sentence. The barrel gets heavier, breathe in, then half out. I can feel my heart jarring, everything is made of rubber. Squeeze the trigger like an orange, like a nipple, like a pimple, like it's glass. The tip of the finger, stroking the bottom of the curling tine. There's a tiny, coy resistance, then black noise. The gun jerks up, the report is a startling flat, hard slap like a huge fist punching the air. I look round at the man with the telescope. He searches. 'Och, yeah, bottom left.'

'Have another go,' says the stalker. 'Take your time, no pressure.'

Three shots scattered at random. 'That's fine,' he says, 'Just fine. As long as you're within the outer circle, that'll kill your beast.'

It isn't really fine. I'm not a great rifle shot. I can't produce those neat little clusters of holes but it'll do. And the stalkers know what to expect.

At this point, we ought to do the man-to-man hardware talk: the gun stuff, barrels and triggers, noses, charges and trajectories. But I'm not really interested. I can fake the chat. I just can't remember any of the numbers. Some people care; Germans and Belgians care. They bring beautiful, huge guns that nestle in foam rubber, with calibres that can punch holes in history. But stalking isn't really about rifles. Or, actually, shooting. Not for me anyway. It's about something else. Something that's just out of the corner of my eye, that's shy of explanation.

But, I should tell you what to expect in the death department. You should try to shoot a stag at about a hundred yards. Closer if you can get there, a bit further back if you have to. But a hundred yards is quite far enough. You'll shoot it broadside, standing still. You'll be lying down. You trace a line up the inside edge of the foreleg and continue halfway up the body. That's where you aim. It's not a heart shot. The heart is too low down in the chest. You'll miss or shatter a leg. You aim for inside the diaphragm, anything mucking about there at speed will be mortal. The stag will take a step or two, maybe run a few yards, but it's not going anywhere – except Germany.

And, I ought to tell you what we're stalking. The red deer is the largest indigenous animal in Britain. Even so, it's half the size of the same species across the Channel. Its natural habitat is forest. Indeed out of respect, they call these barren, treeless hills a forest – and once it was but now it's peat. The Scottish red deer uses most of its energy keeping warm. All its natural predators are extinct so, as it gets smaller, it grows more numerous and ranges ever further.

The deer are a serious problem in the Highlands. Hinds have a calf each year; the mortality rate in the long winter is high. Stags and hinds live separately until the rut, when the stags come down to gather harems and fight. The rut is set by the weather and perhaps the moon that is now huge and bright and full. And the stags are starting to bellow. That's the Attenborough bit.

The red stag is also stupidly handsome. He moves with the sure-footed lightness of a boxer and the stateliness of a king. He carries cupped in his bony head the weight of his artistic, mythological, poetic and heraldic heredity with an elegant, imperious assumption. Deer are magical beasts. You never shoot one lightly. We don't stalk for trophies. This is important. We aim at the weak and the old, particularly switches – stags whose antlers form a single, lethal dirk.

Letterewe is one of the biggest and, by universal consent, one of the best-managed and environmentally sensitive estates in Scotland. But it'll wait until tomorrow. Now it's dinner and a sleepless bed. The moon shines over the loch, the pines sway black across the pewter sky. And the cry of the loon eddies from the island Valhalla.

7.30 am. Breakfast.

Porridgeeggsbaconsausagesblackpuddingtoastcoffee.

But no kippers – they follow you around all day, like the Ancient Mariner. Stalking is also about conviviality; an individual sport, at best, boasted about to a team. But it's not high-testosterone. A lot of women shoot. They shoot better than men – more accurate, unsurprisingly deadly.

For this trip, I've invited along two chaps who've never stalked before. Carlo, an urbane Italian dealer in very modern art with a severe dose of the English wannabes. He's kitted out like Lord Peter Wimsey. And the actor Ross Kemp, whose top half looks like it's going to garrotte towel-heads and his bottom half is going to a gymkhana.

Outside the gunroom, the stalkers – David and Norman – and the pony boys and eager-beaver terriers and the frightful midges wait patiently. Stalkers are singular men, like the captains of ships. You employ them as servants, but, out on the vastness of the hill, their word is iron law. A stalker says what you shoot and when. If he says lie down and crawl, you crawl, even if you are wading a burn. They have an almost uncanny knowledge of country, a sensitivity to wind and the best of them think like stags. They all have soft voices and hard hands and in rural communities they are held in high regard, though their pay is Victorian, their work medieval and their prospects gloomy – rheumatism, arthritis, bent backs and a long, shuffling retirement in a cold bothie, collecting firewood. I've met stalkers that I didn't like, but never one that I didn't admire.

On the first day, Carlo went for his stag and came down the hill caked in gore. It's tradition: after your first stag, you are turned into Driller Killer. Usually it's just a strip on the cheek but Carlo copped a couple of pints because of his impeccable neatness. Norman informed him with a fearsomely straight face that he had to wear it until midnight or have bad luck for ten generations. And being Italian – and therefore more superstitious than a convention of clairvoyants in a ladder factory – and not wanting to flout protocol, he kept it on for dinner, cracking and peeling like an Old Master.

The next day, I shot my stag, an old chap we found sitting on his own on a high plateau. He looked a long way off, but through the sight I could see the individual hairs on his neck, the sweep of his wide head. The tension before you shoot is as extreme as anything I've ever known and there's a moment when you really see what you are about to do. You stare and will the bullet home. There's the double thud, the echo that arrives in the splitting of an atom as the shot strikes. The beast jerks and tenses, absorbing the massive shock, walks a few steps, stands and sways, head dropping under the weight of his crown, flanks heaving, straining at the bubbling wreckage of lung, bone and muscle. And gently he settles onto his haunches so that from the firing position all we can see are his black antlers; slowly they slide sideways, like the masts of the sinking ship.

David, crouching, crabs forward, takes his thick-bladed knife and jabs it into the base of the beast's head. Searching for the axis at the top of the spine, he works the steel back and forth, edging it between the bones. The deer doesn't move; its tongue lolls, still with the fresh grass on it. The soft muzzle shivers with faint breath. David taps the dark eye with the flat of the blade.

I'm always astonished that even in so violent and sudden a death, how gentle and fragile is the departing of life. You can sense it stealing away, evaporating with the slightest whisper. He slits the cheek to age the teeth and he's about ten – younger than he looked. Must have had a hard winter. I gralloch him, slitting the stomach from sternum to pizzle. I reach into the hot cavity, feeling through the slimy entrails for the spleen to grip the top of the stomach and reach the whole ninety-nine yards out onto the heather for corbies (crows) that are already circling and cawing. David sits and smiles and says, after a bit, 'My but that's a fine and expensive watch you've left in there.'

On the last day, Ross and I go for his stag. This is what I like best. The joy of the stalk. Someone else to shoot. We are going to search the distant march of the beat. Stalking is all about wind. Stags have uncanny hearing, excellent sight in black and white; but their black noses are their most reliable long-distance warning. You travel all day with the wind in your face. The wind constantly eddies and backs, bouncing off cliffs and down blind glens. Worst of all are the days when there is no wind, but they're rare in Scotland.

We start out at 8.30 am, working our way up. First thing is always up. You have to be high to spy the deer. And high up is where the stags like to be, for the same reason. Up there, the wind is true. Up, up in slow lung-tugging zigzags: a thousand, two thousand feet in the first two hours. Now, there's a point on every stalk I've ever done where I think with absolute conviction that this is the very last time I'm ever going to do this.

Trudging up a one-in-two incline, with a drop beneath you and a summit that keeps retreating above, I think, 'What a ridiculous piece of asinine, male bravado.' And then you reach the top and breathing is less like sword-swallowing and you look up from your feet for the first time in an hour and it just takes your breath away all over again.

To say that Scotland is beautiful is to turn out a predictable truism, but it's the quality of that beauty. There is a keening melancholy in the emptiness. This is a sad place. A sad country. I've often wondered if I'd enjoy stalking over some other landscape. But I've never had the inclination to shoot fat stags in German oak forests, or scramble up Switzerland for hairy goats. It's the emptiness of the place. It's not an untouched, pristine emptiness. The Highlands are bereft.

We walk up and up and in the neck of a glen, by a sandy loch, a spellbinding place, there's the footprint of a croft. They are dotted all over the hills. I try to imagine the life up here, the savage winters, the unforgiving soil, the shin-splintering rock, the impossibility of comfort, the weeping loneliness. The families who once lived here are now probably bankers in America, shopkeepers in Canada or lawyers in Australia. Scotland's long history of disappointment, heroic failure and exodus has made this stoic, granite landscape a memorial to a million small, personal wars lost to despair, politics and time. Scotland is not that much smaller than England. It has a population of five million, four-and-a-half of whom live in the conurbation between Glasgow and Edinburgh. The rest of it is stone memories.

We walk on, up and up; a covey of ptarmigan fly beneath us, calling like someone winding a large clock. The day grows into a sublime wonder, the light dapples and sidles over the hills. The deer are always ahead of us. In their eerie corries, we can hear the stags roaring to each other; they're rolling in peat, painting themselves black, hanging garlands of grass and myrtle from their antlers. They're maddened and bold with pummelling hormones; too excited even to eat; their necks swollen to make their challenging bellows. Across a glen, we sight a river of them, five, six hundred stags raving across the hillside. Some are huge, holding their great heads up and back to support their crowns of bone. On and on we walk, drinking from tumbling burns. The ravens fly past, their wings creaking like starched linen. And then we're on a crag, a serrated spine of rock above the clouds. Far below are two bible-black lochs with cascading waterfalls. To the east, beyond a rainbow, this rolling, blasted moor flows into the green fields of Inverness-shire. And to the west there's Loch Maree and the sea. And over the sea, the great Cuillin mountains of Skye and, beyond that, shadows in a glittering ocean, the Outer Hebrides, Lewis and Harris. I can see from coast to coast, from North Sea to Atlantic.

Ross finds his stag at about 5.30 pm. He has a tricky, awkward stalk. At 6.30 pm, there's a shot. Gingerly we make our way down and there he is, as red and bald as a pillar box, grinning fit to split.

We drag the stag down to a plateau where the ponies can reach it, heft it onto the complicated Victorian saddle with its dozens of belts and buckles, the head twisted up over its shoulder, leather pulled tight under its breast bone. The ponies are fat, stubborn garrons, the indigenous Scots horse. Sure-footed, unflappable, they pick their way through the bog and shale, carrying the great dead weight, dripping sweat and foam and blood.

Walking back is easier, the wind behind us, the setting sun ahead. I can't disengage my feelings for Scotland from this landscape. They're all one. I suffer the heightened sentimentality of all expatriates. I live in London. I sound English but I was born here. I have a feeling for it that's beyond words. This place is the only inanimate thing in the world that I miss. It's all wrapped up with history and my grand-father, the little, dark Frenchman who escaped here from Verdun. How astonishingly peaceful and grave and grand it must have seemed to him.

We get back to the lodge at 9 pm, eleven hours' hard walking, eighteen tricky and treacherous miles. That's Scots miles, mind, which are longer than your soft Sassenach ones. Then whisky as the moon rises, teasing and banter. A bath, a grouse, a bed. And tomorrow, London, where I can go back to being a Scotsman who sounds like an Englishman, a hunter who stalks with a keyboard.

January 2003

Father

It's got him and it's slowly, capriciously losing him, rubbing him out so that in the end all that will be left is the whine of dementia and a hieroglyph that looks like him. It has a bleak trendiness, Alzheimer's: old Ronnie Reagan had it, Iris Murdoch's has been turned into a book and a film, no doubt somewhere there's the T-shirt.

I know how it works. I've seen it before. We've all seen it before, some grandparent, husband, friend, father. It begins with a misplaced word – so easy to lose a word, we all do it. But as it goes on, language escapes, there's a hole in the vocabulary, memories slip away or take on new significance. So much of the familiar furniture of life vanishes or is rearranged, but there's a growing confusion and often panic. At this point someone – a spouse, a child, a friend – has to make the choice to go to a doctor to confirm what they already secretly know. That's the big decision, because there's a world of difference between dementia and dottiness. Eccentric is an anecdote; Alzheimer's is a sentence. Or, as my dad puts it, 'You know I've got that terrible illness, what's its name?'

I've been trying to remember my first memory of him and, you know, I can't – he's always been there. But one keeps coming back. I must have been about eleven. He's taken us to Venice for a day. Venice was my dad's version of Disneyland. It's getting late, it's hot, we're lost but there's one last thing he has to show me. I've had enough, I want an ice cream and a go in a gondola. He's irritated, I'm bolshie. We walk around the corner and there it is, there's Verrocchio's condottiere, and I burst into tears, just bowled over, thumped in the soul by art. It's only happened to me twice, both times with my dad. The other was the bronze blind Zeus in Athens. Anyway, he hands me his handkerchief and makes the condottiere live and Verrocchio live and it's one of the best moments of my life.

That's it. The handkerchief, that's my first memory of my father: he always carried a handkerchief. It smelt of pipe tobacco.

We didn't really do outside. Never did that father-son thing with rods and rackets, oars or balls. He never taught me to take a penalty or bowl a googly. We stayed in. In museums, galleries, palaces, castles, ruins, anywhere that had a story. He was the best storyteller. Only later did I realise how amazingly capacious his knowledge was and what a rare and winning gift his ability to impart it. When I first went to school it was a surprise to discover I already knew all the Greek and Norse mythology and a fair chunk of classical history.

Books were our thing. All my adult life, whenever he visited, first thing he'd go to the bookshelves, searching for pilfered strays. He was never a best friend or a mate. I've had lots of friends and mates. He's the only father I'll ever have. We didn't do pubs or garden sheds; we just talked and talked and talked. Always in the deep end.

He's eighty this year, born an only, sickly child of first-generation middle-class parents. He was in RAF intelligence during the war and the occupation of Germany after, read philosophy at Edinburgh – the first member of his family to go to university – became a journalist on *The Scotsman* and then the *Observer*, joined the BBC. Made more than 1,000 art documentaries, filmed Giacometti and Bacon, worked with David Sylvester, John Berger and Kenneth Clark, co-producing and directing *Civilisation*. He made a funny, short 1960s movie that went to Cannes, wrote a clever, idiosyncratic book on the nude in art. Married twice, had three children, four grandchildren and along the way became the widest- and furthest-travelled man I know.

He is a man of his time, that wartime generation of cerebral social-ists, instinctive modernists who wanted to build a new Jerusalem on the bomb site of the old world using culture, information and intelligence as their pick, shovel and brick. The last unapologetic intellectuals.

I wouldn't be telling you any of this if something hadn't happened. Prosaically, it came via Age Concern, the Kensington branch. There, a chap called David Clegg has instigated a programme of getting artists to work with the Alzheimered. It isn't art therapy – nothing is as humiliating and demeaning as getting people who have led extraordinary lives to end up colouring in for their own good. This is a collaboration to create a work out of the fractured memory and circular obsessions of dementia.

For some time now Becky Shaw has been visiting Daddy once a week, and together they're creating something. It's meant an enormous amount to him; he's excited by it, and it's so rare to hear of anything positive about our collective treatment of the old, so I went to sit in on a session. I don't know what I expected: stuff about the war, his school days, family things, the shards of life.

When I get there he's sitting on a sofa. In front of him, as ever, there's a scatter of books. He picks one up – H.G. Wells's *A Short History of the World*. We slip into the familiar chat, 'good on the League of Nations and prehistory, not so good in between'. Every time Daddy comes to a pothole in a sentence he pauses, concentrates and searches vainly for the word: 'I can't remember... words.'

Shaw arrives with large, chaotic rolls of papers: 'I thought you'd like to see what we've done.' She starts laying down the sheets; the corners flick up and curl. They are densely written with catches of conversation colour-coded and linked by a road map of lines and circles and arrows to make connections to underline repeated themes. There are collaged images from photographs and postcards, rough line drawings; things are crossed out and new bits imposed and stuck on. The rolls spill out over the floor. Daddy looks at them with a beneficent smile. They are opaquely complex, like a mad family tree or alchemistic experiment.

What I can see is that he's been talking an awful lot about prehistoric shamanism and the relevance to early religions of domesticated animals. There's a page of ancient horses. 'It's strange,' says Daddy, 'that the horse never became a god: it's the most important and... of all the tamed animals but it was never made a god. I wonder why.'

There's miles of it, this stuff about fertility symbols and the role of the earth goddess – then a Mitchell bomber his squadron flew and the Makonde figure he brought back from Tanzania, a photograph of his father.

'What are you going to do with all this; how do you edit it into something coherent?' I ask Shaw. 'Well, I think I'm going to make a

museum of your father, a model for a museum with all these impos-
sible corridors, some that connect and some that don't. An architect's
model that could never be built.'

Daddy smiles and nods. It couldn't be more appropriate, more
right. He is like a curator of a collection that's been sacked by the
philistines. He's trying to rescue the objects and memories of a life-
time while the vandals next door rip up the photograph album and
smash the furniture. Not just appropriate but awfully poignant.

What strikes me as memorable about this project is that it could
only be done with people who are clinging to the wreckage. It's not
one of those pitifully hearty bits of do-goodery that pretend to allow
the physically or mentally compromised some *manqué* padded version
of the able word. Shaw says she reckons the input is 50-50: half hers,
half Daddy's. So you're not just being an amanuesis? 'I'm sorry,' she
says, 'I don't know what that word means.'

Conversations with Daddy are like talking to someone who can
travel through walls. In the middle of a sentence, he can be some-
where else. I have to open empirical, rational doors to follow him.
He elides through time and subjects in a way that logic and language
prevent me from doing. It's a sort of itinerant freedom. He's still
lucid and connected enough for an afternoon spent with him to be
funny and emotional and stimulating and real. All this stuff about the
prehistory and origins of belief, the theories and suppositions based
on ancient ruins and rescued fragments, is inescapably a metaphor, as
have been all the conversations we've ever had about history, aesthetics
and culture. This was our playing field, the language we used to be
together. They were the words between words.

After Shaw leaves I suggest we go for a walk. His face clouds,
'Well, maybe not, I'd rather not, I'm frightened,' he says in a quite
matter-of-fact way, as if the fear were just another vandal in another
room. But reassured that someone will be here when he gets back,
my stepmother gives him a clean handkerchief and we stroll round
Holland Park. He used to bring me here as a child. 'I can't have keys
now, you know; I lose them . . . Are you going to get another dog?'
I haven't had a dog for a decade. 'She's nice, Becky, isn't she? I think
the work might be, might be . . .'

We go and sit in the flower garden and I mention how morbid benches are; always dedicated to the dead. It's like sitting on graves. I ask if he'd like a bench here. He laughs: 'No, no. They might put me next to someone I hate. I might get Deirdre Lawrence.' I've no idea who she was, a name snatched from another room.

There is a late autumnal feeling to our time together now. It's the long walk back to the pavilion. We haven't always made each other's lives easy. I was a tedious and irritatingly difficult son; he could be dismissive and short-tempered. But that's all gone now there are no more positions to defend, points to be scored, no more competition. Along with everything else, Alzheimer's has washed away the friction of expectation, leaving us with just this moment. Fathers and sons are an endlessly retraced journey for all men – it is one of the great themes of our lives. For a time every man is a hero to his son and I can catch again something Homeric in Daddy's last lost battle. This slow parting is sad and precious. We have this moment and we've managed to say everything that needs to be said.

Look, I don't want this to sound like a happy ending, some bitter-sweet violin sob of new-age closure. There is nothing good to say about Alzheimer's. It robs families. It robs the sufferers of themselves. It makes thankless, unremitting demands on those who have to stay and care. The process of loss and grieving is unnaturally mixed with the humbling mechanics of maintenance. Not only will we lose him, but he will lose us. Soon I won't be in any of the rooms at all.

March 2003

Glastonbury

What is it with hippies and fire? You only have to spark up a Zippo and four of them will come and stare contentedly into the flame. At Glastonbury they light up everywhere. In the field in front of the main stage while some deathless bit of old pop flotsam is offering his timeless classic in the middle of 300,000 swaying, wigged-out happy campers, you'll trip over a little family of hippies, cross-legged in front of an improvised bonfire, watching the salamanders and phoenixes in the flames with their third eyes. I saw a bloke stroll down one of the festival's makeshift ley-lines and just put a match to a pile of rubbish. It wasn't so much an act of pyromania as the offering of a small prayer, the elemental, Promethean act of spiritual bollocks. In the age of nuclear fission and quantum physics, plasma screens and 3G cells, hippies can still look into a fire and see the meaning of life and the answer to everything.

So there I am, you see, seven sentences in, and I've started already with the hippy-baiting. You just can't help it; to know them is to mock them. What's amazing is that they've lasted so long. At the bottom of the child-line of bullied pop trends, hippies are now in their third generation. Born in the mid-sixties into a blizzard of mockery, they've suffered, for forty years, the ridicule of almost everyone. They've tried rebranding as yippies, travellers, crusties, hairies, the tribe, the clan, eco-warriors, alternative health practitioners and outreach coordinating social workers. But we all know they're just the same old hippies in a new shapeless jersey. And credit where credit's due, what other useful fad or fashion has lasted as long? No one says, 'Oh, you sad old teddy boy.' Your mods, rockers, suedeheads, soul boys, new romantics, Goths, punks and Bay City Rollerettes are now just embarrassing photographs and a ridiculous pair of shoes at the back of the wardrobe. Only hippies have transcended the natural lifespan of their music and knitwear.

And if you sit down and think about them without sniggering, there's a lot of hippy shit you quite like. Flower power became the green movement, and you quite like that. The don't-work-just-feel-the-vibe-and-roll-a-spliff thing has its points, and as a weekend mini-break you'd rather make love than war. And you wouldn't mind fathering a lot of blond kids from a number of surprisingly attractive and non-judgemental free-spirited women who can bake. Actually, when you get right down to it, there's a bit of you that would like to live in a tepee. Yes, there is. With some mates and Liv Tyler in August. It would be a laugh and you quite fancy having a go on those Celtic drums. (Obviously, you don't want the Hoover-bag hair, the scabies, the compost sleeping bag, a mate called Bracken and a lurcher called Stephen.)

Perhaps we all need to get in touch with our inner hippies. Which is partially why I decided, finally, that it was time to go to Glastonbury. It's funny, Glastonbury. It's a secret password. Whisper it to grey men in offices, your accountant, your MEP, a hedge-fund analyst, and it's likely a look of beatific remembrance will pass like a cloud over the sun and they'll say, 'Yes, I went once, years ago.' Glastonbury is a secret medieval heresy that's remembered with hidden joy. 'I was once a free-love hippy, Mott the Hoople acolyte and hand-painted chillum maker,' is probably not what you want to hear from the merchant banker handling your corporate takeover. Actually, medieval heresy is the decorative theme of Glastonbury, which, by the way, means 'place of woad', or more exactly 'place of the woad people'. Inside, the huge curtain wall of the temporary, self-governing state of Glastonbury is a reprise of the thirteenth century, or at least the Jabberwocky version of it, while outside the Black Death of progress tears up the earth and eats people. Getting into Glastonbury is about as easy as the Black Prince found getting into Calais.

Having made the decision to find my inner hippy at Glastonbury, I had to make a decision as to what sort of hippy I was looking for. Was it Swampy? Or Donovan? Or was it the Marquess of Bath? Over the years there's been quite a variety of hippies. You could, if you so wished, hold a Eurovision Hippy Contest or a Hippy Olympics. I like to think of Glastonbury as Hippy Crufts, a walled, heretic, medieval Hippy Crufts. That just about gets the flavour.

I have an advantage in shopping for an inner hippy because this is my second go. I was there at the start. I'm a child of the sixties, albeit at school in rural Hertfordshire, which wasn't exactly Woodstock or the Prague Spring or even Eel Pie Island. But we had the music and the hair and a bit of Red Leb and I know where my nascent, born-again hippy lurks. He's a cross between Malcolm McDowell and William Blake with a dash of Jethro Tull. This is really the crux. I'm fifty this year. Glastonbury is the last act of my forties. Glastonbury is unfinished business now that I'm closer to an undertaker than I am to boarding school.

When I was a hippy first time round we used to say, never trust anyone over thirty (with shrill, clipped, upper-middle-class accents). Now I'm over fifty I'd add, never sleep in a tent over thirty. I'll do Glastonbury but I'll do Glastonbury Soft, Glastonbury Lite, which is why I'm sitting above the twenty-mile traffic jam in a Winnebago. Not for me the stews and refugee camps of windy canvas, the dank sleeping bag; a Winnebago is the way to go. You see, a mobile home is a great luxury, the stars' accessory, the private box on nature unless – and this is a big unless – it actually is your home, in which case it's trailer trash. Ours appears to be the main residence of the man who's driving it. It has the mildly weird feeling of trying to hold a dinner party in a peculiarly strange man's bedsit with him in the inglenook saying, 'Don't mind me.'

I'm travelling with my girlfriend. This will be the last year I'm able to say girlfriend without sounding utterly Alan Clark. I'm also taking Matthew, my personal photographer, another little luxury you can give yourself after forty-five (going to Boots and sticking the things in the albums is such a bore) and Alice BB, who's a dear and here because when I told her I was going, she became so overexcited I thought she just might rip off all her clothes and do floral finger-painting on her body. So I said she was welcome to tag along, as it was a sort of hippyish thing to say. She is still improbably buoyant, staring out of the window, squeaking like a spaniel going shooting.

Getting in to Glastonbury is like crossing a particularly fraught border: there are thousands of policemen – or pigs as I suppose I must go back to calling them, hundreds of cones and signs and labels, a Kafkaesque amount of paperwork and when you see the security fence marching across the country it's a reminder that the price of freedom, to be a bit of an anarchist and a fire-worshipper, is a lot of razor wire and a bulk discount from Group Four.

We finally park in the private, behind-stage, Bands and VIPs field, which is like a pilot for a Channel 4 sitcom: *Celebrity Trailer Trash*. Over there is Kate Moss, the pin-up sprite, the Bardot of postmodern Notting Hippydom. I go and find the press tent to get more passes and paperwork, and bump into Roland White, a man whose hidden hippy has probably been sold for medical research. He does my television column when I'm not there. I'm only introducing Roland as a walk-on here because he made one very clever observation and I don't want him to think I'm stealing it. 'Have you seen the tented village yet?' he asked. 'Well, when you do, you'll notice it's become a tented suburb. Well, a number of suburbs. It's rather John Betjeman; there are people laying out gardens and putting up carriage lamps.'

Inside the press tent the latest news is that no one's managed to make it over the wall but security guards with dogs have apprehended ten people and they're all Liverpudlian (the liggers, not the dogs). It's like the punchline to a joke, isn't it? '. . . And they were all Scousers.' The tickets are now £100 each so naturally, in a right-on, hippy-ish way, we're all for people breaking in over the wire. But on the other hand we're jolly pleased when they get caught. There's a lot of nostalgia about Glastonbury: people who've been here every year since they did it without microphones say they miss the gangs of Hell's Angels, the drug-dealers' turf wars, the endemic thievery, the adulteration and overdoses, which just shows you can be nostalgic about anything.

The truth is that this alternative weekend nirvana all comes down to plumbing and waste management. There are armies of kids who've been given tickets in exchange for picking up rubbish, of which there is an extraordinary amount. But it's bogs that are really the central leitmotif of Glastonbury. It's all about one thing: colonic endurance.

Can you go the full three days without going? Because the very thought is so nauseous, so utterly medieval, it makes a colostomy bag sound like a civilised option. There are plenty of loos laid out like back-to-back miners' cottages. You can see the rows of feet in the morning, the whole-earth pasty-shoe next to the Nike Airs, next to Doc Martens. That's the thing that's rarely mentioned about hippies – they've managed to achieve completely unisexual footwear but, my darling, the smell.

By the third morning it's, well, it's half a million turds and all the trimmings. There are horror stories of dropped stashes, of tripping and slipping, of horrible, horrible rectal explosions. But for me the most poignant, the most grisly, is the girl who told me she'd been putting off the call of nature for as long as sphincterally possible and until she was so comprehensively stoned and drunk she could face the drop. So at 2 am she gingerly made her way to the pitch-black amenities block. Opening the door, she dropped her pants and with the tense precision of a Romanian gymnast, lowered her posterior over the open sewer. Something cold and clammy squidged between the cheeks of her buttocks and in a sudden dark, repulsive flash of third-eye insight she realised she was squatting on the pointy turtle's head of the last occupant's offering, which itself was the high peak of a mountain of shit that had risen like the devil's soufflé from the bowl. She said her scream woke at least 4,000 people.

Glastonbury is all about plumbing, 100,000 sloppy bladders. I came across my goddaughter, Florence, a gamine French girl with the most beguiling look and syrupy accent. She's an art student and therefore penniless, so she was here on a green ticket, her job to stop men peeing in the little river that runs through the site. In years past it has become so urically toxic that it's cleared out all the animal and vegetable life for a couple of miles downstream. It's also so pharmaceutically complex that frogs have been found copulating with mushrooms, and sheep lying on their backs baaing 'Green, Green Grass of Home' in three-part harmony.

I asked Florence how it was going. 'It's going a lot. Zer are many, many very drunk boys and zey don't listen. I say, "No, no, put it away, you must not pee-pee, it will damage zee nature." But it is too late, and I am 'aving to jump.'

On that first night we walked out into the humming darkness and stood at the crossroads in an improvised street along a hedge under a stunted hawthorn. A cold moon gave everything the silvered look of an old photograph. Thousands of people walked past in the dark. As Alice said, it was like those films of city streets where all the car lights make long red-and-white streamers. Every single person who passed us was off their face. Not just a little tipsy, not a bit mellow, but utterly slaughtered, mullered, wrecked, legless, shit-faced, arseholed, fucked – deeply, deeply irretrievably fucked. They were like sleep-walking commuters. Faces would leer out of the dark, glassy-eyed, beatific. Occasionally the very undone would stand and rock before being taken up again by the stream of alternative humanity.

What made it all the more weird was that I was utterly, utterly straight. I was so chemical-free you could have tattooed the Soil Association logo on my forehead. I have been straight since the Falklands, since before most of these kids could eat with a fork. It was a straightening feeling to know that I was the only person within a city mile who could, as the label says, safely operate heavy machinery.

But an even weirder thing happened and I still can't really explain it. I never take notes. I trust my memory to edit out what's not needed, and in a decade of reporting it's never let me down until Glastonbury. As if in sympathy, as if by osmosis, it pressed the delete button and I have forgotten pretty much everything that happened. I can't remember coherently, even less chronologically. I've looked at Matthew's photographs and unarguably I'm in them. There I am in a pixie hat and a harlequin velvet coat. Where the fuck did they come from? It jogs only static. My memories of Glastonbury are like putting your head in the sea and staring at the bottom. It's another medium, another world.

'You must remember free hugs,' said Alice. 'That big man who was giving away free hugs, he gave you lots; and the banana shaman, the man dressed in a black bin-liner with a banana skin.' No, but I do remember the girl standing in front of her crudded boyfriend, grooming him like an ape, delicately picking coke-bogies out of his nose and eating them. And I remember standing at seven in the morning in the middle of tented suburbia, as the chill and full bladders woke the weekend hippies far too early, and the transcendent look of pain and nausea on their faces as they poked their heads out of their tents to confront a bright good morning. It was like a slap. I stood and watched it happen over and over again like open auditions for a silent movie. And I remember the lost boy in the middle of the night, fucked and buggered, stopping one in three to ask: 'D'you know where my tent is?' What's it look like? 'It's green.' Right, and is it near anything? 'Yeah, yeah. [Excited] It's next to another tent, a blue one.' Sorry, can't help you, mate.

And I remember buying Florence a fairy ball gown so she could go to a late-night costume party that looked like an Otto Dix painting. And I remember the T-shirt stalls: 'Dead Women Don't Say No' and 'I am Spartacus' – I so wanted one of those. I wanted one that said, 'I am the Eggman', and I wanted to give Matthew one that said, 'I am the Walrus'. And I remember the Welsh 'Te A Tost' stall where the bloke said, 'What you want is a feast, see? That's two rounds with my Auntie Wendy's marmalade and a cup of tea.' And that's exactly what I did want. And it was a feast.

And I remember the nude wanker. Occasional nudity is respected at Glastonbury. It is the original flavour and spirit of non-violent alternative protest, where hippies came from. Where would your flower power happening be without some flaxen-haired, clear-eyed child of the morning getting her tits out and flicking peace signs at the world? This one wasn't exactly from central casting.

In front of the un-amplified folk gazebo where real, head-shaking, lonely mandolin-pluckers and finger-in-ear, off-key whingers attracted a crowd of two or three delicate souls so hammered and wrung-out that their heads had been turned into iPods, there was a lady who had been so carried away by a folk combo that she'd taken all her clothes off. Nothing wrong with that. She'd been so transported by the music she was moved to give herself a bit of a wank. Not a gentle, feel-good fingering, but the complete, top-of-the-range, brace-yourself-Doris, blurred-wrist seeing to. No, maybe not too much wrong with that either. But there's an over-twenty-one age limit and it's Glastonbury.

The half-dozen pigs walk round with blinkers on doing community relations funny-hat-wearing. Lord Lucan jacking up with Osama Bin Laden would have difficulty getting arrested here, but the trouble was that this wasn't some buff, fit, pert hippy chick with flowers in her hair and plaited pubes. It was an old, fat, hideous, meat-faced nutter bagwoman and something had to be done on purely aesthetic grounds. She was putting the folk off their protest songs, and they were complaining.

Two large security guards spent a lot of time animatedly shouting into their walkie talkies before gingerly approaching the frotting troll with rubber gloves and a blanket, the old trout desperately trying to finish off the full Meg Ryan while at the same time telling Securicor to fuck themselves, like what she was doing. And they danced around her trying to grab her wrists without getting the finger. I watched with bated breath on tenterhooks. Would they? Will they? And then one of them did. Gave me the punchline. 'Oh, please, love. Come quietly.' Yes!

And I can remember the alternative health field, with every variety of absurd astral chakra voodoo hokum known to people under forty who've never been really ill. There were lots of circles for noddy-humming away cancer or drumming for a better back and world peace. But what I remember most was a bloke in the door of one tent doing utterly perfect yoga sun salutes. He must have been about my age and as supple as pollard willow. He drew an admiring crowd, they'd all tried a bit of yoga and they knew how difficult it is to link your fingers on the soles of your outstretched feet from a sitting position. But all I could think of was that in the time he'd learnt to do this, Tony Blair had gone from being in a band called Ugly Rumours to being Prime Minister, J.K. Rowling had become a billionaire and most of the blokes he was at school with had got careers, bought houses, had wives and kids, built things, made stuff, taken an interest. And in all that time he'd mastered the sun salute. I looked at him and I thought, there but for the grace of God, if I hadn't fortuitously lost my inner hippy.

And, finally, what I remember is the tepee field. In hippy terms this is the dock at St Tropez. Living in a tepee makes you traveller mega

A-list royalty. This is having it all, in that it's having hardly anything. The rest of us are just here rubbernecking in avaricious awe. The tepee field really does look like a glimpse into another world: hippy Jerusalem. And the dwellers go about their blessed daily chores with the sort of casual insouciance that comes from having been stared at a lot. The difference between these and the mega-yachts of the South of France is that these aren't hideous. These are the essential accessories of the wilfully modest. There are a few ethnic blankets, a log or two, black pots hanging over state-of-the-art fires, a brace of shaggy, blond children in thirteenth-century jerkins and jellybean sandals, a couple of lurchers, a Merlin staff, and a tom-tom finishes off the look that makes the rest of us want to burn our central islands with breakfast bar and trash the Range Rover.

We know in our hearts that our Philippe Starck is stupid bollocks, the espresso machine and *sorbetière* dust and ashes in our mouths, the weight and vast amount of our stuff is a rock about our necks. It's vacuous, unnecessary petty snobbery, a terrible indictment of our insecurity, our earthbound, hoarding dullness. We look at these soaring tents and the fragility of devoting our precious existence to things with plugs and keys. What do you give the man who has everything? A tepee and the opportunity to have nothing but his life back and some self-worth and maybe a dose of goodness and bravery. Bravery and goodness and nits. Bravery, goodness, nits and bad breath. Bravery, goodness, nits, bad breath and cold water with bits in, a bird with organic wilderness body hair and a shit in a shrub.

The tepee field was where I finally faced my inner hippy and found that he was wanting. He was wanting under-floor heating and dinner at the Wolseley. So that was Glastonbury as far as I can remember. I have this feeling it was a life-changing event. My life has a no-returns policy but I got a credit note. The girlfriend loved it; Matthew the snapper, I think, loved it; Alice BB adored it and for Florence the goddaughter it was just another weekend in that gilded time of your life. I have a picture of her in her dressing-up frock on my desk.

You will have noticed that I haven't mentioned the music. Well, it was there, it's the reason for Glastonbury but it's really not the point.

And that's another good thing about the Winnebago. You can watch it on the telly.

I asked Nick Mason of Pink Floyd what he thought of Glastonbury. 'Well, it's like the English hajj, it's going to Mecca.' And I reckon that's pretty spot-on. Glastonbury's a secular pilgrimage. Music and getting off our tits are the only things we all still believe in. Did you ever play there, I asked? 'No, I don't think we did.' Have you ever been? 'Good grief, no,' he replied with a look of mild horror. This is a man who really, honestly, doesn't know how many cars he owns to the nearest ten.

June 2004

Dog

I'm looking at a bunch of flowers. It's expensive, hand-plaited and knotted, £70 minimum. They're for me. I've been bunched. Someone wanted to say it with flowers. The note that came with them says, 'Sorry' but the flowers say, 'You're a fucking monster.' They say it in *a cappella*, colour-coordinated, greenly scented harmony. They're from a man. When men send each other flowers it means one of four things. It means one of them is a gardener, one of them is an interior decorator or cheating on an interior decorator, one of them is dead, or one of them is a monster. The man who sent them to me was an editor, so none of the above. I checked my pulse and it must be me: I'm either the interior decorator or the monster. I have become a diva, the Pavarotti of print. I'm toying with the idea of insisting on my own personal sub-editor. I want Mario to do my picture and Nicky my hair. I want my name above the headline. I want my name to *be* the headline. I want my prose in bold. I want editorial control of readers' letters. I want control of readers. I want, I want . . . How did it end up like this? How did I get bunched by an editor? Because I'd behaved like Lady Victoria Hervey at a TV soap opera awards party.

My Great-Aunt Netta used to say, 'If it's a choice between being brilliant and being nice, be nice. And if you don't have the choice (and you don't) be nice, because you don't have to be brilliant to be nice.' I know what kicked all this off, when my inner monster came out of its closet. It was the dog. An editor (not the floral one, another one) called to enquire politely, nicely, about a piece I owed. It was late, exceedingly late, later than a Bulgarian tackle, later than the USA joining a world war, later than Jools Holland and David Letterman, so late, in fact, that the entire magazine was waiting on the printers' slipway, so did I think perhaps I might let them have it?

Instead of saying sorry, which would have been the Aunt Netta, nice option, I said, 'I'll give you the piece by Friday, if you give me a puppy on Monday.' And instead of saying, 'Fuck off, you megalomaniac little madam,' which would have been the normal sane reaction, the editor waited a beat and said, 'What breed?' And then instead of me saying, 'Ho, ho, ho, I was only joking,' I stepped through the door marked Barking Monster and growled, 'A Parson Russell Terrier. A bitch with a pedigree.'

And so it was that I morphed from mild-mannered hack to loony man of letters and became an eye-rolling anecdote: 'What's the worst job you ever had?'

'Getting a small bitch for that A. A. Gill.'

With a disturbing sense of unreality I filed the piece on Friday and on Monday a pair of editorial assistants appeared, who presumably had double-firsts from ivy-clad academe and had beaten off hundreds of other applicants to gain a toehold in publishing, presuming that it would be, well, God knows what people presume magazine publishing would be, but certainly not driving to Norfolk and back pretending to be a puppy-less couple on behalf of some columnist with a stratospheric ego crisis.

'It's very sweet,' said one of the young over-achievers, 'it's been sick on my lap twice. We called it Biscuit.' *Her* Biscuit.

'Did you? Can I get you anything? No, well, bye-bye.'

I was beginning to understand why very famous, very mad people are often seen as bad-mannered and distant, and can end up as recluses. It's the look on other people's faces, the shadow of mild disgust insufficiently covered by polite disbelief that exposes the bad behaviour.

So there I was, alone in the house, with a Parson Russell puppy, long-legged, wire-haired, a question-mark tail, a tan face with a white blaze. She became Putu, the Zulu word for maize porridge. Naming pets is a glimpse into the prosaic flights of ego, like the naming of celebrity children. You're not giving the thing an identity; you're putting a label on the new extension of you.

Now I'm not going to give you a long, winsome description of dog and man: the runs through the long grass, the amusing little adventures in the shoe cupboard, the heartache of the worm pills, the crisis of the turd in the early morning kitchen. Humans' stories about dogs come just after their stories about dyspraxic children for their utter hell. Suffice it to say, in the language of Californian self-help gurus, I had a dog-shaped hole in my life that Putu filled neatly.

What's always fascinated me is how our species ever got a dog-shaped hole in the first place. Why didn't we have a sloth-shaped or a Noah's Ark-shaped hole? I understand this is rather deflecting the subject from my bad behaviour, but actually it's more interesting. Dogs are the oldest of all domesticated animals. Before sheep or cattle, long before horses and arable farming, man shared his hearth and his bones with dogs, and no one knows quite why. The relationship between horses, sheep, chickens and men is obvious. We eat them and sometimes fuck them. With dogs it's not as straightforward. The hominids that walked out of Africa came with dogs at their heels, but why?

The first question that everything in the world asks itself every morning is: 'So, what's in it for me?' It's not clear what was in it for man or dog at the start. Later, of course, dog would herd, guard, catch crooks, find people in earthquakes and be Shep. To see what's in it for the dog, you only have to compare the number of dogs with wolves. Domestication is a vast advantage for a species. The original progenitor of the domestic cow is long extinct. Happily, animals don't have romantic, new-age, green problems with a free life as opposed to a housebound-and-fed life. But in the beginning, the hunter-gatherer and the dog must have been competitors. Packs of dogs would have been after exactly the same food as people and it's safe to imagine that given the opportunity they'd have killed and eaten each other.

Selection and survival are all about opportunity. What the precise set of circumstances was that made dogs and men cohabit we'll never know, but a likely scenario is that a clan of hominids found orphaned puppies. They wouldn't have been an immediate threat, neither would they have been much of a meal. And a human, probably a child, looked at them and went, 'Ah!' And in that instant there was one of those turning points for a species that is the difference between an evolutionary early bath and a seat on the sofa with your own doctor. It was a moment that went into slow motion and had violins as a soundtrack. The dogs recognised the opportunity. This was what dogs had been born for. This was the once-in-a-lifetime opportunity for an entire species.

Hominids and dogs were opportunistic. Most animals made their living by being specialist tradesmen, working to be the most efficient in a particular habitat or circumstance. They play all their evolutionary cards in one hand. But some are generalists, doing a bit of everything, always competing with specialists but able to adapt. It's tougher to begin with, there are a lot of risks and a lot of casualties, but in the end it seems that nature favours the dilettante. Adaptation is the name of the beautiful survival game. And these puppies saw an opportunity. They saw something they couldn't understand, but they saw that they might exploit it. The puppies noticed that humans had a range of expression and behaviour that was outside dog experience, but that 'Ah!' showed they could manipulate it. They were the first animals to see and understand the importance of human emotions. To live with men, dogs had to do a pretty swift makeover. You can't have small kids and an adult wolf in the same tent, trust me. So dogs do something called neoteny. They remain in a juvenile state for their whole lives. Domestic dogs grow up to be childish wolves, never getting to adulthood because that would make them unpredictable and violent and a blanket.

Dogs are naturally pack animals so they found it easy to fit in. The biggest problem in becoming domesticated is not for the species who can't live with humans, it's for the ones who can't live with each other. For thousands of years we tried to domesticate cheetahs. They're readily trainable, but you can't breed them because they're solitary. Cheetahs have never managed to get over themselves and now they're endangered. Dogs, on the other hand, now live on every continent and country on earth. They've gone into space, though they didn't know why and they didn't come back. They managed to do one other incredibly clever thing: they mutated faster than any other animal. A new variety can be made in less time than Ferrari can make a new car.

You might say that inventing breeds is wholly human – and choosing the colour swatches and size is – but it can only be managed with the acquiescence of the dog. We've been breeding horses for 3,000 years and a horse is still a horse; there's nothing like the variation between a Chihuahua and a Great Dane. Dog species may come and go but their genes are pooled infinitely.

The first dogs realised that, alone in the natural world, humans crave variety. Everything else wants continuity and certainty; people want novelty. And dogs provided it. What they came up with is the cleverest thing in all of nature: reverse-Darwinism – not the survival of the fittest but the survival of the least fit, the most needy. The Chinese Crested is a completely naked Chihuahua except for a tuft of old man's pubes on its head and tail. It has large, lachrymose eyes, huge ears and a tiny little nose. It feels like dry chamois leather and it'll go floppy in the crook of your arm and stare up at you. It's imitating a human baby. What's even cleverer is that its temperature is a couple of degrees higher than normal. It's imitating a sick baby, so you'll care for it. As an animal, it's a fucking disaster. As a dog, it's supremely successful.

Dogs have understood that they can use their genes to become smaller, furrier, weaker, worse hunters, reedier-voiced. Wolves went on being better and better wolves and now they're just behind the cheetahs in extinction's waiting room. Dogs, meanwhile, have their own doctors and holiday homes, their own laws, their own human police force (the RSPCA), their own professional association (the Kennel Club), and they have welfare. They live with all the benefits of the most civilised humans. They even have people who follow them round picking up their shit. (This is an utterly inexplicable waste to a dog, but then everything we do is utterly inexplicable to dogs.) They recognise our emotion. Over a thousand years they've learnt to read it and react to it, but they can have no idea what it means or why we do it. All they know is how to exploit it.

The most fascinating thing about them is that they are no closer to understanding what it is to be human than they were 10,000 years ago, but they pander to our feelings with an infinite subtlety. It's like a play where only half the cast understands the language it's written in. The irrefutable rules of evolution say that there must be something in this relationship for us. And plainly there is: dogs sniff, lead, herd and fetch slippers, but those things don't account for

1 per cent of dogs. They do something more complex for us. They're nature's yes men. A dog is the ultimate lifetime sycophant. A junkie tramp sitting on a pavement in his own wee can have a dog whose look says, 'You're a god among men.' Dogs allow us to be stars in our own lives. They're an endlessly appreciative audience, our most assiduous fans and obsessive stalkers. It's not for real, of course. They just read us in the way a wolf reads a caribou, and if the caribou had opposable thumbs and a tin opener then the wolf would probably let it get dinner instead of ripping its throat out.

When you fall over and break your hip and can't reach the phone, your dog will try his damnedest to help. He'll bark and jump and whine and wag. But when no one comes, have no doubts: he'll eat you. He's a dog. In the way of things, when I turned the corner and stepped through that door marked 'Ooh, get you!' and became the monster, God and Darwin (who are an item) had a bit of a laugh and gave me an antidote, brought on the Fool to my Lear.

As I write, Putu's lying on her chair that used to be my chair, and she's watching me. She can watch me for hours and hours. Her expression looks very like devotion. The eyebrows twitch. She rests her chin on her paws in adoration, except she doesn't. Those emotions are exclusively human. What she's doing is learning me. She's reading me like a book. The truth is, I'm the Fool to her Lear. Dogs are bigger and better monsters than we can ever be. They've found the weakness in our huge brains: we're slaves to our sentiment and emotions. For dogs, we're just a resource. We're prey.

September 2004

Fatherhood

There are any number of design glitches in the human frame: the precipitous decision to stand upright instead of trundling on all fours, which embarrassingly rearranged the visibility of our gonads thereby demanding the manufacture of the Y-front; a columnar spine instantly invented the chiropractor. But as consolation we got oversized female breasts as a secondary compensation for having made their lady bits downward-facing instead of backward-facing at nose level.

But perhaps the worst of all ergonomic glitches was that we were born not knowing how to blow our noses. I don't expect this worries you much because you've probably got nose-blowing covered and most of the people you want to kiss are pretty tidy in the nose department. But you weren't born like that. There was a time in your life when the contents of your nose ran free.

I'd forgotten about the magic of nasal flubber until my new two both got colds on Christmas Day and one grew a geological outcrop that resembled an inverted Old Man of Hoy and the other had two spigots of effluvia that trickled on to her extended tongue. Neither had any idea of the concept of blowing but they did instantly glean that bogies were edible, which is an interesting Darwinian footnote. We are obviously born with the pick and chew gene.

The sight of them, blocked and soggy, reminded me of something I saw in Africa. I was covering the war in Darfur from a refugee camp on the border with Chad in an old tent that passed a Médecins Sans Frontières waiting room packed with women and their desperately dying children. There was one mother who stood out as strikingly beautiful. I mean, really memorable-looking. A face that was strong and implacable – huge eyes and cheekbones cast in toffee-coloured bronze, framed in a single bright shawl. I signalled to Tom the photographer to take her picture. It was an easy opening spread.

She regarded him and his camera with her obsidian eyes devoid of emotion; she was as beautifully inscrutable as a sphinx.

As he kept snapping, the child was wrapped in the folds of her shawl, making that soft mewing that is the exhausted way of children who are losing the light. Shrivelled with dehydration and malnutrition, her nose was clotted with a huge soggy goitre of snot. The mother never took her eyes from Tom's lens, and slowly and deliberately lent down and gently put her mouth over her child's little nose and sucked, then swallowed. It was properly shocking on so many levels.

First, of course, it was disgusting, an act passively aimed at the gaze of strange men from a woman who had probably lost her husband, her family, who had nothing but this little scrap of life in a shawl. Many of the women in this room had been raped. Her face was a terrible liability. The act was overtly sexual but repellent, but that's not the overriding image or the memory that I carry. It was a profound act of love.

At the edge of coping, there was very little this woman could do for her child; she had nothing left to give. No more milk, no more protection, no more security or hope. But she could clean it. And at the margin of life, when all the options are spent, what's important is the simple and practical. And love is like that. Messy and basic and animal. It isn't romantic or subtle when it's all we have left.

The first lesson of being a parent, of being a man, is that you have no idea of what love is, or like, or for. That urgent, delicious groin-magnet feeling that you understand as being love is the tease, the taster, the glimpse – it is a warm bath compared to the riptide of the real thing. And that arrives with fatherhood. Up until then you've just been paddling in love. Nobody ever tells you this, nobody ever explains that you can't feel the bottom, that you drown in the stuff. Other men never mention that love, which is remiss of us, and our dads never tell us, never really tell us. You can write 'love you' on a birthday card, whisper love to a sleeping tousled head, but to explain to an adolescent, a teenager, that terrifyingly transcendent fundamental act of nature that is loving your children, is too difficult and choking. But you should know, you should be aware, that you can't be prepared for it, nothing prepares you. But you shouldn't be surprised. The funny and sad thing is that the time when it's easiest to say it, when there is the greatest paternal emotion, when it's most obvious and strong, you never remember. Those first years when you can't blow your own nose, when your father picked you up and rocked you and watched you speechlessly as you slept, are blank. Later, as you grow up, the relationship is muddled with practicality, with the resentment and the accidents, with the dull rigmarole of discipline and bedtimes and homework, inappropriate behaviour, tantrums and tiredness. And that's what you know of your childhood. You remember dodging through it. But there were four scant years when you slept in an ocean of love and your father never forgets and it never goes away and it will come to you.

And you realise the greatest design fault of human beings is that they don't remember their childhood and you can't recall their first words or first steps – the first time they tasted chocolate or falling asleep on their father's shoulders in dark kitchens. You need to know it's coming and you need to know it's already there.

March 2008

Nelson Mandela

The corridors of the InterContinental hotel smell of the uneaten, unchanged and unloved. The mezzanine floor is a miasma of exhausted, reconditioned air and scream-absorbing carpet. It's one of those constructions of bleak, utilitarian comfort that make you despair of human ingenuity. Here, past the press/business facilities, is a conference room – one of those large open spaces at a premium in cities, used for the amplification of grand, commercial lies and celebrations.

It's 10 a.m. and the room's been fitted up for a big day. Men in shorts and work boots, wearing T-shirts boasting past crusades and convictions, move about with the concerted, head-down purpose of an imminent, immovable deadline. They are the international free-masonry of fitters, riggers and roadies. Blokes who are never without a corkscrew, a light and four yards of gaffer tape.

Every public event, anywhere on the globe, is built by these leftover medieval artisans who step lively, yelling unintelligible single syllables, testing sound systems, putting up podiums, lighting interactive screens and constructing bullet-point display boards with an air of smiley cynicism. You just know that at the final trump, an army of these bantering blokes with 'Iron Maiden on the road!' hair will rise up and dismantle the world overnight.

Keeping out of their way are other men, in suits, with airport ties and multiple phones. They text pleading demands into BlackBerrys. In turn, they are circled by girls with high heels and fussed hair and get-off-me grins. This is the public-relations commissariat. They go with riggers the way vultures go with jackals, employed by customers who want to avoid relations with the public. To a man and woman they look wrung out and worried like sheep. They are employed to be wrung and worried, to suck up and absorb all the anxiety of the organised, money-go-round world. Today, they're overseeing the *mise-en-scène* for a photo call: a simple stage, a backdrop, a couple of cardboard posters saying something portentous, sentimental and forgettable. It might be a product launch, an employee-of-the-month award or the declaration of an invasion.

Actually, it's the stage for Nelson Mandela to have his ninetieth-birthday picture taken with a hundred folk he doesn't know, but who know him. More precisely, it's the stage for a hundred people to have their picture taken with Mandela.

Stephen from Budapest, an economic refugee drone, pushes a vacuum cleaner across a tennis court of nylon carpet. He wears the dull overalls of public invisibility. He's too old to be chasing dust in a foreign country, prematurely bald with sad eyes. He says he likes London, what he's seen of it. But he's tired and, no, he doesn't know what this event is.

Terry O'Neill, the chosen photographer for Mandela's birthday tour, is sitting on the far wall while his assistants set up the big-format camera and the synchronised, megawatt hose-you-down lights. They check the focus on a chair for the umpteenth time. We all stare at it. The chair is the centre of the room; the riggers and roadies regard it with a professional respect, as if it were the apotheosis of Meat Loaf. It's a plush, overstuffed chair, a Louis XXXIII chair, the sort of international chair used for filling up corners in big hotels.

'Go and see how it looks,' Terry tells me. It feels mildly sacrilegious to sit on the chair, like sitting on the throne while the monarch's having a pee. Already, this ugly piece of hotel furniture is imbued with the saintliness of Mandela, and he hasn't even sat on it yet. The assistant snaps the shutter at me, pretending to be the best person in the world, and Terry, pretending to be Bono beside me. He's better at it than I am, and rubs the Polaroid, like trying to get warmth into a corpse.

He looks at the chair and says: 'Change it. Change it for something simpler.' The chair's moment is over. It goes back to being just hotel furniture, a nearly-chair.

This is all displacement activity. The photographers are bored and nervous. There will only be a few seconds for each shot, no margin for error or interpretation or finesse. No space to tell them they've got something in their teeth. Around the edges of the room are the napkinned trestles of inhospitable hospitality – the Thermoses of stewed, lukewarm, coffee-style bitterness, the plates of biscuits you've never seen in a shop or in a home, that only exist in corporate hotels. Guarding them are girls from the distant heart of Europe, who stand in unflattering uniforms waiting for something big to turn up and rescue them from the biscuits.

Most people drift in and collect in the room's dark marches. Sleek, older men with carefully managed grey in their hair, in better suits, worn with sleeker shoes and silk ties chosen by a tie-choosing assistant. Each of these men has another man or two for their support and affirmation. These are the captains of consumption, the herders of money, the gents who move the First World and shake the Third. Blue-chip CEOs who sponsor and fund and finesse this occasion, this happening. They have come to be photographed with Mandela: a small memento, a religious image to be displayed discreetly on the huge desk or in the annual report, or above the bar in the den. You can tell they're not used to being kept waiting – they rather enjoy the hair-shirtness of it. It's sort of appropriate before meeting a saint. In the topsy-turvy world of charity and celebrity, these plutocrats who have chancellors and finance ministers on their speed dials come at the bottom of the cheek-pecking, arm-clasping, back-slapping order. The talent comes first, and they are being corralled in a separate holding room.

One of the PR ulcers whispers 'Bring on the celebrity' into his secret-squirrel radio, and through the big double doors they come, gambolling like spring bullocks, beaming and dazzled by each other, the occasion, the event, but mostly just by themselves for having got here to this room. What a relief to be excited and giggly, not to be surly and cool, to talk all at once. In one corner behind a hastily erected cordon for their own safety are the cast of some multicultural, Milk Tray-coloured, feel-glad and horny musical. These perky, pretty teenagers have been mainlining adrenaline and endorphins. They started out as nature's hyperactive show-offs, but now they're levitating and vibrating with excitement, tumescent with joy and hormones.

They involuntarily bop into little routines, jigging and staggering with a manic, incoherent happiness. They're hazy about who Nelson Mandela is, but they all know Will Smith is awesome.

Slightly apart is an old black man in a suit, the arms too long. He is unmistakably African. He's brought the stillness with him; the guarded eyes, the private face, the quiet politeness. He is Mandela's driver and has been since the beginning – since Robben Island. He looks at the gaggle of humming talent – it's not the worst thing he's ever seen.

Behind him is an open door and slowly, like the entry of shadow puppets, a phalanx, a protective crèche of people, sidles across the light. In the centre, one shuffling silhouette is unmistakably the figure of Nelson Mandela.

Walking with a stick, supported on each side, the radiant tableau moves towards the arena. The pop stars and the dancers, the plutocrats and PRs and photographers and all their assistant managers, handlers and agents don't know that he's just there and Mandela doesn't yet know that they're just here. It's the lull between colliding worlds.

He comes into the room slowly, slowly, his damaged feet in big, comfy slippers, sagging in the trademark African shirt, and they erupt – whistle and clap and whoop, and generally can't believe it. It's like *The X Factor*.

Terry says: 'Let's get the group shot over first' – he doesn't know how long he can hold back the hyperventilating show bunnies. Mandela is ushered to sit in the middle, in the new star chair, helped by his formidable Afrikaans secretary, one of those terrifyingly admirable women only Africa produces. He looks up and around, like a child who's just woken in a strange room, and sees all the folk who have come to see him, and smiles this brilliant, beatific smile, a smile that could break your heart. It is the most conscience-tugging, soul-moving facial expression in the world, and he got it in jail. Go back and look at all the photographs of Mandela before the island, and he is another righteous black lawyer with the ebony, private face and the guarded eyes. But he comes out twenty-seven years later with this miraculous face, moulded and creased by injustice into a transcendent African mask, this expression that speaks every language.

The stars fall in behind and around him, like confetti at an arranged marriage. Annie Lennox sits on his left, transported. The seat on his right is kept empty. Will Smith slips in behind him, flicking peace signs. The pack of drama-school kids squirm at his feet like Labrador puppies. Where you sit is important, not just because closeness is a blessing but because this picture will be cropped for the papers and social gossip magazines, and only those at the epicentre are going to get the publicity fix. The empty seat on the right is filled by the ample thighs of Leona Lewis, Simon Cowell's latest vibrato-rich crooner of the beyond-irony transfusion, 'Bleeding Love'.

'Smile. Look this way, smile,' the snappers call. 'Madiba, Madiba, over here. Madiba!' It's a familiar patronymic of respect, but in a Cockney accent it sounds like mockery.

Mandela regards the camera only fleetingly, not ignoring it, just perhaps not entirely aware of it. His eyes wander around the room at all these people and all this attention, all this expectation, all this love. And he smiles the smile. Behind him Will Smith – who by happy coincidence is promoting his film *Hancock* – grins and leans forward with the Vs, and everyone else arranges their hands in the semaphore of pop eloquence, and their faces into that contortion of egotism and charity. The flashes flash, the moment is caught. Terry turns away and gives me a look that isn't in the camera, and I wonder who on earth thought a pop concert was an appropriate gift for a ninety-year-old-man with bad feet.

But, then, pop concerts seem to be our culture's response to most things – the catch-all celebrations, commemoration and commiseration of everything: the Queen's jubilee, famine, hurricanes, birthdays and small, messy wars.

And why here? Why does Mandela come to London for his birthday? Simply because here he can raise money to combat AIDS. We could have sent him a cheque, he could have sat at home, but then these people wouldn't have had their photograph, and we wouldn't have had the pop concert.

Now it's one-to-one time. The entertainers sit next to him looking nervous, some hold his hand, put an arm round his neck. Beside me, one of Mandela's carers mutters, 'Don't touch him,' with sadness and anger. But only I hear it.

Through all this, he sits quiescent and patient, listening without hearing, knowing without understanding, smiling the great warm smile. His fearsome secretary is fearsome on his behalf, moving people on, holding them back: 'No managers today, no hangers-on, just performers.'

When the talent's all done, the businessmen scuttle in, uncomfortable in their suits, fiddling with their tie knots like vestigial scrotums, taking Mandela's hand firmly and meaningfully, looking deep into the camera's blinking eye, as if sealing some moral deal.

Why do they want all this so badly? This picture with an old African whose deification by the West is such an indictment of all other Africans. We can't help adopting worthy people from the developing world – suspending criticism like debt to make them worthier, investing them with a Christmas tree of wholesome goodness and blameless simplicity. There is more than a stain of racism here, an echo of colonial assumption. We see a good man and promote him to an impossibly great man by virtue of his having come from a bad and frightening place.

Poor, dark, benighted Africa; a continent of corruption, violence, megalomania, ignorance, sickness and superstition. How much greater is Mandela in our eyes because he's risen from the heart of darkness rather than, say, Tewkesbury or Oslo. They hug him and get speechlessly lumpy because he inoculates us against the fears and prejudices about the Third World in general, but Africa in particular. In the process of worshipping him, he is allocated patronising characteristics – an innate, natural wisdom, an avuncular sympathy for children. Someone here said that Mandela was 'Gandhi for our generation'. This is a wishful, fairy-tale nonsense that denies him his history, his anger, his blackness, his Africanness. Mandela was a revolutionary. Far from a pacifist, he organised and led Spear of the Nation, the terrorist wing of the ANC. In adopting Mandela as a smiley face, T-shirt slogan, album-cover vision of happy otherworldliness, we take him from his real family: southern Africa. We make him the West's boy.

He is a real hero, he's an African hero. His struggle and his triumph are their struggle and triumph. We can't buy them with an AIDS donation and a song. He's called Madiba because of his black African-ness, not despite it. He should be at home with his family on his birthday. Africans venerate age. He has lived twice as long as most African men can expect to.

There is a votive quality about these images – the great and the powerful once had themselves painted with saints to fool God and the neighbours. There's also something less edifying, something of the game hunter's trophy shot.

And it's over. Mandela is helped to his feet, slowly, slowly. The performers and plutocrats crowd the exit, stabbing BlackBerrys, shouting into their phones for cars and lunch.

Mandela is handed his ivory stick, and hobbles painfully. This, then, is where the long road to freedom ends. He looks exhausted, beaten down by the adoration of strangers, tired by the demands of so much love.

This has not been an edifying occasion. It's nobody's fault – everybody had good intentions, or at least enough good intentions. But altogether it's been sad, dispiriting. Nobody comes out of the photo call looking good. Already the roadies are tearing down the evidence, packing up the metal boxes. The photographers look at their screens, feeding the images into the river of celebrity and curiosity.

As he gets to the door, for the briefest moment Mandela pauses and looks at the wall where, unnoticed, the coffee girl in her uniform of invisibility still stands guarding the biscuits. She smiles at him. And Mandela bathes her in the great, hot African sun of his grin, and there are tears in her eyes.

July 2008

Old Age

I want you to do something for me. Think of it as a game, a quiz, a trick. Go and find an old person – one who's not related to you or a neighbour. Just a random, strange old person, a lurking crusty. It doesn't matter what sex – sex really doesn't matter to old people. They don't do or have or belong to sex any more, they're just old. Old is the third sex: girls, boys and the aged. So, look at this old person, stare at them, get really close. Don't be frightened – they won't hurt you. They're not contagious; they're more frightened of you than you are of them. Right, here's the game bit. Can you tell me how old they actually are? Look carefully at that face, at the wrinkles, the crêpey, sunken cheeks, the frail, eroded jaw, the thin folds of wattle. Count the archipelagos of age spots, examine the wind-coloured hair patted into the habit of a lifetime. Look into the fretted, damp eyes, their lids sagging like ragged bedroom curtains, and add up the years. Pick a number, like guessing the weight of a cake or the height of a steeple. You'll see it's much more difficult than it looks.

You can discern the years between sixteen and twenty. You know a twenty-one-year-old from a twenty-eight-year-old, but I bet you can't mark a decade between sixty and ninety. You can't read the gradations and patinas. Not that old people hide them; you can't tell because you don't look. And you don't look because you don't care. Really, who cares how old the old are? Old is a destination. There is nothing after old. Just nothing. Now, just one more thing: take another look at your old person and tell me, what was it that determined that they were old? What made you think they weren't just young with a lived-in face and a hangover? If you can't tell what age old is, how do you know when they've got there? Do you think they just wake up one morning to discover they're past everything but care and caring? Old is not a number. It's not a date. It's simply the absence of youth,

the absence of attraction, interest, new friends, society. The absence
of conviviality, warmth, choice, or surprise, or life.

We have a problem with old age, a huge problem. If we arbitrarily
cut the birthday cake at sixty-five, then that makes the old 16 per
cent of the population, which will rise to 22 per cent by 2031. The
old use up more than 40 per cent of the National Health budget.
But the old aren't the problem – it's the rest of us. It's you and I that
have the problem. It's our collective refusal to look at the old, to be
in a room with them, to ask them into our lives. The great terror of
our age is age. We would rather consign the old to a netherworld, a
waiting room where they are out of mind and out of sight. The fear
is plainly not of the old: it is that we will become them. The old are
the zombies at the end of your own home horror movies.

St Leonards-on-Sea was built by an old man. James Burton bought
a lump of farmland on the coast and conceived a new town, a town
of bracing gentility. This collection of gleaming, po-faced streets, the
promenades of probity, the municipal gardens for civic reflection,
became journey's end for the retired civil servants of empire and the
imperial military, a final move for the widowed spouses of industrial
engineers and provincial department-store magnates, the rheumatic
and the consumptive, the dun-achieving tricked down here to the sea's
reflected glister that bounced off the white-cliff-stucco guesthouses
and sedate residential hotels.

They came to play vicious bridge and smiley bowls, formed ex-
clusive societies, had tea dances and charabanc outings, and filled
stuffy rooms with Benares brass, Burmese teak, Turkey rugs and care-
ful china. They hung gilt-framed views of Table Mountain and dead
boys in khaki, and dusted the parsimonious riches of adventurous
lives lived with a gingerish prudence.

St Leonards was, from the start, mildly risible, a crepuscular com-
munity twinned with the letters page, the Conservative Party and
the crematorium. But it was also a reward, a just desert, a symbol of
a life lived with standards, with napkins and polished shoes. And if
you had to be old, it was a good place to be old in at a time when
being old was an achievement. But those old black-and-white granny
ghosts should see it now.

The steely Channel still dowses the front with a squinting bright-
ness, but the streets are gap-toothed, the shops boarded up or given
over to charity. In the pub, the motes of wasted time dance in the
light over yellow-eyed men in tracksuits, who measure the day in
toothpick roll-ups. There is nothing genteel about St Leonards. Like
the rest of the south coast, it has been given over to the long-term
useless, the invalidity addicted, the flotsam of refugees and carelessly
relocated. But they haven't displaced the old. They're still here, the
indigenous community, but hiding. St Leonards has one of the high-
est populations of aged in the country.

On the sixth floor of a caretakered block, an old man sits quietly in
his front room surrounded by pottery, china, wood, cats, none living.
He has an untouched leatherette-bound edition of Dickens, and above
the mantel a print of eighteenth-century huntsmen quaffing in front
of a roaring fire. Their conviviality mocks his stifling solitude. The
room has the smell of exhausted air. A clock strikes a cacophonous
quarter that would infuriate anyone who had something else to listen
to. Here the time doesn't go quietly. Everything harks to an absent
woman. Her knick-knacks and mementos, the holiday souvenirs,
the jolly vanities now fight for space and memory with the detritus
of communal care: crutches, bottles of pills, easy-grip utensils. This
man has diabetes, a heart condition, swollen ankles, but that's not
what ails him. He's old and alone. His tracksuit bottoms are stained.
Food is delivered every two days by a nice agency worker from the
Philippines who does a bit of shopping for him. I am here with the
district nurse, who wants to check his blood is not too sweet. She asks
how he is; the question is rhetorical. He has a bottle of gin and the
telly. Once he lived in Malta, once he was a private detective, once he
kept real cats, once he had a wife and friends. He's not uncared for;
he has the tablets and the tinctures, and a string in the corner that, if
pulled, will summon a man in the call centre, who will phone to ask
what the matter is and, if nobody answers, will send an ambulance.
We as a caring society will fend off his creeping death, insulate his
awful loneliness for as long as possible. We just can't supply him with
anything worth living for. In another small flat along the seafront, an-
other man sits in another chair that seems to have grown around him

like a fungus. He sits with his back to the bright sea view. The room
has hardly any other furniture. There is naught for comfort. In the
corner is a glass cabinet containing a collection of china princesses.
'They're nice,' I say. 'Did you collect them?'

'Do you want to buy them?' he replies.

This man also has diabetes, and depression, and an ulcer on his leg
that won't heal. He's had it for years. They think the best cure is to
cut off the limb. He doesn't use it much anyway. He worked on the
railways at Paddington, met all sorts – royalty, stars. Every day was
different. He had a wife. She died. He had a son and a daughter. They
don't see him or call. He wants to die. The loneliness, the sadness, has
made living a mortal sickness. I ask him how old he is: sixty-nine.
Only sixty-nine. He could reasonably expect to live like this, minus
a limb or two, for another fifteen or twenty years.

These two chaps are not exceptional. There are people like them
in every street, in every block of flats, above every parade of shops,
in every dripping-laurel cul-de-sac, up communal stairs and down
muddy lanes. The old sit in mushroom chairs, never further than two
feet from a radiator, a phone and the TV. They don't go out much
because out is frightening, panicky, hostile for the old. Outside is
a country they don't belong to any more, where they're no longer
included. Just think how few old people you notice, how relatively
few there are among us, bustling and dodging in the streets, shops
and restaurants. You will see none after dark. The old live like Tran-
sylvanians, terrified of the young, the swift and supple, loud and late,
irritable young. Even when they do venture out among us we don't
look at them, we don't see them; they cling to the wall, curl up like
dead leaves in bus shelters, press themselves into corners.

I have become haunted by the absence of the old. Ever since the
death of my father three years ago, I have got into the habit of
asking middle-aged friends about their parents. There is a common
narrative to their answers. They list the deficiencies, the problems, the
conditions, the failings, the diminutions, usually with a tired fondness
and a growing hum of exasperation. I sat next to a woman at dinner
recently who told me how wonderful her father was because he'd died
so well, so quietly and quickly, ne'er a fuss. And then with a sigh,

'Now my mother, she's always complaining, miserable, I think she's scared of letting go.' It wasn't said carelessly or without a decorous dab of concern, but mostly it was with annoyance.

You hear it, too, among the professionals who care for the old, reciting illnesses and shortages. You hear it in the media, where old age is a collection of problems. The old are slow and cold, brittle and cancerous, breathless, toothless, sexless, forgetful. And, most newsworthily, they're victims – of bugs, of councillors and chancellors, or welfare and weather. They're also the victims of grief and pity and comedians. To be old is to be stalked by taxes and frost, flights of stairs, and, finally, God. To be old is to vanish behind the sum of incurable, piteous conditions.

For many, the final furlong of a life is spent immobile in a chair, in a bright room in what's euphemistically called a 'home'. It isn't a home, just as Battersea Dogs Home isn't a home. It's a hospice for those who've been put out of a home. These villas standing back from the road in the outskirts of provincial towns, discreet as brothels, hidden behind leylandii, with bland, forgettable names, are run by opaque, care-dispensing companies that are the shallow end of health care.

It is estimated that a quarter of all nursing homes fall below care guidelines, which are themselves set disgustingly close to the earth. If you walk up the steps of an old people's home, holding the rail to steady yourself through the swinging doors into the little reception area with its pot plants and notice boards pinned with safety warnings and activity sheets, be under no illusion. If you ever leave, it will be in an ambulance or a hearse. You are here until you decide to let go, and the sooner and the quieter and the neater you can manage that, the better. Residential people's homes get less care and attention than prisons. They don't have to rehabilitate anyone. Every inmate is on a life sentence. These bright, wipe-down, neon-lit, disinfected rooms, smelling of fish, piss and Cif, are death row for the blameless.

I'm sent to be shown round a residential home in Putney. This is top of the range – they're proud of this one. Very nice, very busy and efficient. The directors and the PRs and the housekeepers who come to meet me all have the gimlet, spearmint keenness of folk on a no-nonsense, long-distance goodness mission. The walls are collaged with old record sleeves, Perry Como and the Carpenters, Jimmy Shand and Cliff. The doors and lifts work with security swipe cards; the rooms are full of inmates, 'guests', who sit for the most part in a ruminative stasis. A circle of old men sit together, none acknowledging the presence of the others. Their rheumy eyes swim, tufts of missed stubble prickle whitely. Only their fingers are restless, worrying a hem or blindly searching for something lost and forgotten. One holds a large teddy bear with a blue-knuckled hand, like a prize from a long-decamped funfair.

In another room three hunched old ladies watch *Oklahoma!*. 'I'm just a girl who can't say no.' In another, there's a church service. We sing 'Praise My Soul the King of Heaven'. In another room there is painting by numbers. The place is a hamster wheel of activity, singsongs and seated exercise, all purposeless. There is nothing left to learn, nothing to be fit for, nobody to give the paintings to, no more skills needed, no new tunes and no new verses. This is merely collective time-whittling.

Visitors often comment how similar old people's homes are to infant schools. There is a sort of neatness, a return full circle to the innocence of toddlers. It's a comfort to believe that the destination of life is to end up where you started – in nappies, being fed mush, drinking from a sippy cup with a matey, loud kindness that excludes dignity or respect. It's rarely mentioned, though, because it's a sensitive subject, that almost all the staff in care homes are imported from nations that have a far greater veneration for age than our own. As one Filipino cleaner said to me, 'You don't want to live with your old, and you're too guilty to even feed them.'

These homes are the final resort. When you fail at basic one-room, single-bar life, this is where you come. The government will make you sell everything you own to get here. Nearly all 'guests' have some form of dementia. This is the great unspeakable plague of our medically privileged times: dying from the inside out. Outside hospital, dementia isn't even classed as a medical problem: it's a concern of social workers. If it were medical, local authorities would have a statutory obligation to treat it.

In an acute old people's ward in a central London teaching hospital, almost all the beds are taken up with Alzheimer's patients being treated for their related conditions: the broken limbs, the burns, the cancers, the failing organs of tired, forgetful bodies. I ask their consultant, who specialises in geriatric medicine, if the treatment patients get is relative to the amount of outside support they have from their families. She grips her clipboard protectively and stares hard into my face, looking for reassurance or a reason to answer. Finally she says: 'Yes, of course. If a frail old person, probably with multiple conditions and a limited prognosis, is brought in, we think about where they're going to go after we've treated the most chronic condition. Who is going to look after them if they go back to live on their own? Yes, the quality of life is...' she searches for a word. 'If there's not much quality, we may well not do procedures that demand a lot of aftercare. We'll just make them comfortable. We're not talking about killing people, or even letting them die, just not prolonging unhappy, lonely lives.'

Now that thoughtful reply won't come as a surprise to anyone working with geriatrics or in the health service, but it might come as a bit of a shock to anyone whose granny is on a ward that's just too far away to conveniently visit. As a society we run old people's care like a donkey sanctuary. Perhaps that's OK – we're very nice to donkeys.

I ask the consultant if she'd leave her parents to the state. 'No,' she said without hesitation. 'They came from a very tight community – they didn't put the old out on the ice floes. I'd go home and take care of them.' And would you be happy to be treated in an NHS home yourself? 'No. It's not that I think they're bad – I think staff do their best. But it's not something you'd look forward to.'

Not one of the health care or social services personnel I spoke to said they would want to end up in their own care. They all said they thought the service they offered was exceptional in its diligence, that the staff were devoted, that everything that could be done given budget, staffing, red tape, directives, etc., etc., was done. But they'd rather die at home.

All life ends in failure. However much you've laid aside for the package tour of an afterlife, it ends in failure: heart failure, failing eyes and limbs, the failure of bladders and balance, the failure of memory and hope. But it should also be a long moment of success – the pleasure of a race well run, the pride in a family born, nurtured and fledged, a validatory break on the bench to remember times transcended and misfortunes overcome or stoically subdued.

We are one of the very few cultures in all the world, down all the ages, that don't treat age as an achievement in and of itself. There are no old people's homes in Africa, because the old live with their families and in their communities. They earn honorific titles – white hair and a stick are owed respect. There is a polite assumption of wisdom in experience. But we are terrified by the loss of youth. We kick against the clock, like infants trying to put off bedtime. We dress younger than we are, talk younger, stretch, freeze and stitch our sagging bodies to fool those younger than ourselves, and our genes, as if a cocktail of lentils, beetroot juice, positive thinking and hip-hop talk will make us thirty for ever, until we kick off in the middle of a dirty dream. We pray ardently without belief for a painless, switch-flick demise.

Ageing is so frightening in part because we treat the old so badly, and we treat them badly because we're so frightened of them. We ignore them and consign them to horrible solitude because we can't face the truth that some day someone will banish us. Most people in this country die weepingly lonely – cold, starved, and left in no doubt that they have overstayed their welcome. This is the greatest shame and horror of our society and our age.

The cure for this youth-tormented terror is blindingly simple. Reclaim the old. Include them in our lives. The antibiotic for loneliness is company. I wouldn't patronise the aged by claiming that everything they say is wise or steeped in the rare tincture of experience. They talk as much repetitive bollocks as the rest of us. But we never listen to them; we're deaf to the old. We assume they have nothing to tell us, nothing but loopy non sequiturs and circular complaints. Even when the news is about them, nobody asks an old person what they think. Young professionals paraphrase on their behalf.

You know, you really should spend an hour listening to someone who's lived twice as long as you, not as social philanthropy or goodness, but for your own sake, for the sake of your self-worth, to calm your speechless fears about ageing, and because you'll hear something funny and clever, touching and probably astonishing. Most old people are more interesting than most young people, simply because they're older. Experience may not bring wisdom, but it does make for some cracking stories. Every old person you ignore has lived through times and done things, seen stuff that you never will, and it's worth hearing about.

There is a towering, pitiful irony that the most popular use of the net, after watching fat Germans have shaky sex, is unravelling genealogy. We will spend hours picking through turgid ledgers and ancient lists to discover who we are, but can't bring ourselves to listen to the first-hand account of where we come from and what it was like.

We should, at the very least, ensure that nobody, none of our kin, compatriots, kith or countrymen, ever sits alone wishing for their own death because they know of nobody who wishes them to live. We will abate our own fears of ageing by ensuring that someone else isn't fearful and lonely. You get back what you give.

I look at the veneration of Harry Patch, the longest-living Tommy from the Great War. He was the man who didn't just cheat death but transcended it – all those millions of deaths. People queued to see him, they nodded and committed to memory his whispered, papery thoughts. The great and the powerful stooped to shake his hand. He was a living memorial. When I was a boy, every old man I met had served in the Great War. Gardeners coughed up gas-ravaged lungs, publicans wore county regiment ties. The chap with the pinned-up sleeve who sold my dad a box of matches every morning at the train station had lost his arm at Loos.

Harry Patch wasn't a special case; as a young man he did what all young men did. He was exceptional because he beat the indifference of age: he lived long enough to come through the line and be reborn as interesting and wanted again.

March 2009

Dyslexia

I didn't write this, I'm not writing this. Amy is writing this. Say: 'Hello, Amy.' I speak into Amy's crooked ear, and she types on my behalf. Amy can tell the difference between a lower case 'b' and a 'd' with one eye closed, after three gins. She minds her ps and qs, and she'll mind mine if I ask her. Amy is comfortable with all the many and subtle ways of 'ough'. Words are her open book, as simple as ACB. So she writes with an assured dexterity, without even looking down. But what you hear, the timbre, the cadence of the clusters and chicanes, those are mine. The voice that is whispering into your shell-like is mine. And that is a great and subtle alchemy. These squiggles, these secretive, revealing spoors are only desiccated sounds – the dried minestrone of speech. It's the voice that matters, warm from the mouth. Not these cold, black letters.

The first alphabet with vowels is Greek, eight hundred years before Christ. The word comes from alpha and beta, plagiarised from the Phoenicians: the pictograms for 'ox' and 'house'. A stable. The alphabet is a stable for words, for ideas, declarations, statements, jokes, orders, denials, rhymes, reasons, lies and last testaments. And you know what else stables are full of.

It was suggested that we should print this the way I write it, just so you could see, get some idea of the mess, the infantilely random alphabetti muesli of my fifty-five-year-old writing. You'd get a kick out of it. No, it would really amuse you. People still laugh at me on paper: 'Oh my God, is that real? Is that how you write? You've got to be joking.' I'm not immune, but I've grown thick-skinned, if a little defensive. After all the awards, the pats on the back, the gimpy words that put the kids through school and put a chicken in the pot, you can scoff all you like. You can scoff for free. I get paid for these words, and I gave up caring when I discovered the rest of you spell phonetic with a 'ph'.

There are better things to do on a miserably wet night than to come to a charmless church hall. Inside is the familiar setup of self-help: the table with pamphlets and privately published books of obsession, the industrial teapot, the semicircle of plastic chairs, the posters of concern and encouragement. There are perhaps twenty people here, talking in little groups, with the familiarity of a cause that is also a social life. A pair of women see me and beam. They are the vestal stewards of church halls everywhere: solid, energetic, intimidating. 'Ah, there you are!' says one. 'We're so pleased you could come. Have you got a cup of tea?' 'Have a biscuit,' says the other, producing a tin of chocolate ones. There's a plate of plain digestives. 'These are the VIP biscuits,' she whispers. This is probably the only hall where I'm a VIP: the monthly get-together of the Bexley, Bromley, Greenwich and Lewisham Dyslexia Association (founded 1974). And I am a dyslexic. A dyslexic who writes a lot – 1,500 words, give or take, a day. And if I let the spellchecker get its bureaucratic little pince-nez within squinting distance of any of them, it would say 1,000 are spelt wrongly. I am a grammar cripple, a functioning illiterate. Literally, I write for a living, and, like blind mountaineers and limbless golfers, I am a straw to be clutched at by these quietly desperate and bravely determined people whose lives and dreams for their children have been overwhelmed by twenty-six characters in search of orthodoxy.

The meeting gets under way. Four experts – an expert being someone who knows more than you do – sit in front of us: a teacher, a helper, a student and a learning-difficulties coach. The parents, mostly mothers, their faces taut with worry and incomprehension, listen intently. One or two have brought their children, who sit with their heads down, drawing, trying to be invisible. I'm with them. The questions swiftly become long, anguished stories of uncaring schools, intransigent authorities, lax teachers, jobsworth governors and thwarted children. At every hardship and symptom, the experts and regulars exchange knowing, conspiratorial grins and raised eyebrows. A desperate mother, twisting her fingers into knots, says the social services are trying to have her committed as an overanxious parent. There's a chance they'll take her child into care. The room shakes its head and tuts with the commiseration of the vindicated paranoid.

After too long, the meeting closes. It has answered all the questions with more questions. Doors have opened to reveal corridors filled with more doors. It has helped only to concern the concerned, whose anxieties mostly revolve around statements. Children with learning difficulties need to be statemented – that is, given a series of tests by a professional that take a long time and are, if not arbitrary, then not altogether precise, a bit like a *Cosmo* quiz for the semiliterate. They are useful, and they are craved by the parents of children who are failing.

A statement imposes a statutory obligation to give the child special attention. Education authorities and school boards don't want to do this because they don't have any money. They do have time. Time is everything. Children grow older, grow out of their shoes and, with luck, out of their schools. Everyone agrees that the sooner you treat dyslexia the better – so they connive to put off statementing. They don't return phone calls, they cancel appointments, lose forms and files, hoping the problem will go to another catchment area, another school, and probably the private sector. They're not uncaring or cruel. They know that the help they can give a dyslexic child will probably amount to no more than an unpaid, untrained teaching assistant doing a bit of nursery rhyme reading a couple of afternoons a week. Everybody understands that the urban comprehensive system isn't going to step up to the needs of a dyslexic child. Still, most parents have no choice but to make bigger and bigger nuisances of themselves. The children find they do have a choice: they can check out. They can turn up, but they can turn off. They can be in the room but not present. They can get their self-worth by being disruptive and too clever by half. They stop offering up their self-confidence to the blackboard to be squashed and mocked.

I hover by the book stand. There's a list of famous dyslexics – Lee Ryan, Tommy Hilfiger, Benjamin Zephaniah, Steve Redgrave, Richard Branson, Zoë Wanamaker, Eddie Izzard, Toyah Willcox, Albert Einstein, Jackie Stewart. It sounds like a really horrible reality TV show. I could make a starrier list to advertise consumption or syphilis. 'We're a bit in two minds about Einstein,' says the book monitor. 'He was probably autistic.'

I buy a pamphlet called *The Perplexed Parent's Guide to Special Needs*. It is £8. It contains a glossary, four pages of jargon, eighty-seven learning abbreviations. So much easier to tell a parent their child has PMLD than 'profound and multiple learning difficulties'. The well-meaning ladies ask if I'll write for the dyslexic newsletter. I make my excuses. On the way out I am approached by a mother with her daughter, who's had her head bent over a notebook. She must be seven or eight. Her drawings are clever and accomplished, fluent doodles of fantasy things, things that aren't in this room. We smile at each other. 'So good at art,' says one of the vestal ladies. 'Typical dyslexic – so much creativity.'

Maybe I'm too hard on these people, but I've been avoiding meetings like this all my life. I've been avoiding writing this article for as long as I've been writing. I was diagnosed dyslexic when I was at a state junior school in north London, bottom of the class at pretty much everything except the nature table. We were given IQ tests, and apparently mine was disproportionately higher than my academic achievement. This was the way dyslexia was diagnosed in the 1960s. Although not a new disease – it was originally noted in the nineteenth century – it was new to the newly comprehensive school system, and a solid majority of teachers imagined it was either a dubious American import or a euphemism made up by middle-class parents for their dim sprogs. There was certainly no provision for it other than extra homework, which I got and resented, then lost and forgot, dropped in puddles, used as goalposts, fed to the neighbours' dog. So I was sent to a boarding school, St Christopher's, in Letchworth. They said they not only understood dyslexia, but could sensitively help.

At my interview the headmaster asked me to read from the paper – the *Guardian*, naturally. The Commonwealth Conference was on in London. The first paragraph was an exotic list of African and Asian names. I fell at every one. He beamed. Seven years later, as he shook my hand and I left without a meaningful or useful qualification, he wished me good luck without conviction. The careers adviser had suggested a career in hairdressing. 'I'm sure you'll talk your way into something,' said the headmaster. 'I don't think we've ever had a pupil who's spent as much time doing special extra study on Saturdays.' And he laughed, and so did I. Neither of us meant it. It was only afterwards that I wondered if perhaps, after so many years of punishing my inability to understand, they might have thought of some alternative to taking away the only morning I had to myself.

In retrospect there was a prophetic encounter. I loved history. It was taught by a man who always gave me low marks for the work I struggled over at the expense of every other subject. One day I went to him in tears and said I thought my history was better than he gave me credit for. He said he thought my history was very good, but my writing was appalling, and he marked me as an examiner would: 'You have a problem with your writing, Gill.' And I thought, actually, no I don't. You have the problem with my writing. To me it makes perfect sense. And I pretty much decided then and there always to make my dyslexia someone else's problem.

There was, though, the 'one' teacher. The one that, if we're lucky, we all manage to find. He taught English. Peter Scupham. He didn't teach me how to write, he didn't do phonics or useful tricks to distinguish endings; he taught me how to read. He didn't even do that, really. He just showed me how to read. He read all the time – often out loud. He would come to our dormitory late at night and read M. R. James's ghost stories by the light of the full moon. He deconstructed Blake. 'The Sick Rose' was the first poem I ever learnt by heart. I read very slowly, but I forget very little. And it doesn't matter – books aren't a race. A book doesn't melt or go off. The author's still dead, the words still live. Peter Scupham showed me the breadth of what was possible. It wasn't *Dead Poets Society* or Helen Keller, it was just going to the shelf. I found him very early one morning sitting on the floor of the English department, ripping up dozens of copies of Shakespeare. He looked up without surprise and said: 'You've got to show them who's boss.'

I was never going to make university or poly. I stumbled into art school via the labour exchange, manual and menial work: shops, warehouses, building sites, gardens, kitchens, waiting, nannying, modelling. And I did five years at Saint Martin's, then the Slade, where I took my art history exams with a dip pen. I cut my own quills and wrote with an elegantly illiterate, romantic scrawl. A lot of dyslexics end up in the art room or the drama department. Along with the worry of perceived dimness, there is a parallel and concomitant assumption among mothers that dyslexics are artistic. As amputees grow stronger in their remaining limbs, so children with deficient spelling will develop a heightened aesthetic, have natural affinity to line and colour, bias-cutting and spinning clay. In the church hall there'd been a lot of knowing smiles when I said I'd been at art school. 'Of course, we're all artistic, aren't we?' said the woman who claimed she hadn't discovered her inner dyslexia until after she'd completed her doctorate, and was wistfully still trying to uncover her innate creativity. I stayed with art until I was nearly forty. I got quite good at drawing. But I'd done it for twenty-five years, so I should have been competent. There is no proof that dyslexia makes you any more culturally sensitive or artistically dexterous than people who can spell. We end up holding brushes instead of pens because it's where we find some self-confidence. I don't regret the art, but when I finally did sit down to write, oh my God, it was like coming home. This is what I'd been trying to say with chiaroscuro and perspective. Why didn't I ever think of words? I was amazed at how easy writing is if you take away spelling and grammar. If you just say it.

Julian Elliott is a researcher into special needs, a teacher and an expert on dyslexia. Or, rather, he would be if he thought it existed. But last year he caused a lot of asterisks to be inserted into exclamations by questioning the very existence of dyslexia. I called him: I was rather looking forward to a fight. After all these years to discover that I'd been suffering from some imaginary disease, that I was just dim and backward all along. Happily, Professor Elliott's own written style is as wooden as Pinocchio's best-man speech. It is what's technically known as 'academic remedial'. Less fortunately, within three minutes I agreed with almost everything he said. Far from being a chalk dust and elbow patches grammarian, he's a liberal, sensitive soul.

His point is that dyslexia the label has become a meaningless catch-all. So many symptoms and conditions are attributed to it: word blindness, innumeracy, short-term memory loss, low self-confidence, truncated attention and untidiness, sensitivity to light, poor hand-eye coordination, inability to tell left from right, and various choice incapacities from the lighter end of the autistic spectrum. This is no longer a medical condition, it's a social one. He emphasises again that there is no link between IQ and dyslexia. We are not innately smarter, nor is there any provable link with artistic talent, theatricality or interior design. On the other hand, being a brilliant speller isn't an indicator of high IQ either, nor is reading a lot. But still, there is a huge weight of parental pressure behind the acceptance of dyslexia as a cause for special treatment and an indicator of aesthetic sensitivity.

Elliott does not deny that some children have difficulty reading and writing, but he says that the difficulty simply falls into the general bucket of special needs. The treatments for dyslexia and for other learning difficulties are identical, and if the cure is the same, so, possibly, is the condition. But there is consternation at the thought of disbanding the dyslexics' club, not only from parents but from a host of commercially interested schools and experts. There is a lucrative dyslexia industry. Where the state system has been unable and unwilling to offer help, it has colluded with the private sector, all too happy to offer a service and to exploit the worries and fears of parents. So now there are legions of specialists and gurus whose cards mothers exchange at school gates with a desperate trust. Teachers sell proprietary cures, from coloured cellophane to gymnastics to computer programs. A devoted, sympathetic department geared to dyslexia is now one of the best selling points of a private education.

I mentioned to Elliott that I have a son who is dyslexic in exactly the same way as I am, with pretty much the same IQ I had at his age. 'Ah, yes,' he says, 'there does seem to be a genetic link, particularly between fathers and sons.'

I asked Ali's permission before mentioning him here. He said it was fine, as long as I didn't make him look like an illiterate poster boy. He's now seventeen and struggling with exams. The provision for dyslexics is almost exactly the same as it was when I was at school – more work, extra reading, extra writing, one-to-ones with a woman with ethnic jewellery who speaks in a slow, loud voice.

Fairley House is a school that specialises in dyslexia and its associated learning difficulties. This is the gold standard for specialist help, and it needs to be: it's not cheap. They take children at the end of primary school to help them make the jump into secondary education. This is the great nightmare for parents; the competition for big school, both public and private, is fierce. Fairley House is a bright and jolly place in Pimlico, named for Gordon Hamilton-Fairley, the oncologist murdered by the IRA. I remember hearing the bomb that killed him. The school is noisy and energetic. Every wall, door and ceiling is covered in information – pictures, mobiles, labels. It's like being inside a hyperactive thirteen-year-old's scrapbook, a great, tie-dyed stampede of spangly encouragement and useful rubrics.

The headmistress might have stepped off one of her own walls, a lady with Day-Glo energy of the sort that seems to exist only in education and the more charismatic fundamentalist churches. She bobs down the school corridor like a cork in a millrace of children, shouting encouragement and cosy admonishments with a pantomime zeal. She has assigned me to shadow an attractive and winning lad called Zinzan. We go to his maths class with Millie, George and Lewis, taught by Mr Taylor, who's been bitten by the same dog that got the headmistress. We're learning percentages using packets of sweets. They try to teach everything with a practical example or a stick-in-the-head image; they learn pi using real pies. I sit on the little chair behind the desk, and the oddest thing begins to happen: I can feel myself regressing, the panic begins to constrict my chest. I can't follow what Mr Taylor is saying. I don't understand.

Millie leans across and helps me, not as a politeness to a grownup who's older than her dad, but with the fellowship of the impaired; another word-blind, number-paralysed school sufferer. It all rushes back over me: everything falling off my brain, like hearing through double glazing, the fog of incomprehension, the panic of being left behind. I'd completely forgotten the loneliness of classrooms where it all makes sense to everyone else. I look down at the page and my handwriting belongs to a child. I get it all wrong. 'Never mind,' says Millie. No, never mind. This is the most salutary of lessons. I had utterly buried this feeling: being here in this place. To fail with the kindness of professionals willing you on, egging you to understand, just to grasp the simplest corner of a concept that is forever opaque and ghostly. I still can't do long division, or short division. I have no idea how grammar works. I can't name the parts of a sentence. And, do you know the weirdest thing? If I were Chinese I wouldn't have any of this. It seems there is no pictogram for dyslexia. If I were being taught in Finnish, it's unlikely I'd be dyslexic. This is an overwhelmingly English condition. It's the language, stupid, our irrational, fraught and contrary written tongue, that breeds misconceptions and misunderstandings that some of us never get into our thick heads. We can't deal with the memory cards, the exceptions to rules, the little charming eccentricities.

English was only recently regulated and systematised, when public schools had to turn out a large civil service and the mercantile class of clerks who all needed examining and filing. Before then, English was firstly a declaimed, sung, spoken, hot language. Not the chilly, starched memo-for-your-files, cc'd written one. But there's no going back on it. It won't return to the glorious free-for-all, extempore, idiosyncratic, phonic whoop of the seventeenth century. This is the way it is. And school's currency is forever going to be words and numbers. If you can't collect them and order them, it doesn't matter how many sweets you count or pies you make or colourful drawings or pasta pictures. You are never going to be rich here. And we just have to live with that. Get on with the rest of our lives. If you offered most parents, indeed, most dyslexics, the opportunity to spell like a Scrabble champion but that the price would be ugliness, they'd never take it. And, anyway, how much do the rest of you remember about schoolwork?

The galvanising headmistress asked me if I'd talk to a few of the children about my experience with dyslexia. Of course, I said, through a pasty grin. She led me into assembly. *You want me to take assembly?* 'Just a few words. They're all very excited you're here.' How long shall I talk? 'Oh, twenty or thirty minutes, then questions.' I stood in front of this sea of blameless little faces, knowing that behind each of them there was already a room full of low self-esteem, full of catalogues of failure, a great weight of parental concern, and I wondered again at the horrible obstacle course we make of other people's childhoods after we've fucked up our own. And I caught sight of Zinzan, and I felt the anger, the hot fury for the wasted, tearful, silently worried, failed years of school, and I had a Spartacus moment. I started talking, rather too loudly. I told them this was their language, this English, this most marvellous and expressive cloak of meaning and imagination. This great, exclamatory, illuminating song, it belonged to anyone who found it in their mouths. There was no wrong way to say it, or write it, the language couldn't be compelled or herded, it couldn't be tonsured or pruned, pollarded or plaited, it was as hard as oaths and as subtle as rhyme. It couldn't be forced or bullied or policed by academics; it wasn't owned by those with flat accents; nobody had the right to tell them how to use it or what to say. There are no rules and nobody speaks incorrectly, because there is no correctly: no high court of syntax. And while everyone can speak with the language, nobody speaks for the language. Not grammars, not dictionaries. They just run along behind, picking up discarded usages. This English doesn't belong to examiners or teachers. All of you already own the greatest gift, the highest degree this country can bestow. It's on the tip of your tongue.

And then I caught sight of myself, standing like a declamatory tick-tack man, bellowing like a costermonger, and I stopped and stared at the faces staring at me with expressions of utter, dyslexic incomprehension. From the back of the room, a teacher coughed.

March 2010

Morrissey: *Autobiography*

As Noël Coward might have said, nothing incites intemperate cultural hyperbole like cheap music. Who can forget that the Beatles were once authoritatively lauded as the equal of Mozart, or that Bob Dylan was dubbed a contemporary Keats? The Beatles continued to ignore Covent Garden, and Mozart is rarely heard at Glastonbury; Dylan has been silently culled from the latest edition of the *Oxford Companion to Modern Poetry in English*. The publication of *Autobiography* was the second item on Channel 4's news on the day it was released. Krishnan Guru-Murthy excitably told the nation that Morrissey really could write – presumably he was reading from an autocue – and a pop journalist thrilled that he was one of the nation's greatest cultural icons. He isn't even one of Manchester's greatest cultural icons.

This belief in high-low cultural relativity leads to a certain sort of chippy pop-star feeling undervalued and then hoitily producing a rock opera or duet with concert harpsichord. Morrissey, though, didn't have to attain the chip of being needily undervalued; he was born with it. He tells us he ditched 'Steve', his given name, to be known by his portentous unimoniker because – deep reverential breath here – great classical composers only have one name.

Mussorgsky, Mozart, Morrissey. His most pooterishly embarrassing piece of intellectual social climbing is having this autobiography published by Penguin Classics. Not Modern Classics, you understand, where the authors can still do book signings, but the classic Classics, where they're dead and some of them only have one name. Molière, Machiavelli, Morrissey.

He has made up for being alive by having a photograph of himself pretending to be dead on the cover. The book's publication was late and trade gossip has it that Steve insisted on each and every bookshop taking a minimum order of two dozen, misunderstanding how modern publishing works. But this is not unsurprising when you read the book. He is constantly moaning about record producers not pressing enough discs to get him to No. 1. What is surprising is that any publisher would want to publish the book, not because it is any worse than a lot of other pop memoirs, but because Morrissey is plainly the most ornery, cantankerous, entitled, whingeing, self-martyred human being who ever drew breath. And those are just his good qualities.

The book falls into two distinct passages. The first quarter is devoted to growing up in Manchester (where he was born in 1959) and his schooling. This is laughably overwrought and overwritten, a litany of retrospective hurt and score-settling that reads like a cross between Madonna and Catherine Cookson.

No teacher is too insignificant not to be humiliated from the heights of success, no slight is too small not to be rehashed with a final, killing *esprit d'escalier*. There are pages of lists of television programmes he watched (with plot analysis and character criticism). He could go on *Mastermind* with the specialist subject of *Coronation Street* or the works of Peter Wyngarde. There is the food he ate, the groups that appeared on *Top of the Pops* (with critical comments) and the poetry he liked (with quotes).

All of this takes quite a lot of time due to the amount of curlicues, falderals and bibelots he insists on dragging along as authorial decoration. Instead of adding colour or depth, they simply result in a cacophony of jangling, misheard and misused words. After 100 pages, he's still at the school gate kicking dead teachers.

But then he sets off on the grown-up musical bit and the writing calms down and becomes more diary-like, bloggish, though with an incontinent use of italics that are a sort of stage direction or aside to the audience. He changes tenses in ways that are supposed to be elegant but just sound camp. There is one passage that stands out – this is the first time he sings. 'Against the command of everyone I had ever known, I sing. My mouth meets the microphone and the tremolo quaver eats the room with acceptable pitch and I am removed from the lifelong definition of others and their opinions matter no more. I am singing the truth by myself which will also be the truth of others and give me a whole life. Let the voice speak up for once and for all.' That has the sense of being both revelatory and touching, but it stands out like the reflection of the moon in a sea of Stygian self-justification and stilted, self-conscious prose.

The hurt recrimination is sometimes risible but mostly dull, like listening to neighbours bicker through a partition wall, and occasionally startlingly unpleasant, such as the reference to the Moors murderers and the unfound grave of their victim Keith Bennett. 'Of course, had Keith been a child of privilege or moneyed background, the search would never have been called off. But he was a poor, gawky boy from Manchester's forgotten side streets and minus the blond fantasy fetish of a cutesy Madeleine McCann.'

It's what's left out of this book rather than what's put in that is strangest. There is an absence of music, not just in its tone, but the content. There are emetic pools of limpid prose about the music business, the ingratitude of fellow musicians and band members and the lack of talent in other performers, but there is nothing about the making of music itself, the composing of lyrics, the process of singing or the emotion of creation. He seems to assume we will already know his back catalogue and can hum along to his recorded life. This is 450 pages of what makes Morrissey, but nothing of what Morrissey makes.

There is the peevishness at managers, record labels and bouncers, a list of opaque court cases, all of which he manages to lose unfairly, due to the inherited stupidity of judges. Even his relationship with the audience is equivocal. Morrissey likes them when they're worshipping from a distance, but he is not so keen when they're up close. As an adolescent he approaches Marc Bolan for an autograph. Bolan refuses and Morrissey, still awkwardly humiliated after all these years, has the last word. But then later in the book and life, he does exactly the same thing to his own fans without apparent irony.

There is little about his private life. A boyfriend slips in and out with barely a namecheck. This is him on his early sexual awakening: 'Unfathomably I had several cupcake grapples in this year of 1973 . . . Plunge or no plunge, girls remain mysteriously attracted to me.' There is precious little plunging after that.

There are many pop autobiographies that shouldn't be written.

Some to protect the unwary reader, and some to protect the author. In Morrissey's case, he has managed both. This is a book that cries out like one of his maudlin ditties to be edited. But were an editor to start, there would be no stopping. It is a heavy tome, utterly devoid of insight, warmth, wisdom or likeability. It is a potential firelighter of vanity, self-pity and logorrhoeic dullness. Putting it in Penguin Classics doesn't diminish Aristotle or Homer or Tolstoy; it just roundly mocks Morrissey, and this is a humiliation constructed by the self-regard of its victim.

October 2013

Europe

It was the woman on *Question Time* that really did it for me. She was so familiar. There is someone like her in every queue, every coffee shop, outside every school in every parish council in the country. Middle-aged, middle-class, middle-brow, over-made-up, with her National Health face and weatherproof English expression of hurt righteousness, she's Britannia's mother-in-law. The camera closed in on her and she shouted: 'All I want is my country back. Give me my country back.' It was a heartfelt cry of real distress and the rest of the audience erupted in sympathetic applause, but I thought: 'Back from what? Back from where?'

Wanting the country back is the constant mantra of all the outies. Farage slurs it, Gove insinuates it. Of course I know what they mean. We all know what they mean. They mean back from Johnny Foreigner, back from the brink, back from the future, back-to-back, back to bosky hedges and dry-stone walls and country lanes and church bells and warm beer and skittles and football rattles and cheery banter and clogs on cobbles. Back to vicars-and-tarts parties and *Carry On* fart jokes, back to Elgar and fudge and proper weather and herbaceous borders and cars called Morris. Back to Victoria sponge and 22 yards to a wicket and 15 hands to a horse and 3 feet to a yard and four fingers in a KitKat, back to gooseberries not avocados, back to deference and respect, to make do and mend and smiling bravely and biting your lip and suffering in silence and patronising foreigners with pity.

We all know what 'getting our country back' means. It's snorting a line of the most pernicious and debilitating Little English drug, nostalgia. The warm, crumbly, honey-coloured, collective 'yesterday' with its fond belief that everything was better back then, that Britain (England, really) is a worse place now than it was at some foggy point in the past where we achieved peak Blighty. It's the knowledge that the best of us have been and gone, that nothing we can build will be as lovely as a National Trust Georgian country house, no art will be as good as a Turner, no poem as wonderful as 'If', no writer a touch on Shakespeare or Dickens, nothing will grow as lovely as a cottage garden, no hero greater than Nelson, no politician better than Churchill, no view more throat-catching than the White Cliffs and that we will never manufacture anything as great as a Rolls-Royce or Flying Scotsman again.

The dream of Brexit isn't that we might be able to make a brighter, new, energetic tomorrow, it's a desire to shuffle back to a regret-curdled, inward-looking yesterday. In the Brexit fantasy, the best we can hope for is to kick out all the work-all-hours foreigners and become caretakers to our own past in this self-congratulatory island of moaning and pomposity.

And if you think that's an exaggeration of the Brexit position, then just listen to the language they use: 'We are a nation of inventors and entrepreneurs, we want to put the great back in Britain, the great engineers, the great manufacturers.' This is all the expression of a sentimental nostalgia. In the Brexiteer's mind's eye is the old Pathe newsreel of Donald Campbell, John Logie Baird with his television, Barnes Wallis and his bouncing bomb, and Robert Baden Powell inventing boy scouts in his shed.

All we need, their argument goes, is to be free of the humourless Germans and spoilsport French and all their collective liberalism and reality. There is a concomitant hope that if we manage to back out of Europe, then we'll get back to the bowler-hatted 1950s and the Commonwealth will hold pageants, firework displays and beg to be back in the Queen Empress' good books again. Then New Zealand will sacrifice a thousand lambs, Ghana will ask if it can go back to being called the Gold Coast and Britain will resume hand-making Land Rovers and top hats and Sheffield-plate teapots.

There is a reason that most of the people who want to leave the EU are old while those who want to remain are young: it's because the young aren't infected with Bisto nostalgia. They don't recognise half the stuff I've mentioned here. They've grown up in the EU and at worst it's been neutral for them.

The under-thirties want to be part of things, not aloof from them. They're about being joined up and counted. I imagine a phrase most outies identify with is 'women's liberation has gone too far'. Everything has gone too far for them, from political correctness – well, that's gone mad, hasn't it? – to health and safety and gender-neutral lavatories. Those oldies, they don't know if they're coming or going, what with those new-fangled mobile phones and kids on Tinder and Grindr. What happened to meeting Miss Joan Hunter Dunn at the tennis club? And don't get them started on electric hand-dryers, or something unrecognised in the bagging area, or Indian call centres, or the impertinent computer asking for a password that has both capitals and little letters and numbers and more than eight digits.

We listen to the Brexit lot talk about the trade deals they're going to make with Europe after we leave, and the blithe insouciance that what they're offering instead of EU membership is a divorce where you can still have sex with your ex. They reckon they can get out of the marriage, keep the house, not pay alimony, take the kids out of school, stop the in-laws going to the doctor, get strict with the visiting rights, but, you know, still get a shag at the weekend and, obviously, see other people on the side.

Really, that's their best offer? That's the plan? To swagger into Brussels with Union Jack pants on and say: 'Ello luv, you're looking nice today. Would you like some?'

When the rest of us ask how that's really going to work, leavers reply, with Terry Thomas smirks, that 'They're going to still really fancy us, honest, they're gagging for us. Possibly not Merkel, but the bosses of Mercedes and those French vintners and cheesemakers, they can't get enough of old John Bull. Of course they're going to want to go on making the free market with two backs after we've got the *decree nisi*. Makes sense, doesn't it?'

Have no doubt, this is a divorce. It's not just business, it's not going to be all reason and goodwill. Like all divorces, leaving Europe would be ugly and mean and hurtful, and it would lead to a great deal of poisonous xenophobia and racism, all the niggling personal prejudice that dumped, betrayed and thwarted people are prey to. And the racism and prejudice are, of course, weak points for us. The tortuous renegotiation with lawyers and courts will be bitter and vengeful, because divorces always are and, just in passing, this sovereignty thing we're supposed to want so badly, like Frodo's ring, has nothing to do with you or me. We won't notice it coming back, because we didn't notice not having it in the first place.

You won't wake up on 24 June and think: 'Oh my word, my arthritis has gone! My teeth are suddenly whiter! Magically, I seem to know how to make a soufflé and I'm buff with the power of sovereignty.' This is something only politicians care about; it makes not a jot of difference to you or me if the Supreme Court is a bunch of strangely out-of-touch old gits in wigs in Westminster, or a load of strangely out-of-touch old gits without wigs in Luxembourg. What matters is that we have as many judges as possible on the side of personal freedom.

Personally, I see nothing about our legislators in the UK that makes me feel I can confidently give them more power. The more checks and balances politicians have, the better for the rest of us. You can't have too many wise heads and different opinions. If you're really worried about red tape, by the way, it's not just a European problem. We're perfectly capable of coming up with our own rules and regulations and we have no shortage of jobsworths. Red tape may be annoying, but it's also there to protect your and my family from being lied to, poisoned and cheated.

The first 'X' I ever put on a voting slip was to say yes to the EU. The first referendum was when I was 20 years old. This one will be in the week of my 62nd birthday. For nearly all my adult life, there hasn't been a day when I haven't been pleased and proud to be part of this great collective. If you ask me for my nationality, the truth is I feel more European than anything else. I am part of this culture, this European civilisation. I can walk into any gallery on our continent and completely understand the images and the stories on the walls. These people are my people and they have been for thousands of years. I can read books on subjects from Ancient Greece to Dark Ages Scandinavia, from Renaissance Italy to nineteenth-century

France, and I don't need the context or the landscape explained to me. The music of Europe, from its scales and its instruments to its rhythms and religion, is my music. The Renaissance, the Rococo, the Romantics, the Impressionists, Gothic, Baroque, Neoclassicism, Realism, Expressionism, Futurism, Fauvism, Cubism, Dada, Surrealism, Postmodernism and Kitsch were all European movements and none of them belongs to a single nation.

There is a reason why the Chinese are making fake Italian handbags and the Italians aren't making fake Chinese ones. This European culture, without question or argument, is the greatest, most inventive, subtle, profound, beautiful and powerful genius that was ever contrived anywhere by anyone and it belongs to us. Just look at my day job – food. The change in food culture and pleasure has been enormous since we joined the EU, and that's no coincidence. What we eat, the ingredients, the recipes, may come from around the world, but it is the collective to and fro of European interests, expertise and imagination that has made it all so very appetising and exciting. The restaurant was a European invention, naturally. The first one in Paris was called The London Bridge.

Culture works and grows through the constant warp and weft of creators, producers, consumers, intellectuals and instinctive lovers. You can't dictate or legislate for it, you can just make a place that encourages it and you can truncate it. You can make it harder and more grudging, you can put up barriers and build walls, but why on earth would you? This collective culture, this golden civilisation grown on this continent over thousands of years, has made everything we have and everything we are; why would you not want to be a part of it?

I understand that if we leave we don't have to hand back our library ticket for European civilisation, but why would we even think about it? In fact, the only ones who would are those old, philistine scared gits. Look at them, too frightened to join in.

June 2016

Dying

It seems unlikely, uncharacteristic, so un-'us' to have settled on sickness and bed rest as the votive altar and cornerstone of national politics. But there it is: every election, the National Health Service is the thermometer and the crutch of governments. The NHS represents everything we think is best about us. Everyone standing for whatever political persuasion has to lay a sterilised hand on an A&E revolving door and swear that the collective cradle-to-crematorium health service will be cherished on their watch.

When you look at our awkward, lumpy, inherited short-tempered characters, you'd imagine we might have come up with something more brass-bandy Brit: a bellicose, sentimental military fetishism, perhaps, or sport, or nostalgic history, boastful Anglophone culture, invention, exploration, banking avarice. But no. It turned out that what really sticks in our hard, gimpy, sclerotic hearts is looking after each other. Turning up at a bed with three carnations, a copy of the *Racing Post*, a Twix and saying, 'The cat misses you.'

We know it's the best of us. The National Health Service is the best of us. You can't walk into an NHS hospital and be a racist. That condition is cured instantly. But it's almost impossible to walk into a private hospital and not fleetingly feel that you are one: a plush waiting room with entitled and bad-tempered health tourists.

You can't be sexist on the NHS, nor patronising, and the care and the humour, the togetherness ranged against the teetering, chronic system by both the caring and the careworn is the Blitz, 'back against the wall', stern and sentimental best of us – and so we tell lies about it.

We say it's the envy of the world. It isn't. We say there's nothing else like it. There is. We say it's the best in the West. It's not. We think it's the cheapest. It isn't. Either that or we think it's the most expensive – it's not that, either. You will live longer in France and Germany, get treated faster and more comfortably in Scandinavia, and everything costs more in America.

I've wanted to write about the National Health Service for a long time, but it's resistant to press inquiries. While the abstract of the NHS is heart-warming, the truth for patients is often heart-stopping. And junior doctor strikes, executive pay, failing departments, slow-motion waiting times and outsourcing tell a different story, and I'm regularly, ritually refused access by PRs and administrators, or they insist on copy approval or preplanned stories.

One of the doctors I approached was Professor Brian Gazzard, who has a reputation mostly for being an exemplary and inspirationally brilliant physician, but also as something of an ocean-going eccentric. He treats, teaches at and runs the Chelsea Aids clinic. I asked him what had changed most about his job.

'When I started, I told every patient that they were going to die. I could make it easier, make them live a little longer, but everyone died. Now I tell every patient they will live. They will need to do what I tell them, they've been silly, but they'll live to die of something else. That's astonishing.' He paused so I would understand the effect it has on a doctor. 'Look, I really don't want to be written about. You won't remember, but we met once before.'

A decade ago, Gazzard diagnosed my foreign correspondent's dodgy tummy as acute pancreatitis, the result of alcoholism. 'Of course I remember. You told me I could never drink alcohol again and I said, "You haven't read my notes, I've been teetotal for 20 years." And you gave a sigh and reached into a drawer and lit a cigarette and said you'd been dreading telling a restaurant critic he couldn't have a glass of wine.'

Gazzard laughed. 'You're one of the lucky ones,' he'd said as he walked onto the street clutching an armful of patient files and raised a hand in farewell. He repeated again: 'You're one of the lucky ones. I can always tell.' It was his first misdiagnosis of the day.

What neither of us could know is that my pancreas was already a stuffed wallet of cancer, though not pancreatic – a migrated, refugee, desperate, breathless lung cancer.

I stopped smoking 15 years ago and as a gift to myself, proof of the clarity of my lungs, I would spend a week stalking on Loch Maree in Wester Ross. Every autumn since, I have climbed the same hills, chasing the deer, and, trudging upwards, recited a doxology of mostly extinct snouts I no longer puff: Weights, Guards, Navy Cut, Olivier, Black Cat, Passing Clouds, Number 6, Sovereign, Gitanes, Gauloises (does anyone remember when Paris smelt alternately of Gauloises, pissoirs and Chanel?), Winston, Camel, Sobranie, my father's pipe in the cinema – clouds of sweet latakia smoke in the flickering projec tion. A Greek cigarette in a red box with a lasciviously smiling girl that called itself Santé, without irony: an untipped fag called Health.

This year, for the first time, I couldn't make it to the top of the hill. I knelt in the heather, weak and gasping. It was the first time all was not well. There was also a pain in my neck that my doctor said was probably a cervical spine thingy and I should get a scan.

He sent me to Harley Street, where another doctor said: 'You haven't got insurance, it's going to be expensive. Why don't you get it done down the road and send me the pictures. A third of the cost.' I said: 'I'm here now, just do it.' And he shrugged. A couple of hours later I went back for the results. He had the bland bad-news face.

'That was the best money you ever spent.' He turned the screen around and there was a beautiful spiral of colour clinging like an abstract expressionist collar to my spine. 'This is cancer.'

That afternoon I was back in my doctor's surgery. He was wearing the antiseptic face, the professional-doctor tragedy mask. I'm getting to see this a lot now. It is as much a protection against the infection of catastrophe for them as a respect for its victim. They glaze the bad news with sweet spittle. They'll say: 'The test results were not quite what we hoped. It might be trapped wind or it might be the thing that hatched from John Hurt's stomach. Realistically, we'll have to assume it's more alien than fart.' My alien was the most common cancer in old men, our biggest single killer: an aggressive, nimble cat-burglar lung cancer that is rarely noticed till it has had kittens.

Guy has been my doctor for 30 years – 32 to be precise. He was the doctor who put me into treatment for addiction and he's looked after me and my kids ever since. He's private, so I pay. If I need a test, an X-ray, a consultant, I'll pay. If I need anything more than a couple of antibiotics, I'm going to the NHS.

Within 24 hours I have an NHS consultant oncologist and early-morning appointments, for scans, blood tests and X-rays.

You couldn't make up Charing Cross Hospital. Well, not as a hospital you couldn't. It's a monstrous, hideous, crumbling patched-up mess – the Elephant Building. On the way in I notice a couple of posters on the street saying 'Save Charing Cross Hospital'. They're stuck on a municipal noticeboard that's falling over. It's plainly the result of dozens and dozens of attempts to make things better and, in fact, it is the physical embodiment of how most of us, trying to make our way through the teetering automatic doors, feel. It has a very good collection of contemporary British art. In some back corridor there is a series of Peter Blake's best silk screens.

I love it: it's how I feel. The lifts take hours to arrive, emphysemically, wheezingly opening their doors, and when they do, it's without confidence or conviction. A man going up to the cancer ward puts his hand in front of the door and gets out. 'I'm too frightened to take this lift,' he says.

In a waiting room, hundreds of us take numbers to sit like wilted potted plants in an autumn garden-centre sale, to take it in turns to meet the antiseptic face. If this were a set for a film, all the actors and extras would be pulling looks of agony and sadness and fear, but the face of real cancer wipes our expressions to a pale neutral human.

The NHS has one of the worst outcomes for cancer treatment in Europe. It's something to be borne in mind when you're deciding to combine chemotherapy with a safari, or want to embark on a bar-thumping argument about health tourism. It was the first question I asked my oncologist, Dr Conrad Lewanski. 'Why is this such a bad place to get cancer, when we have lots of hospitals, when we teach doctors from all over the world, when we've won more Nobel Prizes than the French?'

'It's the nature of the health service,' he says. 'The key to cancer outcomes is the speed of diagnosis and treatment.' The health service was set up with GPs separate from hospitals. The system means you probably have to wait a week or so for an appointment to see first your GP, or a clinic. The average time for that consultation will be seven minutes. Perhaps your cough isn't a priority. And then if your doctor thinks it does need a second opinion, he'll suggest you see a consultant, and that's likely to take a month. If the GP suspects cancer, that referral time is reduced to two weeks. He or she will probably write a letter, often two – all doctors still carry fountain pens.

And then there are all the appointments – for tests, a cancellation, a missed X-ray, a scan – which can put months on a diagnosis. It's not the treatment, it's the scale of the bureaucracy and the Attlee-reverential, immovable-but-crumbling structure of a private-public doctor-consultant arrangement, which was the cornerstone laid down by the 1945 government at the insistence of doctors. That is the chronic tumour in the bowel of the system.

I'm given a talk by a nurse on the consequences of chemotherapy. She uses three pens. Two of them have three coloured barrels each. The scribbling, the underlining, the stars, the acronyms, the exclamation marks become ever more emphatic and decorative. Finally she hands me a notebook that is unintelligibly runic, but says not to worry because it's all on the computer, which she then turns on to show me a heart-warming film about sexual infections and high temperatures.

The hospital flutters with bits of paper like mayflies. They're propped up against screens, wedged up against keyboards, stuffed into teetering files, and then there are the constant Tourette's questions, 'When's your birthday? What's the first line of your address?', all to collide you with the right cancer, to go with all the forms, the signatures, the screens, the machines, the radiation disclaimers and destiny. It makes Kafka look like ee cummings.

I like my oncologist. He doesn't have the morphine face; he looks amused, inquisitive, like a shaved, garrulous otter. All he does is lung cancer. This is his river, tumours his trout. He's been a consultant for 15 years. Two years in, his father got it and died: 'The worst thing I've ever had to go through. I do know what this is like – so how much do you want to know?'

'Everything, and the truth.'

I've never Googled cancer, but I've discovered that every one of my friends who owns their own house has a preferred cancer specialist and a hospital to go with them. They also have a perfect gardener, an ideal interior decorator and a masseur that they insist – insist – I use, because they are all the best and, of course, you only get what you pay for. Lots of them are astonished I'm still in this country of catastrophic cancer statistics.

Those who don't have money for their own homes have magical diets, homeopathy and religious new-age cures, or at least a conspiracy theory about big pharma hiding the efficacy of vitamin C, kale, magnetism and mistletoe. If it doesn't make you better, at least you get snogged a lot.

And everyone, but everyone, will have a mantra story of their secretary's husband or a woman they used to work with who was given three weeks to live and is still stacking shelves or conducting operas 10 years later. These little homilies are handed out with the intense insistence of lucky heather, using the language of evangelical religion and locker-room encouragement.

Why is our reaction to cancer so medieval, so wrapped in fortune-cookie runes and votive memory shards, like the teeth and metatarsals of dead saints? Cancer is frightening. One in two of us will get it. It has dark memories, unmentionably euphemised. In the public eye, not all cancers are equal. There is little sympathy for lung cancer. It's mostly men, mostly old men, mostly working-class old men and mostly smokers. There is a lot more money and public sympathy for the cancers that affect women and the young. Why wouldn't there be?

'How do men react when you tell them their cancers are fatal?' I ask Dr Lewanski. 'Always the same way – with stoicism.'

'Bollocks,' I think. 'I thought that was just me.' Actually it's not being told you've got cancer that is the test of character, it's the retelling. Going home and saying to the missus: 'That thing, the cricked neck. Actually it's a tumour, the size of a cigar.' It ought to come with a roll of thunder and five Jewish violinists, instead of the creaky whisper of fear.

People react differently to different cancers: most women think they'll survive, and statistically they're right. Most men think they'll die – and likewise.

'So, what's the treatment?'

'Chemotherapy. Platinum in your case. It has a very good chance.'

Someone should write a paper on the euphemistic size comparisons for tumours. There should be an e-site, Euphotumours. The images are very masculine: golf balls, cricket balls, bullets, grenades, ruminant testicles. No one ever says, 'I've got a cancer the size of a fairy cake.'

And what about after the chemo?

'Well, there's a new treatment, immunotherapy. It's the biggest breakthrough in cancer treatment for decades. Cancers camouflage themselves as chemical markers that tell your body's natural defences that there's nothing to see here, move along. These new drugs strip away the disguise and allow your body's natural system to clean up. It's new and it's still being trialled, but we're a long way along the line and it is the way cancer treatment is bound to go. It's better for some growths than others, but it's particularly successful with yours. If you were in Germany or Scandinavia or Japan or America, or with the right insurance here, this is what you would be treated with.'

The doctor looks at Nicola, the missus. His otter face has grown a little sphinxy.

'You remember asking if the treatment Adrian got on the NHS would be any different from being a private patient? And I said a better cup of coffee and more leeway with appointments. Well, this is the difference. If he had insurance, I'd put him on immunotherapy – specifically, nivolumab. As would every oncologist in the First World. But I can't do it on the National Health.'

The National Institute for Health and Care Excellence (NICE), the quango that acts as the quartermaster for the health service, won't pay. Nivolumab is too expensive – £60,000 to £100,000 a year for a lung-cancer patient; about four times the cost of chemo. And the only way to see if it will work for an individual patient is to give it to them all, and the ones it doesn't work for will weed themselves out.

What NICE doesn't say about the odds is that immunotherapy mostly works for old men who are partially responsible for their cancers because they smoked. Thousands of patients could benefit. But old men who think they're going to die anyway aren't very effective activists. They don't get the public or press pressure that young mothers' cancers and kids' diseases get.

As yet, immunotherapy isn't a cure, it's a stretch more life, a considerable bit of life. More life with your kids, more life with your friends, more life holding hands, more life shared, more life spent on earth – but only if you can pay.

I'm early for my first eight-hour stint of platinum chemo. The ward in Charing Cross looks like a cross between a milking shed and an Air Koryo business lounge. I am settled into a hideous but comfortable chair and a tap is jabbed into the back of my hand. A series of combative and palliative cocktails in plastic bags slowly dribble into my body and every 10 minutes I have to shuffle to an invalid's loo to dribble it out again.

I like it here. The nurses are funny and comforting, optimistic, and bear the weight of the sadness, the regret and the pity in the room on their shoulders with an amused elegance and sincerity that comes from their years of experience, or the naivety of inexperience. The other patients shuffle in with their partners to share sandwiches, talk about shopping and the cousins in New Zealand and window boxes. There are children with ageing parents, happy/sad to be able to repay an infant's debt.

I manage to find the one dealer in the ward, or rather she finds me. Her boyfriend's making hash cakes – they've definitely shrunk his tumour, I should definitely have some. I smile, shrug apologetically and say sadly I'm already a junkie. I don't take drugs.

'Really? Even for this?' I'm not giving up 32 years of clean time for some poxy lung.

And there are the ones who sit alone, who don't have any friends to play cards with them, to drip the will and the strength and the faith to face this. I don't know how anyone manages to do this on their own.

An old friend sits through the mornings with me, Nicola comes with lunch and Flora and Ali, my grown-up kids, share the afternoon. If it wasn't for the cancer, that would be a really lovely day. If it wasn't for the cancer.

There's a natural break in the article here. It should have been finished two weeks ago, but I had a bad night, a really bad night.

Nicola called Guy, the GP, and he came round and took a look and said: 'He needs to be in A&E now.'

So I'm on a gurney in Charing Cross at nine in the morning. On the other side of the blue plastic curtain, a bloke is being held down by three policemen shouting, 'Don't flick your fucking blood over here, I don't want what you've got.'

A young doctor comes and asks me questions. All doctors in A&E are preternaturally young. One of the questions after 'What's your date of birth and the first line of your address?' is inevitably 'Can I put my finger up your bottom to see if there's any poo or blood?'

The other question is: 'On a scale of 1 to 10 – 1 being a scratch and 10 unspeakable agony – what do you think you're suffering at the moment?' You wouldn't describe this as thin pain. It's 10 out of 10. My stomach is agonised with a terrible wrenching distension. I've lived a middle-class, sheltered, uncombative, anti-violent life, so I don't know how this compares to other more manly men's pain, but this is by miles and miles the worst thing I've ever been through, thank you for asking.

More X-rays and blood tests and the surgeon returns with the complete granite face and says: 'Well, it could be a burst ulcer, but of course it isn't. The tumour in your pancreas has increased in size very fast. It's as big as a fist.' And he shows me a fist in case I'd misplaced the image.

I've decided to call the pancreatic tumour Lucky, as a nod to prophetic Professor Gazzard. So the chemotherapy isn't working. I ask my oncologist what's next.

'It's a bugger,' he says. 'It looked so hopeful, but you're right, it isn't working. The pancreas is a bad place. We can't operate and the side effects of radiation aren't worth the risk.' And there's pancreatic pain, which is famously in a league apart, so at least I can be stoical about that.

'What next?'

'Well, on the NHS we can give you another round of chemo, a bit rougher with slighter outcomes ... but there is really only one treatment for you: nivolumab.'

From behind the blue curtain, the nurse asks the policeman: 'What do you want to do with him?'

'Oh, let him go,' says the copper.

'I thought you'd arrested him?'

'No. Let him go.'

That evening I'm sitting in bed on the cancer ward trying to get the painkillers stabilised and a young nurse comes in.

'There you are. I've been waiting for you all day. You're supposed to be with me down in chemotherapy. I saw your name. Why are you up here?'

'Well, it turns out the chemo isn't working.' Her shoulders sag and her hand goes to her head. 'Fuck, fuck, that's dreadful.' I think she might be crying.

I look away, so might I.

You don't get that with private health care.

December 2016

Credits

Dinner Parties	*The Sunday Times*
Cabbage	*Tatler*
Morning at the Ivy	*The Ivy Cookbook*
Pomegranate	*Tatler*
Vegetarians	*The Sunday Times*
Stow-on-the-Wold	*The Sunday Times*
Concert	*The Sunday Times*
Starbucks	*The Sunday Times*
Pubs	*The Sunday Times*
Turtle	*Australian Gourmet Traveller*
Ramadan	*The Sunday Times*
Markets	*Australian Gourmet Traveller*
Last Suppers	*Australian Gourmet Traveller*
Noma	*The Sunday Times*
Hotel	*The Sunday Times*
Paris	*The Sunday Times*
Steak	*Vanity Fair*
Burger Pizza	*The Sunday Times*
Fäviken	*The Sunday Times*
Scotland	*The Sunday Times*
Refugee Camp Café	*The Sunday Times*
Sudan	*The Sunday Times*
India	*The Sunday Times*
Aral Sea	*The Sunday Times*
Uganda	*The Sunday Times*
Monte Carlo	*GQ*
Pakistan	*The Sunday Times*
Haiti	*The Sunday Times*
Iraq	*The Sunday Times*

New York	*Australian Gourmet Traveller*
Towton	*The Sunday Times*
Essex	*The Sunday Times*
Airports	*Australian Gourmet Traveller*
The Congo	*The Sunday Times*
Lampedusa	*The Sunday Times*
Refugee Journey	*The Sunday Times*
Victoria Falls	*The Sunday Times,*
GMTV	*The Sunday Times*
Just William	*The Sunday Times*
Prime Suspect	*The Sunday Times*
Jane Austen	*The Sunday Times*
Teletubbies	*The Sunday Times*
Brideshead. Revisited.	*The Sunday Times*
Sportsmen	*The Sunday Times*
David Attenborough	*The Sunday Times*
D-Day	*The Sunday Times*
The Queen	*The Sunday Times*
Sex and the City	*Vanity Fair*
Peppa Pig	*The Sunday Times*
Big Brother	*The Sunday Times*
Alan Bennett	*The Sunday Times*
Alan Whicker	*The Sunday Times*
Rev.	*The Sunday Times*
World War One	*The Sunday Times*
Doctor Who	*The Sunday Times*
Strictly Come Dancing	*The Sunday Times*
Autumnwatch	*The Sunday Times*
Ageing	*The Sunday Times*
Clouds House	*Tatler*
Fashion	*The Sunday Times*
Pornography	*GQ*
Stalking	*GQ*
Father	*The Sunday Times*
Glastonbury	*GQ*
Dog	*GQ*

Fatherhood	*GQ*
Nelson Mandela	*The Sunday Times*
Old Age	*The Sunday Times* March 2009
Dyslexia	*The Sunday Times*
Morrissey: Autobiography	*The Sunday Times*
Europe	*The Sunday Times*
Dying	*The Sunday Times*